Afghanistan after the Western Drawdown

Afghanistan after the Western Drawdown

Edited by Rohan Gunaratna and
Douglas Woodall

ROWMAN & LITTLEFIELD
Lanham • Boulder • New York • London

Published by Rowman & Littlefield
A wholly owned subsidiary of The Rowman & Littlefield Publishing Group, Inc.
4501 Forbes Boulevard, Suite 200, Lanham, Maryland 20706
www.rowman.com

Unit A, Whitacre Mews, 26-34 Stannary Street, London SE11 4AB

Copyright © 2015 by Rowman & Littlefield

All rights reserved. No part of this book may be reproduced in any form or by any electronic or mechanical means, including information storage and retrieval systems, without written permission from the publisher, except by a reviewer who may quote passages in a review.

British Library Cataloguing in Publication Information Available

Library of Congress Cataloging-in-Publication Data

Afghanistan after the western drawdown / edited by Rohan Gunaratna and Douglas Woodall.
pages cmp
Includes bibliographical references and index.
ISBN 978-1-4422-4505-1 (cloth : alk. paper)—ISBN 978-1-4422-4506-8 (electronic)
1. Afghanistan—Strategic aspects. 2. Strategic culture—Afghanistan. 3. Internal security—Afghanistan. 4. Postwar reconstruction—Afghanistan. 5. Terrorism—Prevention—Afghanistan. 6. Geopolitics—Asia. 7. Security, International—Asia. I. Gunaratna, Rohan, 1961– editor of compilation. II. Woodall, Douglas, 1971– editor of compilation.
DS371.4.A3335 2015
958.104'7—dc23
2014038835

∞™ The paper used in this publication meets the minimum requirements of American National Standard for Information Sciences Permanence of Paper for Printed Library Materials, ANSI/NISO Z39.48-1992.

Printed in the United States of America

Contents

Afghanistan-Pakistan Border Region		vii
Time Line of Key Events		viii
Preface and Acknowledgments		xii
Introduction		xiv
1	What Does the Future Hold for Afghanistan? *Halimullah Kousary*	1
2	Pakistan's Inextricable Role in Afghanistan's Future *Abdul Basit*	13
3	An American Perspective for Afghanistan's Future *Douglas Woodall*	35
4	India's Key Role and South Asia's Security Concerns *Iftekharul Bashar*	51
5	The Endgame in Afghanistan Will Affect Central Asia *Nodirbek Soliyev*	63
6	Iran's Strategic Designs for Afghanistan *Halimullah Kousary*	77
7	Why Afghanistan Matters: The Global Threat of Terrorism *Rohan Gunaratna*	85

| **8** | Threat Group Profiles
Halimullah Kousary and Abdul Basit | 113 |

Notes 237

Index 265

About the Editors and the Contributors 269

Afghanistan-Pakistan Border Region

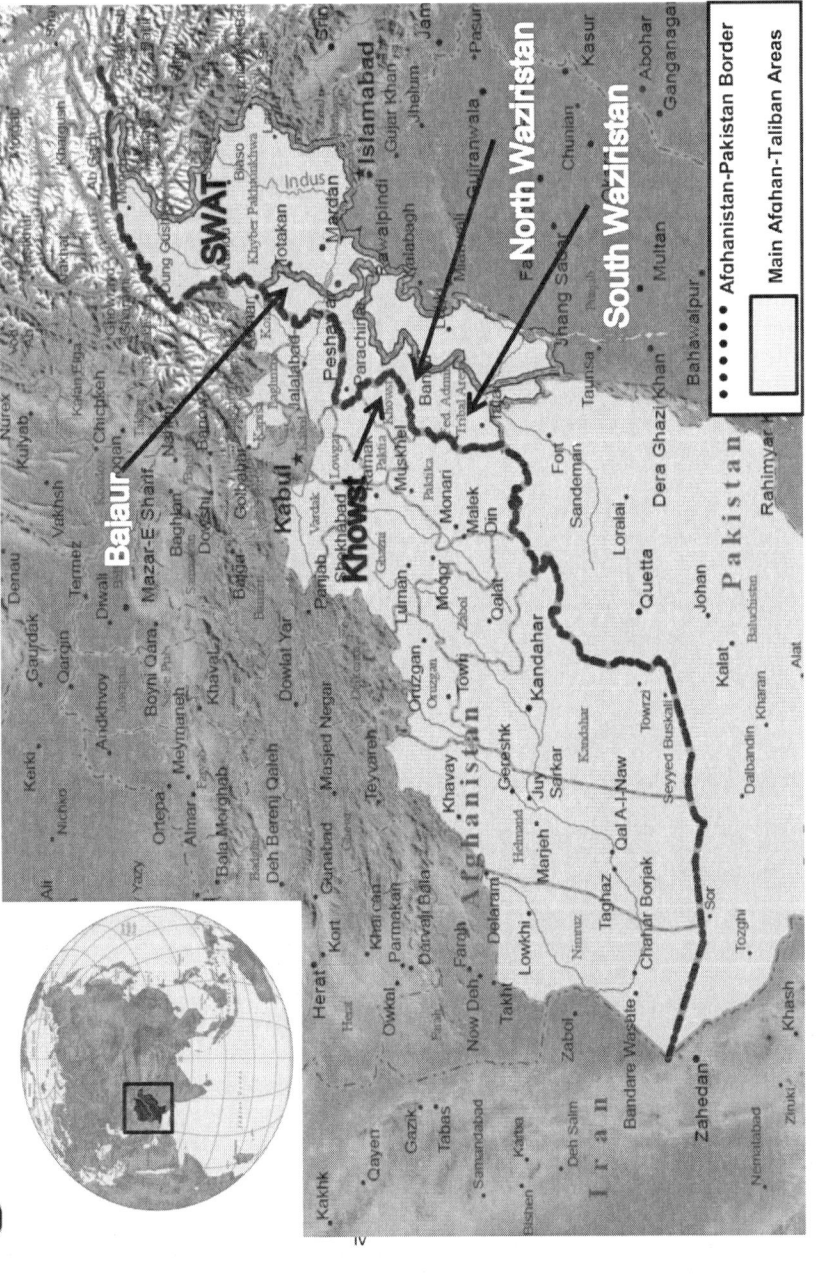

Time Line of Key Events

JUST BEFORE THE WAR

2001 September—Ahmad Shah Masood, the leader of the Northern Alliance, is assassinated by the Taliban and Al Qaeda.

FLIGHT OF THE TALIBAN

2001 October—US-led assistance to Afghanistan quickly follows the attacks of September 11, 2001. Special Operations Forces help to enable the Northern Alliance to enter Kabul and hasten the departure of the Taliban.
2001 December—Afghan groups, excluding the Taliban, agree to a peace deal in Bonn, Germany, for an interim government. Hamid Karzai is shortly thereafter sworn in as the interim leader of the government.
2002 January—The first contingent of coalition forces are deployed. The International Security Assistance Force (ISAF) is established and commences operations in Afghanistan.
2002 June—Loya Jirga convenes and elects Hamid Karzai as interim head of state.
2003 August—NATO assumes security responsibilities for Kabul, its first-ever operational commitment outside Europe.

FIRST ELECTION

2004 January—Loya Jirga adopts new a constitution, paving the way for a new political system.

2004 October–November—Hamid Karzai wins the presidential election.
2005 September—Afghans vote in first parliamentary elections in more than thirty years.
2006 October—NATO assumes security for the entire country.

ESCALATION OF THREAT ACTIVITIES AND THE AFGHANISTAN SURGE

2008 July—Suicide bomb attack on the Indian embassy in Kabul kills more than fifty people.
2008 September—The United States sends additional troops to Afghanistan.
2009 January—US Defense Secretary Robert Gates tells Congress that Afghanistan is the US administration's greatest test.
2009 February—NATO pledges to increase military and other commitments in Afghanistan after the US announces 17,000 extra troops.

NEW STRATEGY

2009 March—US President Barack Obama unveils new strategy for Afghanistan and Pakistan. An additional 4,000 US personnel will train the Afghan National Security Forces (ANSF), and there will be limited support for civilian development.
2009 August—Presidential and provincial elections are targeted by Taliban attacks and serious allegations of election fraud.
2009 October—Mr. Karzai is declared the winner of the August presidential election, after his opponent, Abdullah Abdullah, pulls out before the second round of elections.
2009 December—US President Obama decides to boost US troop numbers in Afghanistan by 30,000, bringing the US total to 100,000. Simultaneous announcement of withdrawal of surge forces by 2011 is declared.
An Al Qaeda double agent kills seven CIA agents in a suicide attack on Forward Operating Base Chapman, in Khost Province.
2010 February—NATO-led forces launch major offensive, Operation Moshtarak, in Southern Afghanistan to remove Taliban presence in Helmand.
2010 June—General Stanley McChrystal is relieved of command by President Obama.
2010 July—General David Petraeus takes command of US, ISAF forces.
2010 August—Dutch troops quit.
Karzai demands that private security firms must cease operations.

2010 September—Parliamentary polls are influenced by Taliban violence, widespread fraud, and long delays in the announcement of results.

2010 November—NATO agrees at the summit in Lisbon to hand control of security to Afghan forces by the end of 2014.

2011 September—Ex-president Burhanuddin Rabbani, the lead peace negotiator in talks with the Afghan Taliban, is assassinated by the Afghan Taliban.

2011 October—As relations with Pakistan worsen after a series of attacks, Afghanistan and India sign a strategic partnership to expand cooperation in security and development.

DEVELOPING MILITARY ALLIANCES

2011 November—President Karzai wins the endorsement of tribal elders to negotiate a ten-year military partnership with the United States at a Loya Jirga traditional assembly. The proposed pact involves US troops remaining after 2014, after the NATO mission ends.

2012 January—Taliban agrees to open an office in Dubai as a move toward peace talks with the United States and the Afghan government.

2012 February—At least thirty people are killed in protests about the burning of copies of the Koran at the US Bagram airbase.

2012 March—US Army Staff Sergeant Robert Bales is accused of killing sixteen civilians in the Panjwai district of Kandahar.

2012 April—Taliban announces its spring offensive with an audacious attack on the diplomatic quarters of Kabul. The government blamed the Haqqani Network. Security forces kill thirty-eight militants.

THE NATO RETROGRADE

2012 May—NATO summit endorses the plan to withdraw foreign combat troops by the end of 2014.

New French President Francois Hollande says France will withdraw its combat mission by the end of 2012—a year earlier than planned.

Arsala Rahmani of the High Peace Council is shot dead in Kabul.

2012 July—Tokyo donor conference pledges $16 billion in civilian aid to Afghanistan up to 2016, with the United States, Japan, Germany, and the United Kingdom supplying the majority of the financing.

2013 June—Afghan army takes command of all military and security operations from NATO forces. The ANSF are in the lead for all security operations in Afghanistan.

President Karzai suspends security talks with the United States after Washington announces it plans to hold direct talks with the Taliban. Afghanistan insists on conducting the talks with the Taliban in Qatar itself.

2013 November—Consultative Loya Jirga assembly of elders backs the bilateral security agreement with the United States, entailing enduring security assistance from the United States after NATO troops withdraw in 2014.

KEY FUTURE EVENTS

2014 April—Afghanistan's presidential elections are held, in which President Karzai is expected to peacefully transition power to the newly elected president.

2014 December—The NATO mission in Afghanistan ends and all foreign forces are scheduled to be withdrawn.

NOTE

Reference Source: http://bbc.co.uk/news/world-south-asia-12024253

Preface and Acknowledgments

This project brings scholars together to provide insights into one of the most critical crossroads in the history of Afghanistan. However, the ramifications for regional and global security merit careful consideration in analytical circles, given the increases in global terrorism and the undiminished desire for terrorists to radicalize and maintain enduring threats to security. At S. Rajaratnam School of International Studies (RSIS) at Nanyang Technological University (NTU), the International Centre for Political Violence and Terrorism Research (ICPVTR) brings terrorism experts together to address and maintain careful analysis of the most pressing and incipient threats to regional and global security.

Given the vast personal and professional expertise of the researchers here at the ICPVTR, our goal is to provide diverse perspectives concerning the future of Afghanistan, in light of concrete decisions that will likely happen prior to 2015. Discrete events that will transpire, to include the status of the bilateral security agreement between the United States and Afghanistan, the upcoming presidential elections for Afghanistan, and the status of the reconciliation talks with the Afghan Taliban, provide a simple, but relevant foundation for formulating future scenarios.

The results of these analyses provide critical relationships across cultural lines, underscoring the common perspectives and potential fractures in our common understanding of the conflict. It is imperative to recognize areas of common agreement and expand those recommendations to address confrontational issues concerning security in South Asia. This work seeks to provide a simple framework for a security situation not easily understood, and even more complicated and twisted by media outlets and publications seeking to further agendas with respect to their anticipated perceptions of what the future holds for Afghanistan.

Many thanks to Marie-Claire Antoine, senior acquisitions editor, and Monica Savaglia, assistant editor, at Rowman & Littlefield for ushering the book through the publishing process. I also want to thank Stephanie Scuiletti, associate production editor at Rowman & Littlefield, for organizing the production of the book; Erin Cler for copyediting; and Beth Easter for proofreading. I would like to thank all the researchers and contributors to this important work, with special thanks to our collaboration across South Asia and those scholars who are working to improve the security situations in their respective countries. I also want to recognize the United States Army War College's efforts, and its visionary approach to place its counterterrorism experts here in Southeast Asia. Its partnership with the ICPVTR, and engagement with Singapore, paved the way for dispatching the first Army War College Fellow in the history of the United States Army to NTU and the ICPVTR. The Armed Forces of the United States could not have chosen a better ambassador with visionary insights for U.S. Armed Forces' engagement in the Pacific than Lieutenant Colonel Douglas Woodall. His efforts in coordination with the ICPVTR surpassed all of my expectations for a visiting fellow, and I know his work will serve as the successful foundation for our enduring partnership.

Asia's future is important for global security, and we must remain vigilant to ensure that terrorists do not restore the capacity to train in sanctuaries beyond the will and capabilities of nation states to intercept them. South Asia holds enormous potential for security cooperation, but investment in security and stability must be enduring and necessary to prevent terror from escalating beyond the confines of the Middle East and of South Asia.

Rohan Gunaratna
January 2015
Singapore

Introduction

After the Western drawdown in Afghanistan, global and regional security landscapes are likely to change dramatically. After a protracted, decade-long fight, the world's most dangerous terrorist alliances still pose a threat to the US-led coalition. Seasoned to fight the world's best armies, al Qaeda and the Afghan Taliban and their allies are now poised to return to Afghanistan and reconstitute their sanctuary. Called the land of jihad, the "mujahidin" in the tribal areas of Pakistan may once again draw the support of free-floating pools of fighters. For the coming decade, Afghanistan will continue to remain the most important battlefield for two generations of fighters. The intent of this book is to offer a predictive framework to understand the ramifications of the Western drawdown and the potential security concerns that may arise. As global terrorism continues to evolve, allowing terror groups to return to Afghanistan will threaten global security.

Not unlike many assumptions that US forces would remain in Iraq, most scholars and security professionals automatically assume that the bilateral security agreement between Afghanistan and the United States will gain concurrence from Afghanistan's next president. Based on public statements from Afghanistan's presidential candidates, this is a very likely scenario. However, what is lacking is a framework for providing predictive analysis for the spectrum of discrete options involving Afghanistan's future scenarios. Specifically, even if approval of the bilateral security agreement is complete, assuming that US forces would stay for more than a few years is dangerous. Therefore, regardless of the status of the bilateral security agreement, the most dangerous scenarios accounting for little Western assistance to Afghanistan must be included in any future scenarios.

This book draws from the experience of researchers and scholars with experience on the ground in their respective regions of expertise. The depth and breadth of experience represented here provides valuable insights for the strategic implications of the security situation in the Afghanistan–Pakistan region. Armed with the key insights from this book, it is our desire to underline the looming increases in global terrorism that should warrant renewed focus and increasing resource allocations to continue the fight in this region. The majority of the world remains separated from the dangers of terrorism—the wars in the Middle East and the Afghanistan–Pakistan region continue to draw terrorist fighters and resources. The focus is shifting, and those countries that benefited from terrorists focusing their energies in these locations may awaken to fresh attempts to export terror to other regions of the globe—albeit with a higher and more sophisticated ability to prosecute attacks. Given this backdrop, the book is organized and focused on the key players that influence regional security and, more important, on Afghanistan's future security.

Chapter 1 provides our ground truth perspective from that of an Afghan. Halim provides strategic insights and his perspective on the most likely and most dangerous scenarios for Afghanistan. His insights on the Afghan Taliban are prescient, and given the current fluid situation in Afghanistan and the pending decisions about the bilateral security agreement between Afghanistan and the United States, Afghanistan's future may include several potential scenarios. The current uncertainties about Afghanistan's future have raised the question of what might happen after the withdrawal of the International Security Assistance Force (ISAF) in December 2014—a negotiated settlement or the continuation of conflict between the Afghan government and the Afghan Taliban? Halim answers this question by assessing the possible scenarios emerging in Afghanistan after 2014. He highlights the fragility of the Afghan state, posits arguments for and against ISAF withdrawals, and delineates his assessment for future scenarios, to include his assessment for the most likely and most dangerous scenarios for Afghanistan.

In chapter 2, Basit highlights his Pakistani perspective of Western involvement in Afghanistan. He underscores that the drawdown of US and ISAF forces in Afghanistan will have far-reaching implications for Pakistan's political, social, economic, and above all, security landscape. He posits that any transition devoid of intra-Afghan reconciliation and a regional framework of noninterference will lead to more chaos and instability. Moreover, the probable security vacuum will lead to internal wrangling for power and regional jostling for domination inside Afghanistan. To avoid this predicament, he believes Pakistan advocates for an Afghan-led, Afghan-owned, and Afghan-initiated peace process among all political and ethnic groups of Afghanistan, including the Afghan Taliban. He highlights that any solution for the Afghan endgame should consider the constants of history, geography, and religion for a sustainable peace in Afghanistan.

Chapter 3 provides a perspective from an American with combat experience in Afghanistan. In this chapter, Doug highlights the criticality of the bilateral security agreement and delineates how its approval will determine future US involvement in the region. While the Afghan National Security Forces (ANSF) continue to improve, engagement and training assistance from the United States is necessary to ensure stability and to send the global message of a longer-term commitment to regional stability. The Afghan Taliban already outlined untenable conditions for reconciliation negotiations, and the most dangerous scenario entails US disengagement from the region. If the bilateral security agreement is not signed or the United States withdraws security assistance within the next three years, diplomatic initiatives involving Russia and China should be explored. It is imperative to work with neighboring nations that have the capacity and security concerns to create regional security alternatives in the event of a US withdrawal from the region.

Looking to South Asia in chapter 4, Iftekharul provides our South Asian perspective and security concerns involving Afghanistan, with a focus on India's key role in the region. For more than thirty years, the geopolitical upheaval in Afghanistan continues to influence the security environment of South Asia and continues to limit the region's growth potential. Today, substantial threats to South Asia's nontraditional security comes from the Islamist militant groups that formed strong networks among themselves based on their shared experiences during the Afghan jihad in the 1980s. Therefore, the fragile security and threat landscape in Afghanistan will continue to have critical impacts on the overall security dynamics in the South Asian region, especially in India. Because the NATO-led mission in Afghanistan may end in 2014, concerns from South Asia are growing. Although South Asian states do not have a coherent regional strategy to engage Afghanistan, all nations face the same security risks. Can Afghanistan avoid becoming a fragmented and lawless country? Is Afghanistan going to emerge as the epicenter of transnational crime and terrorism? What are the emerging challenges for the region after 2014? Is South Asia ready to face them? This chapter seeks to analyze these key security challenges that India and greater South Asia will likely face after 2014.

Central Asia is oftentimes overlooked when considering the stability of Afghanistan. Nodir provides critical insights into this region in chapter 5. He highlights the security implications from actions in Afghanistan and Pakistan on the Central Asian states and posits his assessment of the future threats the region will face given the potential scenarios in Afghanistan. His chapter also provides critical insights into the terror groups threatening Central Asia and how those groups are tied to the security situation in Afghanistan. This analysis provides a road map for looming troubles ahead in Central Asia if the security situation deteriorates in Afghanistan.

In chapter 6, Halim presents his assessment of Iran's interests in Afghanistan and its role in regional security. With extensive experience working with Iranian influence in Afghanistan, Halim highlights the adversarial relationship between the United States and Iran, and the inherent challenges for Afghanistan to balance its diplomatic ties to both nations. However, the inking of the pending US–Afghanistan bilateral security agreement could render Iran's relationship with Afghanistan combustible, because Iran is staunchly opposed to the continued presence of the United States and NATO in its backyard. This chapter sets out an assessment of Iran's strategic direction in Afghanistan. Halim analyzes the US–Iran–Taliban rivalries, the Iran–India–Russia–China common interests in Afghanistan, and Iran's stance concerning the bilateral security agreement. Halim concludes with assumptions for the most likely role Iran may adopt in Afghanistan after 2014, considering scenarios involving the presence or absence of a US-led residual force.

Finally, chapter 7 brings the entire book together to answer the big question: Why does Afghanistan matter? This chapter highlights the security implications this region poses for the entire world. Some academics and policy makers do not think this region is a threat, whereas evidence to the contrary indicates that taking an unblinking eye off of this region may fuel higher levels of terrorism worldwide. Moreover, regions benefiting from containing and attracting jihadists for the past thirteen years will awaken anew and likely experience a greater propensity for terrorists to once again move to the Asia–Pacific region, Africa, and the Levant. Therefore, it is imperative that the proper counterterrorism strategies and commitment be implemented to address the continuing "will to fight" terrorists. Rohan Gunaratna provides the terror road map and answers this critical question of Afghanistan's importance and also expands the discussion to the implications for China and other nations around the globe.

The book also includes threat profiles detailing the most influential terrorist groups operating in the Afghanistan–Pakistan region. These threat-group profiles provide the background and understanding, at a fundamental level, to help readers gain an appreciation for both the complicated nature of security in the region and the organization of the groups that continue to threaten security.

Chapter One

What Does the Future Hold for Afghanistan?

Halimullah Kousary

INTRODUCTION

In June 2013, the Afghan National Security Forces (ANSF) took overall security responsibility for their country. ANSF is now leading all the military operations against the Afghan Taliban and the International Security Assistance Force (ISAF) continues to support the ANSF with limited military actions and intelligence facilities until the end of 2014.[1] War in Afghanistan will be thirteen years old by the end of 2014, making it the longest recorded war in US history. Once supported countrywide in the United States and Afghanistan, the war has turned increasingly unpopular within the populations of both countries because there seems to be no clear endgame to it.[2] The ISAF troop drawdown proceeds while the war with the Afghan Taliban is in full swing, and no outright winner and no reliable prospects for peace talks appear hopeful.

The US-led intervention in 2001 accomplished initial success in Afghanistan, resulting in the collapse of the Afghan Taliban regime and driving al Qaeda into hiding across the border in Pakistan. Initial success was overshadowed in subsequent years by the Afghan Taliban's comeback from Pakistan and its expanding influence in Afghanistan. The ISAF-led counterinsurgency fight against the Afghan Taliban is limited to the confines of Afghanistan's boundaries. The external dimensions of the insurgency were underestimated, despite evidence that the Afghan Taliban was resilient because of its foreign support and sanctuaries. On one hand, Pakistani Taliban and al Qaeda remnants in Pakistan actively participated in the insurgency in Afghanistan. On the other hand, Pakistan adopted accommodative policies toward the Afghan

Taliban that allowed them to organize, train, and raise funds on its soil. This very factor, the Afghan government and public argued, was the major catalyst for the Afghan Taliban's sustainability and ability to remain as an existential security threat to the Afghan state.

Both the US and Afghan governments accelerated attempts at a negotiated settlement with the Afghan Taliban. Currently, there seems to be no breakthrough progress made on that front. The Doha process failed, in part due to the Afghan government's angry reaction to the establishment of the Afghan Taliban's office in Qatar—with the Islamic Emirate flag hoisted and Islamic Emirate nameplate fitted into the wall of the office. The only new development that emerged from the Doha process was that the Taliban delinked itself from al Qaeda and firmly reiterated its preconditions for a full ISAF withdrawal and refusal to talk to the Afghan government.

Given the current fluid situation in Afghanistan and the pending decisions about the bilateral security agreement (BSA) between Afghanistan and the United States, Afghanistan's future may face several potential scenarios. The current uncertainties about Afghanistan's future raised the question of what might happen after the ISAF withdrawal in December 2014—a negotiated settlement or the continuation of conflict between the Afghan government and the Afghan Taliban? This chapter intends to answer this question by assessing the possible scenarios emerging in Afghanistan after 2014. This chapter will delineate the following key points: (1) the fragility of the Afghan state, (2) arguments for and against complete ISAF withdrawal and its aftermath, and (3) possible scenarios after 2014. The chapter will conclude with an assessed assumption of the most likely scenario and its implications in Afghanistan after 2014.

FRAGILITY OF THE AFGHAN STATE

After twelve years of war with incredible amounts of blood and treasure sacrificed by the Afghan nation and the ISAF member countries, Afghanistan is still a fragile state both militarily and economically. A combination of factors, some internal and others external, are cited for its current fragility. Major internal factors include weak and ineffective governance, rampant corruption at various levels of government institutions, and private sector corruption.[3] External factors include the US shift in focus to Iraq in 2003 and Pakistan's perpetual support for the Afghan Taliban against the Afghan government and the ISAF. The US-led Coalition allowed the fragmented remnants of the Afghan Taliban regime to reorganize and stage a comeback, while the Pakistan fostered them and sustained the insurgency in Afghanistan. The Taliban sanctuaries on Pakistan's soil remain a source of their resilience and maneuvers, which enables them to stand their ground to date and remain a serious security threat to the Afghan state.

Rivalries with India have formed Pakistan's view of the Afghan Taliban as a strategic asset for use in Afghanistan. Pakistan sees Afghanistan through the prism of a zero-sum game vis-à-vis India and perceives India's advances toward Afghanistan as a direct threat to its national security. This perception motivated Pakistan to support the Afghan Taliban while India maintained strong ties with the Afghan government and provided assistance in training the ANSF and aiding the country's reconstruction process.[4]

India's economic advances toward Afghanistan help drive its growing economy, its increasing needs for energy, and its dispute with Pakistan over Kashmir. A friendly and liberal regime in Afghanistan is important to India for access to energy-rich Central Asia. Moreover, denying Pakistan the possibility of having an Islamist regime in Afghanistan that is sympathetic to the Kashmir militancy is extremely important to India. India heeds the strong nexus that exists between the Afghan and Pakistan Taliban, and the Afghan Taliban and the Pakistani establishment.[5] The Pakistan Taliban repeatedly comments on the Kashmir dispute. In January 2013, Tehrik-i-Taliban Pakistan (TTP) pledged to send its militants to Kashmir to wage a struggle to establish Islamic rule in Kashmir and beyond.[6] India is concerned that such a nexus can be a catalyst for the Afghan Taliban's support toward the Kashmir militancy. Therefore, it wants to see a liberal regime in power in Afghanistan—of which the Afghan Taliban are not part or in which they are not holding a strong position.[7]

Realizing that India and Pakistan are crucial (India economically and Pakistan in terms of security), the Afghan government tries to remain non-aligned, negates the India–Pakistan rivalries in Afghanistan, and continues with "Pakistan is our twin brother; India is a great friend" policy to keep balance between the two rivals.[8] Afghanistan realizes that constructive engagements with both India and Pakistan are not an option for it, and thus has adopted a balanced position. However, the trust deficit between Afghanistan and Pakistan exacerbates the negative relationship and complicates Afghanistan's efforts for stability.

Iran remains another important player that espouses a dual policy toward Afghanistan. While it engaged with the Afghan Taliban (not to the scale Pakistan has), much of Iran's intervention in Afghanistan has been through soft measures. It spent millions of dollars every year over the past decade funding Afghan media and various political organizations in pursuit of its long-term political and strategic interests.[9] Iran opposes the US presence in Afghanistan and meanwhile wants to see a regime in power that is inclusive of all the ethnicities. Iran thinks that an inclusive regime could safeguard its sectarian influence in Afghanistan through empowering the Shia Hazara minority. The current Afghan government can be an example of the type of regime Iran wants see in Afghanistan, where the Hazaras enjoy unprecedented clout.

In the meantime, Iran supports the Afghan Taliban because it looks at the Afghan Taliban as a useful short-term ally against the United States. Both sides recognize that the United States is the common enemy and that they can work together to stand in the way of US interests and the BSA.[10] However, Iran also perceives the dominantly Sunni Afghan Taliban as a long-term sectarian threat, and its concurrent support to the Afghan government and anti-Taliban Afghan political parties is to prepare in the long term to confront that threat in Afghanistan.

In addition to the Shia political leadership in Afghanistan, Iran also enjoys considerable support among the Sunni Tajik political leaders. Afghan Minister of Water and Energy Mohammad Ismail Khan is closely allied with Iran. Ismail Khan is a warlord from western Herat province and has a strong support base there. In 2012, he recommended to create militias and arm them to fight the Afghan Taliban after the ISAF's withdrawal.[11] Ismail Khan's announcement was interpreted by some Afghans as being early effort's by Iran to prepare in anticipation of future Afghan Taliban threats to its interests. Atta Mohammad Noor—the governor of the northern Balkh province and a possible presidential candidate in the 2014 elections—is another high-ranking government official known to have ties with Iran. Mr. Atta emerged as one of the influential political leaders in northern Afghanistan after 2001, and his clout grew steadily among the supporters of the Northern Alliance. In May 2013, a survey conducted in Afghanistan by the Moscow-based Contemporary Afghanistan Studies Centre indicated that Mr. Atta was voted the second-most influential political leader, after President Karzai in Afghanistan.[12]

The divergent interests of India, Iran, and Pakistan shaped a regional dimension to the conflict in Afghanistan, which seems hard to ignore in the coming years. These divergent interests resulted in the states supporting non-state actors, such as the Afghan Taliban, and positioned the Afghan state in the middle of a strategic game between large and powerful states. The Afghan state is apparently too weak to turn the dynamics in its interests on its own, without support from the United States and the regional stakeholders.

LOCAL PERCEPTIONS OF THE ISAF'S WITHDRAWAL

Withdrawal—Fraught with Peril in Afghanistan

Segments of the Afghan population fear that a complete ISAF withdrawal will further destabilize Afghanistan, as it is still fighting a resilient and foreign-supported Afghan Taliban insurgency. Segments of the population think that the United States has not fulfilled what they perceive as a promise to leave Afghanistan as an economically and militarily stable country. They describe ISAF's leaving Afghanistan in its current state as abandonment of the country just as the United States did in 1989, after the Soviet Union's withdrawal. Their fear is that anarchy will likely prevail in Afghanistan, and proxy war could possibly erupt. The Afghan Taliban will likely gain control in the southern and eastern parts of the country. This may threaten control for the entire country, while warlordism will grow in strength in the the central and northern parts. The Afghan government will likely face growing instability, and its writ will gradually shrink to Kabul and some key urban centers in the country.[13]

For people who are against complete withdrawal, the BSA, which comes with the funds to pay, train, and equip the ANSF, serves as a credible deterrence against the above scenario and is the key to the ANSF's sustainability beyond 2014. The ANSF developed significantly during the past twelve years, and its performance in counterinsurgency against the Afghan Taliban is proven.[14] However, given the resilience of the Afghan Taliban and the insurgency friendly geographic terrain across the country, the ANSF still does not seem capable of rapid deployments to all parts of the country, without ISAF support.[15] The ANSF is underresourced, and its air force and intelligence capabilities are vastly limited, while it requires robust advising and training to professionalize itself. In the absence of ISAF support, all of this could affect the ANSF's fighting strength against the Afghan Taliban from 2015 onward.

The opponents of complete ISAF withdrawal also believe that such a withdrawal could lead to the sacrifice of achievements made over the past decade and that Afghanistan pulled itself out of international isolation to engage with the world through growing diplomatic relations with many countries. Millions of boys and girls go to schools, and the number is increasing year by year. Infrastructure was rebuilt to a considerable degree, and the country's agricultural sector improved a great deal. People's fears are that all these improvements could be reversed once the ISAF withdraws with the zero troop option. The withdrawal already had its fallout in different forms, triggering numerous uncertainties about the security situation after 2014. Aid agencies working in Afghanistan refused to prepare plans beyond 2014, and most NGOs have signed contracts with their employees until 2014.[16] The proponents of the BSA fear that things can get far worse if the withdrawal is completed with no residual US forces left behind in 2014.

Withdrawal—An Opportunity to Restore Peace in Afghanistan

There are those who argue that the ISAF withdrawal from Afghanistan is a step toward bringing peace to the country and urging the Afghan Taliban to hold talks with the Afghan government. President Karzai also supported the withdrawal, stating that it will help ensure peace in Afghanistan.[17] The supporters of ISAF's withdrawal mostly live in rural Afghanistan, and they believe that once ISAF's forces are out at the end of 2014, the Afghan Taliban can no longer claim they are liberating the country from the "foreign invaders." Their recruitment and hate propaganda will be weakened, and it will be hard for them to justify fighting against the Afghan government. The Afghan Taliban's rhetoric of insurgency is heavy on ideology and light on strategy, and ideology alone is not enough to sustain fighting. The Afghan Taliban might gain control in certain rural parts of the south and east after the ISAF withdrawal, but they will not be able to overthrow the government nor come to power in the country.[18] They are already unpopular with Afghans, and their system of governance (the Islamic Emirate, which the Afghan Taliban want to reinstate) in Afghanistan is unpalatable for Afghans across all the ethnicities due to their 1990s experiences.[19]

Another argument made in support of ISAF's withdrawal is the still vivid recollection by Afghanistan's population of the Soviet's withdrawal in 1989, the subsequent collapse of the Afghan communist government, and the resulting chaos that sprang from the collapse and ushered in the Afghan Taliban. Miseries of the Mujahideen factional fighting and the Afghan Taliban regime followed. Therefore, this time with ISAF's withdrawal, the population, unlike after the Soviet withdrawal, will side with the Afghan government, and the Afghan Taliban will have to accept that the time for armed struggle has passed. According to an Asia Foundation Survey in late 2012, there was little sympathy among the Afghan population for the Afghan Taliban insurgency, and the majority of them favored the government's efforts toward reconciliation with the Afghan Taliban.[20] Elements in the Afghan Taliban also realize the need to forsake fighting once the ISAF leaves. In August 2012, the Afghan Taliban's former finance minister and important member of the Quetta Shura, Agha Jan Motasim, called on the Afghan Taliban to shift beyond armed struggle and resolve their differences with the Afghan government through dialogue and negotiation.[21] The government also indicated confidence that the members of Afghan Taliban's leadership support the peace process. According to Masoom Stanakzai, the head of the Afghan High Peace Council (HPC) secretariat, the majority of the Afghan Taliban leaders support the peace process to move forward, but announcing that publicly is a difficult issue for them.[22]

The difficulty and hesitance of the Afghan Taliban leadership to support peace talks in public with the Afghan government may stem from Pakistan using its influence on the Afghan Taliban's strategies. In the past, members of the Afghan Taliban leadership expressed willingness toward negotiation with the Afghan government, but Pakistan hindered their efforts by arresting them or urging them into exile out of Pakistan. The arrest of the former number two leader of the Afghan Taliban, Mullah Baradar, by Pakistani authorities in February 2010 is a case in point. He was arrested when Pakistan, as reported, realized that he was secretly holding talks with the Afghan government. Agha Jan Motasim, another high-ranking member of the Afghan Taliban leadership, supported a shift from military to political strategies and survived an assassination attempt in the Pakistani city of Karachi. He subsequently went into exile in Turkey.[23] Afghans believe that Pakistan was behind both of these incidents, hindering any reconciliation initiatives that do not proceed on its terms.[24]

POST-2014 SCENARIOS

Bilateral Security Agreement Signed and Negotiation with the Taliban Successful

The mandate of the BSA between Afghanistan and the United States is to provide training to the ANSF and conduct counterterrorism missions in the Afghanistan–Pakistan region. The troop numbers are not yet decided, but the most probable range is from 10,000 to 20,000, which will also include troops from other ISAF member countries.[25] According to the Afghan government, the United States wants nine bases in Afghanistan, to which it agreed, as long as it receives security and military and economic guarantees in return.[26] The United States insists that the BSA be signed by October 2013 to send a clear message to the Afghan Taliban that the international community will not be waited out.[27] The Afghan government, however, states that it is in no hurry and demands assurances from the United States regarding stability, military, economic support, and defense against external threats.[28] All this triggered delays in signing the BSA to date.

The United States seems interested in concluding the BSA in the soonest possible way, probably thinking that it will urge the Afghan Taliban to either go away or negotiate with the Afghan government. However, the Afghan Taliban categorically opposed the BSA and preconditioned zero presence of foreign forces to end the war. Negotiating with the US and/or the Afghan government during BSA negotiations will result in political death for the Afghan Taliban, as it could lead to serious frictions within their ranks and put their stated goal (driving the foreign forces out) under question. The Afghan Taliban agreed to disassociate itself from al Qaeda and global jihad, and they manifested a policy shift regarding the government system in Afghanistan.[29] Mullah Mohammad Omar in his August 2013 Eid message hinted that the Afghan Taliban are not interested in monopolizing power but rather want to reach an understanding with the Afghans on inclusive government based on Islamic principles. Nevertheless, Mullah Mohammad Omar remains firmly opposed to the BSA, which he said would rule out the possibility of an end to fighting against the foreign forces and the Afghan government beyond 2014.[30]

BSA Signed with Status Quo

The BSA with status quo means that Afghanistan and the United States sign it and the conflict between the Afghan government and the Afghan Taliban continues. The United States will provide limited assistance to the ANSF and conduct counterterrorism missions focused on the remnants of al Qaeda. The Afghan issue with this scenario is that it could lead to positive effects against the Afghan Taliban insurgency but not long-term outcomes. Missing in this deal is the regional element of the war. US policy toward Pakistan has already been a source of tension between Afghanistan and the United States, and it seems now to be at the forefront of the BSA. The Afghan government realizes that as long as the Afghan Taliban sanctuaries on Pakistan's soil remain intact, they will remain a threat to Afghanistan, even after signing the BSA. Thus, it wants to address the issue of sanctuaries as an integral part of the BSA, as these sanctuaries are the key to ending the conflict in the country.[31] The Afghan government demands that the United States must commit to using decisive force against the Afghan Taliban's sanctuaries in Pakistan and apply serious diplomatic, political, and military measures to urge Pakistan to cooperate.[32] This will place costs on Pakistan but could deter insurgency in Afghanistan, which is the priority of the Afghan government. The delay in signing the BSA depicts a fundamental difference in the Afghan and US threat perceptions in the region. The US concerns are primarily with al Qaeda, whereas Afghanistan feels threatened by the Afghan Taliban and their associated groups in Pakistan.[33]

The United States failed to pressure Pakistan into neutralizing the Afghan Taliban sanctuaries during the past twelve years, despite providing billions of dollars in aid to Pakistan. This adds to the concern of the Afghan government. The Afghan government believes that the sanctuaries will continue to exist, thus making the conflict between the Afghan government and the Afghan Taliban continue, despite the US residual footprints on the ground. The BSA can still be a sufficient reason for the Afghan Taliban to continue "jihad" against the Afghan government and for Pakistan to continue supporting the Afghan Taliban. Other than India, all the other countries in the region, to include Pakistan, Iran, China, and Russia, are opposed to the US residual presence in Afghanistan. In the backdrop of the BSA, Pakistan's and Russia's military authorities made visits to each other's countries, and both sides agreed that the US bases in Afghanistan could be a source of confrontation and friction in the region.[34] Iran will consider the bases as its encirclement by the United States and will adopt a more friendly and supportive role toward the Afghan Taliban beyond 2014.

Complete Withdrawal with Continued Aid

If the United States stops its combat mission in Afghanistan, it will be costly in blood and treasure. It wants to have a residual presence in Afghanistan beyond 2014, but it will continue with the zero troop option if the Afghan government does not agree to it.[35] The recent statements made by US authorities regarding the zero troop option insinuated that it would be more harmful to the security interests of Afghanistan and its immediate neighbors rather than to those of the United States. The United States already proclaimed that its major objective of eliminating al Qaeda from Afghanistan is accomplished and that al Qaeda no longer poses a serious threat to US national security from the Afghanistan–Pakistan region.[36]

The complete withdrawal may not lead to direct threats to US national security from the Afghan and Pakistan Taliban, in the short term, but it could undermine US enduring and vital strategic interests in South Asia in the long run. Just as in the 1990s, abandoning the region will allow the Taliban and remnants of al Qaeda to thrive in the Afghanistan–Pakistan region. Therefore, deterring the stability of the Afghanistan–Pakistan region against the Islamist groups influenced by al Qaeda is critical to US security interests globally. It can feasibly pursue this deterrence by staying on in the region.

Some argue that the United States can continue counterterrorism missions in the Afghanistan–Pakistan region with its intelligence power and drone strikes, even without having bases in Afghanistan. Moreover, there is conjecture that the United States perceives it can kill any al Qaeda or Taliban leader anywhere in the region. However, such missions will not stop the groups from expanding their control, as demonstrated in the Federally Administered Tribal Areas (FATA) of Pakistan. The United States conducted hundreds of drone attacks on al Qaeda, the Pakistan Taliban, and the Haqqani Network in the FATA, killing numerous militant leaders. Nevertheless, they did not change the militant landscape in the broader region.[37] The militants as groups remain at large, and the Afghanistan–Pakistan region suffered increased violence and more intense attacks by them.

The argument of US intent to stay on to pursue its geostrategic interests in the region is also relevant in the context of the BSA. Having footprints in Afghanistan is important for the United States, given a resurgent Russia and assertive strategic rival China in Central Asia. The footprint in Afghanistan will allow the United States to monitor the activities of Russia and China as well Iran in the region.

Afghanistan is the last opportunity for the United States to ensure its presence in the region. Central Asia already has refused to accommodate it. In 2005, Uzbekistan closed down the US base on its soil, and the Kyrgyz government ordered the closure of Manas by July 2014, which is a key transit US facility in Central Asia. For more than ten years, Kyrgyzstan was wheeling and dealing between the United States and the Russian Federation until it banked $300 million as advanced aid promised by Moscow in exchange for closing the base.[38] Uzbekistan initially courted the United States as a counterbalance to Russia. However, relations between the two countries started to deteriorate after the Andijan killings in May 2005, when Uzbek troops fired on crowds of demonstrators to crush an antigovernment protest.[39] The closure of the two US bases in Uzbekistan and Kyrgyzstan shifted the geopolitics of Central Asia against the United States. Kyrgyzstan, for instance, is moving fast to join the Eurasian Union—a project toward achieving close integration among the former Soviet republics and bringing them back into the Russian orbit. Russia already began to consolidate its military presence in Kyrgyzstan and agreed to commence a major military aid program for it, which could be worth over $1 billion.[40] Afghanistan's proximity to Russia, Iran, and China renders the US residual presence there as a strategic asset for the United States and NATO as well.

Therefore, if the United States compromises its security and geostrategic interests in the region, the zero troop withdrawal will be a setback for the United States in the long term, as much as it is for Afghanistan and the region. The zero troop option will be a major setback for Afghanistan, because it will rule out military assistance and training for the ANSF and will lead to huge cuts in civilian aid flowing to Afghanistan. The dwindling economy of the United States will be a factor in discouraging its commitment to continue aid to Afghanistan without having bases there. Complete withdrawal and no continued military support for ANSF could gradually push Afghanistan toward further insecurity and could pave the way for a proxy war reminiscent of the 1990s conflict. Afghanistan could turn into a ground of regional interference, with India more involved this time. Indo–Pak rivalries may continue to be a major dimension of the possible proxy war, where India will align with Iran in support of the groups opposed to the Afghan Taliban.

CONCLUSION

Afghanistan is embroiled in a multifaceted war fought to pursue various competing interests of states and nonstate actors. These competing interests resulted in the states supporting nonstate actors, such as the Afghan Taliban, and positioned Afghanistan in the middle of a strategic game between large and powerful states. Afghanistan is apparently too weak to turn dynamics in its interests on its own, without sincere support from the United States and other regional stakeholders.

The United States desires an endgame in Afghanistan that includes a negotiated settlement with the Afghan Taliban and a successful BSA with the

Afghan government. However, a signed BSA and negotiations with the Afghan Taliban are mutually exclusive, as the Afghan Taliban indicates no flexibility on the BSA. The argument that the pragmatist elements of the Afghan Taliban will be open to compromise on the BSA for their long-term survival seems unlikely. These elements, if there are any, will not have adequate influence within the Afghan Taliban's ranks, and their defection will not exert adequate impact on the mind-set of the overall Afghan Taliban. This is primarily because they link their survival to the complete withdrawal of the foreign forces.

Negotiations with the Afghan Taliban find support by a cross-ethnic consensus and seem to be the best way forward to ensure stability in Afghanistan. However, the major obstacles to negotiations assessed so far are the preconditions set by the Afghan Taliban. Afghans might agree with the Afghan Taliban about ISAF's withdrawal, but not on the constitution and the governance system. They want a democratic governance system as opposed to the Islamic Emirate and consider the constitution as Islamic, drafted by Afghans, and recognized by religious scholars, among other experts, in 2004.

However, the Afghan Taliban refuses to accede on the constitution and to negotiate with the Afghan government. This renders the Afghan Taliban as uncompromising and the possibility of negotiating with them elusive. This in turn will likely foster support for the BSA among not only the Afghan government and political parties but also among the Afghan population. Many Afghan political leaders do not view a zero troop option as being in the best interest of Afghanistan. While they share President Karzai's preconditions for signing the BSA, they also argue that letting such an agreement pass will intensify internal conflict and invite increased meddling by Pakistan, India, and Iran and even by China and Russia. They believe that the BSA is important, as it will make Afghanistan the largest recipient of US security and economic assistance. The performance of the ANSF is promising so far, but the concern is how they will perform when the assistance from the United States and ISAF member countries evaporates.

Thus, it is highly likely that the BSA will successfully conclude between Afghanistan and the United States. In the meantime, armed opposition might continue, as the Afghan Taliban will not walk away nor will they negotiate. Reintegration of the Afghan Taliban's foot soldiers into the Afghan government might relatively increase, but prospects for progress on reconciliation, which engages the Afghan Taliban's top leaders, will remain elusive.

The most the BSA can do is ensure the sustainability of the ANSF, but to undermine and weaken the Afghan Taliban, a government based on intra-Afghan consensus and ability to deliver is the key. Fair and transparent presidential elections in 2014 are of paramount importance to the credibility and legitimacy of the future government. This may promote an improved sense of belonging among the population to the government and play a supportive role for the government in conflict with the Afghan Taliban after 2014. Thus, the future government must undertake measures to curb corruption and improve its ability to deliver goods and services to the people. The Taliban is already a tested group, and the Afghan population did not have great experiences with their regime in the 1990s.

Chapter Two

Pakistan's Inextricable Role in Afghanistan's Future

Abdul Basit

After years of fighting in Afghanistan, the United States and its NATO allies are winding up their war efforts in Afghanistan. Ahead of the 2014 deadline, the collective realization by the insurgents and international coalition forces that there is no military solution to conflict in Afghanistan has given way to a political approach to end the war.[1] Given the 2014 drawdown deadline, it appears impossible to achieve a military victory over the Taliban in such a short time span.

Notwithstanding initiation of a political approach to bring the decade-long war to an end, the current Afghan peace process looks confusing and is inconsistent.[2] So far, it has spiraled around "talk about talks."[3] The quest for peace is elusive because of the lack of clarity among the Afghan stakeholders about Afghanistan's outlook beyond 2014.[4] This vagueness has given rise to speculative scenarios. Such peacemaking efforts are like fishing without bait.[5] Moreover, the focus of the transition is on security and reconciliation with the Taliban insurgents. Discussions on political and economic aspects of the transition have been missing from the wider debate.

The single-most important element for the peace process and transition in Afghanistan is the April 2014 Afghan presidential election. The election will set the tone for future debate. More importantly, the elections are coinciding with the drawdown of international troops. The legitimacy of the April 2014 elections and the next president is important for the peace process. During this crucial time of transition, any attempts to delay or efforts to rig the April 2014 elections, like the 2009 presidential elections, can derail the entire peace process.[6]

After 2014, Afghanistan will enter a new phase in its history. So far, peacemaking efforts in Afghanistan have shown that there is no clear strategy and clear vision about the future.[7] It is unclear whether the external powers will leave the Afghans alone to sort out their internal issues and reconcile.[8] The future political and economic outlook also looks bleak. Moreover, given the pending status of the bilateral security agreement between the United States and Afghanistan, it is still unclear what level of troops the United States will keep in Afghanistan after 2014. To a great degree, the future will also depend on the amount of aid available to Afghanistan.

Moreover, the emphasis seems to be on the 2014 deadline rather than on the complex realities on the ground. After announcing a change in its policy toward Afghanistan in 2011, the United States focused on hardening the deadlines. Any peace deal that is calendar driven instead of conditions based will likely not lead to viable peace. For instance, at the Third Trilateral Summit held on February 4, 2013, the leaders of Afghanistan, Pakistan, and the United Kingdom set a six-month time line to reach a peace settlement with the Taliban. Such plans are not only unrealistic but also damaging to the credibility of the peace process.[9]

The current peace process needs a major course correction for a more realistic resolution of the conflict in Afghanistan.[10] Without a negotiated settlement, a medium- to low-level conflict will continue, which neither side can win nor lose. It is the last opportunity for the international community to set the course right in Afghanistan.

While seeking any solution to the Afghan conflict, careful consideration of the history, geography, culture, and religion should not be ignored. Making war is easier than achieving peace. It is better to follow a systematic approach leading to less, but more sustainable, gains. Achieving less with sustainable peace is better than temporary peace that may lead to violence in the future.[11]

Against this backdrop, the endgame in Afghanistan has to be examined within the context of transition, reconciliation, and the post-2014 US mission in Afghanistan. The interplay of these factors and the role of the regional countries will determine the outlook of Afghanistan beyond 2014.[12] All of the stakeholders in the Afghan endgame are operating in a highly complex and uncertain environment where the shared goals of a peaceful and stable Afghanistan means different things to different actors.

After 2014, the possibility of peace and stability in Afghanistan will have far-reaching consequences for Pakistan.[13] This chapter will underline Pakistan's perspective of the endgame in Afghanistan and its likely implications for Pakistan in light of three emerging scenarios: continued conflict, breakout of civil war, or peace and stability. Each scenario will have a different set of consequences for Pakistan and will require different policy responses from Islamabad. Pakistan's endgame in Afghanistan is linked to emerging internal security challenges on its western borders due to the changing situation in Afghanistan, India's involvement, and the uncertain future US role in Afghanistan.

A PEACE PROCESS GOING NOWHERE

So far, the initiatives employed to engage the Taliban have not moved beyond preliminary contacts and confidence-building measures.[14] In retrospect, US officials and Tayyab Afghan, a close aide of the Taliban leader Mullah Muhammad Umar, held exploratory talks in May 2011.[15] In October 2011, Pakistan brokered a meeting between two midlevel American diplomats and Ibrahim Haqqani, brother of the Haqqani Network's top leader Jalaluddin Haqqani, in the United Arab Emirates.[16]

In January 2012, Afghan Taliban and US officials met in Qatar, but the talks broke down after the United States refused to release five Taliban prisoners from Guantanamo Bay. In October 2012, the Afghan Taliban opened their office in Qatar to restart the stalled peace process.[17] However, the Taliban closed the office within days of its opening after the Afghan President Hamid Karzai objected to raising the flag of the Islamic Emirate of Afghanistan.

PERCEPTION GAPS AND AMBIGUITIES IN THE AFGHAN ENDGAME

The multiple competing and conflicting interests of regional actors also lead to uncertainties in achieving peace in Afghanistan. The linkage between a responsible drawdown and safe power-sharing mechanism in Afghanistan is very weak. This widening gap further complicates the transition process and long-term stabilization of Afghanistan. If the key stakeholders and the neighboring countries—especially India, China, Iran, and Russia—do not bridge these gaps for constructive solutions, the entire process is likely to collapse.

The role that Pakistan is capable of playing and willing to play in the Afghan endgame remains a subject of intense debate and controversy in the policy-making circles around the world. The divergent policy perceptions in the Pak–US relations and Pak–Afghan relations are the most obvious manifestations of this. These divergent perceptions prevented these three actors from complementing each other's efforts to achieve a peaceful settlement in Afghanistan.[18]

The United States and Afghanistan accuse Pakistan of playing a double game. They believe Pakistan's Afghan strategy remains that of the 1990s. The theory is that Pakistan is using the Taliban as a hedge to create a Pakistani client state in Afghanistan after 2014.[19] They also believe Pakistan wants to use Afghanistan for strategic depth in the event of a war with India, as well as to tackle the unresolved issues of the Durand Line and Pashtunistan.[20]

Pakistan has been involved in the Afghan imbroglio for the past three decades. Pakistan is viewed both as part of the problem and part of the solution for the peace process. Pakistan's security-focused Afghan policy further cements these perceptions.[21] In October 2011, during a press conference with Afghan President Hamid Karzai in Kabul, the former US Secretary of State Hillary Clinton elucidated this frenemy (friend and enemy) role of Pakistan as follows: "We are expecting Pakistanis to support the efforts at talking. We believe they can play either a constructive or a destructive role."[22]

The United States and Afghanistan continually accuse Pakistan of not keeping its end of the bargain. The duo believes Pakistan's inaction against the sanctuaries of the Haqqani Network, the most lethal Afghan militant group in the Federally Administered Tribal Areas (FATA), is destabilizing Afghanistan. In an interview with the BBC, Afghan Army Chief General Sher Mohammad Karimi maintained, "Pakistan controls the Afghan Taliban. If Pakistan wants, the fighting in Afghanistan can end in weeks. If Pakistan puts pressure on the Taliban leadership and convinced them what can be done, that can help a lot."[23]

Pakistan's premier intelligence service, Directorate of Inter-Services Intelligence (ISI), is blamed for providing support to the Haqqani Network for furtherance of its interest in Afghanistan. In testimony before the US Senate Armed Forces Committee on 22 September 2011, former US Joint Chiefs Chairman Admiral Mike Mullen noted, "Pakistan is exporting violence in Afghanistan." He said, "Haqqanis are the veritable arm of Pakistan's Inter-Services Intelligence."[24]

Meanwhile, Pakistan has its own apprehensions about US goals and ambitions in Afghanistan and the region. Pakistan continues to view America's Afghan policy as highly inconsistent, confused, and problematic to Pakistan's interests and durable peace in Afghanistan.

Many in Pakistan believe Washington has a tilt toward India in its Afghanistan policy. The United States' support for a bigger Indian role in post-2014 Afghanistan increased Pakistan's reservations that the United States wants to marginalize Pakistan's legitimate concerns and interests in Afghanistan.[25] The signing of the India–Afghanistan strategic partnership agreement in October 2011, when the Pak–US relations were at their lowest ebb, further strengthened Pakistan's fears.[26]

Moreover, in 2010 the coalition's efforts to directly contact the Afghan Taliban without the knowledge of the ISI and Pakistan's military also raised suspicions in Islamabad.[27] The fact that the Afghan Taliban accepted negotiations, without the involvement of the ISI, made Pakistan even more apprehensive.[28]

The lack of clarity on the ultimate US objectives in Afghanistan adds to the complexity of the situation. Despite America's expressed desire to leave after 2014, if the Afghan government does not sign the bilateral security agreement (BSA), Pakistan believes the United States will not leave the region. It will likely retain its long-term security presence in the region to safeguard its strategic interests concerning China, Central Asia, Iran, and Russia.

Pakistan fears that the United States is making Pakistan a scapegoat for its own failures in Afghanistan. In September 2011, when the Pak–US relations touched their nadir, the former ISI chief Javed Ashraf Qazi said, "US is pressuring Pakistan to hide its own failures in Afghanistan." This statement came in the backdrop of the killing of al Qaeda chief Osama bin Laden in Abbotabad by US Navy Seals and twenty-six Pakistani soldiers killed in a NATO air raid in the FATA.[29]

The hostility between India and Pakistan lies at the heart of the current war in Afghanistan. Both countries are fighting a low-level proxy war in Afghanistan. The fact that Pakistan advocates the Afghan Taliban's inclusion in future political scenarios in Afghanistan directly opposes India's desires.[30] Currently, both are vying to fill the possible gap that will likely be created during the current drawdown of coalition forces in Afghanistan.[31]

The India–Pakistan rivalry in Afghanistan is not new. During the Afghan civil war (1992–1995), India and Pakistan supported opposing factions. Pakistan supported Gulbuddin Hekmatyar, the current head of Hizb-e-Islami, whereas India backed the former Afghan president Burhunuddin Rabbani.[32] Similarly, during the Afghan Taliban's rule in Afghanistan (1995–2001), India supported groups that were part of the Northern Alliance and were the main opposition forces to Pakistan's support to the Afghan Taliban's movement.

India believes the drawdown of coalition forces from Afghanistan will allow Pakistan to dominate Afghanistan's political landscape. India fears that Pakistan will try to minimize India's influence in Afghanistan.[33]

India also alleges that Pakistan has been hurting India's interests in Afghanistan. These fears center on the pro–Pakistan Kashmiri jihadi groups' use of Afghanistan as a base to launch terrorist attacks in the Indian-administered Kashmir or against India's interests in Afghanistan.[34] In March 2013, a spokesperson for the Indian External Affairs Ministry Syed Akbaruddin said, "There is a history of Afghan soil being used for terror attacks on India. We can't have that again."[35]

Balancing India's influence in Afghanistan is an important part of Pakistan's future Afghan policy as well as a goal in the Afghan endgame. Pakistan believes India is using its embassies and consulates in Afghanistan as a base for fueling the insurgency in Pakistan's Khyber Pakhtunkhwa and Balochistan provinces. Therefore, Pakistan is adamant to stop India's designs to sow the seeds of trouble in Pakistan through Afghanistan. India's training of the Afghan National Security Forces (ANSF) is also a cause of worry for Pakistan's security establishment. In 2001, Pakistan's Army Chief General Kayani said, "Strategically, we cannot have an Afghan army on our western border which has an Indian mindset and capabilities to take on Pakistan."[36] Pakistan believes an Indo–Afghan partnership will increase India's hegemony in the region. Pakistan fears being encircled between its western and eastern border by India through any alliance with Kabul.[37]

The Afghan Taliban has its own set of apprehensions and policies regarding the peace process. The Afghan Taliban believe that the willingness of the United States to negotiate with them reflects not only Afghan Taliban strength but the legitimacy of the Afghan Taliban movement as well. They cast the coalition forces' drawdown and willingness to talk as their victory and America's defeat.

More recently, the Afghan Taliban softened their stance on talks, after the United States dropped its conditions-based approach. From their categorical demand of rewriting the entire Afghan constitution, the Afghan Taliban moderated their demands to oppose three clauses. Similarly, they indicated a willingness to work with other Afghan political factions instead of trying to take over Kabul.[38] More importantly, they distanced their movement from al Qaeda. They reiterated their resolve to not allow Afghan soil to be used against any other country. In his November 2011 message, Mullah Omar said, "We do not want to harm other nations and countries." In April 2010, the Taliban issued a statement specifically on al Qaeda, which said, "We have no intention of causing harm to anyone, nor will we allow anyone to use our soil against anyone else."[39]

The West is skeptical of achieving any breakthrough during negotiations with the Afghan Taliban, if any at all. Many in the West doubt the Taliban's capacity to talk on behalf of all the Afghan Taliban groups involved in the fighting in Afghanistan due to the fractured nature of the Afghan Taliban movement. Moreover, they also question the Afghan Taliban's sincerity and incentive to join the peace process. Why would the Afghan Taliban come to the negotiation table when they can outlast the US and ISAF 2014 deadline in Afghanistan? Instead of accepting any agreement, which would favor the US and Afghan governments, the Afghan Taliban will try to use such negotiations to their own advantage and thus violate the agreement when it is convenient to do so. Fears also abound that the Afghan Taliban are treating talks as a delaying tactic, or a means to win the war through political and nonmilitary means.[40]

PAKISTAN'S PERSPECTIVE OF THE AFGHAN ENDGAME

Pakistan shares a porous and poorly guarded border of around 2,600 kilometers with Afghanistan, coupled with unrestricted daily cross-border movements of up to 100,000 people. It is also home to over three million Afghan refugees. Therefore, there is no country directly linked to the situation in Afghanistan the way Pakistan is. Developments in Afghanistan affect Pakistan the most, as seen in the Soviet occupation of Afghanistan (1979–1989) and the US invasion (2001–2014).[41] Therefore, Pakistan has vital interests in securing Afghanistan's peace and stability.[42] Afghanistan is one of the most important countries in Pakistan's foreign policy. Pakistan cannot be a passive player in Afghanistan's endgame, especially in light of the serious challenges and feeble opportunities for Pakistan. Pakistan's major concern is that any solution for Afghanistan should not destabilize Pakistan. As reported in a newspaper article written by a former ambassador of Pakistan, "It is better to live in peace with a neighbor whose history is replete with wars and fighting. It is in the interest of Pakistan to stay away from interfering in the internal affairs of Afghanistan. It is also best to ensure that the world's best warriors are your friends than your adversaries."[43]

Former Pakistani Foreign Minister Hina Rabbani Khar (2011–2013) elucidated Pakistan's perspective of the Afghan endgame in her speech at the Chatham House, a London-based think tank, on 22 February 2012. She said, "Kabul is and will remain the most important world capital for Pakistan. Peace, stability and security in Afghanistan are important to Pakistan's national interests. Pakistan supports all peace initiatives in Afghanistan, which are all-inclusive, Afghan-led, Afghan-owned and Afghan-driven. Pakistan will follow and assist and not lead the peace process in Afghanistan."[44]

Pakistan believes any negotiation process that is not Afghan initiated, Afghan led, and Afghan owned and that does not include all Afghan stakeholders is bound to fail. Moreover, pursuing a peace process must not fail to be sensitive to the history, geography, and culture of the region. Peace built on stability alone will be enduring in Afghanistan. Achieving less that is sustainable is more important than attempting more that is not sustainable.

The major reason behind failures of past political settlements lies in the confusion over desired results. The successes of future engagements need to move far beyond power-sharing agreements and deadline-driven hasty endgame proceedings. For the attainment of a broad-based peace or stability, it is necessary that Afghanistan does not sink into civil war.

Pakistan envisages an endgame achieved through a responsible transition that does not leave behind a security vacuum. It should lead to a power-sharing agreement among all the Afghan ethnic and political groups, including the Afghan Taliban.[45] Reconciliation will not be easily negotiated. However, diplomatic efforts must be doubled to achieve this.[46] In this regard,

Pakistan is ready to extend any support needed to help the Afghan government and other Afghan political groups reach a peace settlement. However, Pakistan's role can only be that of a facilitator.

Pakistan's stance, in this regard, is encapsulated in a fourteen-page document that Pakistan's Army Chief General Ashfaq Parvez Kayani handed over to US President Obama during his visit to the United States in December 2010. The document, titled *Ten Years Since 9/11: Our Collective Experience (Pakistan's Perspective)*, notes, "Pakistan is prepared to help in peace negotiations. However, the extent of this help should be correctly appreciated. We can facilitate but not guarantee. Ultimately it will remain Afghan responsibility."[47]

The Pakistani military establishment and the foreign ministry facilitated contacts between the leaders of the former Northern Alliance and the Afghan Taliban to ensure that Pakistan does not have to pursue its strategy of the 1990s.[48] Pakistan believes a negotiated settlement between the United States, the Afghan government, and the Afghan Taliban will help to end the insurgency in Afghanistan. This will eventually help Islamabad deal with homegrown terrorism.[49]

Pakistan does not want to see the Afghan Taliban win exclusive power in Afghanistan. Pakistan's Army Chief General Kayani underscored this fact on 1 February 2010 during a press conference with Western correspondents and journalists in Islamabad. He said, "We cannot have Talibanization. We want to remain modern and progressive. We cannot wish for Afghanistan what we do not wish for Pakistan.[50]

Many in Pakistan believe that if the Afghan Taliban came to power in Afghanistan like they did in 1996, they are morally and culturally bound to support their Pakistani counterparts the way the Pakistani Taliban supported them after 9/11. In such a situation, it will be difficult for Pakistan to reestablish its legitimacy in the FATA, where the Pakistani Taliban collude with al Qaeda and its Arab, Uzbek, Chechen, and Uighur adherents have formed their de facto Emirates.[51]

Another important aspect of Pakistan's Afghan endgame is to curtail India's ability to foment trouble in Pakistan from Afghanistan. While Pakistan acknowledges the importance of India's economic contribution to Afghanistan and accepts India's economic role there, it is not blind to India's subversive activities against Pakistan from Afghanistan. Pakistani security officials maintain India has been providing refuge, training, financial assistance, and weapons to Baloch separatists from Afghanistan.

Pakistani apprehensions about India's involvement are not without reasons as acknowledged by the US special envoy for Afghanistan and Pakistan, James Dobbins. On 7 August 2013 in an interview with the BBC, he said, "Pakistan's concerns over India's presence in Afghanistan are exaggerated but not groundless."[52] In a talk on Afghanistan in 2011 at the Cameron

University in Oklahoma, US Defense Secretary Chuck Hagel also corroborated Pakistani fears about India's anti-Pakistan designs in Afghanistan. He said, "India had been using Afghanistan as a second front against Pakistan. India has over the years financed problems for Pakistan from Afghanistan, and you can carry that into many dimensions. India took advantage of tensions between Kabul and Islamabad for fomenting troubles in the areas that border Afghanistan."[53] According to leaked US diplomatic cables in 2009, during a briefing to a visiting delegation of US parliamentarians, the former director general of the ISI, Ahmed Shuja Pasha, informed them about India's anti-Pakistan activities in Afghanistan. He said, "India had established nine training camps along the Afghan border where it was providing training to the members of the Baloch rebel groups." In 2007, former Pakistan President General Musharraf also raised the same point with US officials. He informed them that "New Delhi and Kabul were involved in efforts to provide weapons, training and funding for Baloch extremists through Brahamdagh Bugti and Balach Marri, two Baloch nationalists, who were living in Kabul."[54] Moreover, according to former Pakistani Interior Minister Rehman Malik, around 4,000 to 5,000 men received training in these camps. In 2012 when Pakistan requested Afghan President Hamid Karzai to deport Brahamdagh Bugti, head of the Baloch Republican Army (BRA), he was forced to leave Afghanistan. He moved to Switzerland.[55]

Pakistan also proposes a regional framework to ensure the commitment of noninterference and neutrality in Afghanistan's internal affairs. Pakistan believes peace cannot return to Afghanistan, without putting in place a regional noninterference framework.[56] Absence of such a framework will likely prompt regional countries to carve out their own spheres of influence in Afghanistan. In 2010, Pakistan carried out a number of diplomatic initiatives to persuade regional stakeholders about the significance of such a framework. Although a document was produced at the Istanbul Conference in November 2011, no subsequent progress has been made on this front. Pakistan should start a new round of regional diplomacy to reinitiate this process parallel to intra-Afghan peace processes.[57]

SHIFT IN PAKISTAN'S AFGHAN POLICY

Fears of an unstable Afghanistan, and the catastrophic impact it can have on domestic insurgencies in Pakistan, will be realized if the Afghan Taliban come to power in Pakistan.[58] The contours of Pakistan's new policy are developing as the Afghan endgame plays out. Internal security threats from anti-Pakistan militant groups in the FATA, India's growing role in Afghanistan, post-2014 US engagement in Afghanistan, and the attitude of Kabul toward Pakistan will be the main drivers of Pakistan's future Afghan policy. Currently, Pakistan is slowly rebuilding confidence with Afghanistan.[59]

Pakistan's new Afghan policy is that of "no favorites in Afghanistan." According to this approach, Pakistan is not supporting any particular group in Afghanistan. For Pakistan the Afghan Taliban are not a "friend," and the Karzai regime is not an "enemy." Pakistan will continue to deal with the elected government in Kabul that represents the Afghan people. Pakistan's Prime Minister Nawaz Sharif reiterated this in his 31 May 2013 meeting with the US special representative for Afghanistan–Pakistan, James Dobbins, in Islamabad. He noted, "We have no favorites in Afghanistan and our policy will be to allow Afghans to decide their future themselves."[60]

Pakistan no longer considers the Afghan Taliban to be its only option in Afghanistan. In fact, the link with the Afghan Taliban is troublesome for Pakistan. Pakistan's closer cooperation with the Afghan government could be seen in this light.[61] Pakistan moderated its demand for a friendly government in Kabul to a neutral government. Pakistan also opposes an Afghan Taliban takeover in Afghanistan, because this will make it more difficult for Pakistan to eliminate the Tehrik-i-Taliban Pakistan, the umbrella group of the Pakistan Taliban, in Pakistan.[62]

Pakistan's Afghan policies in the 1980s and 1990s focused on seeking strategic depth and countering the India–Afghanistan alliance, which supported the Baloch insurgents in Pakistan's southwestern Balochistan province and promoted the idea of Pashtunistan.[63] However, Pakistan's perception of strategic depth has changed in Afghanistan. In February 2010, speaking to a group of foreign journalists at the army general headquarters in Rawalpindi, General Kayani stated that strategic depth in Afghanistan did not imply controlling Afghanistan. In fact, a peaceful, stable, and neutral Afghanistan would automatically provide Pakistan with strategic depth.[64]

The normalization process with India is part of this shift in Pakistan's approach toward Afghanistan. Pakistan dropped its reservations about the economic role India is playing in Afghanistan.[65] Islamabad believes if the relations with India are peaceful, then the need for strategic depth in Afghanistan automatically vanishes. On the other hand, even if the old pattern of enmity with India continues, a stable Afghanistan leading to a peaceful Western border will suit Pakistan's strategic interests.[66]

Notwithstanding the formidable trust deficit between Kabul and Islamabad, in the past few years, Pakistan has been trying to improve its ties with the Karzai government. Pakistan reached out to non-Pashtun political leaders in the north, who have been Pakistan's historical adversaries in Afghanistan.[67] Both steps are to allay the fears of various Afghan groups concerning Pakistan's future policies in Afghanistan, as well as to build checks on the Afghan Taliban.

One illustration of this outreach strategy is the 10 April 2013 inauguration of the $18 million Liaquat Ali Khan Engineering University, built by Pakistan in Afghanistan's Balkh province. The province is a major stronghold of Afghanistan's second-largest ethnic community, the Tajiks. Historically, the Tajiks have been at odds with Islamabad over the latter's historical support for their foes, the Afghan Taliban.

The release of Afghan Taliban prisoners from Pakistan's jails, to facilitate the Afghan peace process, is also part of Pakistan's new Afghan policy. Over the past year, Islamabad released thirty-four Afghan Taliban, including the former number two leader of the Afghan Taliban, Mullah Abdul Ghani Baradar and former Taliban justice minister Mullah Nooruddin Turabi. Pakistan released the first batch of Afghan Taliban on 14 November 2012, during the visit of the Afghan High Peace Council chief Salahuddin Rabbani. This met the demands of the Afghan government.[68] At follow-up talks between Afghanistan and Pakistan, four additional prisoners were set free.[69] Following the visit of Afghan President Hamid Karzai to Pakistan on 26–27 August 2013, Pakistan released the third batch of Afghan Taliban prisoners.[70]

PAKISTAN'S OBJECTIVES IN AFGHANISTAN

- Pakistan's top priority in Afghanistan's endgame is its internal security challenge from the Pakistan Taliban on its western border. Depending on whether peace is achieved in Afghanistan or not after 2014, Pakistan strives to prevent negative spillover of instability from Afghanistan into its northwestern and southwestern areas.[71]
- A hostile Afghanistan aligned with India is also a major concern to Pakistan. The future Afghan government should not be antagonistic, if not friendly, to Pakistan. It should not allow use of Afghan soil by any state or nonstate actors against Pakistan.[72]
- Policy-making circles in Pakistan accept India's development role in Afghanistan. However, Pakistan wants to ensure India will not create problems for Pakistan by taking advantage of Afghanistan. Pakistan will endeavor to curtail any actions taken by India to foment the Baloch insurgency and destabilize Pakistan's tribal areas.
- Pakistan also seeks to strengthen its trade links with the Central Asian Republics (CARs) by working with Afghanistan for enhancing regional commerce and transportation links with the CARs, just as India does. Pakistan is keen to get reliable and alternative sources of gas supplies from Central Asia, as its existing reservoirs are depleting. Pakistan concluded energy deals with Tajikistan and Kyrgyzstan and offered to build road links through Central Asia. With Chinese assistance, Pakistan built a

deep-sea port in Gawadar, Balochistan, to serve as a gateway for trade with Afghanistan and other countries.

WHY PAKISTAN SUPPORTS THE AFGHAN TALIBAN'S INTEGRATION INTO AFGHANISTAN'S POLITICAL SYSTEM

Pakistan thinks that the Afghan Taliban's inclusion in the future political process is the key to long-term peace and stability in Afghanistan. The following points underline Pakistan's interests and perspectives on approaches to solving this problem:

- Any attempts to isolate the Afghan Taliban will likely prolong the insurgency and increase instability in Afghanistan. In this case, the Afghan Taliban's leaders will see no reason to vacate their sanctuaries in Pakistan. The Afghan Taliban will try to retake power in Kabul through force, resulting in widespread insecurity and civil war in Afghanistan.
- The Afghan Taliban's acceptance of a negotiated settlement will lead to their voluntary relocation to Afghanistan, thus eliminating the possibility of pro-India dispensation in Afghanistan.
- If the Afghan Taliban are not part of a broad-based coalition government in Kabul, Pakistan will face serious difficulties in controlling its own domestic insurgency in the FATA. This explains why Pakistan has been pushing for a balance of power between the Afghan Taliban and anti-Taliban forces.

EXAMINATION OF PAKISTAN'S EFFORTS TO NEUTRALIZE TALIBAN SANCTUARIES

A controversial aspect of Pakistan's Afghan policy is its reluctance to dismantle sanctuaries of the Afghan Taliban in the North Waziristan Agency, which enabled the Afghan Taliban to continue its insurgency against coalition and Afghan forces in Afghanistan. The base issues are as follows:

- Capacity issues: The Pakistan government's scarce resources and overstretched military troops hindered actions against the Afghan Taliban. For the past seven years, Pakistan's army has been stretched thin fighting two domestic insurgencies (Separatist insurgency in Balochistan and the Taliban insurgency in FATA), and guarding the country's eastern and western frontiers. Therefore, the army does not have the capacity to open up a new front to neutralize militants in a comprehensive manner. Pakistan's security establishment believes opening up a new front will neutralize the gains it has made in military operations against the Pakistan Taliban. In 2013,

TTP's attacks targeting foreign mountaineers in Gilgit-Baltistan, Pakistan's northern areas, and the Christian community in Peshawar, the provincial capital of Khyber Pakhtunkhwa, during a Sunday mass are two cases in point.[73] An affiliate of the TTP, Junood ul-Hifsa claimed responsibility for these attacks to avenge the killings of al Qaeda's and the Taliban's leaders in US drone strikes. The TTP created the group in June 2013 specifically to carry out attacks inside Pakistan in retaliation for the US drone strikes.[74]

- The Afghan Taliban is a wild card: Another reason for not going after the sanctuaries are Pakistan's concerns of being sidelined in the Afghan reconciliation process, which may benefit the groups and countries hostile to Pakistan. Pakistan considers the presence of the Afghan Taliban on its soil as an advantage that guarantees Pakistan's involvement in the Afghan endgame.
- Animosity with the Afghan Taliban and extra support for domestic terrorism: Pakistan's security establishment also believes going after the Afghan Taliban will not only turn them against Pakistan but will also result in renewed support for domestic terrorism. The Afghan Taliban will back the TTP against Pakistan's army. There are at least four things that the Afghan Taliban and the Pakistan Taliban have in common: geography, ideology, ethnicity, and financing. This implies that any animosity with the Afghan Taliban is bound to destabilize Pakistan. A case in point is the decision of General (Retired) Pervez Musharraf (1999–2008) to ban the Kashmiri jihadi groups—erstwhile proxies of the Pakistani state—in 2003–2004. Around thirty to thirty-five small factions of the Kashmiri jihadis splintered from their parent organizations and joined the Taliban and al Qaeda in the FATA. They were angry at the state for imposing a ban on their jihadi activities in the Indian-administered Kashmir, closing their offices and training camps and siding with the United States against them. The conglomerate of these groups is known as the Punjabi Taliban. The members of the Punjabi Taliban hail from Jaish-e-Mohammad (JeM), Lashkar-e-Jhangvi (LeJ), Lashkar-e-Taiba (LeT), Harkat-ul-Jihad-ul-Islami (HuJI), and so on. In the past few years, the TTP and al Qaeda carried out most of their terrorist attacks in mainland Pakistan, with the help of the Punjabi Taliban.[75] Initiation of a military operation against the Afghan Taliban can result in similar kinds of attack patterns inside Pakistan.

PROSPECTS FOR PEACE AND STABILITY IN AFGHANISTAN

From the previous analysis, three possible scenarios can emerge in Afghanistan after 2014. This chapter examines the three scenarios: continued conflict, peace and stability, and civil war.

Scenario 1: Continued Conflict

The signing of the BSA between the US and the Afghan governments could possibly lead to continuation and intensification of violence in Afghanistan. Holding talks with the Afghan Taliban for political reconciliation, on the one hand, and negotiating a BSA with the Karzai government, on the other, is incompatible. The Afghan Taliban will never reconcile and become part of the political system if foreign forces do not withdraw from Afghanistan.

The Afghan Taliban clearly articulates this demand. They moderated their stance on all their other demands except this one. In his August 2013 Eid message, the Afghan Taliban's leader, Mullah Muhammad Umar, showed his willingness to work with other Afghan political groups. They also dropped their demand of rewriting the entire Afghan constitution to minor amendments in three clauses.[76]

Talks succeed when two sides are ready to make compromises or one of the two sides is so weak that it agrees to compromise. Neither is true in Afghanistan's context. Actually, the Afghan Taliban can await US withdrawal from Afghanistan.

In this case, the conflict will continue in Afghanistan with varying degrees of violence. However, it will not lead to complete collapse of the government in Kabul. This situation is similar to the situation that Dr. Najibullah's pro-Moscow government faced in Afghanistan after the Soviet withdrawal (1988–1989). Against all popular predictions, Najib survived in office for three years, until April 1992. It was widely predicted that the government in Kabul would fall in months, if not within weeks, of the Soviet's withdrawal. The continuation of Soviet economic assistance enabled the Najib government to survive in office.[77]

US presence and continued economic and military assistance will enable the Afghan government to bar the Afghan Taliban from taking over Kabul. The north will remain in firm control of the government. However, it will not be able to exercise its influence beyond Kabul and urban centers in the south. The Afghan Taliban will continue to dominate the countryside in the southern and southwestern parts of Afghanistan along the borders with Pakistan.

Implications

- This situation will increase the complexities of the Afghan crisis. It will push Pakistan toward more instability and unrest in the FATA, the Khyber Pakhtunkhwa, and Balochistan. This will negatively influence the stability of the entire country.
- The Afghan Taliban and other resistance groups will likely continue fighting. The prevailing situation in the Afghanistan–Pakistan border areas is uniquely suited for a prolonged insurgency. Factors like the Afghan

government's weak control on the periphery, the minimal footprint of foreign troops, the porous border, and the drug financing work to the advantage of these groups.[78]
- The Afghan Taliban will not vacate their sanctuaries in Pakistan's border areas, and their ideological bonding and cooperation with the Pakistan Taliban will increase.
- American drone strikes in the Afghanistan–Pakistan border will continue in pursuit of the Taliban, leading to higher levels of anti-Americanism and the spread of Talibanization in the FATA and beyond.

Policy Options

- Despite the odds, as a long-term approach, Pakistan should continue with its proactive and inclusive Afghan policy and work to convince all the parties in the conflict to reach some settlement through political and diplomatic channels.
- Whether the situation in Afghanistan improves or not, Pakistan should immediately introduce political and administrative reforms packages in the FATA to bring it into the mainstream. Abolishing the Frontier Crimes Regulations (FCR), a set of laws enacted under the British Raj in India in 1901, and creating the Reconstruction Opportunity Zones (ROZs) will provide employment to the tribal youth. There is also a need to extend the jurisdiction of Pakistan's mainstream legal system to the FATA and overhaul the public education system, from primary school to the university level. The government should also reform the local law enforcement agencies, such as the Frontier Constabulary and Khassadars.
- Pakistan needs to deploy troops along the Durand Line on a permanent basis to strengthen border control mechanisms and to improve coordination with Afghan security forces.
- Pakistan must also develop a comprehensive national security policy to deal with the issue of homegrown militancy, which is closely linked to the situation in Afghanistan.
- Pakistan should immediately start serious negotiations with the Baloch insurgents to try to settle the issue by accepting their legitimate demands within the constitutional framework. This will allow Pakistan to focus on its western border and the challenges coming from groups such as the TTP.

Scenario 2: Peace and Stability

Peace and stability in Afghanistan is in the best interests of Pakistan. It will prevent further negative fallout within Pakistan. It will also reduce demands by the United States to "do more."

Pakistan pledged $330 million for reconstruction and nation building in Afghanistan. It built a kidney center in Afghanistan's eastern province of Jalalabad and the 2,000-bed Jinnah Hospital in Kabul. Moreover, Pakistan doubled the number (1,000) of scholarships awarded to Afghan students in March 2010. Over 7,000 Afghan students are studying in Pakistan's universities and colleges, which is around 60 percent of all Afghans studying abroad.[79] Over the next four years, Pakistan intends to provide 2,000 fully funded graduate and postgraduate scholarships to Afghan students in Pakistan's universities and higher education institutes.[80] Currently, over three million refugees reside in Pakistan. The Pakistani government extended their repatriation date until December 2015.[81]

Pakistan, by virtue of its geography, is Afghanistan's window on the outside world just as Afghanistan is the key to Pakistan and South Asia's access to Central Asia and to the wider regional economic network. Afghanistan is the third-largest market for Pakistan's exports in the world, accounting for 6 percent of the total exports. However, the India–Pakistan rivalry has been a major obstacle to unlock the economic potential of South and Central Asia. India–Pakistan cooperation is pivotal to Afghanistan's peace and stability.

Though the rival strategic interests of India and Pakistan pit them against each other in Afghanistan, both countries will gain through trilateral cooperation in Afghanistan.[82] India and Pakistan can follow Professor Carol Bell's reverse partnership model. According to this model, in a situation where costs outweigh profits of any confrontation, the actors involved should adopt an adverse partnership. The adverse partnership does not mean cordial, trusting, or friendly relations. It is only a consciousness, between the dominant powers, that they have solid common interests as well as sharp differences. This can be a good starting point for the two countries to cooperate in Afghanistan. For this purpose, the countries should start a sustained bilateral dialogue.

India and Pakistan can build on transit trade agreements already in place, such as the Afghanistan–Pakistan Transit Trade Agreement (APTTA).[83] Despite viewing India as a main threat to Pakistan's interests in Afghanistan, Pakistan changed its stance on India's involvement in Afghanistan. Pakistan withdrew its opposition to India's participation in the November 2011 Istanbul conference. By cooperating, the two energy-starved nations can gain much. The growing compatibility of their regional economic interests, as evident through their partnership in the transnational Turkmenistan–Afghanistan–Pakistan–India (TAPI) gas pipeline, necessitates cooperation.[84]

India and Pakistan can sort out most of the transit problems regarding Afghanistan if the South Asia Free Trade Agreement (SAFTA) is implemented. This agreement was signed in Pakistan in 2004 and was supposed to be implemented in 2006, but has yet to come into force. Implementation of the SAFTA can revive economic cooperation among India, Afghanistan, and Pakistan.

Implications

- Judicious implementation of SAFTA and APTTA will allow Pakistan to have access to cheaper goods, increase employment opportunities, and open up Central Asia's markets to Pakistan's exports.
- Pakistan will gain access to the energy resources and gas reserves in Central Asia.
- Stable western borders with Afghanistan will allow Pakistan to concentrate on the domestic Pakistan Taliban insurgency and its affiliated groups.

Policy Options

- Pakistan should diversify its Afghan policy with the civilian government taking full control and ownership of Pakistan's Afghan policy with a long-term vision. The government should enhance and strengthen the contacts initiated with the non-Pashtun groups.
- Pakistan should take the lead to unlock the transit potential of Pakistan and Afghanistan to facilitate trade in the region and beyond. Being connected to Afghanistan and having built a deep-sea water port in Gawadar, Pakistan, are key enablers for economic growth. If Pakistan does not take the lead, no other countries will likely assume this key leadership role.

Scenario 3: Civil War

If the BSA is not signed, the United States exercises its zero option, and reconciliation between Kabul and the Afghan government remains inconclusive, then Afghanistan can slide into a civil war.

Pakistan has strong apprehensions that the failure to achieve a political settlement with the Afghan Taliban, coupled with the security transition from the United States to the ANSF, and drawdown of the US forces will create a security vacuum leading to further instability. This will increase instability in Afghanistan, leading to additional spillover into Pakistan's tribal areas and beyond. Moreover, the US counterterrorism policies centered on the continuation of drone strikes in Pakistan's tribal areas will contribute to continuing erosion of the government's credibility. It will also increase the growth of radicalization and violent extremism in the Pashtun-inhabited FATA.

A civil war in Afghanistan will be highly destabilizing for Pakistan and the entire region. It will lead to a Syria-like situation in Afghanistan, where no political or ethnic group will be in a position to take over Kabul. During the past ten years, Afghanistan had changed in all dimensions. It is not the same as it was in the 1990s. People's perceptions have changed and expectations have increased. Similarly, the nature of support and goodwill that the Afghan Taliban received from the Afghan masses has diminished.[85]

Unlike the 1990s, the Afghan Taliban cannot take over Kabul. Since the revival of insurgency in 2006, they engaged in hit-and-run guerilla operations against the US and ISAF troops or coordinated terror attacks in Kabul or other cities within Afghanistan. However, this is not sufficient to retake Kabul and reestablish the Islamic Emirate. They lack the manpower, weaponry, and military capacity required to occupy a city. At the same time, the factions of the Northern Alliance have immensely benefited from their alliance with the United States. They have the modern weaponry, improved organization, and bolstered capacity to resist any attempts by the Afghan Taliban to take over Kabul. This will likely result in a deadlock between these groups, but certainly will lead to more bloodshed.

Implications

- The likelihood of an India–Pakistan proxy war becomes imminent in the event of a civil war in Afghanistan.
- These conditions will likely result in continuing unrest in the FATA along with a reversal of the direction of the Pakistan Taliban insurgency whereby the TTP and its affiliated groups will continue their anti-Pakistan activities from their sanctuaries in the border areas of Afghanistan. It will also increase the radicalization and Talibanization in the FATA.
- There will be a surge in drug trafficking and weapons smuggling, and a huge influx of Afghan refugees in Pakistan.

Policy Options

- Pakistan should work earnestly to preempt this situation by working with all the key stakeholders to persuade them away from adopting military means. The aim should be to raise the incentives for participation in the political process and increase costs for recourse to violence.
- Pakistan should come up with a comprehensive national security policy. The focus of such a policy should be inside out rather than outside in. Historically, Pakistan's approach has been to protect itself from perceived external threats (India, Afghanistan) using internal elements, such as the Islamist militants. However, now the situation has changed. This logic must now be reversed to deal with the current security threats posed by homegrown terrorism. Any future national security policy should look at the internal security situation to determine the external security policies in

relation to India and Afghanistan. Internal security threats should treat homegrown terrorism as a major security threat.
- Cooperative policy approaches should be initiated, which will likely enhance understanding and knowledge of the regional countries about each other's interests and worries regarding security and stability in Afghanistan after 2014. This is why a regional framework of noninterference and neutrality among the neighboring states of Afghanistan is very important.
- The goal in theory and practice should be, through dialogue, to give the Afghan Taliban a chance to transform themselves into a political group from their status as an insurgent group, without any talk of winning or losing.[86] A regional forum such as the Shanghai Cooperation Organisation or the South Asian Association for Regional Cooperation should be used to help the Afghan Taliban move away from their current insurgency and transform their movement into a political group. They would benefit just as in the cases of Hamas, Hezbollah, and al Sadr's militia, all of which successfully transformed into legitimate political groups.[87]

CONCLUSION

There are quick fixes to offer rapid growth for peace and stability in Afghanistan after 2014. The vagueness surrounding the on-again, off-again peace process has made the political settlement a futile series of meetings and conferences over the past three years. The entire peace process needs a major course correction. Achieving less that is sustainable is more important than attempting more that is not sustainable.

The current course adapted to reconciliation with the Afghan Taliban must be conditions based rather than calendar driven. Moreover, a political settlement without political incentives is a nonstarter. There are no quick fixes to the Afghan endgame. Arriving at some agreement with the Afghan Taliban in the given time frame will be a miracle. At the same time, any peace deal pushed from the outside can achieve only short-term stability, but cannot ensure sustainable peace.

US intentions in Afghanistan do not transmit a uniform image, which complicates the post-2014 outlook of Afghanistan. Instead of facilitating the peace process, the United States is trying to control it. Moreover, the United States' insistence on staying on in Afghanistan until 2024, as part of a bilateral security agreement with Afghanistan, in parallel with political reconciliation between the Afghan Taliban and the Afghan government, is incompatible. This is a formula for further unrest in the years to come. The focus should be to consolidate the gains earned in political and economic spheres into a sustainable stabilization and reconstruction process. Peace built on stability alone will be enduring in Afghanistan.

The progress on political reconciliation should be assessed separately from the ongoing transition process. Transition is easy to achieve while reconciliation is complex, slow, and hard to come by in a short time period. As long as vagueness surrounds future US goals in Afghanistan, other regional players will continue with their hedging strategies. Any rush to exit from Afghanistan, as indicated by various US officials when referring to the zero option, will be catastrophic. However, long-term US military presence will be equally destabilizing for the region.

The endgame will not lead to long-lasting peace in Afghanistan until it is addressed in its local and regional context. It is important to keep the constants of history, geography, culture, and religion in view when approaching the peace process. The process of political reconciliation must be Afghan led and Afghan owned, and it will still remain fragile without the active support of the international community and the noninterference of regional countries.

Each of the three mentioned scenarios of the Afghan endgame leaves Pakistan between a rock and a hard place. It is likely that violence and armed conflict will continue in Afghanistan. Pakistan needs to come to an agreement with the United States on Afghanistan, and the existence of militant infrastructures in its tribal areas. Without sorting out the issue of existing sanctuaries in its border areas along Afghanistan, Pakistan's demands of asking the United States to end the drone strikes is likely unrealistic. The ostrich approach of Pakistan's theories that the unrest in Pakistan is the negative spilling over of the war in Afghanistan is not good enough, because that does not solve the problem.

Pakistan's hands-off approach of ignoring the Afghan Taliban groups carrying out attacks in Afghanistan from their sanctuaries in Pakistan is fraught with dangerous and blind assumptions. The same groups can reverse the direction of their terror campaign once their dependence on Pakistan ceases.

If Pakistan does not improve its operations in the FATA, there is a strong likelihood of the reversal of this attack pattern, whereby TTP can carry out terror attacks in Pakistan from their Afghan sanctuaries. Pakistan needs to come up with a comprehensive and long-term national security policy, defining the terrorist threat in explicit terms; otherwise, the militant groups will continue to hurt Pakistan.

At the same time, Pakistan will have to give up the tendency of looking at Afghanistan from a narrow security lens that puts Pakistan's security establishment in the driving seat of Pakistan's Afghan policy. The civilian government in Pakistan should take charge of Pakistan's Afghan policy and diversify it in the political and economic domains. The contacts initiated with the non-Pashtun groups in the north should continue, despite slow progress and challenges in this direction.

Pakistan and India should turn their competition into cooperation in Afghanistan. Pakistan does not have to look at India's presence in Afghanistan with paranoia. The scope of working together and the resulting benefits of cooperation in Afghanistan far outweigh the confrontational approach. India and Pakistan can build on transit trade agreements already in place, such as the APTTA. This is why Pakistan's proposed regional framework of neutrality and noninterference among Afghanistan's neighboring countries should be initiated in parallel to intra-Afghan peace processes.

Despite diverging interests and divided opinions of the stakeholders, the Afghan endgame is at a stage where peaceful and responsible transition will depend on their conduct. If they cooperate, and bring more clarity into their long-term interests, an amicable solution to the war in Afghanistan is still attainable. Cooperation, rather than confrontation, holds the key to the fledgling peace process. Integration of the Afghan Taliban as a legitimate political party, the signing of a regional pact of noninterference and neutrality among the neighboring countries, and the continued international economic assistance to the Afghan government can deliver peace. It takes two to make peace, but only one to make a war.

Chapter Three

An American Perspective for Afghanistan's Future[1]

Douglas Woodall

> We are never prepared for what we expect.
>
> —James Michener[2]

Prior to serving in Afghanistan for the first time, a friend recommended that I read the 1963 book *Caravans*, by James Michener. *Caravans* is a great piece of historical fiction and fits in a genre usually not found on recommended professional military reading lists. However, Michener's extensive experience in Afghanistan provides a fascinating depiction of Afghanistan's cultural and societal dynamics. For readers not familiar with the story, the book describes the search for an American woman, Ellen Jaspar, who disappeared in Afghanistan shortly after her marriage to an Afghan man. The story follows an American diplomat ordered to find her at the behest of Jaspar's parents, who contacted a US Senator to determine the location of their missing daughter. The plot immediately grabs your attention, and most readers instinctively assume that Jaspar's fate was likely tragic and unfortunate. It is a compelling read, and for me it became a race to confirm my assumptions about the outcome of the novel. I was wrong. The novel ended in a completely unpredictable way. For those possessing a solid grounding and understanding of Afghanistan's culture and people, the story is plausible.

In much the same way, numerous assumptions abound that Afghanistan's future prospects are inevitably unfortunate, and most media and political commentaries foretell of a troubled quagmire for the future of the country. All future outcomes will depend on unique amalgamations of key decisions and future engagement strategies selected by political leaders charting the way forward for Afghanistan. Given the changing realities on the ground, it is important to capture the incipient economic and social indicators to inform likely scenarios for the future of Afghanistan. Given a contextual framework to analyze future outcomes, I will consider the best case, the most likely, and the most dangerous outcomes for Afghanistan's future. Discrete events and decisions will differentiate the future projections as follows:

- Best case scenario: The United States and the Government of the Islamic Republic of Afghanistan (GIRoA) agree to a bilateral security agreement (BSA) entailing continuing military advise and assist training support and counterterrorism assistance to remain in Afghanistan post-2014. In parallel, negotiations with the Afghan Taliban are successful and result in the peaceful integration of the Afghan Taliban into GIRoA's legitimate political processes. This scenario also assumes that all political factions and parties will agree to the peaceful return of the Afghan Taliban and Afghanistan's presidential elections occur as scheduled with a peaceful transition of power for the government.
- Most likely scenario: The United States and GIRoA sign the BSA, thus enabling continuing training assistance and counterterrorism support. Peaceful integration of the Afghan Taliban into GIRoA is not successful, and a delay or postponement of Afghanistan's presidential elections transpires.
- Most dangerous scenario: The BSA fails to gain the necessary approvals, and all US military support withdraws from Afghanistan prior to 2015. Moreover, negotiation with the Afghan Taliban fails, and Afghanistan delays or postpones its presidential elections. International aid will continue to flow as promised to Afghanistan but will depend on the ensuing security and diplomatic conditions in the country.

Analysis of these scenarios with respect to security, governance, economic, and regional factors will inform the resulting implications for each. Finally, key lessons for future engagements and regional security strategies will inform greater awareness for countries not directly involved in the region. The region is at a critical crossroads, and the global prosperity enjoyed by many nations is about to end if the international community allows this region to again export terror to other regions of the globe.

WHAT IS THE BEST WAY FORWARD FOR AFGHANISTAN?

The best scenario for the future of Afghanistan will depend on the successful conclusion of three key events prior to 2015. First, that a US and GIRoA BSA will maintain US military advisers and counterterrorism capabilities to support the Afghan government beyond 2014. Next, the successful integration of the Afghan Taliban results from the peaceful entrance of the Afghan Taliban under the legitimate political processes of GIRoA. This assumes that Pakistan allows moderate Afghan Taliban voices to enter the reconciliation process such as that of Mullah Ghani Baradar.[3] Although Mullah Baradar is now free, his ability to influence the Afghan Taliban and freely enter negotiations with GIRoA is still yet to be determined. Third, the transition of presidential power in Afghanistan occurs as scheduled with a peaceful transition of leadership. Finally, this scenario assumes that all political factions and power brokers in Afghanistan agree to the peaceful integration of the Afghan Taliban to GIRoA. These assumptions serve as the baseline for the necessary critical events and key decisions necessary to secure the best possible outcome for Afghanistan's future.

THE KEY TO SECURITY IN THE FUTURE

Both GIRoA and the Afghan Taliban gain the most from this scenario. While greater regional security will also likely result, the immediate gains made through the Afghan Taliban's reconciliation and integration will help facilitate GIRoA's ability to focus on other areas of governance and representation for the population of Afghanistan. The continued presence of the United States will also help contain terrorism from spreading to other parts of the world, while advise and assist efforts with Afghan National Security Forces (ANSF) will provide stability during this critical stage of ANSF's development. Moreover, moderate Afghan Taliban, such as Mullah Baradar, may enable direct talks between the Afghan Taliban and GIRoA, thereby facilitating the relaxing of the Afghan Taliban's radical stance against recognizing GIRoA and conducting direct talks with GIRoA. If moderate Afghan Taliban can conclude a reconciliation agreement prior to the elections, they may provide a mechanism for including the Afghan Taliban in decisions to ratify a BSA to enable continued assistance from the United States. This will also give the Afghan Taliban the opportunity to save face for their inflexible position to demand the complete withdrawal of all coalition forces from Afghanistan. This helps the Afghan Taliban's information operations but, in a more important way, will lend credibility and legitimacy to peaceful means of gaining a voice in GIRoA's politics.

    The Afghan Taliban are quickly losing popularity in Afghanistan. Now that the ANSF have the security lead throughout the country, nearly all of the Afghan Taliban's attacks kill or injure other Afghans. Recently, this served as the catalyst for a GIRoA information operations campaign to label attacks in Afghanistan as committed by the "enemies of Afghanistan," indigenous Afghan initiated insurgent attacks.[4] In a more important way, their indiscriminate attacks are taking the lives of women and children, and that is precipitating anti-Taliban movements across the country. The brutality and growing unpopularity are starting to take root in long-held Afghan Taliban strongholds in Southern Afghanistan, such as Panjwai district of Kandahar province. According to Major General Robert Abrams, the International Security Assistance Force (ISAF) Regional Command South commander, speaking in March 2013, "the uprising in the Panjwai district of Kandahar province began about one month ago, and at this point the Taliban have been 'kicked out' of all but about four villages—not at the initiative of Afghan or coalition troops but that of the villagers. I suspect the rest of those villages will fall here in short order."[5] Moreover, many of the Afghan Taliban's movements and motives involve malign influences from Pakistan, and that is exacerbating the ability of the Afghan Taliban to maintain influence over Afghan villages. In Regional Command East, historic Afghan Taliban strongholds are falling as villagers are similarly rising up in arms against the Afghan Taliban. "One Logar province uprising leader, Farhad Akbari, is said to be working closely with local police. 'Our uprising is aimed at saving our people from terrorism and from the clutches of Pakistan's ISI [intelligence service],' Akbari was quoted in Afghan national television. 'They are all slaves and always martyr our elders, scholars, engineers, and intellectuals. . . . They martyred seven school girls . . . so that's enough, and we can no longer tolerate tyranny.'"[6] Peaceful integration into GIRoA is the best hope for the Afghan Taliban's successful reestablishment of legitimacy and rebranding as an independent political entity independent of foreign control and manipulation. Moreover, the Afghan Taliban increasingly are unable to challenge the ANSF in the field, so they are resorting to atrocities against civilians to instill terror in villages or to desperate measures such as the recent assassination of the governor of Logar inside a mosque using the Koran as the method of delivering the attack.

The ANSF will continue efforts to provide the best security they can for Afghanistan. Now that the ANSF are firmly in the lead for the security of the country, efforts to provide a sustainable way forward, with continued assistance from the United States, will ensure security forces can focus on enduring foundations for success. The ANSF are still at a critical stage of development, and minimal investment in coalition force assistance will help maintain a sustainable security force capable of ensuring the independence of Afghanistan. Moreover, Afghan Local Police (ALP) initiatives will continue to increase local legitimacy for security and further the government's efforts to boost Afghans' confidence in GIRoA.

As for coalition forces, this scenario will likely reduce the number of insider attacks while enabling the continuance of reconstruction efforts across the country. Coalition forces can focus on preventing terrorists from establishing sanctuaries in the region while catering to the maturing needs of the ANSF. More time is necessary for security advisers to focus on the logistical and administrative management of large forces, with particular emphasis on utilizing current resources and equipment for sustainable military operations and training. A peaceful settlement with the Afghan Taliban will enable a higher state of readiness for the ANSF and increase capacity for training and equipping the force.

Continued US security presence will also help reconciliation and integration of the Afghan Taliban by serving as a deterrent to any regime or faction refusing to allow their entry to the legitimate political process. Direct US presence serves to deter regional malign actors and terror groups from operating inside Afghanistan, something with enormous benefit for the global commons. A secure environment will set the conditions for GIRoA to continue its focus on corruption and continue to improve governance concerns in remote and rural areas of the country. One of the biggest challenges in the rural and outlying areas of Afghanistan is direct contact with the people, thus fueling the perceptions of a lack of legitimate representation and increasing perceptions of corruption. The ALP are helping to put a legitimate face on local security while eliminating the gulf between the power center of Kabul and the rest of Afghanistan—but the program is under fire in many areas. While the ALP still has challenges with corruption and tribal complexities, getting feedback and representation in security and governance structures reflective of the local populace is the first step toward transparency and confidence-building measures to accurately portray the central government as responsive to the needs of the people.

GIRoA ENABLED TO BATTLE CORRUPTION

With a more stable security framework and safer environment, GIRoA will be able to focus on boosting the confidence of Afghan citizens and foreign investors through focused efforts to reduce corruption and reinforce transparency and legitimacy for the Afghan people. A renewed focus on governance will ensure that the foreign aid promised to the country, to the tune of $16 billion, will arrive as promised. This amount includes donations pledged during the 2012 Tokyo Conference, where over 70 countries met to provide a $4 billion yearly stream of money through 2015. Some nations have pledged to provide current funding streams through 2017.[7] An Associated Press news article stated, "International donors have reaffirmed pledges of $16 billion in support for Afghanistan, while expressing concern about corruption there."[8] Demands from US lawmakers will place emphasis on transparency and accountability for funds flowing to the Afghan government. On the eve of elections, this poses one of the most critical defining moments for the future governance of Afghanistan—that clear measures demonstrate serious work on fighting corruption and result in independent, secure, inclusive, and transparent elections. This will help to facilitate a peaceful transition of power in the country.

Because of the rural nature of the country, securing outlying areas is imperative to address long-standing desires and concerns to establish local legitimacy and representation in the government. Both corruption and the lack of transparency fuel mistrust of the government's policies and serve to exacerbate GIRoA's challenges and understanding of the population's needs and expectations from the central government. This scenario provides the security apparatus and environment necessary to focus on expanding local legitimacy for security forces and the government by putting a local face on security forces while establishing a presence for legitimate government representation. In many rural areas of Afghanistan, villagers have never seen a representative of the government since the time of the Soviet occupation. Small measures demonstrating personal care will improve the population's national commitment to strengthen identity as an Afghan and imbue a renewed sense of national pride in the government.

SUSTAINABLE ECONOMIC GROWTH IS POSSIBLE

GIRoA is serious about mitigating the effects of the coalition's withdrawal through economic measures designed to bring in more investment. Investor confidence is critical and strongly dependent on the security situation in the country. Increased foreign investment will flow to Afghanistan under this scenario. As numerous analysts fail to highlight, the United States helped to enable a security environment facilitating the largest foreign commercial ventures in the history of Afghanistan. While the merits of that may be debatable, the ability to create a sustainable economy for Afghanistan is certainly not out of reach or impossible for what many people continue to refer to as the "land-locked" country. China also holds the economic stability of this region in its hands. Chinese interests should also factor in its citizens killed in this conflict. Eleven Chinese workers were killed by terrorists in 2004, which prompted a strong response from China.[9] This attack also involved the killing of an Afghan guard, and the Afghan Taliban were likely responsible for the attack. After the recent death of three Chinese nationals, an opportunity for greater engagement by China in the region may be possible, given the enormous foreign investment directed to Afghanistan.[10] As reported by CBS News, "In November 2007, the China Metallurgical Group Corp., a state-owned conglomerate, signed a $3 billion contract with the Afghan Ministry of Mines and Petroleum to mine copper from a barren, mountainous region southeast of Kabul. The area is also a Taliban stronghold. But that's not stopping the Chinese from promising what would be the largest foreign investment in Afghan history. In fact, the company has even said they will build a railroad—the first in Afghanistan—to the mine from Pakistan."[11] As projects of this nature continue to improve Afghanistan's infrastructure, its success will draw even more investors and greater involvement from Afghanistan's regional neighbors.

International aid will continue to flow and likely increase given a security framework under reconciliation and the cessation of hostilities. Recent GIRoA investment incentives will certainly help draw the right investment from new sources of capital while opening up potentially new export markets. The BSA's effects will reinforce international economic signals to reduce financial risk of continuing investment flows to Afghanistan and continue to provide the support needed for GIRoA to continue capacity building to attract foreign investment.

Economic benefits will also extend to Afghanistan's neighbors and the rest of the world. Providing greater regional stability will improve regional focuses on economic stability and partnerships, while preventing terrorists from exporting instability beyond the region—something that the continued US presence will mitigate under the BSA.

GLOBAL COMMONS ARE SAFER FROM CONTAINED EXTREMISM

This scenario provides the best capabilities for enduring regional stability. The presence of US counterterrorism forces will mitigate continuing terror operations by al Qaeda, the Haqqani Network, the Pakistan Taliban, and Lashkar-e-Taiba. Moreover, this scenario will severely degrade foreign malign actors, while GIRoA will continue to improve the delivery of goods and services to the Afghan people. Moreover, the continued targeting of terrorist safe havens will prevent terrorists from transcending the region to other areas of the world—especially Central Asia, China, Southeast Asia, the Levant, the Arabian Peninsula, and Africa.

WHAT IS THE MOST LIKELY WAY FORWARD FOR AFGHANISTAN?

The most likely future scenario for Afghanistan will result in an approved BSA to enable military advisers and counterterrorism capabilities to remain in Afghanistan post-2014. The Afghan Taliban are already establishing clear indicators that US involvement past 2014 is not possible under any circumstances. Based on current election estimates, it is also likely that delayed or postponed presidential elections are possible, as incipient indicators of problems organizing the elections are already occurring and overtures by those in the Karzai administration ponder circumstances that may delay the elections.[12] More troublesome are rumors of Afghans' fears of President Karzai convening a Loya Jirga to substantiate a continuing extension of power for the current regime.

CIVIL WAR WILL CONTINUE

Despite labeling attacks in Afghanistan as perpetrated by the "enemies" of Afghanistan, Afghans are increasingly the focus of attacks, and civilian casualties continue to turn local villages against the Afghan Taliban. Recent comments by Afghan Taliban leaders cite conditions for reconciliation that will make inclusion of ethnic minorities unlikely. The inability to integrate the Afghan Taliban or to provide a framework for reconciliation will serve as the impetus for the continued rhetoric for demands to end the perceived occupation by coalition forces. Of greater concern are visits to Iranian leadership by the Afghan Taliban and the recent conclusion of a bilateral agreement by GIRoA and Iran that includes military training and intelligence sharing.[13] According to a recent report from NBC News, "Omar [the Taliban leader] also made clear that they [the Taliban] will not accept any foreign military base in Afghanistan after 2014."[14] The Afghan Taliban will lose all credibility if they negotiate a settlement that entails continued assistance from the United States beyond 2014. As long as Pakistan and the Haqqani Network continue operations to support the Afghan Taliban's desires to undermine GIRoA, attacks against Afghans will continue, and a protracted civil war will continue in Afghanistan.

Successful BSA negotiations will provide the support necessary to ensure that the ANSF can continue to mitigate attacks against the civilian population while ensuring continued US presence to help governance efforts. Forging a more effective national identity will be possible and will provide an opportunity to further discredit and distance the Afghan Taliban from the population. The effects of the war have already forced the Afghan Taliban to compromise their core values and to change their outlook and fundamental position on the education of females. With new Pakistani leadership, increasing pressure may help influence the Afghan Taliban's leaders in Pakistan.

Other key facets the BSA will influence are the stability of the current government and confidence in future assistance. Numerous ethnic factions will likely not support the return of the Afghan Taliban, and some warlords are strong enough to pose additional threats to the internal stability of Afghanistan if the United States withdraws military assistance. The BSA framework will enable the critical presence necessary to ensure that elections occur as scheduled and will continue to signal enduring support for the constitutional underpinnings of GIRoA.

Potential remains for continuing proxy fights between India and Pakistan executed in Afghanistan. Recent violence against Indian targets in Afghanistan reinforces the malign influence and intentions of Pakistan. Continued security assistance via the BSA will help constructive solutions to the resolution of hostilities in Afghanistan and shed light on self-serving operations launched from within Pakistan against Afghan soil. This will provide a mechanism to highlight continuing malign influences from Pakistan for the purview of the international community.

Recent Afghan agreements with Iran serve to influence the United States at the bargaining table, but the credibility of President Karzai's regime deteriorates daily and there appears to be an acute misunderstanding of US interests in the region. Moreover, other Afghan leaders continue to harbor mistrust of President Karzai and his true intentions—another reason that a continuing coalition presence will help GIRoA's governance and constitutional underpinnings succeed. Failure to successfully conclude the BSA at this stage signals potential delay tactics or the desire to gain more support and offer a Loya Jirga the chance to approve continuing coalition force presence.

ECONOMIC GROWTH WILL BE STIFLED

Protracted conflict will dampen efforts to increase capital flows to Afghanistan and test the patience of countries providing current foreign direct investment in Afghanistan. Continued US presence in the region will assuage concerns and keep financial risk more conducive to foreign investors, but the success of the ANSF and GIRoA will determine the direction of economic growth. Without positive efforts by Pakistan to help the ANSF defeat and deny the Afghan Taliban sanctuary, GIRoA must consider options to partner with other countries to provide enduring frameworks to counter the malign influence of Pakistan—even if it means closer relations with India.

The current situation in Afghanistan represents an opportunity for one of the strongest regional countries to increase investment and take a leadership role in Afghanistan's future economic development. Multilateral economic forums involving the Chinese may provide incentives for all the key players in the region to cooperate across security and economic dialogues designed to stabilize the entire region.

LONGER-TERM SOLUTIONS—ENTER THE CHINESE?

This scenario offers the best prospect for regional stability. The Afghan Taliban have proven their record of duplicity and supporting terrorism, and they cannot be trusted. A failure for the Afghan Taliban to enter the international arena peacefully may call for options that are not currently on the table. Specifically, some UN Security Council members do not agree that a US and GIRoA BSA is the correct mechanism for continued US presence in the region. Russia voiced concerns to implement a UN mandate for continued presence. The best way to pressure Pakistan and the Afghan Taliban would be a sanctioned resolution by the UN for a peacekeeping mission to Afghanistan—but with involvement from one of the largest external economic investors in Afghanistan—China. The entire security dynamic in the region would change with the introduction of Chinese peacekeeping troops into Afghanistan. Since the Russians are advocating a UN mandate, the options for sharing the expense and contributions for securing the region can expand outside of NATO. This will also provide a forum for an engagement strategy between the United States and China that seeks common ground with shared interests and with potentially new possibilities for engagement in the Pacific Theater. Taking this long-term approach is crucial to understanding new horizons for sustainable end states for governance, economics, security, and regional cooperation for the future.

Parallel efforts to provide regional security through the Shanghai Cooperation Organization present additional mechanisms to mitigate security concerns in the region. GIRoA gained observer status in 2012, and the recent conference in Kyrgyzstan focused on the critical need to address security concerns in the region. Specifically, Chinese President Xi Jinping "called for the implementation of a convention on combating the 'three evil forces' of terrorism, separatism and extremism, and the establishment of a center for comprehensive response to security threats and challenges."[15] The organization also stressed the importance of the UN and efforts to use the UN to resolve conflicts. This presents a great opportunity to approach China on post-2014 security agreements in Afghanistan.

In April 2013, the Information Office of the State Council released a white paper on China's armed forces. According to this paper, "China is the biggest troop and police contributor among the five permanent members of the UN Security Council. It also dispatches the most numbers of troops for engineering, transportation, and medical support among all the 115 contributing countries. China pays and contributes the largest share of UN peacekeeping costs among all developing countries."[16] President Xi Jinping also recently referenced the "Silk Road Spirit."[17] This is definitely a practical attempt to tie the economic importance of security in the region to efforts to combat the three evils. Given the economic investments throughout Central and South Asia by China and its internal security concerns, it may be easy to coopt Russia and China to sponsor a long-term security solution for Afghanistan that entails stronger support from regional partners and serves as a stronger deterrent to malign plans by the Afghan Taliban.

MOST DANGEROUS SCENARIO FOR AFGHANISTAN'S FUTURE

The recent options considered by the US government to speed the withdrawal of military forces and not extend military assistance post-2014 as a zero option shocked the world and revealed the nature of the current strained political relationships between key leaders.[18] Moreover, many think it is mere hyperbole and the United States will not pull all military assistance from Afghanistan. Those who remember the negotiations for an enduring presence in Iraq certainly know that a failure to negotiate a BSA will solidify US military disengagement and likely precipitate other coalition partners' departure from Afghanistan too. Moreover, a failed BSA, coupled with failed reconciliation efforts with the Afghan Taliban, will provide ideal conditions for an expanding civil war and will cloud future prospects for transparent elections and the public's confidence in GIRoA. Under this scenario, regional security will likely enable terrorists to engage in activities beyond the region, thus affecting countries that have benefited from the umbrella of security provided by operations in the Middle East and South Asia.

INCREASING OPTIONS FOR CIVIL WAR

The ANSF are still developing and at a critical transition period, recently assuming the security lead for Afghanistan's security. Withdrawal of US military support at this critical juncture will remove future advise and assist military training efforts by US and NATO forces, and will serve to hinder counterterrorism efforts against the world's most dangerous terror organizations. Moreover, a departure of coalition security forces enables Afghanistan's warlords and ethnic groups to reevaluate their participation in GIRoA and possibly restructure power relationships within the country. A US presence is needed to ensure that historical societal fractures do not threaten the hard work and consensus that enabled building GIRoA's constitutional underpinnings.

In a rare interview and as pretext for what may lie ahead, northern warlord General Rashid Dostum provided insightful comments about the ability to defeat the Afghan Taliban. A reporter asked him if it was possible to defeat the Taliban: "'Tell your government,' he roars, letting out a great belly laugh, moustache bristling, 'that the Taliban amount to no more than around 9,000 individuals. We know who they are and where to find them. Given the order, I estimate it would take less than a year to destroy their ringleaders. I have said this on many occasions.'"[19] Over the past decade, he is one example of a warlord who has amassed greater wealth and now commands more troops and influence than ever to serve as a destabilizing factor in the country. Just recently, General Dostum highlighted that the silence of ethnic minorities does not mean they are not without capabilities and cannot chart their own course forward. Since the start of the war, the Afghan Taliban has diminished in strength and capacity, while the warlords have grown resources and followings that are now greater than those prior to the war. Moreover, they are not afraid of the Afghan Taliban, and removal of coalition presence may lower the barriers to expanding resistance to GIRoA and further divisions in the country.[20] It is likely that ethnic factions may target Afghan Taliban leaders for atrocities committed before and during the war. Almost all ethnic minorities oppose or fear the return of the Afghan Taliban under any conditions.

With the recent security agreement GIRoA signed with Iran, there is good reason for minorities to have concerns for the future. Given recent meetings by the Afghan Taliban with Iranian officials and historical support within Iran for the Afghan Taliban, it is likely that escalation of conflict and instability will certainly continue.

GOVERNANCE CHALLENGES

The withdrawal of US forces from Afghanistan may precipitate a desire to lobby for President Karzai to remain in power due to the instability and uncertain conditions created. Many fear a call for a Loya Jirga or more calls for consensus measures that will eliminate the mandate to elect a new president. At a minimum, the delay or postponement of presidential elections is likely in this scenario. Trust in GIRoA's leadership is rapidly deteriorating, with many people believing that fair elections are not possible under the current leadership.

President Karzai is responsible for setting the standard and example for future generations of Afghans to follow. His brinksmanship with the United States and nonconstructive engagements are failing to provide a vision that inspires confidence for Afghanistan's future. Factions are coalescing against him, and ethnic minorities are hedging the return of the Afghan Taliban and a return to violence. There is hope, however, with the recent passage of the election laws signed by President Karzai, which are designed to establish the electoral complaints commission and how the vote will be held.[21] Presidential elections need to adhere to clearly established time lines, and time is running out to set the correct path for transparent and fair elections. President Karzai may be abrasive in his external dealings with the international community, particularly with the United States, but at least he is trying to chart the proper way forward to transition power seamlessly and peacefully for the Afghan people. His recent initiatives and measures demonstrate positive results to enable secure, fair, transparent, and inclusive elections.

ECONOMIC DOLDRUMS

The security prospects and ensuing conflicts under this scenario will cause investment activity to be suspended. Unless investing countries establish their own bilateral military assistance agreements with Afghanistan, the ability to improve economic conditions outside of the promised international aid commitments will quickly place Afghanistan's economy in an untenable position. According to a report from an Asian source, based on concerns about GIRoA's ability to provide even a modicum of local security, "China signaled its intention to undo a multi-billion-dollar agreement that had been underpinning Kabul's plans for creating a mining industry."[22] China is already relooking at its investments in Afghanistan, and the prospects for security that involve the infrastructure improvements necessary to support mining operations will not be possible in an uncertain security environment.

Countries seeking to safeguard their investments or solidify regional security interests may escalate proxy fighting between states. If India increases military aid, training, and assistance to the ANSF, it will serve to catalyze a reaction from Pakistan in terms of attacks against Indian interests. According to an Asian source, "It [India] has already committed around US$2 billion in developmental aid to Afghanistan, making India one of the country's biggest donors. In 2011, the two countries signed a Strategic Partnership Agreement, in which India agreed to assist in the training and equipping of Afghan security forces, forces that will eventually take on the Taliban without the support of Western troops."[23] The recent strategic cooperation agreement signed by Afghanistan and Iran is one more example of a confused and desperate foreign policy executed by GIRoA, with little forethought to future second- and third-order effects for Afghanistan's best interests or security.[24] Short-term agreements and convenient alliances will enable aid to continue, but future long-term prospects for security will be tenuous.

International aid may well continue as promised, but demands and conditions placed on GIRoA will be more stringent, with gradual disengagement from donor nations for lack of transparency or governance challenges. Strategies can address mitigation of capital flight through multilateral forums, and transparency must increase to stop directing capital investment elsewhere and into the coffers of personal bank accounts abroad.

REGIONAL SOLUTIONS MAY MITIGATE THE RISKS

Bringing the largest regional investors and power brokers to serve as international peacekeepers under a UN mandate may be the best hope for stability in this scenario. Engaging the Russians and Chinese to sponsor a UN peacekeeping mandate force to mitigate a wider regional conflict and to mitigate the continued flow of terrorists from the region is in the best interests of all the major power brokers involved in South Asia. Moreover, this region is renowned for the ability of key nonstate actors to affect other nations across the globe, something that the Russian government has dealt with firsthand. The enormous potential for instability across a wide swath of Asia is possible.[25]

In this vein, Russia and China have more to lose from this scenario than the United States does. The US involvement in the Middle East and South Asia has kept terror regimes in check for much of the rest of the world. The potential for terror conflagration is greatest under this scenario for a large portion of the world. It is conceivable that violence could spill into the central Asian states, the most important being China, to Xinjiang. China spends more money on internal security than on its military. According to a Reuters news report, for 2013, "[s]pending on the People's Liberation Army (PLA) will rise 10.7 percent to 740.6 billion Yuan ($119 billion), while the domestic security budget will go up at a slightly slower pace, by 8.7 percent, to 769.1 billion Yuan, according to the budget released at the opening of the Chinese parliament's annual meeting."[26] The report goes on to say that internally, "the number of 'mass incidents' of unrest recorded by the Chinese government grew from 8,700 in 1993 to about 90,000 in 2010, according to several government-backed studies. Some estimates are higher, although the government has not released official data for recent years."[27] Radical, ungoverned spaces in China connect to the central Asian states in what was once a formidable territory not easily accessed and that possesses interior lines that are secure and conducive for transnational terrorism. Russia is also concerned about the drug trade and the effects on its society—something the Chinese should also be concerned with, as illicit drugs deteriorate the fabric of societies and weaken nations from within.

The United States can lead change in an increasingly dangerous environment for transnational terrorism. Taking a multilateral approach to Afghanistan's and the region's security is something that countries outside of NATO must become active participants in. Moreover, it is time for our long-standing standoffish global partners to usher in a new era of security cooperation to address terrorism. Even among the biggest military rivals in the world, there is consensus on the desire for internal security from terrorist threats. Taken from that frame of reference, it is possible to engage in dialogue to move forward for better multilateral security on the global front.

NOW IS THE TIME TO ACT

The world will quickly know the course of action that lies ahead for Afghanistan. This fall, resolution on signing the US and GIRoA BSA should be complete, and the status of preparations for the 2014 elections will be evident. As the BSA issue is resolved, the Afghan Taliban's progress for negotiations prior to 2015 will likely come to fruition too. In a more important way, now is the time to build security frameworks to set Afghanistan on the right path for building capacity in security, governance, and economics, and for improving ties with regional partners.

As a fledgling nation, Afghanistan is already feeling out other nations and cooperation on many different fronts. While not all diplomatic initiatives of GIRoA are agreeable to the United States or NATO partners, what is important are the security effects from this region on the rest of the world. Moreover, even though many nations did not bear any burdens from fighting in Afghanistan, most are certainly safer and have economies that have grown as a result. Terror ties held in check will reestablish new connections, and conditions in Southeast Asia are a prime example of what could go badly wrong: with the release of Abu Sayyaf detainees in the Philippines and the relaxation of legal tools to pursue terrorism in Malaysia, many regions of the world may awaken anew to a terror potential not experienced since September 11, 2001.

We are entering dangerous crossroads in world affairs. The region may be on the cusp of creating conditions that precipitate the emergence of a new era in terrorism, one where we see the emergence and increase in entropy that may usher in charismatic terror leadership to spread from inside China through Central and South Asia, Southeast Asia, the Middle East, and Africa. Therefore, countries with direct economic and security interests, like Russia and China, must help to provide enduring security and to create security structures that enable Afghanistan to serve as a stabilizing force in South Asia instead of as a battleground for proxies to continue war against each other at Afghanistan's expense.

Chapter Four

India's Key Role and South Asia's Security Concerns

Iftekharul Bashar

INTRODUCTION

The stabilization of Afghanistan remains a significant work in progress, even after more than a decade of effort by many members of the international community. The threat from the Afghan Taliban continues, and despite overtures for peace talks between the Afghan Taliban and the international community, violence continues incessantly. For more than thirty years, the geopolitical upheaval in Afghanistan continues to influence the security environment of South Asia and limits the region's growth potential. Today, substantial threats to South Asia's nontraditional security comes from the Islamist militant groups that formed strong networks among themselves based on their shared experiences during the Afghan jihad in the 1980s. Therefore, the fragile security and threat landscape in Afghanistan will continue to have critical effects on the overall security dynamics in the South Asian region. Because the NATO-led mission in Afghanistan may end in 2014, concerns from South Asia are growing. Although South Asian states do not have a coherent regional strategy to engage Afghanistan, all nations face the same security risks. Can Afghanistan avoid becoming a fragmented and lawless country? Is Afghanistan going to emerge as the epicenter of transnational crime and terrorism? What are the emerging challenges for the region post-2014? Is South Asia ready to face them? This chapter seeks to analyze the security challenges South Asia will likely face post-2014.

AFGHANISTAN IN SOUTH ASIA'S THREAT LANDSCAPE

The linkages between Afghanistan and South Asian countries are historic. As a region on the rise, South Asia views Afghanistan as a potential trading partner. Located at the strategic crossroads between South Asia, Central Asia, and the Middle East, a peaceful and secure Afghanistan is the key to the region's economic prosperity. Afghanistan holds tremendous influence over South Asia's security landscape.

If coalition forces withdraw from Afghanistan in 2014, a challenging threat environment may emerge in South Asia. The threats not only affect individual countries but also threaten the region as a whole. Over the past decade, most of the countries in the region experienced terrorist activities and attacks on their homeland. There are several reasons Afghanistan cannot be isolated from South Asia's security predicament. The region witnessed the rise of Islamist militant groups that possess ideological, and in many cases operational, linkages with the Afghan Taliban. The turbulence and chaos in the Af–Pak region influences and inspires militant Islamism across South Asia. The region faced two major challenges. First, there was a rise of transnational Islamist militant groups that flourished in the region. Specifically, the Pakistan-based Harkat-ul-Jihad-al-Islami (HuJI), Lashkar-e-Taiba (LeT), Jaish-e-Mohammad (JeM), and Hizbul Mujahideen expanded and firmly entrenched themselves in the region. Second, countries like India, Bangladesh, and the Maldives experienced rising numbers of homegrown Islamist militant groups seeking to use violence to attain their political ends.

South Asia is a complex region with diverse conflicts and unrest. The region's countries possess large populations, competition over scarce resources, and protracted governance crises. Prolonged political and economic crises in the region are creating disgruntled, intolerant, and extreme youths on the fringes, who are highly vulnerable to radicalization. In many cases, these youths are ripe for terrorist recruitment. Since 2001, the region faced a constant diffusion of radical Islamist ideologies that further penetrated into the existing radical milieu. The use of religion in the public sphere is clearly visible and on the rise. Religion is a more dangerous tool, and its misinterpretation mobilizes mass support for terrorism. For a diverse region like South Asia, this is clearly a regressive development. During the past few years, a large volume of jihadist ideological and tactical information proliferated in several South Asian languages. Global ideologies like Wahhabism and Salafism are increasingly gaining an audience in several parts of the region. This indicates South Asia's vulnerability to terrorism and extremism.

During 2001–2013, South Asia witnessed several large-scale attacks that led to some changes in the way states perceive and respond to terrorism. Countries in South Asia largely looked inward to find solutions to counterterrorism. There were significant changes in domestic legal responses and in the operational capability of counterterrorism special forces. Because of the zero-sum nature of regional politics marked by the India–Pakistan rivalry, South Asia has not been able to reach a regional consensus on how to combat terrorism regionally.

As 2014 approaches, South Asia should expect a new threat environment influenced by security challenges concerning Afghanistan. There are key trends and perceptions in South Asia that the Afghan Taliban remain a force to reckon with. Ahead of 2014, the Afghan Taliban in Afghanistan escalated the scale and scope of attacks and serve as a reminder of their undiminished determination and operational capabilities.

Since 2011, the Afghan Taliban adopted new tactics against international troops, as well as against the Afghan government. The targeted killings of high-ranking government officials, progovernment local elders, and key political figures increased. Insurgents stepped up their attacks throughout Afghanistan, including attacks conducted in the nation's capital, Kabul. The Afghan Taliban's attack on Camp Bastion in Helmand in September 2012 is one example. The Afghan Taliban's attacks conducted in 2011 and 2012 reveal increasing use of improvised explosive devices, suicide attacks, and "green-on-blue" insider attacks. The attack against the Afghan presidential compound and the ISAF headquarters in Kabul on 25 June 2013 is an important example of the fragility of the security situation. The Afghan Taliban planned and conducted these attacks to destroy the partnership between the Afghan National Security Forces (ANSF) and the International Security Assistance Force (ISAF).

The ANSF still lack capabilities, and they lack equipment needed to detect and disable roadside bombs. Afghan capabilities may not be ready for several years.[1] Moreover, the ANSF has yet to reach the level of professionalism needed to provide security to the Afghans. Many observers are of the opinion that the ANSF remain fragmented along tribal and subtribal lines.

Building the ANSF is an enormous project that needs adequate resources and time, and a strong partner with the capacity and willingness to rebuild Afghanistan. The Afghan Taliban, al Qaeda, and dozens of like-minded groups located near the Afghanistan–Pakistan border survived a decade of global counterinsurgency and counterterrorism measures. The Taliban's sanctuaries in Pakistan are behind their survival.[2] These groups slowly and steadily returned to Afghanistan and recreated pre-9/11–like sanctuaries in the pockets that remain beyond the control of Afghan and the ISAF.[3] With the prospect of the withdrawal of NATO-led coalition forces, the success of Afghan security forces to neutralize the influence of the insurgents will be limited. Besides, the insider threat stemming from the Afghan Taliban is affecting Western capacity building. In this scenario, a security vacuum in Afghanistan might result in an expansion of terrorism threat in South Asia.

THE THREAT IN AFGHANISTAN

Currently, there are three major groups that pose security challenges to Afghanistan and to the South Asian region: the Afghan Taliban, the Haqqani Network, and the Hizb-e-Islami Gulbuddin.

The Afghan Taliban are the leading insurgent group in Afghanistan. The Afghan Taliban today are largely a decentralized and loosely networked insurgent/guerilla group controlled by the Quetta Shura.[4] The Afghan Taliban emerged in the early 1990s in northern Pakistan following the withdrawal of Soviet troops from Afghanistan. As a predominantly Pashtun movement, the Afghan Taliban came to prominence in Afghanistan in the autumn of 1994. They took control of Afghanistan's government in 1996 and ruled until 2001. Quickly thereafter, the Afghan Taliban relinquished and fled from power after the US-led invasion. The US-led invasion of Afghanistan precipitated the fall of the Afghan Taliban, who later relocated to Pakistan, where they had ethnic, religious, and linguistic ties to the local people. In Pakistan, the Afghan Taliban control areas in the northwest and conduct suicide bombings and other attacks. The group is renowned for providing safe havens for al Qaeda, as well as for its rigid interpretation of Islamic law. The regime is also infamous for its public executions for criminals, and intolerance and uncompromising policies concerning the education of women. The Afghan Taliban's current strength is approximately 25,000–30,000 fighters.[5] The Afghan Taliban's leaders enjoy support and sanctuary in Pakistan. The main leader of the Afghan Taliban movement is Mullah Mohammed Omar. Since 2010, both US and Afghan officials have pursued talks with members of the group, in pursuit of a negotiated settlement to end the conflict in Afghanistan.

The threat emanating from the Af–Pak region is not a homogeneous movement but rather a collection of movements that are currently cooperating under the umbrella of the Afghan Taliban, as well as a number of other groups that sometimes align with the Afghan Taliban when conditions necessitate cooperation among groups. Together, these groups maintain a significant presence throughout Afghanistan.[6]

Though often categorized as an independent group, the Haqqani Network (its commonly known name) is a group that pledged its allegiance to Mullah Omar, the supreme leader of the Afghan Taliban. The Haqqani Network is a terrorist group operating against the Afghan government and the NATO-led coalition forces in Southeastern Afghanistan. This group was founded by Jalaluddin Haqqani. Currently, his son, Sirajuddin Haqqani, is leading the group. The Haqqani Network originated from Afghanistan's Khost province, which shares its border with Pakistan's North Waziristan. The group allegedly has strong ties to Pakistan's Inter-Services Intelligence (ISI), as well as with the Pakistani Taliban based in South and North Waziristan. The Haqqani Network's estimated current strength is around 15,000. Some of the major terrorist attacks carried out by the Haqqani Network include the attacks against a US military base in Wardak, the Hotel Intercontinental, the British Council, and the US Embassy in Kabul in 2011. The Haqqani Network also likely has links to Pakistan-based militant groups.

The Hezb-e-Islami Gulbuddin is an insurgent group in Afghanistan led by former Afghan prime minister and Mujahideen leader Gulbuddin Hekmatyar. The group is leading those factions opposing a foreign presence in Afghanistan. In early 2007, the Afghan Taliban entered an alliance with Gulbuddin Hekmatyar in the fight against US forces and the Afghan government. Gulbuddin Hekmatyar led the largest jihadi faction, Hezb-e-Islami Hekmatyar, against the Soviet forces in Afghanistan. After the US invasion in 2001, Hekmatyar returned to Afghanistan and began operations against the Afghan government and coalition forces. The Hezb-e-Islami Gulbuddin has linkages to Lashkar-e-Taiba, a Pakistan-based militant group that was involved in a number of attacks in India, which included the 2001 attack on the Indian Parliament and the 2008 Mumbai attacks. According to Afghan authorities, Lashkar-e-Taiba was involved in the August 2013 attack on the Indian consulate in Jalalabad.[7]

TALIBANIZATION IN SOUTH ASIA

Since the Soviet Union's invasion of Afghanistan in December 1979, the Af–Pak region remains an epicenter of militant Islamism, a phenomena that influenced South Asia's politics and security. The Afghan jihad, as it is widely known in the Muslim world, provided foreign fighters with a tremendous opportunity to fight the battle against the "atheists," which in due course turned into a global terrorist group known as al Qaeda. In fact, that became the first raison d'être of jihad for South Asian Muslims. The rise of Islamic militancy in Afghanistan was phenomenal for South Asia. In many ways, it left far-reaching effects upon the region. For example, it created a new crisis within South Asia's Muslim societies—now referred to as Talibanization.[8]

The Afghan Taliban's resurgence in Afghanistan and the significant rise in terrorist activity in Pakistan have not only exacerbated regional tensions but also caused erosion of the writ of both states in their respective territories. This is especially disconcerting in the Southern Pashtun–dominated provinces of Afghanistan and in the Federally Administered Tribal Areas (FATA) of Pakistan. Today, the FATA has the largest sanctuary of terrorist groups, which include Tehrik-e-Taliban Pakistan, Muqami Tehrik-e-Taliban, the Haqqani Network, Tehreek-e-Nafaz-e-Shariat-e-Mohammadi, Lashkar-e-Islam, Ansar-ul-Islam, Hizbullah, Mahdi Militia, al Qaeda, Islamic Movement of Uzbekistan, Islamic Jihid Union, and Punjabi Taliban.

Though the existing literature on Talibanization focuses on the Af–Pak region, several countries in South Asia remain at long-term risk of Talibanization. The Afghan Taliban movement influences religious extremist groups as far away from Afghanistan as India, Bangladesh, and the Maldives.

The expansion of radical ideologies in South Asia is evidence of a new borderless reality for the region. It is important to examine how the Talibanization process originated and evolved in this region.

When the Soviet Union invaded Afghanistan, a new front for jihad attracted Muslims from all over the world.[9] South Asia was no exception. It is important to note that many of the terrorist and extremist groups in South and Central Asia originated after the Soviet Union's withdrawal from Afghanistan in 1989. Examples include the Islamic Movement of Uzbekistan in Central Asia, and Jamaat-ul-Mujahideen and Harkat-ul-Jihad al-Islami both in Bangladesh. These organizations formed strong networks among themselves based on their shared experiences during the Afghan jihad in the 1980s.

INDIA

During the rise of the Afghan Taliban, South Asia's threat landscape started to evolve and become more transnational. Several South Asian groups found their sanctuary in Afghanistan. The Harkat-ul-Jihad-ul-Islami (HuJI) is an example. This group started working closely with the Afghan Taliban and al Qaeda. The group started in Pakistan, in 1980. HuJI's area of operation extends throughout South Asia, with their terrorist operations focused primarily in India and Pakistan. HuJI's relationship with al Qaeda flourished after the Taliban's rise in Afghanistan. They provided fighters for the Afghan Taliban in Afghanistan and training of HuJI members in al Qaeda's training camps. HuJI carried out numerous terrorist attacks. On 2 March 2006, HuJI were responsible for the suicide bombing of the US Consulate in Karachi, Pakistan, which killed four people, including US Diplomat David Foy, and injured forty-eight others. HuJI also executed terrorist attacks in India, to include the May 2007 Hyderabad mosque attack, which killed sixteen and injured forty. Furthermore, they spearheaded the March 2006 Varanasi attack, which killed twenty-five and injured one hundred. In January 2009, a federal grand jury indicted HuJI's leader Mohammad Ilyas Kashmiri for terrorism-related offenses in connection to a terrorist attack against the Jyllands-Posten newspaper in Denmark.[10] HuJI work closely with the Afghan Taliban and al Qaeda. They formed in Pakistan in 1980. Currently, the group operates across South Asia, especially in Pakistan, India, and Bangladesh.

Over the years, they have established collaborations with local militant groups. On 6 August 2010, the United States and the United Nations designated HuJI as a foreign terror group.

For post-2014 South Asia, Lashkar-e-Taiba (LeT) might emerge as the major threat group. LeT have extensive networks in South Asia, especially in India, Pakistan, Nepal, and Bangladesh. The US government designated LeT as a Foreign Terrorist Organization in December 2001. The Pakistani government banned the group in January 2002, but this did little to stymie its operations. The group renamed itself the Jamaat-ud-Dawa and resumed business as usual. Although LeT operates their own command structure and network, they are subordinate to al Qaeda in many ways. The groups often train in each other's camps in Afghanistan and Pakistan, and fight side by side in Afghanistan. Hafiz Saeed, the emir of LeT, and several other leaders gained recognition on the list of Specially Designated Global Terrorists. Over a period of years, the LeT established an organization that rivals the Lebanese Hizballah. The group succeeded in providing aid to earthquake-ravaged regions in the Kashmir in 2005 while the Pakistani government was slow to act. The LeT is active in fund-raising across the Middle East and South Asia, and recruited scores of foreign fighters to train in their camps. It is important to note that during the Afghan Taliban's rule, terror camps in Khost trained militants from Kashmir, Pakistan, and other states to fight against Indian rule in Jammu and Kashmir. Destruction of the camps by US missile attacks in 1998 facilitated degradation of Hizbul Mujahideen, the Harkat-ul-Mujahideen (formarly known as Harkat-ul-Ansar), and the Markaz Dawa Al Irshad and their militant wing, the Lashkar-e-Taiba.[11] In December 1999, the Indian Airlines flight hijacked from Kathmandu to Kandahar by Pakistani hijackers received assistance from the Afghan Taliban in Kandahar.

BANGLADESH

Being geographically far from Afghanistan, Bangladesh did not experience mass recruitment of jihadis to fight in Afghanistan. For most of the Bangladeshis, the Afghan war was a remote issue. However, for radical groups of Islamists in Bangladesh, as Ali Riaz points out, it was "a clarion call to dedicate their lives to a greater cause for Islam." Some 3,000 people under the leadership of Abdur Rahman Faruki were "motivated" to travel in several batches to Afghanistan and fight alongside other volunteer mujahideen. Over the following four years, at least twenty-four of them died and ten became disabled. In 1988, a delegation of ten self-proclaimed Ulema from Bangladesh visited Afghanistan.

After the Soviet Union's withdrawal in 1989, most of the Bangladeshi mujahideen returned to Bangladesh. The returnees maintained close contact and celebrated the Afghan mujahideen's capture of Kabul in 1992. By then, Shafiqur Rahman, a returnee of the Afghan war, already established contacts with a Pakistani Islamist organization called Harkat-ul-Jihad-al Islami.[12] A week after the Mujahideen emerged victorious, Bangladeshi participants in the Afghan war launched the Harkat-ul-Jihad-al Islami (HuJI)-Bangladesh. The operational training and ideological consolidation played a vital role behind the emergence of HuJI-Bangladesh. Today, the HuJI-B is a major Islamist militant group in Bangladesh. HuJI-B formed under the guidance of Bangladeshi jihadist veterans of the Soviet–Afghan war. HuJI-B's objective is to establish an Afghan Taliban–like regime in Bangladesh through armed jihad. HuJI-B aims to establish Islamic rule in Bangladesh by waging war and killing progressive intellectuals and politicians. It draws inspiration from Osama bin Laden and the erstwhile Afghan Taliban regime of Afghanistan. HuJI-B carried out major high-profile terrorist attacks in Bangladesh. HuJI-B reportedly has linkages with other Islamist militant groups in South Asia, and in 2005, Bangladeshi authorities banned HuJI-B.

The Bangladeshi mujahideen set up another organization called the Jamaatul Mujahideen Bangladesh (JMB). It is a major Islamist militant group operating in Bangladesh. The primary objective of the JMB is to impose a rigid, extremist interpretation of Islamic Law on Bangladesh. To achieve this end, it sought to undertake terrorist activities to undermine the authority of the state. The JMB started in the Jamalpur district by Shaikh Abdur Rahman, one of the jihadist veterans of the Soviet–Afghan war. The JMB carried out a spectacular attack on 17 August 2005, when they detonated 510 bombs within a span of less than an hour throughout Bangladesh. In recent years, the group is decentralizing its command structure by establishing independent cells. Although the JMB's leadership is in disarray and most of its leaders apprehended to face the justice of Bangladeshi authorities, their operational strength and networks remain a security concern. The group maintains suicide squads and is currently a banned terrorist group in Bangladesh.

THE MALDIVES

Extremist ideology first took root in the Maldives in the 1980s, when Maldivians went to study in Saudi Arabia. Since then, Maldivian families, especially belonging to the lower socioeconomic segment of society, send their children to study in Islamic schools (madrassas) in Pakistan. Thus, the presence of extremist ideologies promulgated in the Maldives. The Adhaalath extremist political party enjoys a strategic relationship with the government of Mohamed Nasheed and receives funding by foreign groups—especially those from Saudi Arabia. They are likely spreading extremism in the Maldives. These individuals and groups in the Maldives succeeded in converting a segment of the traditionally tolerant Maldivian society into religious extremism.

Working with the Afghan Taliban, Ali Jaleel, a Maldivian suicide bomber, attacked the ISI headquarters in Lahore, Pakistan, on 27 May 2009. This attack killed thirty-five and injured more than 250 individuals. On 29 September 2007, there was a terrorist attack in Sultan Park in Male, killing twelve tourists. On 7 February 2012, six Islamist extremists destroyed thirty-five images of the Buddha and Hindu gods in the Maldivian National Museum, with the objective of purging the pre-Islamic heritage of the Maldives. Furthermore, nine Maldivians arrested by Pakistani authorities for involvement with violent extremist groups were operating in the Waziristan region in March 2009. Three Maldivians detained in Sri Lanka in 2006 were under suspicion that they were enroute to join a jihadi training camp in Pakistan.

US–AFGHAN BILATERAL SECURITY AGREEMENT (BSA) IS CRITICAL FOR SECURITY

The BSA envisages continuing a security presence and a force of 5,000 to 10,000 soldiers, which the United States will leave behind while withdrawing the bulk of its forces from Afghanistan at the end of 2014. The US objectives for post-2014 include providing a train, advise, and assist mission under NATO leadership and a Counterterrorism capability to assist the ANSF against the resurgence of al Qaeda.[13]

The troops will provide limited intelligence and reconnaissance and close-air support, because Afghan capabilities will not be ready for several years. Close-air support and intelligence capabilities, along with detecting and disabling roadside bombs, are the biggest weaknesses of Afghan security forces.[14] There will likely be a small number of trainers for the ANSF as part of the security assistance package designed to help Afghanistan.

WORST CASE SCENARIO: US ZERO OPTION

The issue of immunity from Afghan laws for US troops remains a precondition for the BSA. Although it is unlikely, failure to negotiate a BSA will compel the United States to withdraw completely from Afghanistan.[15] If Afghanistan does not give US troops legal immunity, a complete withdrawal from Afghanistan might become a reality. In this case, international troops will completely withdraw, and the regime will not have the security assistance it needs for sustainable growth. Disgruntled Afghan Taliban will likely wage a war of vendetta. It is critical to gauge civil society and groups who do not want the Afghan Taliban to react. A Pentagon report states that the insurgency is now less capable, less popular, and less of an existential threat to the government of Afghanistan than it was in 2011.[16] Therefore, it may take some time for the Taliban to gain momentum to launch a full-scale nationwide civil war and reoccupation of territories. The ANSF, which already lead security efforts for Afghanistan, will face challenges without the ISAF's support if all assistance terminates. The ANSF have yet to emerge as an enduring professional, mature, and disciplined security force.[17] According to observers, in the absence of a strong partner, the ANSF will face a serious challenge in the post-2014 scenario. Factionalism within security forces might increase. Although highly unlikely, post-2014 Afghanistan might resemble post-1989 Afghanistan. The southern and eastern parts of Afghanistan might emerge as sanctuaries for South Asia's militant groups, which will eventually pose increasing threats to South Asia. Tensions in the Kashmir and geostrategic flashpoints will escalate.

MOST LIKELY SCENARIO: BSA SUCCESSFUL AND TALKS WITH THE TALIBAN FAIL

This is the most likely scenario. It will be in India's best interests for a successful BSA. At the very least, it will formalize the mechanisms of security cooperation between the two countries and address uncertainty about sustained commitment on both sides. This will lend more transparency to what has recently been a less than ideal relationship. Indian observers are of the view that the Afghan Taliban are still under the control of the Pakistani military. Therefore, there needs to be negotiations between the Afghan government and the Pakistani military, and these talks need brokering by the United States because it is the only country maintaining economic influence over both countries. Therefore, the talks, as structured today, are likely to fail anyway. Even if they succeed, they will not likely have any material effect on the insurgency. It is mostly window dressing; the talks do not address the fundamental causes of the insurgency. The Afghan Taliban is not a monolithic entity. Their leadership continues to enjoy sanctuary in Pakistan. The insurgency still receives enormous support from the Pakistani military.[18] Unless the Pakistani military is supportive and sincere about finding a political solution that addresses the domestic concerns of Afghanistan as well as regional sensitivities, there is simply no enduring stability in sight.

BEST CASE SCENARIO: BSA SIGNED AND TALKS ARE SUCCESSFUL

This would be a win–win situation. This is a positive scenario for Afghanistan and the South Asian region as well. Results will lead to relative stability, to decreasing terror attacks, and to civilian governments maintaining control of the security situation. Trade, commerce, and connectivity will flourish under these conditions. This is beneficial for South Asia and enables trade links and pipelines across Central Asia to work.[19]

CONCLUSION

Afghanistan today is much different from the Afghan Taliban's era of governance. The NATO-led ISAF played an instrumental role in ensuring security and stability in Afghanistan since 2001. Nearly 80 percent of the population is safer from the Afghan Taliban's violence, which is mostly concentrated in the country's more remote regions. The country made significant progress in human development, especially in access to education and health care. Although the Afghan Taliban's hold in many parts of Afghanistan is disconcerting, the presence of the ISAF is important for countering the Afghan Taliban and degrading their operational capabilities. Moreover, the ISAF continues to augment the capacity of the ANSF, enabling them to take over security responsibilities for an eventual post-NATO Afghanistan.

As the mission draws down in 2014, there are concerns about whether the ANSF are in a position to take over security responsibilities for post-NATO Afghanistan. Although the ANSF's capabilities have greatly increased over the past two years, they have yet to demonstrate the ability to operate independently on a nationwide scale.[20] As Afghanistan stands at a critical crossroads in its nation-building efforts, a new wave of instability will be highly detrimental to the nation's achievements over the past ten years. The future of Afghanistan's economy will depend on its security, and the performance of the state's institutions will indicate whether the nation can endure. It is still too early to say whether Afghanistan will emerge as a sovereign, stable, and prosperous country or once again disintegrate into chaos.

Today, Afghanistan is far more critical to South Asia than at any time before. The drawdown of NATO troops has effects on Afghanistan but also has significant implications for the South Asian region in terms of security issues. Particularly, failure to address regional security concerns will affect the intensity of transnational security threats such as terrorism, narcotics trafficking, and small arms proliferation. This is a major reason Afghanistan cannot be isolated from South Asia's security landscape. Instability in Afghanistan poses long-term challenges to the region as a whole. Across South

Asia, there are terror groups supporting or sympathizing with the Afghan Taliban. Therefore, post-2014 Afghanistan will potentially present enduring security challenges to South Asia's security. South Asia's states must work together to ensure that Afghanistan does not fall into the hands of extremist forces, who desire to reverse progress in South Asian countries. A peaceful and secure Afghanistan is in the best interests of South Asia and the region.

Chapter Five

The Endgame in Afghanistan Will Affect Central Asia

Nodirbek Soliyev

> [U]nlike other wars, Afghan wars become serious only when they are over.
> —Sir Olaf Caroe [1]

INTRODUCTION

As the International Security Assistance Force (ISAF) drawdown from Afghanistan continues to its likely terminus in 2014, the countries in Central Asia are increasingly concerned about the future scenarios in Afghanistan and their probable implications for the region.

For almost thirty-five years, the Central Asian region continues to remain close to the armed conflicts in Afghanistan. Today, preeminent challenges for national and regional security in Central Asia derive from Islamist militancy that is often driven, influenced, and sustained by the Afghan conflict. Although Central Asian militant groups based inside Afghanistan suffered serious blows during counterterrorism initiatives by the ISAF since October 2001, they are not entirely defeated. Their support and sanctuaries in the tribal areas of Pakistan pose enduring security challenges for Central Asia post-2014. Furthermore, there is an increase in the transit of Afghan drugs through the so-called northern routes into Central Asia on their way to Russia and Europe. Obviously, with the departure of US troops from Afghanistan, the situation will only get worse. This will have direct effects on all of the Central Asian nations.

This chapter examines the challenges for Central Asia and its regional security post-2014 and explores how the countries in the region symbiotically depend on a safe and stable Afghanistan. What future scenario for Afghanistan will likely emerge after the potential US military withdrawal? If Afghanistan descends into chaos again, what effect will it have on Central Asia?

US–AFGHANISTAN BILATERAL SECURITY AGREEMENT

Today, ongoing instability in Afghanistan appears likely to persist, with no end in sight. More than a decade of military engagement by the US-led coalition forces in Afghanistan highlights that military options may not be the most effective solutions for lasting peace.

To delineate terms of settling the war and the political future of Afghanistan, the United States entered into negotiations with the Government of the Islamic Republic of Afghanistan (GIRoA) and the Afghan Taliban. The bilateral security agreement (BSA) between the United States and the GIRoA is important to reinforce political and security frameworks for Afghanistan. The proposed agreement allows for a limited US military presence in Afghanistan after 2014, with a mandate of continuing assistance to the Afghan National Security Forces (ANSF) with limited counterterrorism support. This counterterrorism support is crucial for managing transnational threats emanating from Afghanistan post-2014. The Afghan government sees a US peace deal with the Afghan Taliban as one of the preconditions to achieve the BSA. For the United States, a peace deal with the Afghan Taliban is "the surest way to end the conflict in a peaceful manner."[2] The United States outlined the following conditions for the Afghan Taliban: to put down their arms, to pledge not to use Afghanistan as a safe haven for transnational terrorism, and to disown its links with al Qaeda.[3] The Afghan Taliban stipulates that all foreign troops must leave the country as a precondition to join in legitimate political processes in Afghanistan.[4]

As of April 2014, the future of the BSA is still in limbo. The negotiations with the Afghan Taliban also remain a daunting work in progress. All future outcomes will depend on two key factors. First, the status of the BSA and second, the peace talks with the Afghan Taliban.

The ISAF withdrawal may affect regional security in Central Asia. Post-2014, Central Asian countries will grapple with two main challenges: (1) the spillover of radical ideologies and terrorist activities from Afghanistan and (2) an increase in the transit of drugs along the infamous "northern transit route" through Central Asia to Russia and Europe. Three scenarios in this analysis are critical for understanding Afghanistan's effects on Central Asia's future. Each probable scenario will have different effects on Central Asia's future security and the ensuing dynamics inherent therein. The three scenarios considered here are as follows:

- The BSA is not signed and talks with the Taliban are not successful.
- The BSA is successful and talks with the Afghan Taliban fail.
- The BSA is signed and the Afghan Taliban talks are successful.

BSA IS NOT SIGNED AND TALKS WITH THE TALIBAN ARE NOT SUCCESSFUL

For the Central Asian region, this is the most dangerous scenario. The critical point of failure under this scenario is the failure to conclude a BSA between the United States and Afghanistan. A failure to negotiate a BSA will cause all US military support and other international coalition forces to withdraw from Afghanistan by 2015. In parallel, if peace talks with the Afghan Taliban are unsuccessful, then the conditions are ripe for continuing violence.

If all coalition troops withdraw from Afghanistan, the future stability of Afghanistan will be questionable. The key question is whether Afghan government institutions can provide stability and security for the Afghan people. Another question is whether the ANSF will be able to counter the Afghan Taliban or other transnational militant groups. Full withdrawal of US troops will enable al Qaeda and other militants to recuperate inside Afghanistan and likely allow the Afghan Taliban to solidify their influence in the south. Achievements accomplished to date likely may not endure without sustained external support by the international community post-2014.

During the past decade, the United States and NATO have been fighting against al Qaeda and the Afghan Taliban. Per the new military strategy by Washington for Afghanistan in 2009, the primary aim of the US military mission there was to "defeat" al Qaeda and to "degrade" the Taliban.[5] With the death of Osama bin Laden in 2011 and other top leaders of al Qaeda, US objectives appear successful and are successful in restricting al Qaeda's organizational and operational capabilities in Afghanistan. However, al Qaeda and their allied groups have not yet been completely defeated.[6] They continue to operate in the Federally Administered Tribal Areas (FATA) of Pakistan, which continues to offer safe haven for them since October 2001. Al Qaeda and its allied Central Asian associate groups, such as the Islamic Movement of Uzbekistan (IMU), Islamic Jihad Union (IJU), Jamaat Ansarullah (JA), and Jund al-Khilafah (JaK), have strong nexuses with each other. Subsequently, it would be a serious security issue for Central Asian countries if these terrorist groups start expanding and growing their operations after a coalition exit from Afghanistan.

EXPANSION OF TERRORIST ACTIVITIES

There is a general perception in the Central Asian region that the departure of US troops from Afghanistan will precipitate the spillover of radical ideologies and terrorist activities from Afghanistan and Pakistan. To understand this, it is important to outline current threats by transnational terrorism emanating from Afghanistan.

Central Asia consists of five countries: Kazakhstan, Kyrgyzstan, Tajikistan, Turkmenistan, and Uzbekistan. The total population of the region is about sixty-four million, out of which fifty-five million, or 86 percent, are Muslims.[7] In 1991, the five republics in Central Asia announced their independence from the Soviet Union and declared a secular and democratic form of state building.

Prior to 2001, Central Asian militants, with significant support from the Afghan Taliban and al Qaeda, posed serious threats to the region's security by carrying out several large-scale attacks. For instance, on 16 February 1999, the IMU detonated car bombs in Tashkent, Uzbekistan—killing thirteen civilians and wounding 128 people. In 1999 and 2000, about 700–1,000 IMU militants attempted to infiltrate into Uzbekistan through Kyrgyzstan and Tajikistan. Militants took eight Kyrgyz military personnel hostage, in addition to four Japanese geologists and four American climbers, among other foreigners. Japanese officials paid the ransom to secure the release of the hostages.[8] Two military incursions also resulted in the death of dozens of Kyrgyz and Uzbek soldiers. The Kyrgyz authorities claim that 120 militants died and more than two hundred were injured in operations involving extremists.

Over the course of the US-led military campaign in Afghanistan, Central Asian militants' safe sanctuaries, training bases, and networks of support in Afghanistan ceased to exist. This includes operations resulting in killing or capturing several prominent leaders. As a result, their operational capabilities significantly degraded, and these groups found safe refuge in the Afghanistan–Pakistan border areas. Since 2005, the attacks in Central Asia occurred less often as these groups focused their fight on survival against the US-led security operations in Afghanistan.

THE WORST CASE SCENARIO AND THE LOOMING TERROR THREATS TO CENTRAL ASIA

The most serious threat to the security of the countries in Central Asia—particularly Uzbekistan, Tajikistan, and Kyrgyzstan—comes from the IMU. The IMU, currently based in the FATA of Pakistan, is the al Qaeda–linked international terrorist group. It also has strong ties to the Afghan Taliban, the

Haqqani Network in Pakistan, the IJU, the East Turkestan Islamic Movement (ETIM, aka Turkestan Islamic Party), and the Caucasus Emirate (CE). Since its formation in 1998 in Afghanistan, the IMU's main goal has been to establish an Islamic state across Central Asia. This objective, conceived with the demise of the Soviet Union, gained traction when the newly independent Central Asian states were going through a critical transition in the early 1990s.

The Fergana Valley, which is divided between Uzbekistan, Tajikistan, and Kyrgyzstan, was chosen to be the core of this state. The valley is the most densely populated area in the region, with twelve million people (mostly ethnic Uzbeks), comprising almost one-fifth of the total population of Central Asia.[9] Because it connects three Central Asian countries, any unrest in one part of the valley can easily spread to other parts and across national borders. Therefore, stability in the Fergana Valley serves as the thermostat for stability in Central Asia.

The IMU was listed as an International Terrorist Organization by the US State Department in 2000 and the Russian Supreme Court in 2003. Currently, the IMU's activities are banned in Uzbekistan and other Central Asian countries.

After the US invasion of Afghanistan in October 2001, the IMU suffered a serious blow and later lost its sanctuaries in Afghanistan. Subsequently, the IMU fled to the Afghanistan–Pakistan border areas. The loss of sanctuaries in Afghanistan effectively severed the group's logistical lines of communication from Central Asia. Furthermore, the IMU floundered after the death of its leader, Tohir Yuldoshev, by a US drone strike in the FATA of Pakistan in 2009. Currently, the group is led by Usmon Ghazi. Since its move to Pakistan, the IMU focuses less attention on Central Asia and more on targeting coalition forces in Afghanistan and against the government of Pakistan to secure and maintain local support for al Qaeda, the Afghan Taliban, and other militant groups operating in the FATA. The IMU is not the only group Central Asia is growing concerned with and must monitor closely for likely expansion in the worst case scenario.

WORST CASE SCENARIO AND THE ISLAMIC JIHAD UNION

There is growing concern regarding the IJU. The IJU splintered from the IMU in the early 2000s forming a new group in March 2002 and training in Pakistan's North Waziristan. The main objective of the group is to impose Sharia law by conducting military jihad against the government of Uzbekistan and other governments: Afghanistan, Pakistan, the United States, and Germany. Despite its independent status, the group operates under the support and direction of al Qaeda and Afghan Taliban leaders in Afghanistan and Pakistan. Of note, in 2002–2009, the Libyan ideologue Abu Laith al-Libi was a contact person between the IJU and al Qaeda while the IJU operated alongside the Haqqani Network of Pakistani terrorists.[10] The IJU's current leader is Abdulloh Fotih.

Over the past few years, the IJU has conducted numerous assassinations in the northern and northeastern Afghan provinces, such as Takhar and Kunduz, places predominately populated by Uzbeks and Tajiks. Their concentration of activity in these areas suggests an eventual plan to infiltrate from northern Afghanistan back into Central Asia and present a very dangerous security threat to these countries.

WORST CASE SCENARIO AND THE JAMAAT ANSARULLAH

The JA pose the preeminent threat to Tajikistan's national security. The JA is the IMU's branch in Tajikistan and is another affiliate of al Qaeda. The JA aims to establish a Sharia-based government system in Tajikistan by toppling its secular regime. Amriddin Tabarov is the emir (leader) of the group. Reportedly, Amriddin has close ties to the Afghan Taliban leader Mullah Omar,[11] and he was a candidate for al Qaeda's top post after Osama bin Laden's death.

The JA were responsible for several bloody incidents in Tajikistan in 2010. On 3 September 2010, a suicide attack on a police station in Khujand city killed two police officers and injured thirty others. The suicide bomber, who was a local resident, Akmal Karimov, reportedly trained in al Qaeda camps in Afghanistan and Pakistan. On 19 September 2010, a defense ministry convoy seeking to apprehend the prisoners who had escaped came under grenade attack in the Kamarob Gorge in the Karategin Valley, resulting in twenty-eight Tajik soldiers killed. This group has the potential to grow and conduct even deadlier attacks if allowed to expand.

WORST CASE SCENARIO AND JAISH AL-MAHDI

The Jaish al-Mahdi (the Army of the Righteous Ruler, JM) is a terror group targeting Kyrgyzstan. Established in 2007, the JM consists of mostly local Kyrgyz people. The group also has members from Kazakhstan. The main objective of this group is to overthrow the secular Kyrgyz government and establish an Islamic state in Kyrgyzstan. They have links to the IJU and to the Afghan Taliban.

In March 2011, the group pledged allegiance (bay'at) to the Afghan Taliban leader, Mullah Omar.[12] Saliev Kairat is the leader of the group. On 9 September 2010, the JM carried out bombings in the courtyard of a synagogue in Bishkek, the capital of Kyrgyzstan. There were no injuries. On 30

November 2010, a bomb exploded near the sports center in Bishkek, where the trial of twenty-nine former government officials was taking place. Three people were injured. The JM reportedly possess advanced military technologies, such as satellite communications and night vision devices, and they have the ability to conduct successful terror attacks.[13]

WORST CASE SCENARIO AND THE JUND AL-KHILAFAH

The JaK is an Islamist terrorist group. The group was started in 2011 by Kazakh nationals operating under al Qaeda's tutelage in the Afghanistan–Pakistan border area. The JaK have links to the Afghan Taliban, the Haqqani Network in Pakistan, the IMU, and the IJU. The group's objective is to overthrow the secular government and to create an Islamic state in Kazakhstan. The current leadership of the JaK is questionable. The group's former leader, Moezeddine Garsallaoui (aka Abu Moez al Tunisi), was killed in October 2012 as a result of a US drone strike in Pakistan's tribal region of North Waziristan. Moezeddine was al Qaeda's senior operative in the FATA who recruited and trained new members from Europe.[14]

The JaK recently conducted several terrorist attacks in Kazakhstan and Afghanistan. On 31 October 2011, a JaK suicide attacker blew himself up near a five-story building in Atyrau, a city in western Kazakhstan. No damages or casualties were reported among the civilian population. Alarmingly, it was the first successful terrorist attack in Kazakhstan. In November 2011, an armed attack took place in the southern Kazakh city of Taraz, resulting in the death of seven people. The JaK took responsibility for the attack. On 12 November 2011, the group carried out attacks in Taraz city, which resulted in the death of seven people. In 2012, the JaK claimed responsibility for a terrorist attack in Toulouse, France, in March 2012. Its slain leader, Moezeddine Garsallaoui, was responsible for training Mohamed Merah, who killed seven people in Toulouse, including three children and a teacher from a Jewish school.

Operating from the Afghanistan–Pakistan border area, the JaK continues to receive ideological and logistical support from al Qaeda and the Haqqani Network. There is a strong likelihood of increasing operations in Kazakhstan by the JaK, especially after the withdrawal of the ISAF from Afghanistan in 2014. In the short-term, the JaK will likely continue to target Kazakh security forces and government installations, similar to the increasing patterns of attacks already established.

However, as the country has no common border with Afghanistan, the opportunity for militants in Afghanistan and Pakistan to travel directly to Kazakhstan is limited. The JaK is actively conducting online propaganda campaigns to recruit new members, especially among the population of Kazakhstan.

CIVIL WAR IN AFGHANISTAN IS THE MOST DANGEROUS OUTCOME FOR CENTRAL ASIA

Thirteen years of US military operations in Afghanistan have severely degraded the Afghan Taliban's operational capabilities. However, the Afghan Taliban's insurgency continues, especially in the southeast and eastern parts of Afghanistan.[15] The Afghan Taliban's persistence and "invincibility" can be attributed to Pakistan's proximity. Since 2001, the FATA of Pakistan offers safe havens for the Afghan Taliban's political and military leadership. For Pakistan, influence over the Afghan Taliban allows Pakistan to manipulate them during the negotiation processes with Washington and Kabul.[16]

However, the Afghan Taliban may not possess the capability to recapture Kabul nor the public support to impose the establishment of its rigid sharia-based regime across the entire country. First, although continuing political, economic, and social issues endure, Afghanistan is not the same country as it was in the 1990s. When the Afghan Taliban came to power in Kabul in 1996, Afghanistan was a chaotic and desperate country. Today, there is no anarchy in Afghanistan. Although it is still evolving, there is a functioning central government with a regular army, government agencies, and public offices. There are local and international businesses. Second, the Afghan Taliban do not enjoy the previous popular support that they did in the 1990s. The Afghan people do not want their return to power. The people in Afghanistan believe that the Afghan Taliban's return to power will not bring lasting peace and stability. With their negative historical baggage, the perception of the Afghan Taliban changed. The people also perceive that the Afghan Taliban are not a sovereign government—that they are run by Pakistan.[17] Next, the international community will likely not abandon Afghanistan post-2014. Many countries in the world, including regional and global powers, have a stake in Afghanistan. Nontraditional transnational threats such as terrorism and drug trafficking are changing traditional security paradigms, and these threats require global strategic responses. The international community wants a secure and stable Afghanistan, and is willing to continue efforts to attain that.[18]

Although continued statements by US military leadership in Afghanistan that the ANSF are capable of leading security and can contain the Afghan Taliban, Central Asian countries are skeptical about the future scenarios in Afghanistan. The common view of the neighboring Central Asian states is that the departure of the US military from Afghanistan will exacerbate the severity of the security situation in Afghanistan. The widespread expectation is that without sustained support by the international community, the central Afghan government may not be able to hold power post-2014.[19] Consequently, there is widespread expectations of a future civil war.

If Afghanistan descends into chaos again, it will emerge again as a catalyst for the expansion of terrorist activities, to include forming an enduring source of instability for Central Asia. Central Asian militants in Afghanistan and Pakistan may gain important training grounds and robust support sanctuaries for a jumping-off point into the Central Asian region. From 1998 to 2008, there were networks of training camps for the IMU in the Afghan provinces of Balkh, Herat, Nangarhar, Wardak, Paktia, and Takhar, which all formerly belonged to al Qaeda. Using these bases, IMU militants conducted military incursions and infiltration operations into Central Asia.

Moreover, any further deterioration of the security situation in Afghanistan may lead to an inter-ethnic armed conflict between Pashtuns and Tajik-dominated ethnic groups in Northern Afghanistan, just like those clashes involving the Uzbeks and Hazaras in the 1990s.[20] With the fall of the Soviet-supported Najibullah regime in Kabul in 1992, Pashtuns (including the Afghan Taliban) and the so-called Northern Alliance, led by Ahmad Shah Massoud, an ethnic Tajik, commenced fighting each other. Thus, Afghanistan plunged into a civil war, and the Afghan Taliban never gained control of all areas of Afghanistan.

A civil war or the Afghan Taliban's eventual return to power in Afghanistan would be the most dangerous scenario for Central Asia. It would destabilize not only the separate countries in neighboring Central Asia but also the entire region. Because of its geographic and ethnic proximity, Tajikistan will be the first country in Central Asia affected by this scenario.[21]

The internal security of Tajikistan remains fragile, with more instability influenced by post-2014 Afghanistan. The July 2012 clashes between Tajik military forces and armed militants of local warlords in Tajikistan's Gorno-Badakhshan Autonomous Province, located along the border with Afghanistan, are evidence of looming security concerns. The clashes that resulted in the death of more than two hundred military personnel and civilians fomented concerns in the region about the possibility of a new civil war in Tajikistan.[22] The incident highlighted that the division of Tajikistan into local power centers persists even after the end of the Tajik civil war in 1997. The strong ethnoregional and political divisions, alongside economic stagnation, corruption, organized crime, arms smuggling, and drug trafficking, were internal conditions and factors precipitating the eruption of the Tajik civil war in 1992. Any destructive factors from Afghanistan post-2014 may exploit these existing internal vulnerabilities in Tajikistan to stimulate disorder and replicate the previous civil war.

Afghanistan may again become a major destination for small arms transfers from different parts of the world. For instance, Pakistan's FATA, the world's largest illegal firearms market, supplies the Afghan Taliban, al Qaeda, and its allied Central Asian associates with small arms.[23] In fact, illegal arms smuggling through porous Tajik–Afghan borders was one of the main outside factors for the eruption of the Tajik civil war.[24] With significant numbers of arms obtained from locations inside Afghanistan, the opposition, the United Tajik Opposition (UTO), a coalition of Islamists, nationalists, and Pamir-speaking ethnic groups, resorted to arms in their resistance against the secular-oriented central government. Afghanistan also provided safe havens for Tajik opposition fighters. The Tajik civil war left at least 100,000 people dead and one million others displaced.

The Afghan border with Tajikistan, along the eastern edge of Afghanistan, makes up about 1,344 kilometers, the longest shared border after the border shared with Pakistan. Most of the Tajik–Afghan border is porous and poorly demarcated—making it difficult for the Tajik border guards to police it. This helps to facilitate easy access for militants in Afghanistan to slip into Tajikistan, with aims of further incursions into the region. The proximity also lends itself to refugee flows from Afghanistan.

Any possible armed conflicts in the north of Afghanistan may lead to a refugee crisis for its Central Asian neighbors. Refugees from the south and east of Afghanistan have predominantly flowed into Pakistan or Iran in the past. Tajikistan, Uzbekistan, and Turkmenistan may face a serious risk from the influx of refugees, because of their shared ethnic identities with northern Afghanistan. The Tajiks are the second-largest ethnic group, 27 percent, in Afghanistan, after the Pashtuns, 42 percent. The Uzbeks and Turkmens comprise roughly 12 percent of the Afghan population.[25] Tajikistan does not possess the capacity to handle large numbers of refugees, and it could not meet the logistical or financial requirements to accommodate Afghan refugees flooding its borders.

The security situation in Kyrgyzstan continues to be volatile. Over the past decade, the country experienced the overthrow of two regimes, in 2005 and 2010. The latest took place after bloody inter-ethnic clashes between the ethnic Kyrgyz majority and Uzbek minority in southern Osh and Jalal-Abad province in June 2010, leaving about 470 people dead, and 400,000 others displaced.[26] There is also growing trends of extremist and radical ideologies among the population in these areas. Thus, the situation in the southern provinces of Kyrgyzstan is extremely susceptible to destructive factors from external influences. The conditions are ripe for Central Asian militants fighting in Afghanistan and Pakistan to turn their focus back home, thus igniting a hotbed of extremist activity post-2014. Kyrgyzstan's weak internal security enables terrorists and drug traffickers to transit illicit weapons and narcotics into other countries in the region. Terrorists may also evade capture in Kyrgyz territory and further evade detection by slipping across borders into its neighboring countries.

Any political instability or rise of Islamist militancy in Kyrgyzstan or Tajikistan can easily spill over into the other neighboring countries in the region, to include China and Russia. China's Xinjiang province and Russia's Muslim-dominated southern territories have very strong ethnolingual, religious, and cultural ties with Central Asia's Turkic populations and can easily be manipulated by Islamist militant groups.

A number of preparations are under way by these countries in anticipation of the US withdrawal. Central Asian countries, China, and Russia see the Shanghai Cooperation Organization and the Collective Security Treaty Organization as key platforms to meet possible threats arising from post-2014 Afghanistan. Fearing the worst is still to come in Afghanistan, at the bilateral level, Russia has taken steps to ensure security by strengthening its military presence in Kyrgyzstan and Tajikistan. Russia extended its lease at Kyrgyzstan's Kant Airbase to host its air force units, and in October 2013, the Tajik parliament ratified an agreement with Moscow to extend Russia's military presence in Tajikistan until 2042.

MOST LIKELY SCENARIO: BSA SUCCESSFUL AND TALKS WITH THE AFGHAN TALIBAN FAIL

The most likely future scenario entails a successful BSA and the failure to integrate the Afghan Taliban into the legitimate political process. The proposed BSA allows a limited US military presence in Afghanistan post-2014, with a mandate of continuing assistance to the ANSF and limited counterterrorism support, which is crucial for managing transnational threats emanating from Afghanistan post-2014. The BSA will enable more resources for the Afghan government to improve governance and continue development for the ANSF. Central Asian countries want a continuing US presence in Afghanistan. The presence of foreign troops in Afghanistan post-2014 will prevent the resurgence of al Qaeda and its allies, and will stem the flow of dangerous fighters to Central Asia.

Apparently, the Afghan Taliban remain focused on Afghanistan post-2014. On 1 March 2014, the Afghan Taliban's spokesman, Qari Yousuf Ahmadi, stated that the Taliban seek "good relations with Afghanistan's neighbors and the international community based on mutual respect and did not interfere in internal affairs of others and expect the same from others."[27]

However, Central Asian militants in Afghanistan and Pakistan will likely continue to expand and continue their operations, posing a significant threat to the region. The current capabilities and intentions of these Central Asian militant groups will remain as challenges to the region's stability after the looming US-led coalition forces withdrawal from Afghanistan in 2014. The statements uploaded by the IMU and the IJU in recent years suggest that

Central Asian militants delayed their pursuit of establishing Islamic states in their home countries until the Afghan Taliban's victory is "achieved" in Afghanistan. The IMU and the IJU have been active in conducting numerous assassinations in the northern and the northeastern Afghan provinces such as Takhar and Kunduz, areas predominately populated by Uzbeks and Tajiks. Their concentration of activity in these areas suggests an eventual plan to infiltrate from northern Afghanistan back into their home countries.

However, Central Asian militants cannot achieve their political objectives in Central Asia—to establish Sharia-based government systems by toppling the secular governments that are in power. These militant groups remain limited in their appeal among their own citizens. Muslims in Central Asia are averse to the militant groups' dogmatic insistence of an Islamic state. Nevertheless, the need to promote moderation and efforts to counter extremist ideologies remains, with many Muslims in Central Asia lacking the knowledge of how extremists are misusing Islamic concepts and thus rendering them susceptible to indoctrination by extremist propaganda.

GROWTH IN NARCOTICS TRAFFICKING STILL LIKELY

Central Asia continues to be a transit region, offering a number of northern routes for the Afghan drugs on their way to Russia and Europe. US officials estimate that up to 30 percent of Afghan opium shipments transit through northern routes, which particularly pass through Tajikistan, Kyrgyzstan, and Turkmenistan.[28, 29]

The long-term efforts of the ISAF mission and the Afghan government have not reduced the current growth of drug production in Afghanistan. With a total of over 236,000 hectares under cultivation, illegal opium poppy production reached peak levels—a 36 percent increase in 2012, surpassing the ten-year record high in 2007.[30] Total opium production reached roughly 5,500 tons, an increase of 49 percent since 2012.[31] This trend is a threat to all the countries of the region and the target societies for these drugs, including Russia, the United States, China, the European Union, Iran, and Turkey.

Given the situation with drug production, as well as an analysis of the socioeconomic and sociopolitical situation in Afghanistan, an increase in narcotics trading is expected. This will have direct effects on all of Central Asia's nations. Obviously, with the potential departure of the US and NATO troops from Afghanistan, the situation will only get worse.

Tajikistan is currently one of the main transit routes for transportation of Afghanistan's drugs into Russia and Europe. There are several routes along the Afghan–Tajik borders used for this purpose. One of the main thoroughfares passes through the borders between the northern Afghan province of Badakhshan and the Gorno-Badakhshan Autonomous Province (GBAP) of

Tajikistan. Kalai-Khumb, Ishkoshim, and Khorugh towns are the main entry points for drugs and arms in the GBAP. The Fayzabad city, which it is located in, is a hub for illegal exportation for small arms and narcotics from Afghanistan into Tajikistan.[32] There is a need for continued support for Tajik–Afghan border security.

The production of drugs in Afghanistan also remains a powerful catalyst influencing transnational crime from Afghanistan, such as funding international terrorism and extremism. For instance, from 1998 to 2000, the IMU guerillas were actively involved in the transport of heroin from Afghanistan to Tajikistan and on to Russia and Europe. Regardless of the scenario, the effects of the drug trade will continue to have devastating effects on the region.

BEST CASE SCENARIO: BSA SIGNED AND AFGHAN TALIBAN TALKS ARE SUCCESSFUL

If the United States and the Afghan government sign the BSA, vital continued military assistance to the ANSF will be enabled, and the needed counterterrorism assistance by the United States post-2014 will be maintained. At the same time, peace talks with the Afghan Taliban could lead to their peaceful integration into legitimate political processes in Afghanistan. Violence will decline, and a stabile security environment will likely result.

A stable and peaceful Afghanistan will contribute to the stability and economic prosperity of Central Asia. It will allow the landlocked Central Asian countries to maintain access to the Karachi port of Pakistan and provide a stable route for trade through Afghanistan to the rest of the world. Afghanistan may become an essential constituent of the "material bases" of sustainable developments in Central Asia.[33] Afghanistan also may emerge as an important network of alternative trade routes, especially for energy and raw material supplies, and for regional trade, and be important in the transit of Central Asian hydrocarbon resources to the world market. Many in Central Asia believe that peace in Afghanistan will follow after integrating it into regional cooperation frameworks.[34] Central Asian countries have the potential to play an important role for Afghanistan's future. Their geographic proximity, economic engagement, and ethnocultural linkages with Afghanistan are important to reach a long-term solution.

CONCLUSION

Today, Afghanistan is at a critical crossroads. After the US-led coalition forces draw down from Afghanistan in late 2014, the future stability of Afghanistan is debatable. All future developments in this country will depend on two key factors—the fate of the BSA and the peace talks with the Afghan Taliban. To maintain achievements accomplished to date, Afghanistan needs sustained external support by the international community post-2014. The presence of limited foreign military support is crucial to effectively curb and reduce the potential threats emanating from Afghanistan post-2014.

Security and stability in Central Asia inextricably depend on developments in Afghanistan in post-2014. Any military and political conflict in Afghanistan will have negative effects on the security and stability of the entire region. Any deterioration of the security situation in Afghanistan will precipitate the increase of transnational security threats such as terrorism and illegal trafficking of drugs and small arms. The eruption of a civil war in Afghanistan will be the most dangerous scenario for Central Asia. It will serve as a catalyst for existing domestic vulnerabilities in Tajikistan and Kyrgyzstan to stimulate greater entropy and thus replicate renewed civil war in other countries.

In light of this, countries in the region need to strengthen their security cooperation and take preventive measures at both national and regional levels. To meet transnational threats emanating from Afghanistan more effectively, these countries need to build a collective security network along their borders with Afghanistan. Central Asian states must actively work alongside the international community to ensure that the Afghan government does not collapse and that it ceases to serve as an enduring source of instability. A safe and stable Afghanistan is critical for the security and stability of Central Asia.

Chapter Six

Iran's Strategic Designs for Afghanistan

Halimullah Kousary

INTRODUCTION

Afghanistan sits at a critical stage, as NATO's US-led military efforts against the Afghan Taliban in Afghanistan appear to be at a stalemate. The United States and NATO are destined to withdraw the bulk of their remaining (over 80,000) troops they currently have in Afghanistan prior to 2015. The endorsement of the bilateral security agreement (BSA) by the US and Afghan governments will allow the United States and NATO to leave behind a residual force of 10,000 to 15,000 troops to continue to advise and train the Afghan National Security Forces (ANSF) and to maintain counterterrorism capabilities to pursue the remnants of al Qaeda in Afghanistan.[1] The BSA is currently pending, largely because of an Afghan government precondition that the United States should facilitate practical peace talks with the Afghan Taliban to ensure security in the country.[2]

The course of war in Afghanistan during the past decade was shaped by rivalries within state and cynicism of the India–Pakistan and US–Iran relationships.[3] Iran's hostility toward the United States serves as a catalyst for Iran to play a double game in Afghanistan. Iran initially supported the US-led intervention and played a crucial role in the formation of the new Afghan government, but it also covertly continued to assist the Afghan Taliban in subsequent years.

Iran is Afghanistan's western neighbor, sharing a 560-mile border with it, and has significant cultural and religious ties with the Afghan people. A new chapter commenced in Iran–Afghanistan relations after the fall of the Afghan Taliban regime. Afghanistan described Iran as a "helpful brother and partner,"[4] and Iran delivered unprecedented volumes of aid to Afghanistan.[5] The two countries have fostered a growing economic relationship since the fall of the Afghan Taliban in 2001, with Iran ranking as the second top exporter to Afghanistan after Pakistan.[6] However, the relationship also suffered disparities between the two countries. Apart from Iran's providing measured support to the Afghan Taliban and select Afghan political groups, water is another serious issue that disturbed the Iran–Afghanistan relationship.[7] Water has been the subject of bilateral tensions between the two countries since the 1870s, and both of them claim water rights and disagree about water sharing from the Helmand River in Southern Afghanistan.[8]

Despite these disparities, both countries tried to keep the relationship as amicable as possible, especially Afghanistan. This is difficult, given the adversarial relationship between the United States and Iran, with Afghanistan trying to balance its diplomatic ties to both nations. However, the inking of the pending US–Afghanistan bilateral security agreement could render Iran's relationship with Afghanistan combustible because Iran is staunchly opposed to the continued presence of the United States and NATO in its backyard. This chapter sets out an assessment of Iran's strategic direction in Afghanistan and highlights the following issues: (1) the US–Iran–Taliban rivalries, (2) Iran–India–Russia–China common interests in Afghanistan, and (3) Iran's stance regarding the BSA. Concluding, I will present assumptions of the most likely role Iran might adopt in Afghanistan post-2014, both in the presence and absence of a US-led residual force.

IRAN–US–TALIBAN RIVALRIES

After the CIA planned a successful coup against the government of Mohammad Mossadeq in 1953 and before the 1979 Islamic revolution in Iran, Iran's interests in Afghanistan chiefly focused on the spread of communism. Iran, under the regime of Mohammad Reza Shah Pahlavi, who gained power from the 1953 coup, was a member of the anticommunist Central Treaty Organization (CENTO), along with Turkey, Pakistan, the United Kingdom, and the United States as an observer.[9] The pro-US Shah Pahlavi suppressed the left parties in Iran and jailed thousands of their members.[10]

However, the 1979 Islamic revolution, which overthrew the twenty-six-year-old regime of Reza Shah Pahlavi, marked the end to CENTO and triggered the US–Iran enmity, which has endured over the past three decades.[11] Both countries spared no chance to blame each other for exporting terrorism and violence—the United States describing Iran as an "axis of evil" and Iran labeling the United States as the "Great Satan."[12] The Islamic revolution also softened Iran's anti-Soviet stance at that critical time. Iran's Islamic regime, despite clear recognition that the Soviet invasion of Afghanistan in 1979 was a threat to Iran, was not active in the anti-Soviet Mujahideen resistance on par with assistance provided by the United States, Saudi Arabia, and Pakistan. One major reason for this assessment was Iran's confrontation with the United States, alongside Iran's war with Iraq from 1980 to 1988.[13] The Islamic regime took precautions not to come into direct conflict with the Soviet Union, in a bid to avoid opening one more hostile front because it was already plunged into a war with Iraq and intense rivalry with the United States.[14]

After the Soviet withdrawal from Afghanistan in 1989 and the subsequent disengagement of the United States from South Asia, Iran had more flexibility to foster its involvement in Afghanistan, and it continued arming and funding its proxies during the Afghan civil war from 1992 to 2001.[15] It expanded its influence among the Mujahideen groups hailing from the Hazara Shiite community. When the Afghan Taliban emerged in 1994, bringing much of the country under their control, Iran supported the Northern Alliance, dominated by the non-Pashtun ethnic groups. This included the Hazara and constituted the backbone of the anti-Taliban resistance from 1996 to 2001.[16] The Afghan Taliban regime posed not only an ideological but also a geopolitical challenge to Iran by threatening its interests in Afghanistan and in the broader region.[17] Pakistan created the Afghan Taliban and helped to facilitate support for them from Saudi Arabia and the United Arab Emirates—three countries challenging Shiite Iranian influence in South Asia and the Middle East.[18] Because of its support for the Northern Alliance, Iran came close to getting into a direct conflict with the Afghan Taliban when the latter killed eight Iranian diplomats and a journalist in the northern city of Mazar-e-Sharif in 1998.[19]

Iran welcomed the US-led intervention in Afghanistan because such intervention was certain to change the balance of power in the country in favor of Iran. The Afghan Taliban regime collapsed, resulting in Iran, India, and Russia cooperating to help to establish the new Afghan government.[20] Iran's influence with the Northern Alliance was instrumental in the new government's formation, because the Northern Alliance was reluctant to share power with President Hamid Karzai. Iran's political pressure on the Northern Alliance's leaders during negotiations in Bonn, Germany, influenced a compromise resulting in an agreement to share power. The new government offered many ministerial positions to the Northern Alliance leaders,[21] and with that, Iran assumed a larger role in Afghanistan than it had at any time since the mid-nineteenth century.[22]

Iran used both soft and hard measures to maintain its influence in Afghanistan and counter both the United States and the Taliban—the United States in the short term and the Taliban in the long term. Media strategy has been one strand in Iran's multipronged design of soft power in Afghanistan. Iran backed nearly a third of Afghanistan's media; it has spent more or less $100 million a year in Afghanistan on the media, civil society projects, and Shiite religious schools.[23] Iran pledged $570 million in 2002 and another 100 million in 2006 in aid to the reconstruction process in Afghanistan, most of which was actually delivered.[24] In 2008, it pledged an additional $50 million in aid and $300 million in loans to be delivered to Afghanistan over the next three years.[25] Furthermore, Iran has a growing investment in and trade with Afghanistan. In 2012–2013, annual trade between the two countries totaled over $2 billion, with Iran accounting for about 35 to 40 percent of exports to Afghanistan.[26] Both countries expect bilateral trade to increase with the operation of Iran's Chabahar port, which will be a major conduit for Afghanistan to trade with India and other countries.[27]

The United States and Iran share common ground in Afghanistan—both countries support a sustainable and inclusive Afghan government, strong enough to prevent the return of the Taliban and al Qaeda.[28] Nevertheless, the nature of their broader relationship urged each of them to view their actions in Afghanistan as a zero-sum game. Their relationship worsened when the United States called Iran the "axis of evil" in 2002[29] and when in 2003 it was revealed that Iran was building secret nuclear energy facilities for military uses.[30] The US–Iran rivalry made it difficult for Afghanistan to keep a balance in its relationship on one side with an important ally against the Taliban and on the other side with an influential neighbor. When the United States signed a strategic partnership with the Afghan government in May 2005, Iran demanded a similar agreement with a commitment from Afghanistan that the United States would not use its territory for military operations against it. The United States exerted pressure on the Afghan government to decline Iran's proposition.[31] In 2012, the US Treasury Department urged the Afghan banking and business organizations not to conduct business with Iranian firms as stipulated by the US-led sanctions. However, Afghanistan refused to discontinue the business arguing that it would be in economic crisis if the business were stopped.[32]

The US–Iran rivalry also became the major catalyst for Iran to provide measured support to the Taliban against the US-led NATO forces in Afghanistan post-2001.[33] The most important development in the Iran–Taliban relationship that developed in the aftermath of the US-led intervention was a visit by the Taliban delegation to Tehran at the invitation of the Iranian government in June 2013.[34] The Taliban acknowledged several such delegations, including some of their senior leaders having visited Iran for meetings with the Iranian authorities. They stated that the visits were aimed at removing existing misunderstanding between Iran and the Taliban.[35] During the visit, Iran was said to have raised its concerns about the Shiite Hazara community in Afghanistan and that the Taliban in return asked Iran not to support their opponents after the US–NATO withdrawal in 2014.[36] The Taliban realize that Iran has considerable influence with the anti-Taliban Afghan groups, but they may not know that Iran would not halt supporting the groups against them in the long term. Iran looks at the Taliban as only a short-term ally against the United States to stand in the way of US interests in and the BSA with Afghanistan.[37] Iran fears that continued presence of the United States in Afghanistan could be used to destabilize Iran.[38] In the meantime, Iran perceives the Taliban to be a long-term ideological threat. Therefore, Iran's concurrent support of the Afghan government and the anti-Taliban Afghan political groups is to prepare in the long term to confront that threat in Afghanistan. Iran maintains strong ties with the Afghan government and anti-Taliban groups through providing financial support. In 2011, President Hamid Karzai acknowledged that his office regularly received suitcases of cash from Tehran. He characterized the cash as routine aid from Iran.[39]

IRAN–INDIA–RUSSIA–CHINA BLOCK AND ITS INTERESTS IN AFGHANISTAN

Afghanistan is in a geopolitically sensitive region. This has urged regional and extraregional powers to develop collaborations to protect their convergent interests in Afghanistan and the broader region.[40] Iran, India, and Russia were key supporters of the Northern Alliance against the Taliban in the 1990s,[41] and the three countries have a stake in a stable Afghanistan and do not want the Taliban back in power. But they support the Taliban's joining the Afghan peace process and giving up violence, accepting the Afghan constitution, and cutting all ties with al Qaeda and other like-minded groups in the region.[42] Iran wants the government in Afghanistan to be inclusive of all ethnic groups, which seems impossible while the Taliban are in power and while Russia perceives that with the Taliban in power, the danger of Islamic extremism emanating from the Afghanistan–Pakistan territory could be reinforced. Islamic extremism already has had a notable effect on the Russian provinces of Dagestan, Ingushetia, and Chechnya.[43] India fears that a Taliban takeover of Afghanistan would seriously affect the prospects of stability in its border province of Jammu and Kashmir.[44] Thus, Iran and India have undertaken collaborative projects for the sustainability of the current regime in Afghanistan. The 135-mile Chabahar–Zaranj–Delaram Highway, completed in 2009, is one example.[45] India built the highway to link Afghanistan with the port of Chabahar in Iran, which was also developed with Indian assistance to help create an alternative trade route to Afghanistan to bypass Pakistan. Indian goods to Afghanistan and Central Asia have to go through Iran because Pakistan does not allow the transit of Indian goods.[46] Iran's partnership with China vis-à-vis Afghanistan is also conceivable because both countries view each other as potential allies in maintaining a geostrategic balance in the region against the United States.[47]

However, there are also disparities vis-à-vis the BSA among these four countries. China fears that Afghanistan will be used as a sanctuary for the Uyghur separatists in western Xinjiang region. It, thus, did not indicate strong opposition to the continued US–NATO military presence in Afghanistan as Iran did because the US–NATO presence can be a deterrent for China against Islamist extremists. Xinjiang region shares a short border with Afghanistan,[48] and China already has accused these extremists from neighboring countries of supporting the Uyghur separatists in the region. China even offered to help Afghanistan to fight the "terrorist forces" in the country.[49] India openly endorses the continued presence of the US and NATO forces in Afghanistan.[50] After the Afghan traditional Loya Jirga approved the BSA in November 2013 and demanded that it be signed immediately, Iran opposed the BSA, whereas India underscored its cruciality to security in Afghanistan.[51] India's broader goal in Afghanistan regarding the BSA appears to be to prevent Pakistan from dominating that country.[52] Russia is not comfortable about the US–NATO presence in its proximity.[53] It realizes the risks tied to a full US–NATO withdrawal from Afghanistan in terms of narcotics and terrorism targeting its backyard, but it believes that it can handle it alone. Russia might consider deploying troops along the Tajikistan–Afghanistan border to deter narcotics and terrorism in the event instability increases in Afghanistan after the full US–NATO withdrawal.[54] Russia denies foreign influence in both the Caucasus and Central Asia regions because these regions have significant influence on Russian domestic and regional security establishments.[55]

IRAN'S OPPOSITION TO THE BSA

Iran's relationship not only with the United States but also with Afghanistan could be further combustible if the BSA is concluded successfully.[56] Iran argues that the US military efforts in Afghanistan were not successful in the fight against the Taliban and al Qaeda and that the BSA cannot ensure Afghanistan's security in the future but that it will instead pose a serious threat to the stability of the region, especially to that of Iran. It described the BSA as a US ploy to achieve permanent military presence in Afghanistan and contain it.[57]

The Baloch insurgency in Iran is an important factor in Iran's perception of threat from the United States. The Baloch people, who are predominantly Sunni Muslims, are divided among Iran, Pakistan, and Afghanistan. Out of an estimated seven to eight million Baloch people, over six million live in Pakistan, while about two million live in Iran's Sistan and Baluchestan province. Some 500,000 of them live all across Afghanistan. Prior to the inception of the Islamic Republic, the Baloch insurgency first developed against the government of Reza Shah Pahlavi and gained momentum in 2004 through the efforts of the Jundallah, a militant organization based in Balochistan that fights for the rights of the Baloch population in Iran. Iran labeled the group a terrorist organization and charged the United States with buttressing it.[58] The February 2010 arrest of the Jundallah leader, Abdolmalek Rigi, by Iranian forces reinforced Iran's threat perception of the United States. Before he was executed, Rigi "confessed" on Iranian television to having the support of the United States. Eight months after Rigi's execution, in November 2010, the United States designated the Jundallah as a terrorist group, but even that did not change Iran's assessment of the suspected nexus between the United States and the Jundallah.[59]

In a possible bid to discourage the Afghan government from signing the BSA, Iran inked a strategic cooperation agreement with Afghanistan in August 2013.[60] The agreement stipulates cooperation and exchanges in military training, counterterrorism, and organized crime, as well as joint military exercises and intelligence sharing.[61] Iran believes that instead of the continued presence of the foreign forces, a native and self-reliant security system is the most practical option for long-term security in Afghanistan[62] and that this option can be strengthened with political and logistical support from regional and extraregional powers. According to Iran, the neighboring countries can agree to a solution to the conflict in Afghanistan if the world powers would allow it.[63]

CONCLUSION

Iran's interests in Afghanistan seem to be contradictory and more strategic than economic, urging Iran not to rely on a single option for its foreign policy. Some of its key interests in Afghanistan coincide with the US military efforts to defeat the Taliban and establish a viable and inclusive Afghan government. However, its enmity with and perception of threat from the United States have led Iran to provide measured military assistance to the Taliban even though the Taliban are ideologically opposed to Iran. Thus, Iran's measured support for the Taliban and its strong opposition to the BSA are the direct result of its broader relationship with the United States.

Although any improvement in the relationship will likely facilitate avenues for bilateral cooperation in Afghanistan, the potential for such an improvement seems bleak given the strategic and economic complexities in the greater Middle East. From a US perspective, Iran's nuclear program and its "support for terrorism" are the major issues obstructing efforts to improve the relationship. Israel, an all-weather ally of the United States in the Middle East, views Iran as a security threat because of its support for Hezbollah and Hamas, and the Arab allies see Iran as a strategic, economic, and ideological rival in the region. The Arab states were already against the 2003 war in Iraq, which strengthened Iran's influence in the region, and any effort toward a rapprochement between the United States and Iran will likely require compromise over Arab allies, which the United States seems unwilling to do.

Thus, absent an improved relationship with the United States, Iran will not agree to the continued military presence of the United States and NATO in Afghanistan. In such a scenario, Iran will remain acutely distrustful of any long-term US military presence in its proximity. Iran desires a regime in Afghanistan that not only distances itself from the United States but also refuses an influential role for the Taliban. Iran wants all this to happen with no US military presence in the country after 2014.

Thus, Iran has kept all of its options open to be able to respond to emerging developments in pursuit of its interests in Afghanistan. If US troops remain after 2014, Iran would see this as a threat to its security and would continue helping the Taliban. If the BSA is not completed and the Taliban still refuse to negotiate with the Afghan government and cut ties with al Qaeda, Iran would put its weight behind the Afghan government and the anti-Taliban political groups, as will India and Russia because they also see the Taliban and Talibanization a threat to stability in their backyards.

Chapter Seven

Why Afghanistan Matters

The Global Threat of Terrorism

Rohan Gunaratna

INTRODUCTION

With the US-led coalition withdrawal, the reconstitution of the Afghan sanctuary by al Qaeda, the Taliban, and their associated groups is inevitable. The tone and tenor of the directing figures and the momentum of attacks during the drawdown reflect the looming threat to Afghanistan. The threat will affect not only Afghanistan but also its neighbors, particularly Pakistan, and China, India, and afar. Like the earlier generation of Soviet forces, Western forces failed to sustain and succeed in a long-drawn-out insurgency.

Unlike the earlier generation of fighters, the insurgents and terrorists integrated suicide into their operational art, inflicting high fatalities and casualties. The blowback of the first generation of the anti-Soviet multinational Afghan Mujahideen campaign was its geographic expansion and al Qaeda's attacks on America's most iconic landmarks. Today, a second wave of terror is in the making. With multiple conflict zones and a pool of foreign fighters willing to kill and die, the global threat of terrorism will grow in the immediate (one to two years), the midterm (five years), and the long term (ten years). Complex, fractured, and more lethal, the second-generation fighters are willing to conduct mass fatalities and casualty attacks.

With no global strategy and with the US-led coalition drawdown, the threat is likely to shift inside Afghanistan. The long-range terrorist threat to the West will endure, but the greater and more immediate day-to-day threat will be to the regions around the Af–Pak theater. In the event the Afghan sanctuary is recreated, the immediate neighborhood of Iran, Central Asia, South Asia, and Northeast Asia will suffer from threat groups. Iran and

Central Asia deployed their security forces in strength to better protect their borders. However, in South Asia and Northeast Asia, where the borders are long and porous, the threat will be greatest.

THE CONTEXT

The origins of the current wave of terrorism can be traced back to the Soviet invasion of Afghanistan on Christmas Day 1979. After the Soviet withdrawal from Afghanistan in February 1989, the international community neglected Afghanistan, Pakistan, and the foreign nationals in tribal Pakistan who fought against the Soviets. Internecine warfare in Afghanistan paved the way for the emergence of Taliban–Afghans, who studied in Pakistani religious seminaries, to seize power in Kabul on 27 September 1996. The Taliban seized power in Kabul with military support by Pakistan and financial support by Saudi Arabia. The newly established Islamic Emirate of Afghanistan received partial diplomatic recognition from Saudi Arabia, Pakistan, and the United Arab Emirates. Lacking in good judgment, they hosted foreign terrorist groups supporting Muslim insurgent and terrorist groups in conflict zones worldwide. An ally of the Taliban, al Qaeda formed in Peshawar, Pakistan, in August 1988, hence creating a state of the art training infrastructure in Afghanistan to mount attacks against the United States, its allies, and its friends. After forming the World Islamic Front for Jihad against the Jews and Crusaders in February 1998, al Qaeda, led by Osama bin Laden, provided training, weapons, financing, and ideology to two dozen threat groups.

The Islamic Emirate of Afghanistan, governed by the Islamic movement of the Taliban, brought untold suffering to its people. Muslim leaders worldwide criticized the Taliban's interpretations of Islamic law—sharia. Just like al Qaeda's leadership, Taliban leaders, including its leader Mullah Mohammed Omar, were illiterate and poorly educated in Islam.[1] For ill treating the minorities and women, the Taliban was condemned internationally. With al Qaeda, the Taliban committed massacres against Afghan civilians, especially the Hazaras, and the Taliban also starved a segment of their civilians. The Hindus and Sikhs who lived in Afghanistan for centuries were directed to wear markers. The Taliban issued edicts forbidding education for women and forbade their participation in employment, with the exception being the health sector. In addition to wearing a dress covering the entire body except the eyes, those leaving their home had to be accompanied by a male relative. In addition to destroying the 1,700-year-old Bamiyan Buddha statues by a decree in March 2001, the Taliban entered the national museum in Kabul with hammers and smashed statues and images. In the name of Islam, the Taliban committed the most despicable atrocities and destruction until al Qaeda's attacks on America's most iconic landmarks on 9/11. The US intervention in Afghanistan drove the Taliban into tribal Pakistan. Although the United States successfully dismantled al Qaeda's training infrastructure and dislodged the Taliban from Afghanistan, the threat groups survived and revived in Pakistan. The US intervention in Iraq in March 2003 distracted the United States from completing its mission in Afghanistan and Pakistan. The most powerful militaries, consisting of the US-led European armies, failed to restore stability and security in Afghanistan. The cost of intervention was staggering for the United States.[2] The Afghan Taliban, and their associated groups, were weak in numerical strength, but using tribal Pakistan as a sanctuary, they endured and fought back. Despite the loss of territory, key leaders, and fighters, they never recognized the US-led coalition intervention in Afghanistan starting in October 2001. Claiming troops of Operation Enduring Freedom as "foreign invaders," neither the Taliban nor their associated groups regarded themselves as breaching international law when their fighters target and kill foreigners that play a support role in the intervention. Moreover, the United Nations is also not immune from perceptions of impropriety concerning Afghanistan. "The United Nations cannot claim to be exempt as from the beginning it has taken a partial role and supported the illegal invasion of Afghanistan."[3]

Against the West, the Afghan Taliban and their associated groups seek to achieve a victory comparable to their defeat of the Soviets, the erstwhile superpower. The Taliban regard themselves as "Mujahideen" (fighters of God) and Karzai's Afghan forces as "puppets"! Despite the threat from the Taliban, Karzai was unwilling to sign a security agreement to keep a US force of trainers and operators in the country after the NATO-led coalition ends its mission and withdraws at the end of 2014. In the previous generation, the Afghan fighters, supported by a few thousand foreign fighters, checkmated the Soviets. The defeat of the Soviets in Afghanistan led to their withdrawal and collapse as a superpower.

With military operations by the Pakistani and Afghan forces fighting a common enemy, the epicenter is on the Pakistan–Afghanistan border. Using tribal Pakistan as a staging platform, fighters of Afghan, Pakistani, and other nationalities stage operations into Afghanistan, largely hitting its southeast and the capital of Kabul. The Afghan security forces, without international support, cannot sustain against a persistent and relentless adversary. They are no match against a highly motivated and battle-hardened 20,000 to 30,000 Taliban fighters. The United States intends to maintain a smaller footprint of Special Operations Forces and their enablers, while withdrawing the bulk of the general-purpose forces. In addition to mounting intelligence-led counterterrorism and counterinsurgency operations, the United States will provide trainers and advisers to support Afghan capacity building to fight and develop a range of capabilities.

The Afghan Taliban derive their strength from Tehrik-e-Taliban Pakistan (TTP), also known as the Pakistani Taliban, a conglomerate of groups. Followers of Deobandism—a puritanical sect of Sunni Islam, numbering several hundred foreign fighters, notably al Qaeda, provide support. With news of the US drawdown, they eagerly await to reenter Afghanistan. Because the border is porous, they move back and forth from Pakistan to Afghanistan, capturing bordering towns and villages. Located in tribal Pakistan, these experienced fighters wage an intergenerational war. Their invincible warrior spirit, then driven by a martial culture and today by a politico-religious ideology, reflects the deep belief that Afghanistan is the graveyard of empires.[4]

Without a proper appreciation of the emerging threat, Karzai released several hundred Taliban insurgents and terrorists held in US, British, and other detention facilities in Afghanistan.[5] Karzai's likely successor, Dr. Abdullah Abdullah said, "Taliban are not fighting in order to be accommodated. They are fighting in order to bring the state down. So it's a futile exercise, and it's just misleading. . . . There are groups that will fight to the death. Whether we like to talk to them or we don't like to talk to them, they will continue to fight. So, for them, I don't think that we have a way forward with talks or negotiations or contacts or anything as such. Then we have to be prepared to tackle and deal with them militarily."[6] Considering the sustained threat to the leadership and the government, Dr. Abdullah and Afghanistan face a severe threat from terrorism and insurgency. Like in Iraq, if the United States withdraws without signing the Enduring Strategic Partnership Agreement between the Islamic Republic of Afghanistan and the United States of America, it is very likely that Afghanistan will reemerge as a terrorist sanctuary. With likely attacks directed at the United States and its allies and friends from Afghanistan, US forces will be forced to reintervene in Afghanistan after a few years.

BACKGROUND

Historically, Afghanistan is regarded as the most important battleground for Muslims. Hopeful of victory, al Qaeda and its associated groups regard Afghanistan as the most important "land of jihad." The British in the nineteenth century, the Soviets in the twentieth century, and the United States in the twenty-first century fought the Afghans. The local rulers and the intervening powers they collaborated with also collapsed, demonstrating the futility of the interventions. The Afghan spirit is indomitable, and its capacity to endure is formidable. Six months before the Soviet withdrawal on 15 February 1989 al Qaeda was created on 11 August 1988. Conceptualizing al Qaeda as the "pioneering vanguard of the Islamic movements," the Palestinian–Jordanian ideologue, Abdullah Azzam wrote: "This vanguard constitutes the solid base [qaeda in Arabic] for the hoped-for society. . . . We shall continue the jihad no matter how long the way, until the last breath and the last beat of the pulse—or until we see the Islamic state established."[7] Serving as the unofficial Saudi representative to Afghanistan, Osama bin Laden implemented his mentor's vision by conducting spectacular attacks to inspire and instigate a global fight against non-Muslims.

At its formation, al Qaeda collaborated with the Egyptian Islamic Jihad (EIJ) led by Dr. Ayman al Zawahiri, and al Gamma al Islamiyah (Islamic Group [IG]), led by Sheikh Omar Abdel Rahman. In addition to providing financing, training, and sanctuary in Afghanistan to these groups, al Qaeda also provided support to the Kurdistan Islamic Movement ([KIM] which later evolved into Ansar al Islam and Tawhid wal Jihad), Al-Ittihad al-Islami ([AIAI] The Islamic Union), The Eritrean Islamic Jihad Movement (EIJM), The Moroccan Islamic Combatant Group (Groupe Islamique Combatant Marocain [GICM]), Tunisian Combatant Group, Libyan Islamic Fighters Group, Eastern Turkistan Islamic Movement ([ETIM] which later evolved into Ḥizb al-Islāmī al-Turkistānī [Turkistan Islamic Party, TIP]), Armed Islamic group of Algeria ([GIA] which later evolved into the Salafist Group of Call and Combat), Islamic Movement of Uzbekistan (IMU), Islamic Movement of Tajikistan (IMT), and several Chechen organizations, notably the International Islamic Brigade (IIB). In addition to several Pakistani groups, notably those operating in Kashmir, Harakatul Jihad I Islami Bangladesh (HuJI-B) received training and support. Al Qaeda also coordinated with Southeast Asian groups, to include Myanmar's groups, including Harakatul Jihad I Islami Arakan (HuJI-A), Rohingiya Solidarity Organization (RSO), and Arakan Rohingiya Nationalist Organization (ARNO). In Malaysia, al Qaeda's coordination with Kumpulan Militan Malaysia (KMM) and the Philippines' groups, to include the Abu Sayyaf Group (ASG), Moro Islamic Liberation Front (MILF) expanded the network and goals of the organization. Finally, Thai Muslim groups, specifically, Jemmah Salafi (JS), Pattani United Liberation Front (PULO), Gerakan Mujahidin Islam Patani (GMIP) and Jemmah Islamiyah (JI) received training and support from al Qaeda. JI extended its influence throughout Southeast Asia. In June 2001, al Qaeda merged with EIJ, creating al Qaeda al Jihad, but its most significant partners today are the Afghan Taliban and Pakistani Taliban.

After emerging from the Pakistani madrasahs, the displaced Afghan youths formed the Afghan Taliban. The Taliban collaborated with al Qaeda since Osama bin Laden's relocation from the Sudan to Afghanistan in 1996. The leader of the Islamic Emirate of Afghanistan, Mullah Mohammad Omar, designated the Amir al-Mumineen (Commander of the Faithful), gave al Qaeda the mandate to train the Mujahideen (God's warriors) worldwide. By providing ideology, training, financing, and weapons in Afghanistan and in other theaters, al Qaeda empowered insurgent and terrorist groups in Asia, Africa, the Middle East, the Caucuses, and the Balkans. Initially, al Qaeda trainers, financiers, and operational leaders supported the fight, but later, the local groups produced their own combat tacticians and explosives experts.

THE GLOBAL AL QAEDA STRUCTURE

Afghanistan's sprawling training and support infrastructure for al Qaeda strengthened thirty insurgent and terrorist groups in Asia, Africa, the Caucuses, the Balkans, and the Middle East. To attack the distant and far enemies, al Qaeda built the "World Islamic Front for Jihad against Jews and Crusaders" in 1998. The global network of groups created by al Qaeda, also known as the "Global Jihad Movement," emerged as the most violent terrorist network. As the "pioneering vanguard," al Qaeda conducted an exhibition attack against America's most iconic economic, military, and political landmarks. By staging 9/11, al Qaeda not only inspired and instigated thirty associated groups but also sent a clear message that they can attack inside the United States. Their dual focus was to hit the United States, the "head of the poisonous snake shielding corrupt Muslim rulers" and strike the "ungodly regimes" at home.

The US-led response to al Qaeda's attacks against America's World Trade Center, the Pentagon, and the attempt to attack Capitol Hill on 9/11, was met with quick reaction. The initial phase was led by about one hundred US intelligence and two hundred special operators working with indigenous forces opposed to the Islamic Movement of the Taliban, who served as the ruling regime in Afghanistan. The Taliban's and al Qaeda's sanctuaries in Afghanistan were known to the CIA since al Qaeda's attacks in East Africa in August 1998 and the USS *Cole* attack in October 2000. The ruling Afghan Taliban, al Qaeda, and a dozen other threat groups fought briefly and then retreated in the face of overwhelming firepower. These groups subsequently relocated to tribal Pakistan and Iran. From tribal Pakistan, some leaders and members relocated to mainland Pakistan, including the 9/11 mastermind Khalid Sheikh Mohamed. From Iran, some leaders and members relocated to northern Iraq. Working with their US counterparts, Pakistan's security forces played a central but quiet role in killing and capturing some leaders and members of al Qaeda and other foreign fighters. This includes efforts to capture Khalid Sheikh Mohamed by the Inter-Services Intelligence and Abu Zubaidah, who was captured by the CIA with the assistance of Pakistani police. Iran detained about two hundred al Qaeda leaders such as Saif al Adel, the head of the security and intelligence committee; Abdel Aziz al Masri, the head of the WMD subcommittee; and Abu Khair al Masri, the head of the political committee. Iran deported a few al Qaeda leaders and their families but retained most of them.

The Pakistani government hunted al Qaeda and their supporters that formed the Mujahideen Shura in North Waziristan but not the Afghan Taliban that formed the Shura in Quetta—Rahbari Shura. Pakistani military operations against al Qaeda led to heavy resistance and the creation of TTP, the most violent group in the region attacking both Pakistan and Afghanistan. Al Qaeda influenced TTP to create Umar Media, and their videos called for Shariah-based governance in Pakistan and hostility to those opposing it. The TTP also developed an appetite to carry out operations overseas, from Spain to New York, and Myanmar. Although most of them failed, the New York Times Square car-bombing attempt by Faisal Shehzad in May 2010 nearly succeeded. Pakistani insurgent and terrorist leaders targeting Afghanistan were killed along with civilians by Pakistani ground forces, Pakistani and US proxies, and US drones. However, they were quickly replaced by a long list of younger but more motivated men nurtured in an environment of conflict.

Immediately after the Afghan Taliban withdrew into Pakistan, they lacked the capability to conduct operations against the United States, NATO, and other forces in late 2001 and 2002. This is because US forces maintained good security and focused on threats to Afghanistan. However, as the United States prepared to strike Iraq in 2003, its focus shifted to the Middle East. In 2004, with the deterioration of security in Iraq, the United States started to shift its specialist units to Iraq. In 2005–2006, the tribes that traditionally fought the occupiers of Afghanistan organized themselves, notably the Mehsuds, and started conducting operations into Afghanistan. It was the neglect of Afghanistan and Pakistan and the prioritizing of Iraq that led to the revival of the Taliban in Pakistan, thus creating a shadow government in Afghanistan's regions bordering Pakistan.

The US-led strategy to restore stability in Afghanistan and Pakistan was to kill insurgent and terrorist leaders and to dismantle their infrastructure. The strategy was flawed, because the political environment and economic conditions produced more fighters than the number that could be killed. The Taliban from Pakistan reentered the villages at night that were cleared by security forces during the day; then they killed, maimed, and injured those who cooperated with the International Security Assistance Force (ISAF) and government forces. The strategy changed in 2009, when village stabilization operations were mounted to empower the locals to provide security and to establish closer local relations to the central government in Kabul. On Pakistan's side of the border, stability operations by the Pakistani military were fewer, and the Taliban recruited from the pool of Afghan and Pakistan were displaced. With Middle Eastern and other sources of funding and ideology, young men joined the Taliban from tribal Pakistan.

As the Taliban largely operated from tribal Pakistan, the United States also targeted the Pakistan Taliban's leadership. Although rarely acknowledged publicly, Islamabad approved the strikes. The accuracy of the strikes improved over time. Both Pakistan's ground operations and US drone strikes depleted the leadership ranks. The first leader of the Pakistan Taliban, Abdullah Mehsud, was released from Guantanamo Bay in March 2004. After his death in July 2007, Baitullah Mehsud formed the TTP in December 2007. Killed in a US drone strike in South Waziristan in August 2009, Baitullah was succeeded by Hakimullah Mesud. Also killed in a US drone strike in November 2013, Hakimullah was succeeded by Maulana Fazlullah, the leader of Tehreek-e-Nafaz-e-Shariat-e-Mohammadi (TNSM). Since 9/11, the drone has proved to be the most effective weapon against the terrorist and insurgent leaders. When a drone targeted Hakimullah Mehsud's vehicle in North Waziristan on 1 November 2013, a Twitter user, "Abu Jandal al-Khorasani," called for action against Americans and said, "America will not rest and have security; instead, in place of Hakimullah Mehsud there are a thousand Hakims. We will see, O Obama and your helpers. So have fun for an hour and you will have regret until the Day of Judgment."[8] On the forums, one jihadist asked for a solution to drones, and two posters condemned Pakistan's Prime Minister Nawaz Sharif for the assassination of Hakimullah.[9] Others prayed that God accepts Hakimullah as a martyr.[10] The Taliban, especially the TTP, responded by mounting suicide attacks, to include the suicide bombing by Jordanian Humam al-Balawi aka Abu Dujana al-Khorasani at a CIA base in Khost, Afghanistan, in December 2009. After training in a facility called "Salahuddin Ayyubi Military Training Center" in Pakistan, the terrorist portrayed himself as an informant. The insurgent and terrorist attacks focused on Western forces and on insider attacks after Afghan forces started to play a frontline role. The Taliban continue to maintain pressure on NATO and other forces.

RENEWED THREAT LANDSCAPE

The earlier generation of threat groups that fought the Soviets are fighting Western forces in Afghanistan and the Kabul government. First, the Hezbollah-e-Islami group evolved into the Haqqani Network; second, Maktabil Khadimat evolved into al Qaeda; and third, the Mujahideen formed the nuclei of the Afghan Taliban and the TTP. Having trained, fought, and won in Afghanistan against the Soviets, the leadership of the Afghan Taliban and the Pakistan Taliban and the TTP, especially the Haqqani Network, are determined to defeat the US-led coalition in Afghanistan. In the same way the Afghan and Pakistani Mujahideen leaders fought against the Soviets, Afghan veterans in leadership positions guide the dozen groups fighting campaigns worldwide. The leader of the Haqqani Network, Jalauddin Haqqani, commented, "all the reasons and factors that led to the fall of the Russian Empire at the hands of the Afghan Mujahideen are today facing the American Empire."[11]

The ancient tribesmen and warriors in Afghanistan and Pakistan are culturally martial. Nonetheless, with the introduction of al Qaeda's ideology, the thinking and actions of the populace transformed. The tribal elders, the Maliks, were killed; the tribal system was threatened; and the tribal structure disintegrated. The newly formed militant groups embraced suicide operations, alien to Pakistan and Afghanistan, a concept imported from the Middle East. The culture of death was evident, especially when the head of the Haqqani Network, Jalaluddin Haqqani, congratulated Mullah Omar and himself after his son was killed. Jalaluddin Haqqani commented, "Shaheed Naseeruddin Haqqani was neither the first martyr from our family nor will he be the last."[12] Jalaluddin Haqqani added, "Seeking martyrdom through the campaign for the supremacy of Islamic government and the defense of our beloved nation is the Haqqani family's most ardent desire."[13] Al Qaeda continues their mentoring by indoctrinating TTP, an entity several times the strength of the Afghan Taliban. Although Mullah Muhammed Omar is the Afghan Taliban's leader, TTP strategists and al Qaeda combat tacticians guided TTP's ideology and direction. Because his knowledge of Islam was limited, Mullah Omar was deeply influenced by al Qaeda's philosophy. Like his predecessor Osama, al Zawahiri pledged his allegiance to Mullah Omar. Because of Pakistani military operations using air power and indirect fire, the local elite and population perceived them as the enemy. Intelligence-led Pakistani and US operations eroded the numerical strength of al Qaeda to diminish from a few thousand to a few hundred fighters. From an operational organization that fought in the battlefield and off the battlefield, al Qaeda transformed into an ideological and training organization.

While the battle-experienced Afghan elders in Pakistan actively enable the return of the Taliban to Afghanistan, al Qaeda's leader, Dr. Ayman al Zawahiri, is guiding global campaigns of terrorism and extremism. As the successor to Osama bin Laden, he plays a central role in shaping the international threat environment. In addition to al Zawahiri's focus on Pakistan and Afghanistan, the new al Qaeda leader remains the central player influencing and shaping the human terrain. The threat is not only targeting the West but also India, China, and Muslim governments branded by al Qaeda as "un-Islamic." Like Osama, Zawahiri successfully appropriated local struggles and fused them into a "global jihad." Although al Qaeda in the real space retreated to tribal Pakistan to survive, al Qaeda in the virtual space expanded and operationally coopted an ideologically inspired several dozen groups.

9/11'S LONG SHADOW

With al Qaeda located in the Pakistan–Afghanistan border, South Asia is the epicenter of international terrorism. The intention of al Qaeda, the most influential Islamic movement in contemporary times, is to return to Afghanistan. Despite the denial of the Afghan sanctuary, al Qaeda persists in instigating and inspiring the global threat landscape of jihadist ideology and violence. With al Qaeda at the center of a constellation of affiliated and associated groups, global extremism, terrorism, and insurgency have steadfastly grown. The world witnessed a 43 percent increase in the number of terrorist attacks in 2013, counting 9,707 terrorist attacks.[14] The top five countries in the world suffering from terrorism include Afghanistan, India, and Pakistan. The world's most violent insurgent and terrorist groups are the Pakistani and Afghan Taliban. Threat groups inspired by the ideology and methodology of al Qaeda, such as Nigeria's Boko Haram and al Qaeda in Iraq, present the most severe and enduring threat. Although many of them are not formally associated with al Qaeda, these groups look to al Qaeda for guidance. They maintain high operational tempos in their areas of operation and a cyber presence akin to al Qaeda. If al Qaeda returns to Afghanistan from tribal Pakistan, once again, Afghanistan will reemerge as a sanctuary. Returning to Afghanistan means a new lease on life for its operationally associated and ideologically affiliated groups. The luxury of sanctuary will enable al Qaeda to reestablish its training and operational bases and to regroup and strategically rethink its operations to coordinate operations worldwide in the years ahead.

Despite security measures, terrorism rose during the past decade at the beginning of the twenty-first century. Al Qaeda itself did not mount the bulk of the attacks, but groups associated and affiliated with al Qaeda did. Al Qaeda's greatest strength was their ability to inspire and instigate individuals, cells, and groups. Al Qaeda's ideology and technology were embraced by the existing and new generation of groups. Although al Qaeda remain the most hunted threat group in history, al Qaeda continue to serve as both ideologue and trainer. With the depletion of al Qaeda's capacity to mount attacks due to targeted operations by intelligence, law enforcement, and the military, the group still operates in the shadows. The associated and affiliated groups compensated by acting as the operational branch of al Qaeda. Of the groups, the closest associate to al Qaeda is al Qaeda in the Arabian Peninsula (AQAP), led by Nasir Abdel Karim al-Wuhayshi, the former secretary for Osama bin Laden. In contrast to other groups, many of the AQAP leaders and members came from al Qaeda's core. As such, unlike other groups, AQAP is considered an extension rather than an associated group of al Qaeda.

The threat groups formally associated with al Qaeda are AQAP, al Qaeda in the Islamic Maghreb (AQIM), al-Shabaab al-Mujahideen, and Jabhat al-Nusra. Until February 2014, the Islamic State of Iraq ([ISI] renamed Islamic State of Iraq and the Levant [ISIL]) was al Qaeda's associate in Iraq. Australian cleric Abu Suleiman al-Muhajir, a member of the Shariah Committee of al-Nusra Front, said his leader Abu Muhammad al-Julani tried to settle its differences with the ISIL and even offered to cancel its name if the ISIL canceled its name so that both groups could operate under the banner of "Qaedat al-Jihad Organization in Bilad al-Sham." But ISIL chief Abu Bakr al-Baghdadi rejected the offer.[15] Over disagreements with the leadership of ISIL, al Qaeda's al Zawahiri appointed Jabhat al Nusra as al Qaeda's representative in Syria. Most groups considered it prestigious to be associated with al Qaeda, but al Qaeda has always been judicious in its selection. The latest group to request al Zawahiri to be acknowledged as an associate of al Qaeda is al Qaeda in Kurdistan.[16]

The groups associated with al Qaeda transformed into al Qaeda-like organizations. Both operationally and ideologically, they functioned like al Qaeda, conducting spectacular strikes, especially suicide attacks. For instance, the Shabaab al-Mujahideen Movement promoted its bloody raid in September 2013 on the Westgate shopping mall in Nairobi and threatened additional attacks in Kenya, claiming that there are "hundreds of men who are wishing for such an operation."[17] The threat came in the fourth episode of the "Mujahideen Moments" series produced by the group's al-Kata'ib Media Foundation and was posted on forums on 17 April 2014. The video shows a group of foreign fighters chanting in unison about the danger posed by al Shabab to the enemy and inviting Muslims to come to Somalia for jihad. They stated, "We have entered Westgate, we have reached Nairobi. That's just the beginning, more similar attacks are on the way. We will blow you up until we finish you off." Other threat groups like al Shabab are associated with al Qaeda, but for security and other reasons, they are not formally known as associates of al Qaeda. A dozen groups located in tribal Pakistan currently work with al Qaeda's core on a day-to-day basis. They are either Pakistani or foreign groups. The Pakistani groups consist of the Pakistani Taliban, Haqqani Network, Lashkar-e-Jhangvi (LeJ), Sipah-e-Sahaba Pakistan (SSP), Lashkar-e-Taiba, The Jaish-e-Mohammed (JEM), Harakat-ul Mujahidin (HuM), Harakat-ul Jihad Islami (HuJI), The Harakat-ul-Mujahidin Al-Alami (HUMA), and a few others. The non-Pakistani groups are the Afghan Taliban, Islamic Movement of Uzbekistan (IMU), Islamic Jihad Union (IJU), Jemaah Islamiyah (JI), Turkistan Islamic Party (TIP), Islamic Emirate of the Caucasus (IEC), and a few others. The groups that are operationally autonomous, but ideologically linked to al Qaeda, are the State of Iraq and the Levant, Jamma'a Ahl al-Sunna lil Daw'a wal Jihad (Boko Haram), Jama'atu Ansarul Muslimina Fi Biladis-Sudan (Vanguard for the Protection of Muslims in Black Lands), al Mulathamun (al-Murabitoon, al-Mulathameen Brigade), Tawhid and Jihad in West Africa, Abdullah Azzam Brigades, Ansar al-Dine (Ansaruddin), the supporter of Jerusalem (Ansar Bait Al Maqdis)—Sinai peninsula, Fatah Al Islam, Ansar al Islam, Army of Islam (Jayash al Islam), Asbat al Ansar (League of the Followers), the Students Islamic Movement of India (SIMI), Harakat ul Jihad-i-Islami Bangladesh, Indian Mujahidin, Abu Sayyaf Group, the Rajah Suleiman Movement (RSM), the Moro Islamic Liberation Front (MILF),[18] Jamaat Tawhid Anshoru, al Qaeda in Southeast Asia, and others. The entire Palestinian Salafi Jihadi elements operating in the Gaza Strip—Tawhid wal Jihad, Jaish Al Islam, Jund Ansarallah, and Ansar Al Sunna—were united, forming the consulting council for the holy warriors in the outskirts of Jerusalem, known as Majlis Al Shura Lil Mujahiddin Fi Aqnaf Bait Al Maqdis on June 2012.[19]

A GLOBALIZED AL QAEDA

The US invasion of Iraq in March 2003 reinvigorated existing groups and created several new threat groups in the Levant. After the US invasion of Iraq, the transfer of its limited counterterrorism resources from Afghanistan to Iraq, both regions competed for limited resources. US public support for the continuing deployments diminished, and President Obama, focusing on domestic policy, decided to withdraw troops. After so much blood and treasure, had the United States withdrawn without killing Osama, the intervention in Afghanistan would be a failure. The United States focused on hunting bin Laden by sending one of its most capable Special Operations commanders, William McRaven, to Afghanistan. Because the intelligence was flawed, McRaven said there was only a fifty-fifty chance that Osama would be in the compound, and yet Obama approved the mission. Because it was a clandestine mission, operating directly under CIA Director Leon Panetta, McRaven staged the operation and was concerned about a political storm if his men got into a confrontation with Pakistani forces. When one of their helicopters crashed, an American Pakistani outside the compound spoke in Urdu to the responding Pakistani police that it was an exercise and for them to go back. Meticulous in rehearsing every step, McRaven said he even prepared these men to fight their way back to Afghanistan. As the United States knew Osama was in Pakistan, McRaven relocated to Afghanistan for six years, ultimately successful in locating and hunting down America's number one enemy. The elimination of Osama bin Laden in a joint CIA/US Special Forces operation in Abbotabad, Pakistan, on 2 May 2011, created the conditions for US withdrawal. Osama's death gave face for United States to withdraw.

McRaven and a number of others in the government understood the threat, but President Obama remained convinced that America must withdraw. The United States agreed to keep 10,000 to 12,000 troops in Afghanistan, mostly Special Operations Forces, to enable Afghanistan to develop its own capabilities to fight the resurgent Taliban. The US withdrawal from Iraq left behind a small team of military personnel at its embassy in Baghdad, which was helpless to prevent a further deterioration of the security situation in Iraq. Under Iranian pressure, Iraq rejected the US offer to station a contingent of forces that will train and advise Iraqi forces. In Afghanistan, the Karzai administration resisted signing an agreement with the United States for stationing US forces after withdrawal. Al Qaeda remain intact after Osama's death—although a highly experienced and a competent terrorist leader Zawahiri assumed leadership. Zawahiri himself was in charge of al Qaeda's biological weapons program, including its anthrax project, and successfully led its information committee to shape Muslim attitudes and opinions. Together with his son-in-law, Abdur Rehman Al-Maghribi, a German-trained software engineer from Morocco, he built the online infrastructure—especially the forums. Modeled on al Qaeda's multimedia al Sahab (The Cloud), al Qaeda inspired or assisted to create dedicated media organizations. In turn, this precipitated the creation of AQAP's Al Andalus Media Foundation, TIP's Islam Awazi Media Center, IMU's Jundulloh, and IJU's Badr at Taweed. Today, Shumukh al-Islam, a top-tier password-protected jihadi forum, and other platforms propagate the global jihad ideology by hosting al Qaeda communiqués, videos, etc. His mastery in propaganda was reflected when Zawahiri authorized the use of Twitter and other social media, now the most favored communication tools of al Qaeda and its family of groups. Although the movement of Zawahiri was restricted after his relocation from Afghanistan to Pakistan, armed with a computer, he used his time to strategize and create the content for an online infrastructure that greatly assisted in decentralizing the fight.

The decentralization strategy was not only to enhance the motivation and capabilities to fight in the conflict arenas of Africa, the Middle East, and Asia far away from the Af–Pak theater but also to instigate Muslims living in industrialized countries of North America, Europe, and Australia. English-speaking radical and violent clerics, such as Feiz Mohammad from Australia/Lebanon, Abdullah el-Faisal from the UK/Jamaica, and Anwar al Awlaki from US/Yemen, were successfully radicalized and militarized Muslim migrants exhorting attacks against the West. To create a pool of terrorist sympathizers and supporters, al Qaeda and its associated groups produced propaganda material in English, including dedicated websites in English politicizing diaspora Muslims. The Pakistani American editor and publisher of *Inspire* magazine, Samir ibn Zafar Khan, was killed on 30 September 2011, and propagated in English the writings, interviews, and speeches legitimizing, justifying, and prompting violence. The propaganda created self-radicalized homegrown individuals and cells either supporting or conducting attacks.

THREAT EXPANDS

Afghanistan remains a key focus for Zawahiri, but he aggressively pursued a policy and a strategy for creating several fronts to exhaust his enemies. Of the many fronts, Zawahiri paid special attention to Syria where al Qaeda social media played a central role in politicizing, radicalizing, and mobilizing a new generation of fighters. Zawahiri's call to create an Islamic state in Syria found resonance among Muslim youths worldwide. Providing guidance to the Muslim terrorist and insurgent groups in his video statement titled "Onwards, Lions of Syria," Zawahiri said, "Wounded Syria still bleeds day after day while the butcher, son of the butcher Bashar bin Hafiz [Hafez al-Assad], is not deterred to stop." Zawahiri said, "But the resistance of our people in Syria despite all the pain, sacrifice and bloodshed escalates and grows,"[20] and urged "Muslims in Iraq, Jordan, Lebanon and Turkey to join the uprising against Assad's 'pernicious, cancerous regime.'" Zawahiri warned Syrian fighters not to rely on the West for help.[21] Compared to Afghanistan, the number of foreign fighters is much higher in Syria. With an estimated 10,000 to 12,000 foreign fighters joining the fight within three years, it is a harbinger of a different scale of global threat. Like the previous generation of foreign fighters in Afghanistan, those that started the current wave of global violence, the blowback of Syria is likely to pose a much greater threat. With a new set of skills and linkages to groups and personalities, the return of motivated fighters from Syria to their homelands is likely to pose a larger threat than the blowback from Afghanistan.

Worldwide, the number of threat groups inspired and instigated by the ideology of al Qaeda continues to grow among Muslim communities. With the United States taking a backseat in the intervention in Mali, terrorist propaganda, especially by al Qaeda's leader Zawahiri, interpreted it as follows: "It is an old-new orientation. Perhaps the reason is that America is exhausted after both defeats in Iraq and Afghanistan, and that these jihadi activities fall in the areas of French power."[22] Demonstrating al Qaeda's African interests beyond the Sahel, Zawahiri accused "France of having a role in the aggression on Muslims in CAR, and expressed that the 'confrontation with France is part of the extended Crusader war between the Romans and the Muslims until the end of time.'"[23]

After the Arab Spring, a series of new groups emerged throughout North Africa and in the Middle East. In contrast to the thinking of Western governments that supported the Arab Spring, the revolts did not help to stabilize but rather destabilized parts of Africa and the Middle East. While existing threat groups grew and forged new alliances, thus exploiting the uncertain political landscape, several new threat groups emerged. The Mali-based al-Murabitoon (al-Mulathameen Brigade), established in August 2013, merged with the Tawhid and Jihad in West Africa. Al Qaeda-associated al-Murabitoon leader Moktar Belmoktar alias Khalid Abu al-Abbas was responsible for taking eight hundred people hostage at the Tigantourine gas facility near Amenas, Algeria, where thirty-nine foreign hostages were killed in January 2013.

Naming themselves Ansar al-Sharia, several new groups have emerged in North Africa, from Egypt to Libya and Tunisia to Morocco. Exploiting the ungoverned spaces and porous borders, their influence is shifting from the Maghreb to the Sahel. The Ansar al Sharia, created in the Sahel, includes groups from Mali to Mauritania. With the flow of Salafist Jihadist ideology to Africa, new threat groups and cells are emerging in Mauritania, Mali, Burkina Faso, Niger, Chad, Nigeria, Senegal, Sierra Leone, the Sudan, and Somalia. Spanning the range of experienced and well-established threat groups such as al Qaeda and their associates, these new and emerging groups look for ideological inspiration, training opportunities, financial resources, and access to weapons. To grow, they exploit state-of-the-art media infrastructure maintained by well-established groups, notably by al Qaeda and its associated groups.

Similarly, several new groups have emerged in Asia. With the decapitation of the leadership of al Qaeda's closest associate JI by Detachment 88 (Densus 88), a number of new groups have emerged. The largest Muslim country in the world, Indonesia hosts more than a dozen groups inspired by al Qaeda, and a few South East Asians, such as Umar Patek, traveled to Pakistan to fight in Afghanistan. While JAT is the most capable group, several other groups linked to JAT have emerged. They include Mujahidin Indonesia Timur, a group ideologically inspired by al Qaeda, but operationally autonomous. Also known as East Indonesian Mujahideen, its leader Abu Warda Santoso, incited Muslims to kill members of Densus 88, the Indonesian Special Forces counterterrorism squad, and claimed they are American and Australian agents.[24] Stating that Densus 88 and police forces are responsible for killing their families, claiming that they seek to eliminate them or convert them to Christianity, he claimed that these forces represent the American and Australian armies and act in their interests, not those of the people or Islam, and therefore must be attacked. His speech came in a twenty-minute, English-subtitled video titled "So Fight Against the Allies of Satan," which was produced by Sawt al-Jihad Nusantara and posted by the Global Islamic Media Front (GIMF) on jihadi forums on 20 April 2014. If a sanctuary exists in Afghanistan, Santoso, a tier-one target of D88, will most likely relocate to Afghanistan.

INTERNATIONAL NEGLECT OF AFGHANISTAN

On 20 January 2009, Obama pledged to withdraw troops from Iraq and Afghanistan. This statement boosted the confidence of the Taliban and their associated groups, thus increasing the threat to Afghanistan. Within two years, the Afghan Taliban opined that "the Americans have exhausted themselves in Afghanistan over the last nine years, and now will not stay long in our beloved country. What they could not gain in the last few months with their, then, fresh troops, they will not be able to gain in Kandahar, with their, now, demoralized and fearful troops. It is becoming manifest that the Americans will not be able to conceal their defeat in Afghanistan for too long. Therefore, the White House, instead of counting their mounting casualties in Afghanistan, had better be advised to formulate a withdrawal plan, to at least save those troops, which are still alive."[25] On 16 December 2013, British Prime Minister David Cameron told British soldiers in Helmand that they accomplished their mission and that they could come home in 2014. Although Cameron said they could come home with their heads held high, the message he sent to the Taliban was that they had lost the war.

Domestic electoral and political compulsions led Western leaders to withdraw forces from Afghanistan, prompting the Karzai regime to engage in political negotiations with the Taliban. Afghanistan, Pakistan, and the United States considered political negotiations with the Taliban as a strategy to end the violence. In January 2012, the Afghan Taliban showed in a declaration their readiness to have a diplomatic office in Qatar and even reached preliminary agreement with the government of Qatar. Before that, Taliban envoys reached a settlement with the American side that the Americans will set free the prisoners from Guantanamo and will let them live with their families in Qatar.[26] The Taliban alleged, "instead of fulfilling their promises and paving the road for the forthcoming dialogues, the American media started a kind of propaganda indicative of multi-dimensional talks with the envoys of the Islamic Emirate for the solution of Afghan dilemma which was in total contradiction with the ground realities."[27] The Afghan Taliban said, "In the same time, some secret circles of the enemy published some spurious declarations asking the Mujahedeen to freeze their attacks. This venomous propaganda created anxiety as if, may Allah forbid, a secret deal is ongoing between the Islamic Emirate and the Americans even though it is quite clear that the Islamic Emirate is an Islamic movement based on principles and all its work is transparent and under the supervision of the Amir-ul-Momineen (Leader of the Faithful) may Allah protect him. The political office of Islamic Emirate, just like its military commission, is working for the lofty aims of the ongoing Jihad which are the freedom of the beloved homeland and the implementation of the Islamic Sharia alongside the provision of the benefits of the immense sacrifices of the Muslim masses of Afghanistan in the form of an Islamic government."[28]

As the Taliban was confident in victory, the Taliban was disinterested in genuine negotiations and only wanted Western forces to withdraw. The Taliban alleges, "invading forces repeatedly committed such actions which served the opposite purpose. E.g. the desecration of the Holy Quran in Bagram airbase by the Americans, the slaughter of innocent children in Kapisa, Nangarhar and Ghazni provinces, the defiling of the dead bodies of martyrs and recently the martyring and then burning of the bodies of tens of children and women in Zangabad area of Panjwai district. How can the opposition on the one hand be calling towards a peaceful resolution to the Afghan problem and on the other justify such brutal actions?" While the Karzai regime in Afghanistan was open to the Taliban sharing power, the Taliban were not and attacked meetings convened to negotiate. The Taliban—claiming to be the Afghanistan Islamic Movement Fidai Mahaz (AIMFM) founded by Mullah Dadullah Mahaz (Mullah Dadullah Front)—killed Maulvi Arsala Rahmani, a top negotiator for Afghanistan's High Peace Council (HPC) in Kabul on 13 May 2012. The Afghan Taliban's position was that they will succeed against the Karzai regime sooner or later and they must exploit both the call for talks and the talks itself. In its message for Eid al-Adha 2010, Hakimullah Mehsud said that the TTP is open to "serious" negotiations and a cease-fire but only if the Pakistani government frees itself of pressure from American and Pakistani establishments and the drone attacks in the tribal areas stop.[29] This reflected the pressure the drone strikes brought upon the Mehsuds and in return the Taliban harnessing the call for talks to extract concessions.

When President Karzai convened a meeting, the Afghan Taliban denounced the Jirga and demanded the "restoration of sovereignty for Afghan People" in January 2014. The Afghan Taliban discussed the context of the proposed security agreement between the United States and Afghanistan, suggesting extending the time of the American military presence in the country and promised that American forces will not carry out operations unless there are exceptional circumstances, in which case they would only work jointly with the Afghan forces. The Afghan Taliban argued restoring sovereignty can only be achieved by the Afghan people and not by relying on the promises and agreements of foreign entities. In an Afghan Taliban statement posted to the group's website on 29 January 2014, by spokesman Qari Yousuf, the Afghan Taliban chastised President Hamid Karzai for being inclined to sign the agreement, as were many other participants in the Loya Jirga. The message also stated that the bombing of Afghan civilian homes serves as proof that no promises or agreements can be trusted. It asserted, "whether the security agreement is signed or not, they will kill whosoever they want and will bomb wherever they like. They are not responsible and accountable to anyone for their atrocities, and there is no one who can even question them for their brutalities." The spokesman declared that Afghans must not depend on promises by those who have proved to be deceitful and added, "It is the responsibility of each and every intuitive Afghan to comply with the will of the Mujahid Afghan nation and lend a helping hand to Mujahidin in driving out the foreign invaders and restoring our sovereignty. This is the only way which can save us from the wrath of Allah Almighty and the reproach of history and the future generations."[30] The true intention of the Afghan Taliban is to return to power in Kabul. The Afghan Taliban claimed a total number of 1,088 attacks throughout Afghanistan during the presidential election of April 2014 and reported a suicide bombing in Kandahar province and the shooting down of a military helicopter. A representative from the Afghan Taliban posted an English message on his Twitter account on 6 April 2014, boasting that the group carried out over one thousand attacks, but the number might be higher due to "communication problems" in receiving information from some provinces. According to the SITE Monitoring Service, a provincial breakdown of the strikes shows Nangarhar as the most active with 123, followed by Laghman with eighty-seven. The representative added, "Except for some parts of some fortified cities where ballots were cast and propaganda spread, nearly the entire country was closed down by Mujahideen where none of the people voted with most polling stations closed while in many districts of the country, no polling stations ever even existed."

The Afghan Taliban's position is reflected in their statements as follows: "Today, as the Americans are confronted with an inevitable defeat and international humiliation, they are leaving no stone unturned to obscure it from the outside world. But this plain defeat and the valor of the Mujahid Afghan Nation can never be concealed therefore we are convinced that Insha-Allah (God willing) the trounce of the American forces inside Afghanistan will be the start of their eviction from all the oppressed areas of the world and as it is said that history repeats itself thus the world will be freed from the yoke of another ruthless imperial power very soon, Insha-Allah, and It is never hard for Allah Almighty!!!"[31]

THE RISE OF THE PAKISTAN TALIBAN

The Pakistan Taliban were not marked as different from the Afghan Taliban. The TTP announced the creation of a committee charged with delivering their position to the Pakistani government regarding peace talks. A TTP fighter posted the Arabic announcement on his Twitter account on 2 February 2014. The message, which was signed by TTP spokesman Shahidullah Shahid, stated that the group decided to create a committee that can liaise with the government, and deliver easily the position of the Tehrik-e-Taliban Pakistan to them and to the Pakistan people. The decision was reached during a February 1 meeting of the TTP's Shura Council. The statement named five committee members, including high-profile Pakistani political and religious figures Maulana Abdul Aziz, the imam and preacher of the Red Mosque [Lal Masjid] in Islamabad; Sami'a ul-Haq, director of the Haqqania Akora Khattak University; and Pakistani politician Imran Khan.

The TTP pledged to provide protection for the committee members within TTP-controlled areas. The outcome of talks between the TTP and the Pakistani government, consisted of the following key personalities:

- Maulana Abdul Aziz, imam and preacher of the Red Mosque
- Maulana Sami'a ul-Haq, director of the Haqqania Akora Khattak University
- Imran Khan, chief of the Insaf Movement
- Mufti Kifayatullah, district emir of the Assembly of Islam Scholars
- Professor Ibrahim, district emir of the Islamic Group

Moreover, the political Shura of the TTP will supervise and direct the guidelines to the committee. The TTP agreed to provide protection for the members of the committee in the event they enter areas that are under the control of the TTP. The TTP pledged that they want to conduct talks with "all sincerity and to be taken seriously,"[32] its leaders demanded "Sharia by the gun," and demanded its members wage "continuous jihad." The talks failed as expected and the violence resumed. Confronted by geostrategic challenges and security threats, Pakistan remains one of the most affected countries from terrorism and insurgency. Although many accuse Islamabad, Pakistan is itself a victim of violence. With modest international support, Pakistan contends with a large refugee population and a pool of foreign fighters from the Afghan war.

Today, Pakistan is hopeful of successful talks with the Pakistan and Afghan Taliban, but any negotiations are unlikely to succeed. The Afghan Taliban are determined to capture power in Kabul, with the intention of the Pakistani Taliban to come to power in Islamabad. Unless these two groups are militarily dismantled, they will pose an increasing threat not only to Afghanistan and Pakistan, but also to rising Asia. With the infusion of al Qaeda's ideology and methodology, their lethality presents a serious threat to stability and security for the region and beyond. The scale of violence, especially by the TTP, makes it the most lethal contemporary threat group. Table 7.1 captures the increasing terrorist attacks in Pakistan from 2001–2013.

Pakistan suffered more suicide attacks than Iraq and Afghanistan starting in 2008.[33] "In 2008, Pakistan suffered fifty-nine suicide attacks topping the list of countries suffering from suicide terrorism. The country left Afghanistan and Iraq behind, when it suffered twenty-eight suicide attacks that killed over 471 and left 713 wounded, including civilians and armed forces' per-

Table 7.1. Terrorist Attacks in Pakistan 2001–2013

Year	Terrorist Incidents	Killings	Injuries
2001	3	17	6
2002	25	22	43
2003	10	21	42
2004	17	85	185
2005	17	14	55
2006	657	907	1,543
2007	1,442	3,448	5,353
2008	2,148	2,267	4,558
2009	2,586	3,021	7,334
2010	2,113	2,913	5,824
2011	1,966	2,391	4,389
2012	1,577	2,050	3,822
2013	1,717	2,451	5,438

http://www.terrorismwatch.com.pk/Pakistan%20since%209%2011.pdf; "Pakistan Security Report 2006," Pak Institute for Peace Studies (PIPS), 7 June 2007, http://san-pips.com/index.php?action=reports&id=psr_list_1; "Pakistan Security Report 2007," Pak Institute for Peace Studies (PIPS), 7 January 2008, http://san-pips.com/index.php?action=reports&id=psr_list_1; "Pakistan Security Report 2008," Pak Institute for Peace Studies (PIPS), 19 January 2009, http://san-pips.com/index.php?action=reports&id=psr_list_1; "Pakistan Security Report 2009," Pak Institute for Peace Studies (PIPS), 10 January 2010, http://san-pips.com/index.php?action=reports&id=psr_list_1; "Pakistan Security Report 2010," Pak Institute for Peace Studies (PIPS), 15 January 2011, http://san-pips.com/index.php?action=reports&id=psr_list_1; "Pakistan Security Report 2011," Pak Institute for Peace Studies (PIPS), 4 January 2012, http://san-pips.com/index.php?action=reports&id=psr_list_1; "Pakistan Security Report 2012," Pak Institute for Peace Studies (PIPS), 4 January 2013, http://san-pips.com/index.php?action=reports&id=psr_list_1; "Pakistan Security Report 2012," Pak Institute for Peace Studies (PIPS), 6 January 2014, http://san-pips.com/index.php?action=reports&id=psr_list_1

sonnel. Iraq suffered forty-two incidents of suicide terrorism leaving 463 people dead and 527 others injured. Meanwhile, Afghanistan witnessed as many as thirty-six suicide bombings killing 436 people and injuring 394 others."[34] Table 7.2 shows the number of suicide attacks in Pakistan from 2002–2013.

The terrorist threat in Pakistan and Afghanistan will continue to escalate with the US drawdown starting in December 2014. With the pending US drawdown from Afghanistan, al Qaeda, the Afghan Taliban, the Pakistan Taliban, and a dozen other groups in tribal Pakistan are planning to move to Afghanistan and reconstitute their erstwhile sanctuary. Emboldened by their battlefield attacks, resilience, and persistence, the terrorist threat will spill over to the neighboring regions of the Af–Pak theater. This includes Central Asia, South Asia, and Northeast Asia. Two of the countries bordering the Af–Pak theater are India and China.

Table 7.2. No. of Suicide Attacks in Pakistan 2002–2013

Year	No. of Suicide Attacks	Killed	Injured
2002	1	15	34
2003	2	69	103
2004	7	89	321
2005	4	84	219
2006	7	161	352
2007	54	765	1,677
2008	59	893	1,846
2009	76	949	2,356
2010	49	1,167	2,199
2011	41	628	1,183
2012	39	365	607
2013	43	751	1,411

South Asia Terrorism Portal

With the shift in the center of gravity of terrorism to Asia, the orientation of the threat is to South Asia and Northeast Asia, notably to India and China. While India faces a sustained threat, China faces a growing threat. There is persistent movement of terrorists and supporters from the safe havens to the target countries—India and China. Located on the Afghan–Pakistan border, the rise of international terrorism has the potential to create ethnic and religious disharmony in the neighboring regions. Because Afghanistan and Pakistan border India and China, terrorism is spilling over, creating a growth in extremist ideologies and increased terrorist incidents and if left unchecked, will spawn new insurgencies.

With the exception of Syria, according to START and ICPVTR databases, India is among the top five countries of the world suffering from terrorism. Terrorism in India in the future will not only be from group terrorism but also from homegrown terrorism. For example, "Ansar al-Tawhid in the Land of Hind" released the second episode in its "Lions of Hind" video series and on its social networking account promoting lone-wolf attacks against police.[35] The group's al-Isabah Media produced the twelve-minute, forty-five-second video and posted it on its Facebook account, its website, and its YouTube channel on 18 April 2014. Footage shows fighters preparing for an attack and then firing rifles as a Hadith from the Prophet Muhammad is displayed in Arabic, English, and Urdu, reading "The Messenger of Allah (P.B.U.H) said: 'There are two groups of my Ummah whom Allah will free from the Fire: The group that invades India, and the group that will be with 'Isa bin Maryam (P.B.U.H.).'"[36] On its Facebook page, al-Isabah Media published by an English poster on 4 April recommended that jihadists who wish to join Ansar al-Tawhid can stay in their homeland and attack police. The message states, "Want to Join Ansar'ut Tawheed? Yes you can! But how? Well, you don't need to go anywhere, just stay wherever you are and fulfill your obligation. . . . Targets: Police can be easily targeted using knives, petrol bombs or by burning their cars!"[37] Although authored by others, al-Isabah Media posted two English articles on its website attributed to "Abu Ubaidha Al Hindi." Because there are a number of active Muslim threat groups, homegrown terrorism is not yet a serious threat in India. The most active Muslim threat groups in India are listed in Table 7.3.

Of the Muslim threat groups active in northeast India, the Muslim United Liberation Tigers of Assam (MULTA) is the most active. Several other Muslim threat groups are declining in their operational capabilities. Among these groups are the Islamic Liberation Army of Assam (ILAA), Islamic Sevak Sangh (ISS), Islamic United Reformation Protest of India (IURPI), Muslim Liberation Army (MLA), Muslim Security Council of Assam (MSCA), Muslim Security Force (MSF), Muslim Tiger Force (MTF), Muslim United Liberation Front of Assam (MULFA), Muslim Volunteer Force (MVF), Revolutionary Muslim Commandos (RMC), and the United Muslim Liberation Front of Assam (UMLFA).

EMERGENCE OF AN ASIAN-CENTRIC THREAT LANDSCAPE?

Is there a reorientation of the threat from the West to Asia? Today, China and India, the rising superpowers, face unprecedented threats. The terrorist threat in Asia, originating in the anti-Soviet multinational Afghan mujahidin campaign, has its genesis in the Middle East. The center of gravity of international terrorism shifted from the Syrian-controlled Bekha Valley in Lebanon to Pakistan and Afghanistan after the Soviet invasion of Afghanistan in December 1979. Since then, the single largest concentration of threat groups oscillates between the Afghanistan–Pakistan border, Afghanistan, and Pakistan. The blowback from the multinational Afghan mujahidin campaign (1979–1989) shaped and influenced the global threat landscape. After the return of fighters to the Balkans, the Caucuses, Asia, Africa, and the Middle East, the threat to the West peaked with al Qaeda's attack against America's most iconic landmarks on 9/11. Today, the threat from Muslim terrorism is globalized, with the exception of Latin America. However, the most sustained threat is to Asia.

In addition to India, Pakistan, and Afghanistan, areas that produce a large number of fatalities and injuries from insurgency and terrorism, China faces

Table 7.3. Active Muslim Threat Groups in India

Proscribed Terrorist/ Extremist Groups	Active Terrorist/Insurgent Groups	Inactive Terrorist/Insurgent Groups
1. Hizb-ul-Mujahideen (HM) 2. Harkat-ul-Ansar (HuA, presently known as Harkat-ul Mujahideen) 3. Lashkar-e-Taiba (LeT) 4. Jaish-e-Mohammed (JeM) 5. Harkat-ul Mujahideen (HuM, previously known as Harkat-ul-Ansar) 6. Al Badr 7. Jamiat-ul-Mujahideen (JUM) 8. Harkat-ul-Jehad-al-Islami (HuJI) 9. Al Umar Mujahideen 10. Dukhtaran-e-Millat (DeM) 11. Students Islamic Movement of India (SIMI) 12. Indian Mujahidin 13. Deendar Anjuman (DA	1. Lashkar-e-Omar (LeO) 2. Lashkar-e-Jabbar (LeJ) 3. Tehrik-ul-Mujahideen 4. Jammu & Kashmir Liberation Front (JKLF) 5. All Parties Hurriyat Conference (APHC) 6. Mutahida Jehad Council (MJC)	1. Al Barq 2. Al Jehad 3. Jammu & Kashir National Liberation Army 4. Muslim Janbaz Force 5. Kashmir Jehad Force 6. Al Jehad Force (combines Muslim Janbaz Force and Kashmir Jehad Force) 7. Mahaz-e-Azadi 8. Islami Jamaat-e-Tulba 9. Jammu & Kashmir Students Liberation Front 10. Ikhwan-ul-Mujahideen 11. Islamic Students League 12. Tehrik-e-Hurriat-e-Kashmir 13. Al Mustafa Liberation Fighters 14. Tehrik-e-Jehad-e-Islami 15. Muslim Mujahideen 16. Al Mujahid Force 17. Tehrik-e-Jehad 18. Islami Inquilabi Mahaz

an increasing threat from the Turkistan Islamic Party, an al Qaeda–associated Chinese group operating from tribal Pakistan. Like India, China faces an unprecedented threat from ideological extremism and its vicious by-product, terrorism. With over two hundred attacks in Xinjiang during 2013, China is increasingly coming under threat. This includes a few attacks outside Xinjiang. A vehicle suicide bombing in Tiananmen Square, Beijing, by the TIP on 28 October 2013, killed three occupants of the vehicle and two bystanders including a Filipino, and thirty-eight were injured. Similarly, knife-wielding assailants killed thirty-three civilians and injured about one hundred forty at the Kunming railway station in Yunnan, China, on 1 March 2014. Calling it an "expensive offer" to the Chinese government, the TIP requested China reconsider its "cruel" policies in East Turkistan.[38] A TIP official imran read a message that the attackers purportedly addressed to Chinese President Xi, demanding he end China's influence and policies in "East Turkistan," release Uyghur Muslims from prison, and cease stealing the region's natural resources. Asking Uyghur Muslims to follow the example of the attackers, TIP leader Abdullah Mansour said on 2 March, "If the fighters of East Turkistan are now fighting with swords, knives, and mallets, our dear Allah will soon give us opportunities to fight the Chinese using automatic guns. Know that the blood of those who are killing themselves is not being spilled for nothing, for their blood will bring tens of more to carry out jihad. We are witnessing now that those countries that have the most powerful weapons are running away from Afghanistan because they could not stand against the power of the mujahedeen."[39] In Urumqi, two suicide bombers and knife-wielding assassins attacked a train station, killing three and injuring seventy-nine on 30 April 2014, after President Xi Jinping's visit to Xinjiang. The Chinese leader remarked that "[t]he Kashgar region is the front line in anti-terrorism and maintaining social stability."[40] Although belatedly, the Chinese leader recognized the threat from Af–Pak but only after Uighur militants had established a presence in tribal Pakistan.

With the deepening influence of al Qaeda, the Uighur militancy transformed from an ethnopolitical to a politico-religious movement where they recruit irrespect of nationality. This is reflected in a video by Ṣawt al-Islām, showing the Turkistan Islamic Party's Sheikh Abu Dhar 'Azzam praising the acts of the foreign fighters coming from Eastern Turkistan, and calls upon Muslims to support them. Addressing the "Chinese and Buddhists," Abu Dhar warns them of dire punishment for their crimes against Muslims and Islam, and says that killing them and shedding their blood is "good."[41] He further said,

> I was asked what you know about eastern Turkistan. I answered that it is part of our Ummah (Islamic nation) and the people living there are our brothers and sisters. Thus how can our Muslim fighters not know our brothers and sisters who are living in an oppressed land? I came from Burma and we were oppressed by the Buddhists and Chinese too. I very well know what our brothers and sisters are facing. Initially there is no such thing as eastern and western Turkistan. The west separated the area and thus the western Turkistan is now Uzbekistan, Kyrgyzstan or Uighurs but in fact, all of them are Muslims. When I see the situation in the region, I see it as pain of the Ummah. Muslims are now facing difficulties and oppressions such as Syria and Burma. The widows and orphans are crying. We know Turkistan, and it is a Muslim country. It

must be known to all that this Ummah will win as how it began. If this Ummah perform Jihad, then it is going to be victorious. We will not win through democracy. We are not Uighurs, Pakistanis or Burmese in principle, but we are Muslims inside out.[42]

He added,

> We are Muslims, and you are the enemy, Oh! Buddhists in China, we will do you good. Kill you, spill your blood, cut off your head is a good thing. We're killing and slaughter you with a vengeance. We are going to cut you, piece by piece. You are liars, Oh! Apes and pigs eaters, Oh! Worms and whales eaters, Oh! Worms and snakes eaters. May God curse you and all like you. We are people who love death as much as you love wine and woman of the country. We will come to you. We want to kill the Buddhists of the East and the West. Killing and slaughtering you is a good thing. On the orders of Allah, to purify your filth off the floor is a good thing. You will soon see. We pray God tortures you, with his ability, through the Mujahideen and destroy you.[43]

Reflecting collaboration with other Turkic groups in Western Turkistan, the ETIM changed its name by dropping "Eastern Turkistan" to "Turkistan." Working with other groups, the TIP mounted operations in the Af–Pak theater and adopted al Qaeda–style suicide attacks. The idea of attacking iconic targets, as well as the strategy of attacking the epicenter, was reflected when the TIP hit Beijing and other targets outside Xinjiang. In addition to establishing Awazi Media Center, a copycat of al Qaeda's multimedia unit, the TIP demonstrated the growing influence of al Qaeda on the group when the TIP leaders appeared on video just like al Qaeda's leaders. Reflecting the "no compromise" policy of al Qaeda, the TIP official imran, standing between two armed men said the following:

1. The Chinese are big enemies of the Muslims of East Turkistan. The Chinese have never belonged to East Turkistan and they never will. The actions of the Chinese government are tantamount to fighting. Therefore, all the Chinese people must leave East Turkistan.
2. We are Muslims. We are descendants of Muslims. All the actions committed against the Muslims of East Turkistan forced us to be motivated and to act first against it. Islam is not a religion that is for cruelty, but it replies to cruelty with cruelty and takes revenge. That is why we encourage you to stop immediately all the bad policies that you are implementing against Islam and the Muslim people.
3. Stop the actions that are trying to destroy Muslims in general.
4. Stop trying to ruin the behavior of the Muslim young men and women, and stop trying to distance them from their religion. Return to their parents the young men and women that you sent to different regions of the country for mandatory work, and free them from the politics of making them Chinese.
5. Stop the mandatory education of the Chinese language on the kindergarten children.

6. Free those Muslims who are suffering in dark prisons.
7. Stop publicly and secretly stealing the natural treasures of East Turkistan.[44]

The looming threat to China with the drawdown of US-led coalition forces from Afghanistan is apparent. The threat of insurgency and terrorism is likely to peak in Afghanistan and Pakistan, a theater that borders China. With a failed global strategy to stabilize Afghanistan and the NATO drawdown from Afghanistan starting 2014, terrorism is likely to take a new dimension.

Today, India cooperates on terrorism with the United States, Europe, Australia, and all the South Asian countries except Pakistan. China cooperates on terrorism with Pakistan and Central Asia. Even though terrorism and insurgency presents a tier-one national security threat to India, China, Pakistan, and Afghanistan, counterterrorism cooperation is virtually nonexistent between India and Pakistan and India and China. Superpower and regional geopolitical imperatives affect genuine security and intelligence, law enforcement, and military cooperation to fight the threat of terrorism and insurgency.

CONCLUSION

After the US drawdown, the Afghan arena will remain the central battlefield in the years to come. With implications for the region and the world, the blowback of Western intervention in Afghanistan will be comparable to the Soviet intervention. Both these interventions produced a highly motivated floating group of international fighters willing to kill and die for Allah. Working together with Afghan and Pakistan fighters, they mutually support and reinforce their common vision of creating an Islamic state in Afghanistan. If they succeed in winning in Afghanistan, they are determined to take on Pakistan, a nuclear state. Exploiting the sanctuary in Afghanistan, they will invest in similar projects worldwide to create Islamic states. Afghanistan's and Syria's potential to politicize and radicalize Muslims cannot be underestimated. Although Muslim scholars debate its authenticity and reliability, a segment of the Muslim youths are fixated by a Hadit, "black flag will rise in Khorasan (the region of Pakistan–Afghanistan) and will march westward to Sham (the region of the Levant including Syria)."[45] Among other lands of jihad in the Middle East, Asia, Africa, the Caucuses, and the Balkans, the Afghan and Syrian battlefields are considered the most important. To them, to martyr in a land of jihad is the pinnacle of their faith in God.

Sustained US drone attacks and Pakistani military and intelligence operations against al Qaeda reduced its capabilities significantly. Although al Qaeda, led by Zawahiri, ceased as an operational organization capable of mounting terrorist attacks, it is still the ideological vanguard for global terrorism. If the Afghan Taliban return to Afghanistan, the return of al Qaeda is inevitable. Furthermore, the influence of al Qaeda on the Afghan Taliban, the TTP, and other global structures of extremism and terrorism will persist. The threat of al Qaeda to the United States and to its allies and friends is apparent. Nonetheless, the lack of US public will to commit forces in conflict zones over the long term is leading to a new landscape.

With a lack of public support for Western forces to remain in conflict zones, the rising Asian superpowers should step in to stabilize their neighborhoods cooperatively and collaboratively. The challenges are daunting. The most enduring is the India and Pakistan dispute and Pakistan and Afghanistan dispute. The Indian and Pakistani governments sponsor threat groups, including terrorist groups that are inimical to each other. Although relations between India and China have improved, Beijing and New Delhi do not trust each other. China and Pakistan are allies, and India and Afghanistan are allies. Geopolitics and strategy dominate international relations, but the real threat to India, China, Pakistan, and Afghanistan is from insurgency and terrorism. Pakistan is emerging as one of the four most violent conflict zones in the world. Because terrorism is a common and growing threat to both the countries, rather than criticizing Pakistan, India should cooperate with Pakistan. However, there is a deficit of trust between the two governments. With the US drawdown, the United States should consider the implications for its own security and work with India to forge a partnership with China, an all-weather friend of Pakistan, to stabilize Afghanistan and Pakistan.

Chapter Eight

Threat Group Profiles

Halimullah Kousary and Abdul Basit

AFGHAN TALIBAN GROUP PROFILE

BY HALIMULLAH KOUSARY

Fact Sheet

Name(s)	Taliban, Islamic Movement of Afghanistan, Islamic Emirate of Afghanistan. Also spelled as "Taleban."
Date of creation	1993–1994
Leader	Mullah Mohammed Omar
Estimated strength	In September 2006, the ISAF estimated Afghan Taliban fighters to number between 3,000 and 4,000, plus Afghans paid by the Afghan Taliban to assist in specific operations. The Afghan Taliban's own estimate of their strength is 12,000. More recent estimates by coalition forces put the total number of active Afghan Taliban between 30,000 and 35,000. However, the Afghan Taliban do not declare their numerical strength, and efforts by NATO/ISAF to learn their troop strength remain inconclusive.
Area of operations	The Afghan Taliban conduct operations in all regions of Afghanistan. However, their principal regions of strength are the southern and eastern provinces.
Symbols	Flag of the Islamic Emirate of Afghanistan Taliban "Coat of Arms"
Overview of ideology	Upon seizing power in Afghanistan, the Taliban's aim was to restore order and security to the population, end corruption, disarm the population, and establish a credible government following their interpretation of Islam. Over time, the movement became more extreme, seeking, in the words of Mullah Omar, to "establish the

laws of God on Earth" and to "prepare to sacrifice everything in pursuit of that goal." The leadership claimed to have no expansionist ambitions beyond Afghanistan's borders, but its association with al Qaeda was interpreted to mean that the group was involved in global Islamist extremism.

The Afghan Taliban can be categorized as a political Islamic group because of their support for the establishment of an Islamic state and the implementation of Sharia law. The Afghan Taliban are generally Sunni Muslims from the Hanafi school of thought and are known as Deobandis in the South Asian region.

HISTORY

Taliban Emergence in Afghanistan

The Soviet Union's invasion of Afghanistan resulted in uniting various Afghan mujahideen groups toward a common goal—the expulsion of the Soviet's forces from Afghanistan.[1] Seven Peshawar-based Sunni Mujahedeen groups received assistance from Pakistan, Saudi Arabia, and the United States to fight against the Soviet and Afghan communist governments from 1979 to 1989.[2] After the Soviet Union withdrew militarily in 1989 and the last Afghan communist government collapsed in 1992, the unity of the Mujahedeen disintegrated. The Uzbek commander Abdul Rashid Dostum, who supported the Afghan communist governments, formed an alliance with Jamiat-e-Islami against Hezb-e-Islami Gulbuddin as part of their struggle for power. This led to internal fighting and division of the country into many fiefdoms from 1992 to 1994. Fighting between Jamiat-e-Islami and Hezb-e-Islami Gulbuddin reached the streets of Kabul, and thousands died in the city from shelling from the Gulbuddin forces and other groups. The country was in chaos, and fighting continued around major urban centers in Afghanistan, leading to the emergence of the Taliban in 1994 from the Kandahar province.

The Taliban's creation myth was founded upon the premise that the spontaneous unification of Islamic students who were studying in madrassas in Pakistan answered the call to help the victims of banditry and went to Afghanistan to restore justice and order. The Pakistani madrassas remained a major source of the Taliban's manpower.

The Taliban, led by Mullah Mohammad Omar, captured Kandahar in December 1994. By February 1995, the Taliban consolidated control of southern Afghanistan and advanced to Kabul. The Taliban used Kandahar as their headquarters and ousted Hekmatyar from his base outside Kabul. However, instead of using this position to launch an offensive on Kabul, they moved west and captured Herat. In August 1996, the Taliban pushed into eastern Jalalabad city and then into Kabul in September 1996, forcing Jamiat-e-Islami's commander, Massoud, to flee with his forces to his traditional stronghold in the Panjshir Valley. On 26–27 September, the Taliban murdered and executed President Najibullah in Kabul. Massoud formed an alliance, the Supreme Council for the Defence of Afghanistan, with Dostum and Shia militia leader Karim Khalili, against the Taliban, which came to be known as the Northern Alliance.

The Taliban turned their attention north in the spring of 1997. A deputy commander of Jonbesh, Abdul Malik, defected to the Taliban and ousted Dostum from Mazar-e-Sharif. The Taliban's attempts to wrest the city from Malik led to a bloody fifteen-hour battle between the Taliban and Malik in which the Taliban were forced to retreat with heavy losses. Another attempt on Mazar in September failed when Wahdat guerillas (a Shia militia composed of citizens of Mazar-e-Sharif) forced them to retreat. Mazar eventually fell to the Taliban in August 1998 (probably because of Pakistani support in directing artillery), giving them control of over 90 percent of the country.

During this period, the Taliban had clear objectives for their military campaign in Afghanistan. The Taliban's objectives for Afghanistan at this time were as follows:[3]

- To end the conflict between rival Mujahedeen groups, which continued to divide the country into several fiefdoms and caused lawlessness.
- To unite the people under one central government.
- To restore peace and security for the population and protect their rights and liberties.
- To end the corruption by various parties and establish a credible and accountable government.
- To disarm the population.
- To enforce the Sharia, establish the Islamic state, and preserve the Islamic character of Afghanistan.
- To rebuild war-torn Afghanistan.

After the Taliban succeeded in occupying Kabul in 1996, they became the de facto ruler of Afghanistan. They expanded their objectives to cover Afghanistan's relations with other countries and the international community. While there were no clear official documents outlining the foreign policy of the Islamic Emirate of Afghanistan, some foreign policy objectives are as follows:[4]

- To gain recognition from the international community as the legitimate government of Afghanistan.
- To secure revenue from international sources in the form of aid and investment for the reconstruction and development of Afghanistan.
- To establish fair and friendly relations with all countries based on mutual respect and noninterference.

- To uphold international norms and principles.
- To support the UN and Organisation of Islamic Cooperation (OIC) peace initiatives for Afghanistan.
- To support the operations of all UN agencies and NGOs.

AFGHANISTAN: PARIAH STATE

By 1998, despite controlling most of the country, the Taliban's administration was recognized by only three governments—Pakistan, Saudi Arabia, and the United Arab Emirates. Its international reputation was increasingly damaged by reports of human rights abuses committed in enforcing its version of Islam, as well as its continued hosting of al Qaeda's training camps.

The presence of Osama bin Laden in the country and the increasingly close relationship between al Qaeda and the Taliban resulted in scrutiny from the international community following the August 1998 attacks on the US embassies in Kenya and Tanzania. The United States identified facilities in Afghanistan used for training al Qaeda's members and demanded that these facilities be closed. Bin Laden and other senior figures within the organization were requested to be handed over. However, the "Arab Afghans"—as al Qaeda was known by then—became an important source of both financial benefit and ideological motivation such that the Taliban and Mullah Omar refused to comply. His administration claimed to examine the evidence against bin Laden and declared him not guilty. Further international condemnation of the Taliban ensued in late 1998, when the Taliban's leadership ordered the destruction of the 2,000-year-old giant Buddha statues at Bamiyan, carved into the cliffs located there.

FALL OF TALIBAN GOVERNMENT (NOVEMBER 2001)

The Taliban's refusal to hand over Osama bin Laden and other wanted al Qaeda members following the 11 September attacks, despite intense diplomatic pressure from Pakistan, led to the end of the Taliban's administration in Afghanistan. The United States conducted massive aerial bombardments of Taliban targets in support of the Northern Alliance's forces on the ground. This led to the collapse of the Taliban's hold on Mazar-e-Sharif and across the northern areas of the country. Foreign troops assisted in the drive toward Kabul, which was recaptured by the Northern Alliance on 13 November 2001. Before the Northern Alliance reached Kabul, the Taliban were estimated to have withdrawn the majority of their garrison—between 10,000 and 15,000 troops—most of which fled to the southern Afghan province. The Northern Alliance secured Kabul, while its forces prepared to oust the Taliban from Kunduz. Offensives in the south against Kandahar were largely left to US and local Pashtun forces opposed to the Taliban.

Following the collapse of their regime, the Taliban lost not only huge swaths of territory but also thousands of fighters who were killed or imprisoned or who simply abandoned the organization. What remained was a core radical element that withdrew from the urban centers and regrouped, reportedly with foreign allies and al Qaeda's elements, in the mountainous border region with Pakistan. In 2003, the Taliban and their foreign allies committed themselves to an insurgency against the Afghan government and coalition forces. The Taliban received support from radical madrassas in Pakistan's Baluchistan province and the FATA and enjoyed freedom of maneuver under the protection of Pashtun tribes and their hospitality to the Taliban.

LEADERSHIP

Taliban Leadership Pre-2001

Originally, the Taliban were governed through collective political leadership, based on consultations and consensus building rather than on personalities.[5] The Taliban Shura (council) was, in some conceptions, an Islamist version of a traditional Pashtun tribal jirga, where all clan chiefs take part in resolving the issue at hand. After 1996 however, power became concentrated in the hands of a single man, Mullah Mohammed Omar. The shura became consultative only, with final decisions resting with Mullah Omar. When the Islamic Emirate of Afghanistan was proclaimed on 26 October 1997, Mullah Omar became the political leader and de facto ruler of Afghanistan. The Taliban Supreme Council was first established in Kandahar in 1994 by ten Taliban leaders, all of them mullahs, and chaired by Mullah M. Rabbani. After taking Kabul in 1996, a federal council was established and acted as a provisional government. The Taliban's ruling structure during this time reflected three principal governing bodies—the Supreme Shura and two subcouncils, known as the Military Shura and the Kabul Shura.

As the self-appointed head of the state of Afghanistan and supreme leader of the Taliban, Mullah Omar gave himself the title of Amir ul-Muminin (commander of the faithful). The highest decision-making body of the Taliban, the Supreme Shura, comprised ten members. In addition to the ten permanent members, the Supreme Shura's meetings also involved military commanders, tribal leaders, and religious scholars. The decision process sometimes involved as many as fifty people. Subordinate to the Supreme Shura, the Military Shura was a loose body in charge of devising strategies and implementing tactical decisions but lacked any decision-making authority. Military strategy, key military appointments, and military fund allocations were decided upon by Mullah Omar as the commander in chief of the

Taliban. The Kabul Shura dealt with the day-to-day operations of the government, the city, and the Kabul front against the Northern Alliance. Important issues were conveyed to the Supreme Shura for decisions to be made.

After the collapse of the Taliban's regime post-2001, the Taliban created a variety of shuras to restructure the organization and make it more adept at managing an insurgency as opposed to a government. In October 2006, the Taliban's website published a message from Mullah Omar announcing the establishment of a new Shura Council (Majlis-Al-Shura) with twelve members and three advisers.[6] Currently, the Taliban's command and control is exercised from two power bases, one in Quetta and the other in Peshawar, Pakistan.

The Quetta Shura Senior Leadership

The Quetta Shura consists of the most senior Taliban leadership, mostly Pashtuns from southern Afghanistan, including Mullah Omar. The shura has ten permanent members and a fluctuating number of advisers. It is primarily ideological and maintains connections with al Qaeda and other like-minded groups. Members of the Quetta Shura rarely enter Afghanistan and implement their influence through the combatant commanders fighting in Afghanistan, who rely on Quetta for resources, funding, and strategic military direction. In recent years, the Quetta Shura's leadership came under increased scrutiny as the international community increased its focus on Pakistan.

The Peshawar Shura Military Leadership

The focus of the Peshawar Shura is military operations. The composition of this shura primarily includes Taliban leaders who hail from eastern and southeastern Afghanistan. The shura members are not as senior as the members of the Quetta Shura. More recently, this shura lost prominence as a result of the Haqqani Network, which operates in the same region as the Peshawar Shura but which has eclipsed the shura by launching a number of complex attacks in Afghanistan against coalition and Afghan forces. The shura sustains Afghan operations in eastern and southeastern Afghanistan through a network outside of Afghanistan. The network recruits fighters through jihad ideology and receives training in various madrassas in the Khyber Pakhtunkhwa.[7]

The Taliban's Leadership in Recent Years

As the Taliban-led insurgency gains increasing footholds in the country, certain notable trends have emerged. The two shuras of the Taliban still exist, but the Haqqani Network—part of the Peshawar Shura—is becoming increasingly influential. It solidified its position in the Waziristan areas of

Pakistan, which is adjacent to its main areas of operation in Afghanistan. This area, known in Afghanistan as the Loya Paktia (Greater Paktia) region, includes the provinces of Khost, Paktia, and Paktika (known among coalition circles as P2K). These areas are part of NATO's Regional Command East in Afghanistan, a region that is under the command of US forces in Afghanistan. The US forces in Afghanistan and US officials called the Haqqani Network the greatest threat to their troops in the country. The rising role of the Haqqani Network can have an influential effect on the overall leadership of the Taliban's movement.

Some of these effects are already emerging. In regions that are between spheres of influence, factions within the Taliban are evident. In some areas, the terms "Haqqani's men" or "Mullah Omar's men" describe fighters. There seems to be a dividing line between these networks. This could signify a decentralization or fractionalization of the Taliban movement, which could have important consequences for any counterinsurgency measures that could be implemented.

In terms of possible reconciliation efforts with the Taliban's movement, the fractionalization of the movement could be a weakness that can be exploited, but it could also prove to be a serious challenge. As far as weaknesses go, it can help reconciliation efforts by moving insurgent groups away from the central Taliban movement while minimizing the number of fighters on the battlefield. However, if these different focal points of leadership exist in the Taliban's movement, it could prove challenging for counterinsurgency efforts as well. There will be no central authority to arrange reconciliation efforts or negotiations with that will give the Afghan government and the ISAF confidence that this will be a watershed change in the insurgency. If you negotiate with one element of the Taliban, the other elements will likely continue their fight.

Targeted Killings and the Effect on the Taliban's Leadership Structures

A recent operational trend in the counterinsurgency efforts that has a notable effect on the leadership and organizational structure of the Taliban is that of targeted killings. As part of the evolving counterinsurgency strategy, targeted killings have been carried out in both Pakistan and Afghanistan with powerful effects. In Afghanistan, midlevel commanders are targeted by coalition special forces or, more rarely, drone strikes as part of a plan to disrupt the Taliban's leadership structures. The targeted killing strategy in Afghanistan exploits an organizational weakness of the Taliban. With decentralized "nodes" carrying out attacks, they are more difficult to find, but without their regional midlevel commanders, they may not have the means to contact the military shuras. Without the strategic direction and with the loss of key talent and leaders, the Taliban as group is likely to lose a great deal of its operational capacity.

PERSONNEL AND RECRUITMENT PROPAGANDA

Personnel

The resurgence of the Taliban since 2003 has raised questions about the number of militants that align themselves with the Taliban's movement and casts doubt about early estimates regarding the Taliban's numerical strength. There are several estimates about the number of fighters fighting against the government and coalition forces in Afghanistan. In an interview with Al-Jazeera television in 2005, Mullah Dadullah claimed the Taliban had 12,000 fighters fighting in the four southern provinces.[8] But the spokesman for the Ministry of Defense, General Zahir Azimi, rejected the earlier remarks by the Taliban, saying that these are just "psychological tactics." According to Major General Richard Barrons, a British general responsible for Afghanistan reconciliation, there are up to 36,000 Taliban fighters in Afghanistan.[9] The difficulty of assessing the number of Taliban fighters reveals an important part of their strength. As a predominately Pashtun movement, the Taliban blend in easily with the civilian population of southern and eastern Afghanistan, and their numbers fluctuate depending on the intensity of their activities in the province and the presence of Afghan or coalition forces. Often, if there is an operation by Afghan or coalition forces, the Taliban will slip back into the civilian community or move around to other provinces or bordering areas in Pakistan until it is over.

Many studies, including one conducted by the United Nations Office on Drugs and Crime (UNODC) and the World Bank, highlight the numerical difference between ideologically and financially motivated Taliban militants. Not surprising, this assessment states that ideologically motivated fighters who are fighting in Afghanistan are fewer in number than those fighting for financial gains and that those fighting for ideological motivations form the leadership of the group, whereas those who are fighting for financial gains are low-ranking fighters. This report lends credence to the argument that many of the Taliban are motivated to militancy by chronic unemployment.

The Taliban organize operational fighters into units ranging from thirty to fifty fighters. Each unit has a commander and a specific area of operations where they conduct attacks. Since 2006, there have also been examples of Taliban fighters carrying out attacks in larger groups of several hundred fighters, indicating that the organizational capabilities of the Taliban are growing more powerful. For instance, consider the attack on Sarposa prison in Kandahar in June 2008, where as many as four hundred fighters were said to be involved. The attack succeeded in freeing several hundred Taliban prisoners.[10]

Propaganda Campaign

The Taliban have proven to be very adept in propaganda and information warfare, which entails utilizing the information sphere of influence as a means to coerce the Afghan population and the Afghan government into establishing an Islamic Emirate in Afghanistan and to advance their aims of expelling all international forces. As a report from the Royal Danish Defence College states, "[I]f the ISAF does not win the battle for the information environment, it will not prevail in Afghanistan."[11] Unfortunately, in the information sphere of influence for the war, the Taliban are at a distinct advantage over coalition and Afghan government forces for the following reasons:

- The Taliban have a better understanding of the local culture, history, and society. "The Taliban often refer to themselves as mujahideen, or freedom fighters . . . with the intent of portraying the ISAF as being the same as the Soviet regime."[12]
- The Taliban are able to invoke Islamic rhetoric in ways that the ISAF will never be able to replicate. For instance, the use of "crusaders" or "infidels" as alternative names for the coalition and "martyrs" for suicide bombers effectively distances coalition forces from the population.
- The Taliban are able to use information operations to coerce, not just to influence. Consider Taliban *shabnama* (night letters), handwritten notes addressed to individual Afghans (those who support or work for the government), often outlining what they are doing wrong and what they must do to ensure that they are not killed by the Taliban.
- The Taliban do not abide by legal, political, and ethical foundations that ISAF information operations must abide by. In other terms, the Taliban are able to lie, while the ISAF is legally bound to tell the truth. For instance, sometimes the Taliban will take responsibility for an attack that they did not carry out just for propaganda. The reciprocal event also happens. If a Taliban attack were to inflict too many civilian casualties, the Taliban would not take responsibility.[13]
- Little oversight or bureaucratic structures means that the Taliban's information can be released almost immediately after an event takes place. "Their timing is close to perfect: they exploit ISAF operations and political developments in near real time with great success, often having a spokesman on international media with claims about ISAF collateral damage before the operation is even finished or ISAF HQ is aware of the situation."[14] This decreases the impact and effectiveness of ISAF's rebuttals, which take place several hours after an event.

Recruitment

In the early period of the Taliban's movement, most of the fighters recruited (in Arabic Talib) were studying Islamic education in madrassas in the FATA, Quetta, and Peshawar in Pakistan. They were given initial training on how to fight and use weapons. Madrassas built during the Soviet's invasion of Afghanistan are still training fighters for the current insurgency. Funding for these madrassas came from some Arab countries, especially the Kingdom of Saudi Arabia.

After the reemergence of the Taliban in early 2003, they were in desperate need of fighters to fight against the Afghan and coalition forces. Not only did they recruit fighters from madrassas in Pakistan but also from local people who sympathized with their cause. There are several important developments that enabled the Taliban's insurgency to recruit from people within Afghanistan. They highlighted the heavy-handed tactics used by coalition forces that led to civilian casualties; the rough treatment of Afghans; and the ineffective and corrupt Afghan government, which is unable to deliver goods and services to the Afghan people. This led to many areas in the south and southeast, where coalition forces were most active, to become more sympathetic toward the Taliban's movement. In recent years, the Taliban, with the assistance of al Qaeda's members, established several training camps in Waziristan's area of the FATA. These camps provide training to newly joined volunteers. The methods used during training include both traditional and modern insurgency tactics. They are not only trained to use weapons, emplace land mines, and use remote detonated bombs but also to use communication devices such as satellite phones and the Internet. They are also trained in making homemade explosive devices.

The Taliban's recruitment strategy also includes children trained as suicide bombers. As ruthless as this practice is, there are tactical advantages for the Taliban to use children as suicide bombers. They can pass undetected through most security checkpoints and do not attract attention, as adults might. Initially, all the recruits are shown videos in which ISAF's soldiers conduct search operations and videos of Bagram and Guantanamo prison abuses. They receive indoctrination in the ideology of jihad and the perceived benefits of fighting against "infidels" and committing suicide attacks. Afterward, the instructors teach them how to make explosives, wear suicide jackets, and target the ISAF in Afghanistan.

EQUIPMENT

The Taliban forces are believed to possess only light weaponry. The overwhelming majority of the Taliban's archaic inventory of armor was collected upon desertion by other forces in the mid-1990s, with the more serviceable weapons taken by the United Front (UF) and various regional warlords. The most effective weapons the Taliban uses are explosives and suicide bombers. The explosives are usually improvised devices made from easily accessible materials. In the first half of 2007, machine-made bombs similar to the ones found in Iraq were also discovered in Afghanistan.[15] This may represent the introduction of a new generation of more sophisticated explosive devices in Afghanistan. In comparison to the improvised explosive devices (IEDs) that were used in the earlier years of the insurgency, the ones used in recent years are deadlier and are seen as an important factor in rising casualties within coalition forces. If technology and assistance advance, they could help the Taliban develop new capabilities to continue the insurgency in Afghanistan. In addition, the large quantity of mines, unexploded ordinances, and other remnants of the war in Afghanistan constitute a prime source of materials needed for the fabrication of advanced IEDs.

Although there are regular accusations, there is no clear evidence that neighboring countries are providing weapons to the Taliban. The countries considered most likely to render assistance are Iran and Pakistan. Some of the more advanced and sophisticated tactics and weapons the Taliban acquired recently may come from Iran. The United States called Iran's role in Afghanistan a "double game" on several occasions and accuses it of helping the insurgency.

FUNDING AND ASSOCIATIONS

Financing

International Support

In May 2011 at the Carnegie Moscow Center, Hekmat Karzai, director of the Centre for Conflict and Peace Studies (CAPS), described the conflict in Afghanistan as a "theme park" of conflicts, pointing to the various interests of regional and international actors in the country.[16] These competing interests, especially when it comes to wariness toward an American presence in the region, resulted in state support for certain insurgent elements like the Taliban. In this scenario, the Taliban provide a mechanism for use as "strategic assets" by certain countries, specifically, assets wielding influence within Afghanistan and a country in an important geopolitical position, optimal for use to counter rivals in the region. Particularly, the sanctuaries in Pakistan are an important part of the international support that the Taliban receive.

Taxes

The Taliban imposed taxes and levies in areas that fell under its administration before the fall of Kabul in 1996. Reportedly, the Taliban received 200,000 rupees (USD 5,000) in tolls from transport operators in December 1994 when fifty truck convoys carrying raw cotton from Turkmenistan arrived in Quetta.[17] As the de facto government in Afghanistan, taxes were imposed on the population for various reasons, and the revenue was used to achieve the Taliban's objectives in the country. The Taliban also collected various types of *zakat* (alms), which is a religious obligation for wealthy Muslims.[18] Furthermore, an estimated $3 billion was generated annually for Afghanistan's economy through the Pakistan–Afghanistan Transit Trade Agreement, which the Taliban also benefited from.[19] There are claims made by locals in rural Afghanistan that the Taliban still use taxes as a source of income. They collect revenues and alms in areas where they have a strong presence.

Drug Trade

Despite being ideologically opposed to drugs, the Taliban have made a habit of bending this rule to fund their insurgency. During the 1990s, the Taliban collected a 20 percent tax from the value of truckloads of opium.[20] The Taliban increased opium production in Afghanistan to meet their economic interests, although they denied direct involvement in opium cultivation and drug-smuggling activities.[21] With the toppling of the Taliban regime and their return as insurgents, the movement is widely connected to the narcotics trade in Afghanistan. The drug trade flourished in Afghanistan since the Karzai administration has been in power, with the country supplying more than 90 percent of the world's opium. Although progress on eradicating opium in certain parts of the country is moving forward, the south is still a major producer. The deteriorating security situation in southern Afghanistan and the booming drug trade have strong causal linkages. In areas where insurgents are present, fighters work with drug mafias and receive a portion of the profits. The Taliban's insurgents provide protection and labor for the drugs to be grown. A telling example is the annual fighting season—it usually does not begin until after the opium harvest. According to US State Department estimates, the Taliban receive USD 400 million annually from the drug trade. A large amount of this income is spent buying weapons and vehicles, and paying the wages of foot soldiers.[22]

Jihadist Groups

Jihadist groups' financial aid to the Taliban's regime came mainly in the form of donations collected by them in their respective countries of origin.

This is due to their support for the Taliban's ideology or in return for access to training facilities and/or safe havens. Among the jihadist groups, al Qaeda was the biggest contributor to the Taliban. Reportedly, al Qaeda provided USD 3 million for the Taliban's campaign to capture Kabul, as well as one of its Arab-dominated fighting brigades known as the 055 Brigade.[23] This relationship still exists today. Moreover, key individuals within the Taliban continue to have close relationships with Arabs in the Gulf States and with certain foreign members of the jihadist groups that helped during the war against the Soviets.

Individual Funders

The Taliban received sympathy from Muslims of other countries, especially in the rich Arab states of the Gulf. Fatwas in support of the Taliban supported recruiting efforts, and numerous respected scholars issued these fatwas.[24] Official recognition toward the Taliban's government by Saudi Arabia and the United Arab Emirate contributed to support and sympathy from their respective populations. It is likely that monetary support flowed from these donations to the Taliban. The view that the US attack on Afghanistan was an invasion of a Muslim land and the perception of the Taliban as a resistance force against the occupation contributed to continued support for the Taliban from Muslims all over the world.

An assessment of the current financing mechanism for the Taliban's organization from the Center for Stategic and International Studies is as follows:

> Although Afghanistan provides ready access to weapons and explosives, additional resources are brought into the country through traditional smuggling routes and networks. The Taliban maintain local allegiances with tribes, government officials and most likely drug traffickers who provide assistance at border crossing points in the vicinity of southern Helmand, southeastern Kandahar, Zabul, southern Paktika, southern Nangarhar, Kunar, and Nuristan. The Taliban receive funding from both international donors and indigenous sources (in both Afghanistan and Pakistan). It is believed that elements of the Pakistani Inter-Service Intelligence Directorate—not necessarily working under government sanction—provide resources to the Taliban movement. Additionally, it is believed that the Hawala informal banking system plays a significant role in transferring money from international sources.[25]

The Taliban and its close ally, the Haqqani Network, succeeded in finding several funding sources in the past few years for their ongoing struggle against Afghan and coalition forces. They earn millions of dollars from the drug industry, which expanded several times since the collapse of the Taliban's regime in 2001. The old pipeline funneling money from wealthy Arab Gulf States to jihadi fighters in Afghanistan and Pakistan is ongoing. In an effort to tackle this issue, the United States enlisted the support of countries like Saudi Arabia to investigate the financial support that the Taliban's insurgents receive from abroad. On 22 July 2010, the US Department of Treasury labeled three important individuals for "supporting acts of terrorism and for acting for or on behalf of the Taliban or the Haqqani Network."[26] Under US Executive Order 13224, Nasiruddin Haqqani, the son of Jalal-u-Din Haqqani; Gul Agha Ishakzai, a key figure of the Taliban's financial commission; and Amir Abdullah, former treasurer to Mullah Baradar are now under financial sanctions.[27]

However, it seems that the sanctions are not as fruitful as believed for two main reasons. First, the insurgent groups have established a network of fundraisers in various countries, and Taliban leaders abstain from traveling abroad. Therefore, their sympathizers or other low-ranking officials fulfill the task of fund-raising on their behalf when necessary. Second, the terrorist groups largely use the informal system of money transfer known as *Hawala*.[28] This system gives militants the ability to transfer their money through informal channels with no fear of sums being frozen or traced by governments.

Associations

Haqqani Network

Jalaluddin Haqqani and his sons lead the Haqqani Network, based in the Waziristan area of Pakistan. Jalaluddin Haqqani's health is fragile, but so far, there are no confirmed reports of his death. In March 2008, he appeared in a video, countering rumors that he had died of hepatitis.[29] Haqqani's son Sirajuddin (Siraj) is believed to be the de facto leader of the Haqqani Network today.

There is debate over whether a disaggregation of the Taliban should include the Haqqani Network as an independent militant group operating in Afghanistan or as a subset of the Taliban's movement. After the Haqqani Network brazenly attacked the US embassy in September 2011, the US focus moved against bringing the Haqqani Network to the negotiating table. Shortly after this attack, the Haqqani Network released a statement saying they would be willing to negotiate if the Quetta Shura allowed them to negotiate. This eliminated hopes that the Haqqani Network could negotiate independently of Quetta's leadership.[30] This message also strongly suggests that the Haqqani Network is just one (albeit the most powerful) subset in the larger Taliban movement. This is not to say that the Haqqani Network cannot operate separately from the Taliban for tactical or operational analysis, but it does mean that reconciliation efforts need to focus on the top tier of the Taliban's leadership, the Quetta Shura.

Al Qaeda

Al Qaeda support but do not maintain command and control over the Taliban. They influence through traditional connections with the Quetta Shura. al Qaeda provide foreign volunteers and are an ideological force for attracting fighters for the Taliban.[31] In May 1996, at the behest of the Sudanese government, al Qaeda's leadership, including their top commander Osama bin Laden, relocated to Afghanistan. At that time, the Taliban gained control of southern and western Afghanistan and were on their way to conquering the capital. Initially, bin Laden settled in the Jalalabad area at the invitation of an old ally from the mujahideen period, Yunus Khalis. When the Taliban later that year took control over Jalalabad and Kabul, bin Laden started building his relationships with them and soon became a close associate of Mullah Omar. When the Taliban took power in Afghanistan, they "inherited" not only bin Laden's network but also a number of training camps for foreign fighters financed by al Qaeda.

Although respectful of each other's efforts, the ideologies of the Taliban and al Qaeda did not initially coincide. Whereas the Taliban's desire was to rehabilitate Afghanistan through enforcement of their interpretation of the sharia, al Qaeda saw the Muslim world as being under attack from the West and sought to use Afghanistan as a launching pad for their global jihadi campaign. After 1996, the Taliban opened Afghanistan's borders not only to al Qaeda but also to a host of other foreign militants. Among the many groups hosted by the Taliban were fighters from the Islamic Movement of Uzbekistan (IMU), Pakistanis fighting in the Kashmir, and Chechen fighters battling Russia.[32]

Al Qaeda enjoy close cooperation with the Haqqani Network in eastern Afghanistan. Al Qaeda's fighters were involved in the insurgents' campaign in Afghanistan from the very beginning. Initially, several talented al Qaeda commanders, such as Abdul Hadi al Iraqi and Khalid Habib, served on the Afghan front. Another influential commander was Abu al-Layth al-Libi, based in northern Waziristan, who trained foreign fighters to conduct cross-border attacks into Afghanistan. In 2007, the capture of Abdul Hadi al-Iraqi resulted in detainment at Guantanamo Bay, Cuba. Al Qaeda appointed one of their most senior members, the Egyptian Mustafa Abu al-Yazid, to lead al Qaeda's activities in Afghanistan. This indicates the continued determination of al Qaeda to support jihad in Afghanistan, despite the loss of several veteran commanders. Mustafa Abu al-Yazid was involved in establishing relations with local militant groups on both sides of the Afghanistan–Pakistan border. He also claimed responsibility for attacks carried out jointly by al Qaeda and local groups, to include the suicide attack on a US base in the Khost province in 2008 and the suicide bombing against the CIA base in December 2009, resulting in the death of seven CIA operatives. Mr. Yazid issued a statement praising the work of the bomber, Humam Khalil Abu Mulal al-Balawi, and said that the bombing was revenge for the killings of a number of top militant leaders in CIA drone attacks. Osama bin Laden's death in Pakistan in May 2011 marks a turning point for the relationship between al Qaeda and the Taliban in Afghanistan. After bin Laden's death, the Taliban released a statement saying they would avenge his death by killing coalition forces in Afghanistan.

There is contention about the actual number of al Qaeda operatives in Afghanistan. Recent official US figures estimate around fifty to one hundred al Qaeda operatives are active in Afghanistan, the lowest number since they first arrived in the country in the early 1990s.[33] However, other analysts argue that this number is not accurate when cross-referenced with the supposed number of al Qaeda killed (in 2011 approximately forty al Qaeda operatives were killed in Afghanistan).[34] Whatever the total number, it is a very small contingent compared to the former strength of al Qaeda in Afghanistan, and as numbers decline, al Qaeda's operational capabilities and influence diminish. However, foreign fighters are an active element of both the Haqqani Network's operations and wider insurgent activity, either by facilitating training, in support roles, or as hired guns. These foreign entities in addition to al Qaeda include the Islamic Movement of Uzbekistan (IMU), the Islamic Jihad Union (IJU), Tehrik Nefaz-e-Shariat Muhammedi (TNSM), and Tehrek-e-Pakistan Taliban (TTP). There are also ties to traditionally Kashmir-focused groups such as Lashkar-e-Taiba (LeT).

Interactions with Foreign Parties, Governments, and Intelligence Services

Jamiat-i-Ulema Islam

The Jamiat-i-Ulema Islam (JUI), headed by Maulana Fazlur Rahman, and the Jamiat-i-Ulema Islam, headed by Maulana Sami ul Haq, are associations of religious scholars and madrassas in Pakistan. The JUI's primary base is in Pakistan's Khyber Pakhtunkhwa province and Baluchistan province. These parties run numerous madrassas primarily in the two provinces, as well as in tribal areas, which are the main source of the Taliban's fighters. These madrassas cater to the education of many Afghan refugees' children as well, going back to the invasion of the Soviet Union, as well as ethnically Pashtun Pakistanis. These children are Talibs and form the backbone of the Taliban's volunteers.

Pakistan and Inter-Services Intelligence

Pakistan's Inter-Services Intelligence (ISI) is widely known for its involvement in Afghanistan's affairs since the Soviet Union's invasion. During the

1990s, while Iran and India supported the anti-Taliban warring parties, Pakistan supported the Taliban. Pakistan's support came in many forms: humanitarian aid, technology, and labor for both civilian and military purposes.

Despite Pakistan's proclaiming support for the US war on terror after the attacks of 9/11, it is believed that the ISI maintained close relationships with elements of the Taliban that are currently fighting in Afghanistan. Defense Secretary Robert Gates called Pakistan's intelligence service activities as "hedging bets" and believed the ISI uses elements of the Taliban as "strategic assets" for their purposes in Afghanistan. In David E. Sanger's book, *The Inheritance: The World Obama Confronts and the Challenges to American Power*, he talks extensively of his meetings with senior officials of the Bush administration who monitored Taliban activity in Pakistan and saw active support from official channels in Pakistan's government. In their own statements, as early as July 2009, senior leadership from Pakistan's military admitted that they remain in contact with leaders of the Afghan Taliban and can play a role in reconciliation efforts—providing that their concerns are addressed.

Saudi Arabia

The Saudi government recognized the Taliban government from 1996 to 2001. The Saudi government's support for the Taliban was not only politically motivated to help counter Iran's position in Afghanistan and beyond but also ideologically motivated through its support for the Taliban's Sunni Islamic state. Saudi Arabia maintains close links with the Taliban regime and is believed to help the Taliban's use of Pakistan as an intermediary.

Now that the Taliban's insurgency has gained momentum in Afghanistan, the role of Saudi Arabia is part of the dialogue—this time in reconciliation efforts. Given their close relationship with the United States and their links with the Afghan Taliban some are hopeful that the Saudis will be able to play a constructive role in bringing the two conflicting sides together. Initial talks between former members of the Afghan Taliban and the Afghan government reportedly occurred in early 2009, with Saudi Arabia hosting the meeting location.

Iran

During the past several years, US military officials repeatedly said that Iran's government assists the Afghan Taliban in Afghanistan. Recently, the director of US National Intelligence, Dennis Blair, said that Iran is covertly supplying arms to the Taliban's insurgents while publicly posing as supportive of the Afghan government. According to Mr. Blair, the arms provided by Iran to the Taliban include small arms, mines, rockets, and other explosives. This cooperation is interesting, because prior to 9/11, Shiite Iran and Sunni Taliban were hostile to each other. Short-term interests brought these two closer, as they have a common enemy in the form of the United States. The Afghan Taliban benefit from these relations by receiving weapons and money, and Iran is allegedly benefiting by keeping the United States entangled in Afghanistan.

Aside from US officials, some Afghan officials, particularly from the western provinces bordering Iran such as Herat, Farah, and Nimroz, also believe Iran is channeling money and arms to the Afghan Taliban. For example, arms seized in March 2010 in the western province of Farah were from Iran. The local government's officials of the Farah province said that the weapons seized prove that they are smuggled out of Iran. However, high-level Afghan officials, particularly President Hamid Karzai, refused to support the allegation. This might be because President Karzai does not want to inflame his relations with Iran, as he already has tense relations with Pakistan.

TACTICS, TECHNIQUES, AND PROCEDURES

The Afghan Taliban's tactics, techniques, and procedures against the ISAF and the Afghan government are determined by their strategy and theaters of operation, as well as by ISAF's counterinsurgency gains. The Afghan Taliban's strategy is not to expand their areas of control, as their forces and weaponry cannot match that of the ISAF and the Afghan government. During the past ten years, there are repeated instances of the Afghan Taliban capturing district centers and losing them to Afghan and ISAF forces in a matter of days. In March 2011, the Afghan Taliban captured Bargi Matal district of Nuristan province in eastern Afghanistan but were forced out of the district after Afghan and ISAF forces launched an operation.[35] In August 2010, they captured Muqur district of the Ghazni province in southern Afghanistan and set ablaze its office building. The district fell back to Afghan forces a day later.[36] Thus, the Afghan Taliban continue a strategy to wage guerilla war aimed at bleeding as many Afghan and ISAF forces as possible and to sustain an insurgency to make people believe that "they are not weakened" before the exodus of ISAF and Afghan forces. The Afghan Taliban declared the same strategy in response to President Obama's thirty-thousand-troop surge in 2009. They stated that the reinforcement will only result in further troop fatalities and that it will provide better opportunities and more targets for their offensives.[37]

Summer is the primary fighting season for the Afghan Taliban. They increase attacks in rural and urban Afghanistan from April until November. Afghanistan has harsh winters, making it more difficult for the Afghan Taliban to continue their operations. They spend winters in their homes and rest while preparing for the coming summer. The Afghan Taliban's spring offensives usually start in April. In 2011, they announced their spring offensive on 30 April 2011, aimed at reversing the gains made by ISAF forces in 2010. The Afghan Taliban announced their intent to increase violence across Afghanistan, especially in those areas weakened by ISAF and Afghan forces in the previous year.[38]

Targets

The Afghan Taliban determine their attacks according to targets and the area of operations. The Taliban's attacks since 2003 indicate that the Afghan Taliban's targets have expanded year by year. In addition to combatant targets, which include Afghan and NATO forces and their bases, the Afghan Taliban increasingly targeted Afghan government officials, progovernment civilians, and tribal elders. They also targeted hotels and banks. They targeted the Serena Hotel in 2008 and the Intercontinental Hotel in 2012 in Kabul, which are both popular with foreigners and high-ranking Afghan government officials. They raided UN guesthouses and offices in a number of major cities in Afghanistan. In 2011, the Afghan Taliban targeted hospitals and banks, resulting in the death of numerous civilians.[39] According to the rules of engagement set by the Afghan Taliban, fighters can target the aforementioned groups, and the reasoning behind the attacks is that they are working and supporting the "puppet regime" (government of Afghanistan) and the "infidels" (coalition forces and the international community).

Tactics, Techniques, and Procedures

The Afghan Taliban use various tactics including direct and indirect attacks. They ambush combatants, storm government installations and ISAF bases, and carry out IEDs. In some cases, the Afghan Taliban amassed into company-sized assault forces and attempted to overrun police stations, villages, and towns. The Afghan army and coalition forces responded with ground mobility, helicopters, firepower, and air strikes. The results amounted to grievous losses for the Afghan Taliban. Despite the significant losses suffered by the Afghan Taliban, their ability to reappear in areas from which ISAF forces cleared proved to be a serious challenge for the Afghan government and coalition forces. US Marines launched a massive operation in the southern Helmand province in the summer of 2009 to clear out militants, and this was previously attempted. However, the Afghan Taliban avoided direct confrontations during these intensive operations. The Afghan Taliban's supreme leader Mullah Muhammad Omar prepared a thirty-article code of conduct (Layeha) to give special instructions for commanders and fighters who are fighting against the Afghan government and coalition forces. These rules of engagement addressed interactions with the local people and those who are working for the Afghan government and ISAF forces.

Suicide Attacks

In terms of inflicting casualties, suicide attacks in Afghanistan—unlike Iraq—have a mixed record. In the early years of the Afghan Taliban's insurgency (2004 to 2006), human suicide attacks resulted in either the bomber getting killed and/or civilian and military casualties. For the suicide attacks in Afghanistan for 2007 and previous years, less than 55 percent inflicted casualties beyond the bombers themselves.[40] The deadliest single suicide attack in 2007 was the attack on the Afghan police trainers' bus in Kabul on 17 June 2007, resulting in the death of thirty-five police officers and the injury of ten other policemen.[41]

Because of the inefficiency of suicide attacks, the Afghan Taliban turned to vehicle-borne suicide attacks from 2007 onward. Because this trend proved effective in causing Afghan and ISAF forces high casualties, the Afghan Taliban increased their employment and continued to use various vehicles ranging from cars to small trucks. They equip vehicles with tons of explosives and target Afghan and ISAF convoys and establishments. On 11 September 2011, a suicide bomber rammed a truck equipped with tons of explosives into a US base in Maidan Wardak province, injuring seventy-seven US soldiers working inside the base.[42] In recent years, starting from 2009, the Afghan Taliban introduced another sophisticated trend of coordinated suicide attacks. Using this tactic, a group of suicide bombers armed with grenades, AK-47s, and explosives-laden vehicles targeted government and ISAF establishments, as well as hotels and UN guesthouses in the major cities of Afghanistan.[43]

Recruitment of Suicide Bombers

Perhaps the most disturbing developments involving suicide bombings by the Afghan Taliban are the growing use of adolescents for their operations. Over time, the ages of the suicide bombers have dropped. In the Khost province, a fourteen-year-old bomber was caught with his suicide vest just as he was planning to target the provincial governor, Arsala Jamal, in late 2006. On 24 August 2011, a couple of days ahead of the Muslim religious festival Eidul Fitr, Afghan President Hamid Karzai ordered the release of twenty child suicide bombers, with age ranges between eight and seventeen. President Karzai told Afghan security officials to take these children to their families. In his meeting with them, the children told President Karzai that the Afghan Taliban had recruited them. The Afghan Taliban strapped them with suicide vests and instructed them to detonate them near foreign forces.[44] They explained how they feared threats from the Afghan Taliban, because they surrendered to Afghan security forces before carrying out their attacks. One of them promised to continue jihad against the "invading forces" in Afghanistan.[45] Security forces intercepted all twenty child suicide bombers before they could strike. The Afghan Taliban recruited these children at religious schools or in poor neighborhoods. Afghan children are the most vulnerable segment of society, as they are economically impoverished and illiterate, which eases the Afghan Taliban's recruitment efforts. One of these children, Gul Khan, of Kandahar, admitted in front of President Karzai that his father had sent him to a religious school in Pakistan but that the school had motivated him to conduct suicide attacks in Afghanistan. Another child, Noor Mohammad, said he was studying in a madrassa in the Ghazni province of Afghanistan and that the Afghan Taliban had equipped him with a suicide vest and pistol, and instructed him to target a nearby provincial reconstruction team.[46] Another child said that the Afghan Taliban had recruited him and told him to carry out a suicide attack in Afghanistan, and then told him he would go straight to paradise.

The Afghan Taliban fighting Afghan and ISAF troops largely rely on suicide attacks and roadside bombings. During the past three years, the Afghan Taliban have increased coordinated suicide attacks. For instance, four suicide bombers stormed the British Council in Kabul on 19 August 2012, killing over ten people and injuring ten others. Such attacks need sufficient suicide recruits, and the Afghan Taliban fulfill this need by targeting children and teenagers.

Female Suicide Bombers

In 2010 and 2011, the Kunar province witnessed the employment of female suicide attacks. Kunar province is located in the eastern region of the country and shares a lengthy border with Pakistan. Kunar was hit three times by female suicide bombers since 2001. The Afghan Taliban claim responsibility for all three of these attacks. Unlike male suicide bombers, where identities and names are revealed, the identities of these three female suicide bombers were not revealed. The Afghan Taliban referred to the 29 October 2011 female suicide bomber as "a lone Mujahid combatant of the Islamic Emirate."[47] The female suicide bomber was in her twenties and carried out the attack in Asadabad, the capital of the eastern Kunar province of Afghanistan. She fired a handgun and detonated explosives strapped to her body at the office gate of the National Directorate of Security (NDS) in Asadabad city. The blast resulted in the injury of seven people, including five security officials and two civilians.[48]

The Afghan Taliban commander Qari Zia Rahman in the Kunar province, closely linked to Pakistan Taliban and al Qaeda, claimed responsibility for the second female suicide bomber attack on 21 June 2011 in the Kunar province. The attack injured two Afghan children and killed two US soldiers.[49] On 4 June 2010, the Afghan Taliban claimed responsibility for the first suicide attack in the Marawara district located in Kunar province. That attack resulted in killing three Afghan interpreters for US forces. The Afghan Taliban referred to the female suicide bomber as "Mujahida sister," who they claimed killed twelve US and Afghan troops.[50]

Turban Suicide Attacks

The Afghan Taliban introduce new trends every year. For example, they started with suicide vest attacks or human-borne attacks in the early years. Later, they adopted vehicle-borne suicide attacks from 2007 onward. In 2008, the Afghan Taliban launched commando suicide attacks, a tactic involving a group of suicide bombers equipped with suicide vests, AK-47s, and hand grenades targeting government and ISAF installations in the major cities of Afghanistan. None of the above tactics resonated with specific cultural symbols of Afghan society, other than the trend of the Afghan Taliban's turban suicide attacks in 2011. The turban is an important and common cultural symbol of Afghan society and is not searched and removed from the heads of tribal elders out of respect. Tribal leaders and elders frequently wear these hats. The Afghan Taliban, knowing this sensitivity about the turban in Afghan society, exploited the turban and successfully targeted three critical supporters of the Afghan government.

The suicide bomber wears the turban on his head, laden with explosives, and then detonates it when he reaches his target. The Afghan Taliban carried out turban suicide attacks three times in 2011. On 27 July 2011, a suicide bomber wearing an explosives-laden turban assassinated Kandahar's Mayor Ghulam Haidar Hamidi, in the municipality complex of Kandahar City.[51] The other turban suicide attacks happened on 13 July 2011, just one day after a bodyguard killed President Hamid Karzai's younger brother, Ahmad Wali Karzai, head of Kandahar's provincial council. The bomber's explosive, hidden inside his high turban, enabled him to detonate the bomb inside a mosque, killing four people, including the head of the Ulema Council in Kandahar.[52] The third turban suicide attack was on 20 September 2011, which killed Professor Burhanuddin Rabbani, former president of Afghanistan and chairman of the Afghan High Peace Council.[53] The Afghan Taliban claimed responsibility for the three attacks. Given that these three turban suicide attacks killed two important anti-Taliban personalities, few doubt the increasing use of this technique by the Afghan Taliban in the future.

THE PEACE PROCESS AND THE US/AFGHANISTAN STRATEGIC PARTNERSHIP

Afghan Taliban and the Peace Process

The Afghan government is trying to start a dialogue of peace with the Afghan Taliban, something initiated several years ago. However, negotiations did not involve the international community until the London conference in 2010. In July 2010, the Afghan government hosted an international conference in Kabul, and President Karzai presented his reconciliation plan and received endorsement by the international community.

Prior to the London conference, President Karzai's message to Mullah Omar on 16 November 2008 was the first official message that publically requested that Mullah Omar be present at the peace talks and assurances that the Afghan government would give him safe passage. The reply to this message was from Mullah Baradar, deputy leader of the Taliban, saying, "We are safe in Afghanistan and we have no need for Hamid Karzai's offer of safety." He also said that foreign troops should leave before the start of any negotiations and that any dialogue with the Afghan government prior to the departure of foreign troops would be a waste of time.[54]

The first official step to begin the peace process occurred at the London conference in 2010. The Afghan government was able to convince the international community that peace talks should be Afghan led and started to improve security and stability in Afghanistan. Therefore, a peace Loya Jirga in 2010, endorsed by the London conference, paved the way for the Afghan government to establish a high peace council consisting of sixty-eight influential leaders and politicians from different ethnicities and former jihadi factions led by former president of Afghanistan, Professor Rabbani, as of September 2010.[55] However, the Afghan Taliban's response to the peace dialogue remained negative. The Afghan Taliban believe that the Afghan government is a puppet government and does not have any authority to hold talks with the Afghan Taliban.[56]

High Peace Council and the Afghan Taliban

The establishment of the High Peace Council (HPC) was a step forward for the Afghan-led peace process in September 2010. On 5 June 2011, the head of the High Peace Council, Burhanuddin Rabbani, asked for a meeting with the parliament to discuss the HPC's activities and achievements. Rabbani stated that "it is worth mentioning that in the past five months we have made contacts with those who are involved in armed conflict, including Mr. Hekmatyar, the Council of Quetta and the Haqqani network." However, he did not comment further about how those meetings were progressing and the advancement prospects for the peace process.[57] The HPC and a senior delegation visited Pakistan, Qatar, and Turkey to talk about possible ways to bring the Afghan Taliban to the peace talks. However, the Afghan Taliban showed no signs of willingness to talk to the Afghan government.[58]

On 5 August 2011, the HPC claimed that Mullah Mohammad Omar was ready to talk with the Afghan government. Mr. Ismael Qasimyar, a member and secretary of the International Affairs Committee of the HPC, said that there were direct and indirect contacts made with important sources in a bid to bring the Afghan Taliban to the negotiation table. Unfortunately, the Afghan Taliban's spokesman, Zabihullah Mujahid, immediately dismissed HPC's claims and explained that the role of the HPC in the peace process has not been effective. The Taliban's spokesman categorically stated, "[W]hen our leader Mullah Omar could resist against 49 countries, how come he could say he is ready for talks?" He described HPC claims as baseless and said that the HPC made such claims only to keep foreigners' money flowing into the council. He also said that these claims would not result in anything progressive and that they would not turn into a reality.[59]

Post-Rabbani Peace Process and the Afghan Taliban

The Afghan Taliban sent a messenger under the guise of a message from the Quetta Shura to assassinate Professor Rabbani, the head of the HPC. The suicide bomber put the explosive device in his turban and detonated it when he embraced Rabbani upon greeting him. The death of Rabbani is a great loss for President Karzai and the peace process in Afghanistan.[60] However, the Afghan Taliban did not officially claim responsibility for the attack. Nonetheless, the National Directorate of Security (NDS) stated that the Quetta Shura was behind the attack and that the letter found in the pocket of the suicide attacker verified that the Quetta Shura was involved in Rabbani's death.[61] Rabbani's assassination changed the calculus of the reconciliation process and highlighted that the Afghan Taliban are not reconcilable unless their Pakistani supporters stop giving them sanctuaries and cease support for their efforts to continue fighting against the Afghan government and ISAF forces in Afghanistan.

Taliban and Afghanistan–US Strategic Partnership

The Afghan Taliban, in a statement, opposed the Afghanistan–US strategic partnership agreement and establishment of US bases in Afghanistan beyond 2014. The Afghan Taliban in their statement said, "Afghanistan is under the occupation of America. No treaty and agreement has legitimacy in condition of occupation. These sham treaties do not reflect the aspirations and objectives of the Afghans. And the permanent bases in Afghanistan will turn our country into a de facto hotbed of American conspiracies. They will use these bases to change regimes in Afghanistan and the neighboring countries, utilizing them as instruments of pressures. Therefore, these permanent bases in Afghanistan stand in contravention to our Islamic and national interests and objectives. They can't be acceptable."[62]

The Afghan Taliban's coercive position regarding the Afghanistan–US strategic partnership became clear during a traditional Loya Jirga discussing the Afghanistan–US strategic partnership, held on 16–19 November 2011. The Afghan Taliban called it a non-Islamic jirga that allows Americans to stay longer in an Islamic country.[63]

THREAT ASSESSMENT/OUTLOOK

Based on the information presented in this Afghan Taliban profile, despite increasing efforts by the West and evolving counterinsurgency and stability strategies, the Afghan Taliban remain a complex and capable threat to Afghanistan. The Afghan Taliban's forces are growing stronger in the eastern and southeastern regions of Afghanistan and are threatening the writ of the Afghan government. In the current security context, if the West leaves Afghanistan, there could be dire consequences for the government, society, and economy of Afghanistan.

In the near future, the pace of the conflict is unlikely to wane uncharacteristically. This year, the Afghan Taliban proved they could follow through with their proposed objectives laid out at the beginning of the fighting season. While attacks will likely decline for the winter, it is unlikely that next year's spring offensive will be any less potent than it was this year. Sustaining an urban insurgency is the key to the Afghan Taliban's publicity—both nationally and in international circles. The Afghan Taliban will try to insert insiders into government institutions, while attempting to create cells in major cities. This insider help will enable the Afghan Taliban to continue their high-profile coordinated attacks in urban Afghanistan. Post-2014, the Afghan Taliban will likely sustain their insurgency through indirect operations. In rural areas, they will sustain the insurgency through IEDs and in urban areas through the continued use of suicide and insider attacks.

UPDATED KILL/CAPTURE LIST OF SENIOR TALIBAN MILITANTS[64]

Updated Kill/Capture List of Senior Taliban Militants

No.	Name/Position	Date Killed/Capture	Circumstances/Means
1.	Bari Ali Midlevel Taliban commander; acted as intermediary between low-level Taliban and senior leadership	4 November 2011	Arrested in eastern Laghman province
2.	Inayatullah Taliban military commander based in North Waziristan	3 September 2010	Killed in air strike in Pakistan
3.	Mullah Abdul Ghani Baradar Taliban's second in command and operational commander of Taliban	January or February 2010	Arrested in Karachi by Pakistani forces and released at the request of the Afghan government on 20 September 2013
4.	Mawlavi Abdul Kabir Head of Peshawar Regional Military Shura; Taliban's former shadow governor of Nangarhar province; governor of Nangarhar during Taliban regime	February 2010	Arrested in Peshawar
5.	Mullah Mir Muhammad Shadow governor of northern Baghlan province	February 2010	Arrested in unknown location
6.	Mullah Abdul Salam Shadow governor of northern Kunduz province	February 2010	Arrested in Afghanistan
7.	Mullah Younus Known as Akhundzada	February 2010	Arrested in Karachi
8.	Anwarul Haq Mujahid Member of the Peshawar Regional Military Shura; commander of Tora Bora military front located in Nangarhar	June 2009	Arrested in Peshawar

No.	Name/Position	Date Killed/Capture	Circumstances/Means
	province; son of Mawlavi Muhamad Younus Khalis		
9.	Mullah Ustad Muhamad Yaser Head of the Recruitment Committee and Taliban's spokesman	January 2009	Arrested in Peshawar and allegedly killed by Pakistani authorities in jail in 2012
10.	Mullah Obaidullah Akhund Defense minister during Taliban regime from 1996 to 2001	January 2008	Arrested by Pakistan security forces in Quetta; said to have succumbed to a heart attack while in jail; news of his death became public in late 2011
11.	Mullah Mansour Dadullah Akhund Also known as Mullah Bakht Muhamad; replaced his brother Mullah Dadullah Akhund as the Taliban's top commander for southern region in the summer of 2007	January 2008	Arrested in Pakistan and released in September 2013 at the request of the Afghan government
12.	Mullah Dadullah Akhund Top military commander of Taliban in southern Afghanistan	May 2007	Killed by British special forces in Helmand province
13.	Akhtar Muhamad Osmani Member of the Quetta Shura and a commander of Taliban's military operation in Oruzgan, Nimroz, Kandahar, Farah, Herat, and Helmand	December 2006	Killed by ISAF forces in southern Afghanistan

LIST OF QUETTA SHURA MEMBERS AS OF SPRING 2010[65]

List of Quetta Shura Members as of Spring 2010

Name	Remarks
Hafiz Abdul Majeed	Current leader of the Quetta Military Shura and serves as the Taliban's intelligence chief
Mullah Muhamad Hassan Akhund	Governor of Kandahar province and Minister of Foreign Affairs during Taliban regime
Mullah Muhamad Hassan Rahmani	Very close relationships with Mullah Omar and was the governor of Kandahar during Taliban regime
Mullah Abdul Qayum Zakir	Leads the Gerdi Jangal Regional Military Shura and serves as Taliban surge commander in southern region of Afghanistan
Agha Jan Mohtasim	Son-in-law of Mullah Omar and finance minister during Taliban regime; no longer part of the Quetta Shura; lives in exile in Turkey and supports dialogue with the Afghan government
Amir Khan Mutaqi	Leads the Information and Culture Committee
Siraj Haqqani	Head of the Haqqani Network and leads the Miramshah Regional Military Shura, which strategizes operations in Loya Paktia region, including Paktia, Khost, and Paktika provinces
Mullah Muhamad Rasul	Served as the governor of Nimroz during Taliban regime
Gull Agha Ishaqzai	Head of finance committee; works as Mullah Omar's personal financial secretary and one of Mullah Omar's advisers
Abdul Latif Mansour	Commander of Abdul Latif Mansour network in Loya Paktia region; member of Miramshah Regional Military Shura; was the minister of agriculture during Taliban regime; said to have led the Peshawar Regional Military Shura
Mullah Abdul Razaq Akhundzada	Served as Interior Minister during Taliban regime and commander for northern region of Afghanistan

Name	Remarks
Mawlavi Hamdullah	Taliban representative for the Gulf region; was the head of Finance Department during Taliban regime
Mullah Akhtar Muhamad Mansour	Served as the Minister of Aviation and Transportation during Taliban regime
Mawlavi Qudratullah Jamal	Head of Investigation Committee to which the local people submit their complaints against local Taliban personnel; maintains relationships of Taliban with its international supporters; worked as the head of propaganda from 2002 to 2005
Mawlavi Aminullah	Commander of Taliban in Oruzgan province
Mullah Abdul Jalil	Leads the Interior Affairs Committee of the Taliban
Qari Talha	Head of Kabul operations of the Taliban
Sheikh Abdul Mana Niyazi	Shadow governor of the Taliban for Herat province

AL QAEDA GROUP PROFILE[66]

BY INTERNATIONAL CENTER FOR POLITICAL VIOLENCE AND TERRORISM RESEARCH

Fact Sheet

Name(s):	Jama'at Al Qaeda al-Jihad/Tanzim Al Qaeda al-Jihad
Date of creation:	1998; Transnational Jihadist Group
Leader:	Ayman Zawahiri (founder was Osama bin Laden)
Estimated strength:	Current strength is less than 1,000 fighters, located primarily in the Afghanistan–Pakistan region. Its ideological influence affects millions of aspiring jihadists, and affiliated organizations under its umbrella account for its global presence.
Area of operations:	Al Qaeda conducts operations in all regions of world. Affiliated groups in the Arabian Peninsula and Afghanistan–Pakistan regions continue to pose a significant threat to stability.

LEADERSHIP

The founder of al Qaeda, Osama bin Laden, was killed by a US Navy SEAL team known as "SEAL Team 6," in Abbottabad, Pakistan, on 2 May 2011 during Operation Neptune Spear around 00:50 hours. Reportedly, he had lived in this Abbottabad compound for six years. His death was the culmination of a decade-long hunt.[67] From al Qaeda's inception to his death, Osama bin Laden remained the leader of al Qaeda. Born in the Saudi capital Riyadh in 1957, bin Laden was raised in a wealthy family that made its fortune from Saudi Arabia's oil-fueled construction boom. In the 1970s, Osama bin Laden went to the King Abdulaziz University in Jeddah, where he initially studied at the economics college.[68] During his time at the King Abdulaziz University, bin Laden and his close friend and brother-in-law, Muhammad Jamal Khalifa, received lectures from Muhammad Qutb, who was a visiting professor at the university. Qutb was the brother of the Egyptian Sayid Qutb, whose books *Milestones* and *In the Shade of the Quran* would later serve as the ideological foundation for al Qaeda. In Jeddah, bin Laden also met the charismatic cleric, Palestinian Sheikh Abdallah Azzam, who taught at Abdulaziz University until 1981 and later moved to the International Islamic University in Islamabad, Pakistan.[69] Together, they established the Maktab al Khidamat (MAK) in 1984, commonly known as the Afghan Services Bureau.

Osama bin Laden was the deputy to Abdullah Azzam. At the height of the foreign mujahideen influx into Afghanistan and Pakistan from 1984–1986, MAK recruited several thousand Arab and Muslim youths to fight the former Soviet Union. MAK received several billion dollars' worth of financial and material resources for the Afghan jihad and facilitated travel to Afghanistan for many recruits through the safe house Beit al-Ansar and into Afghanistan. MAK also established the Khaldan training complex in the Khost province of Afghanistan.[70] However, in 1985 bin Laden ventured into Afghanistan for the first time to fight the Soviet Union and the forces of the Afghan communists. The year after, he formed his own Arab unit and training camp (Masada or Lions' Den) at Jaji in Afghanistan. This created a rift between bin Laden and Azzam, who did not believe that foreigners should have their own units but instead chose to disperse them among the Afghan units. Azzam did not believe that the foreigners coming to Afghanistan should interfere in the Afghans' internal affairs. Azzam believed that Afghans' internal affairs should be left to the Afghans and that the foreigners should focus on uniting and supporting the Afghan fight against the Soviet Union. This rift increased as bin Laden came increasingly under the influence of members from the Salafi Egyptian group, al-Jihad. The Egyptians were very antagonistic toward some of the Afghan warlords, especially the Tajik warlord Ahmed Shah Massoud, who was admired and supported by Azzam and MAK.[71] Compounding these differences were allegations by bin Laden and his followers that MAK was being mismanaged. In August 1988, bin Laden and nine followers formed al Qaeda (The Base).

This organization was established on 18 August 1988, during a meeting in bin Laden's house in Peshawar. During this meeting, a nine-member Majlis al-Shura (Advisory Council) was also formed.[72] According to a summary of the meeting, as reproduced in Peter Bergen's book, *The Osama Bin Laden I Know*, the goal of this organization was to "lift the word of God, to make His religion victorious."[73] After Soviet military forces left Afghanistan in February 1989, bin Laden returned to Saudi Arabia in November 1989. However, with the introduction of Western, and especially military forces from the United States to Saudi Arabia, and after the Iraqi invasion of Kuwait in 1990, bin Laden became increasingly opposed to this presence of Western military forces and the regime, which was responsible for inviting them. After voicing his opinions, the House of Saud removed bin Laden's passport, effectively barring him from traveling abroad. However, in early 1991, bin Laden managed to convince members of the royal family that he had to go to Pakistan to liquidate his investments there and then return to Saudi Arabia. The Saudi authorities subsequently issued bin Laden a temporary passport, with which he could travel to Pakistan and return to Saudi Arabia.[74] However, instead of returning to Saudi Arabia, bin Laden stayed in the Afghanistan–Pakistan area. After witnessing the warlords fighting and squabbling over power in Afghanistan, bin Laden, in early 1992, decided to leave for the Sudan. In the Sudan, he established several businesses and training camps at farms in Damazine, near the Ethiopian border, and at Sobhi, near the capital.[75]

In 1994, the Saudi authorities revoked bin Laden's citizenship, and since then the Saudi government has refused to recognize bin Laden as a Saudi citizen. In 1994, bin Laden survived an assassination attempt by the group Takfir wal Hijra (Excommunication and Withdrawal), which judged him to be a heretic because of his theological and ideological views. In 1996, the Sudanese government was forced through international pressure to evict bin Laden. In May 1996 he traveled on a private plane to Afghanistan, where he was hosted by the late leader of the Hizb e-Islami Yunus Khalis faction, Maulavi Muhammad Yunus Khalis, in the mountains near Tora Bora in Nangarhar province. Here bin Laden would frequently host various members of the international press.[76] His other main base was in Khost, where al Qaeda's training complex, encompassing the al-Faruq, Khalid bin Walid, Jihad Wal, and Abu Bakr al-Saddiq camps, was hosted by the Afghan warlord, Jalaluddin Haqqani, since the 1980s. In mid-1996, bin Laden's headquarters in Nangarhar province came under the control of the advancing Taliban, but after a negotiation process, of which very little is known, his presence was accepted by the Afghan Taliban regime (1996–2001).[77] In August 1996, bin Laden announced his first declaration of war against the

United States and Israel and declared a boycott of US products.[78] In 1997, he was asked by the Taliban's supreme leader, Mullah Muhammad Umar, to move from Nangarhar to the Taliban's stronghold and headquarters in Kandahar. The motivations behind Umar's request are unclear. The reasons vary, ranging from Umar's desire to increase control over bin Laden's activities to increasing his safety after the assassination plans were uncovered.[79] Osama bin Laden followed Umar's wishes but did not move into the city of Kandahar, preferring instead to stay at the Tarnak Farm's housing complex, close to Kandahar airport. In February 1998, bin Laden and four other members and leaders of various Islamic militant groups signed a statement signifying the formation of the "World Islamic Front for the Jihad against Jews and Crusaders."[80] In this statement, they declared that killing Americans and their allies was Fard al-Ayn (a compulsory duty upon all Muslims) to liberate al-Aqsa Mosque in Jerusalem and the Kaabah in Mecca from crusader occupation.[81]

These statements were followed by a press conference in May 1998 at al Qaeda's training complex in Khost, where bin Laden formally declared the formation of the "International front to do jihad against the Crusaders and the Jews."[82] In August 1998, al Qaeda conducted simultaneous attacks against the US embassies in Dar es-Salam, Tanzania, and Nairobi, Kenya. Immediately following these attacks, US armed forces executed cruise missile attacks against an alleged chemical plant in the Sudan and al Qaeda's training camps in Khost, Afghanistan. After the attacks, efforts by the moderate factions of the Taliban increased pressure to hand over bin Laden, but according to the former head of the Saudi security service (Mabahith), Prince Turki al-Faisal, Mullah Umar only hardened against any plans to hand over bin Laden. Al Qaeda rebuilt its al-Faruq camp, which was destroyed in the US cruise missile attack, in an old copper mine near Kabul, located in Mes Aynak, within Logar province. However, this was a small camp, not able to support more than twenty trainees at a time, and it was often on the front lines between the Taliban and the Northern Alliance. In 1999, bin Laden was ordered to refrain from giving interviews to the press by Mullah Umar because it was creating trouble for the Taliban regime.[83] Although bin Laden did abide by this order, he did not follow the spirit of the order from the Taliban. Instead, al Qaeda created their own media company, al-Sahab (The Clouds), which produced al Qaeda's own films, which were then distributed to the press.[84] In 1999, bin Laden was convinced by Khalid Sheikh Muhammad, who would later mastermind the attacks in New York and Washington on 9/11, to train militants in the use of civilian airliners in operations against targets in the United States.[85] In 2000, after strengthening his relationship with Taliban leaders, Mullah Umar, bin Laden, and al Qaeda opened a larger al-Faruq camp in the immediate vicinity of his living quarters at Tarnak Farms.[86] In 2000, al Qaeda attacked the US naval destroyer, the USS *Cole*, in Aden harbor in Yemen. This successful attack followed the previous failed attempt against the USS *The Sullivans*. These al Qaeda attacks came after bin Laden had changed his initial order, given in 1998, to attack an oil tanker in favor of a US military ship.[87] Immediately before the attacks in the United States on 9/11, al Qaeda merged with the Egyptian al-Jihad group. After the merger, which took place in June of 2001, al Qaeda changed their name to Jama'at al Qaeda al-Jihad (The Base and Jihad Group) or Tanzim al Qaeda al-Jihad (The Base and Jihad Organization).[88] Ayman al-Zawahiri, who was also a signatory to the 1998 statement announcing the creation of the Islamic Front for Jihad against Jews and Crusaders, had already joined al Qaeda in 1998.[89] Al-Jihad's merger with al Qaeda occurred after al-Zawahiri was reelected as the leader of al-Jihad.

After the 9/11 attacks in the United States, the Taliban and al Qaeda were routed from the battlefield and subsequently retreated toward the Pakistani border. There was substantial reporting by individuals who were on the ground at Tora Bora, including Gary Berntsen, who led a CIA team in the Nangarhar province during November and December of 2001, suggesting that bin Laden had escaped into the mountains around Tora Bora.[90] According to Ron Suskind's book, *The One Percent Doctrine*, on December 15, 2001, bin Laden was overheard speaking on a handheld radio at Tora Bora as follows: He praised his "most loyal fighters,"[91] and asked for forgiveness for drawing them into a defeat, decrying that he had led his Mujahideen into the catastrophe they were facing. However, despite being heavily bombarded and driven out of the main Milawa camp, bin Laden managed to escape. According to Ron Suskind, quoting internal CIA reports, bin Laden took the northern route, "past the Khyber Pass—and into the province of Konar."[92] In a television interview with Pakistani television channel Geo-TV, which was broadcast in January 2007, Gulbuddin Hekmatyar claimed that he had ordered his men to assist bin Laden with his escape. While this is likely the case, we also believe that bin Laden's initial host in Afghanistan, Maulavi Muhammad Yunus Khalis, provided assistance for his escape.[93]

After that, information about bin Laden's movements was not clear.[94] According to the Abbottabad Commission Report, after the US invasion of Afghanistan bin Laden moved to the Waziristan region of the FATA, near the Pakistan–Afghanistan border. From there, he moved to the Shangla district of northwestern Khyber Pakhtunkhwa (KP) province. He stayed in Shangla for about eight months with his family. Then he moved, along with his two Pashtun bodyguards, to the Haripur district, where he lived for around two years. Ultimately, he settled in Abbottabad. Until his assassination[95] in Abbottabad, he remained in contact with other leaders in the al Qaeda organization and the Taliban. He used these contacts to issue strategic guidance and directives to instigate new policies, such as his order for al Qaeda to commence attacks against targets in Saudi Arabia and his cease-fire offer to the Europeans in 2004. This included his policy of mergers, which started with the merger of Ahmed Fadil Nazzal al-Khalaylah's group, Jama'at Tawhid wal Jihad, in October 2004. The mergers increased during 2006, with the merger of factions of the Egyptian Gama'at al-Islamiyah and the militant Algerian group, Groupe Salafiste pour la Prédication et le Combat (GSPC). Osama bin Laden's last speech was an audiotape aired on Al-Jazeera in April 2006.[96]

Dr. Ayman al-Zawahiri

After Osama bin Laden's death, his deputy Dr. Ayman al-Zawahiri became the patron in chief and head of al Qaeda. Zawahiri was born on June 9, 1951, in the Cairo suburb of Maadi, into an aristocratic family. He joined the Faculty of Medicine at Cairo University in the academic year 1968–1969. He graduated in 1974, receiving his bachelor's degree with the mark of Jayyid Jidan (Very Good). He received his master's degree in surgery, completing it in 1978.[97] On 23 October 1981, Zawahiri was arrested as a suspect in the assassination of former Egyptian President Anwar Sadat. He was jailed for three years before managing to escape to Saudi Arabia in 1985. In 1987, Zawahiri moved to Peshawar, the provincial capital of Khyber Pakhtunkhwa province of Pakistan, where he started reassembling his al-Jihad group.[98] He also struck up a close friendship with Muhammad Atef aka Abu Hafs al-Masri and Ali al-Rashidi aka Abu Ubaydah al-Banshiri, both of whom would later be founding members of al Qaeda.[99]

However, numerous disagreements inside al-Jihad, including disputes over Zawahiri's close relations with al Qaeda's more international agenda (versus al-Jihad's initial Egypt-centric agenda), eventually fractured al-Jihad. Examples of factions that broke away from Zawahiri's line were the leader of al-Jihad in Egypt, Nabil Naim, who declared a unilateral cease-fire in Egypt in 1995, and Ahmed Husayn Agiza, who broke with al-Jihad and founded Tala'i al-Fatah (Vanguards of Conquest) in the early 1990s.[100] However, Agiza's organization was hit hard in its infancy by arrests in Egypt. Both the remnants of al-Jihad and the Vanguards of Conquest were also hit extremely hard by the arrests preceding the "Returnees from Albania" case in 1999, in which Zawahiri was also sentenced to death in absentia.[101] The case was named after a number of al-Jihad members who were returned to Egypt by the local authorities in Albania after they were arrested there. Zawahiri's brother, Muhammad Rabie, was also a high-ranking member of al-Jihad and managed to escape the Albanian dragnet.[102] He was later caught in the United Arab Emirates and extradited to Egypt in 1999.[103]

In June 1999, Zawahiri was ousted as the leader of al-Jihad because of a lack of support among al-Jihad's members and because of his entry into the World Islamic Front for Jihad against Jews and Crusaders in February 1998. He was replaced by his lieutenant, Tharwat Shehata, who continued to focus the group on overthrowing Egyptian President Hosni Mubarak and the Egyptian government.[104] Immediately prior to his ousting from al-Jihad, Zawahiri formally joined al Qaeda, under the leadership of Osama bin Laden. After joining al Qaeda, Zawahiri and al Qaeda's military commander Abu Hafs started developing a biological and chemical warfare program,[105] referred to as the Yoghurt project and run under the direct supervision of Zawahiri. It also involved Midhat Mursi, aka Abu Khabbab, who had been running al-Jihad's chemical warfare program since 1995.[106] Part of this effort involved attempts to obtain and develop a virulent strain of anthrax, as well as creating an anthrax laboratory in Kandahar, Afghanistan.

Zawahiri initially chose a Pakistani microbiologist, Abdur Rauf, to develop these weapons. Rauf traveled widely in the West and managed to buy the necessary laboratory equipment, which was shipped to Kandahar. However, when he was scheduled to move to Kandahar, he decided to abandon his work with al Qaeda. During his time as the operational leader of al Qaeda's anthrax efforts, Rauf managed, in 1999, to purchase a virulent strain of anthrax.[107] In 2001, his work was transferred to a Malaysian, Yazid Sufaat, who was initially a member of the militant Malaysian group known as Kumpulan Mujahidin Malaysia before being recruited into al Qaeda by Riduan Isamuddin, aka Hambali. Sufaat had a bachelor's degree from the University of California, where he majored in clinical laboratory technology and minored in chemistry.[108] Soon after he had started work in Kandahar, the Taliban regime fell, and Sufaat escaped into Pakistan. From there he moved to Malaysia, where he was arrested upon arrival at Kuala Lumpur.[109] Throughout the period from 1999 until the fall of the Taliban in 2001, Zawahiri and Abu Hafs al-Masri oversaw the Yoghurt project. After the detention of Sufaat and the death of Abu Hafs al-Masri in November 2001, Khalid Sheikh Muhammad, Jama'at al Qaeda al-Jihad's head of external operations, took control of the anthrax program until he was detained in March 2003.[110]

Before the attacks in the United States on 9/11, Zawahiri had successfully convinced al-Jihad to merge with al Qaeda. Although successful in this endeavor, the merger between al Qaeda and al-Jihad is still a divisive issue, especially among former al-Jihad members. The merger took place in June 2001, and al Qaeda thereafter became known as Jama'at al Qaeda al-Jihad.[111] After the attacks in the United States on 9/11 and during the subsequent US and Northern Alliance military campaigns in Afghanistan, Zawahiri lost his wife and two girls and a boy during a US bombing raid on his house, located in the Tora Bora area.[112] Although he has since remarried, this loss remains an open wound for him.

After becoming the head of al Qaeda, Zawahiri appeared in several Internet video messages, speeches, and sermons. In his videos and audiotapes, he urges Muslims to join the jihad against the United States and its allies. Very little is known about his current whereabouts. Several reports suggest that he resides in the Bajaur Agency, inside the FATA, near the Afghanistan–Pakistan border area. An unmanned US Predator drone targeted a seminary in Damadola town of Bajaur in Janaury 2006, where Zawahiri was believed to be hiding. However, Zawahiri had left the seminary fifteen minutes before the strike.[113] He is also reported to have been a frequent visitor to the madrassa (Koranic School) in Chingai in the Bajaur Agency, which was attacked by Pakistani attack helicopters in October 2006.[114] Chingai and Damadola are within 1.5 miles of each other, and both are situated in the areas of the Bajaur Agency, inhabited by members of the Mahmund tribe. Among his closest allies are leading members of the militant Deobandi movement, Tehrik Nifaz Shariat Muhammadi (TNSM), which mobilized ten thousand members to fight with the Taliban against US forces in Afghanistan in 2001. This includes Maulana Faqir Muhammad, who leads TNSM, and Liaquat Hussein, who ran the Ziaul Uloom Taleemul Quran seminary in Chingai, located in the Bajaur Agency, until his death in October 2006, when his madrassa was attacked by Pakistani helicopters.[115] The US State Department has offered a $25 million reward for any information leading to the capture of Zawahiri.

Muhammad Atef

Among the leaders killed by the United States in Afghanistan was the head of Jama'at al Qaeda al-Jihad's Military Committee, Mohammed Atef. He was killed by a US Hellfire attack in Kandahar on 14 November 2001. A former police officer in Egypt, Atef joined the Mujahideen fighting the Soviet and Afghan communist forces in Afghanistan. In 1988, he became one of the early members of al Qaeda.[116] After the death of one of the founding members of al Qaeda and the first leader of the Military Committee, Ali al-Rashidi aka Abu Ubaydah al-Masri, in Uganda in April 1996, Muhammad Atef assumed this command. He was subsequently involved in the planning of all al Qaeda operations from 1996 until 2001, including the bombings of the US embassies in East Africa, the USS *Cole* attack, and the 9/11 attacks in the United States. He was al Qaeda's member who had overall responsibility for the operations of al Qaeda's 055 Brigade, which fought with the Taliban against the Northern Alliance, and ran al Qaeda's training camps, its nuclear program, and Osama bin Laden's security detail. However, most of these tasks were delegated to commanders or subsection commanders, who administered these programs and units on a daily basis.

Khalid Sheikh Muhammad (KSM)

Following Atef's death, Sayf al-Adel became the head of the al Qaeda's Military Committee. Sayf al-Adel headed al Qaeda's Security Committee and was Atef's deputy. However, he refused to return to Pakistan from Iran, citing security concerns, and Osama bin Laden and Ayman al-Zawahiri wanted their military/operations commander within their reach. Therefore, they appointed the Kuwaiti-born Pakistani, Khalid Sheikh Muhammad (KSM), aka Mukht (The Brain) and Muktar (The Chosen One), to head al Qaeda's operations outside the Pakistan–Afghanistan area. KSM attained huge prestige within al Qaeda for planning the Ghazwah Manhattan (The Manhattan Raid) in the United States. However, before appointing KSM, bin Laden had divided al Qaeda's operational structure into two parts: external and internal operations. The head of external operations was tasked to conduct attacks outside the Afghanistan–Pakistan area, which became the domain of the head of internal operations. KSM was appointed to head Jama'at al Qaeda al-Jihad's external operations, while Mistafa al-Uzayti Abu Faraj al-Libi assumed leadership of internal operations.[117] As head of external operations, KSM financed and planned numerous executed and foiled attacks across the globe.[118] Before assuming command of al Qaeda's external operations, KSM headed the group's Media Committee, which he assumed command of in 2000. He also led the Bait al-Shuhadah (Home of Martyrs) after it had moved to Kandahar in 2000.[119] Before joining al Qaeda in 2000, KSM had worked independently. During the early and mid-1990s, he worked with his nephew, Ramzi Ahmed Yousef, in the Philippines, targeting the pope and eleven US airliners in planned, but foiled, attacks.[120] KSM was arrested in Rawalpindi, Pakistan, in March 2003 and was initially moved to a secret CIA detention facility before being transferred to a US detention facility, known as Camp X-Ray, in September 2006.[121]

Abu Faraj Al-Libi

Mustafa al-Uzayti, aka Abu Faraj Al-Liby, is a Libyan who also operated under the names of Dr. Ibrahim and Dr. Tafeeq. He headed al Qaeda's internal operations from 2002 until he was captured in May 2005. He became the third-highest-ranking al Qaeda member after the capture of KSM in March 2003.[122] According to the Office of the Director of National Intelligence in the United States, Abu Faraj was a communications conduit for al Qaeda managers to bin Laden from August 2003 until his capture in 2005. He was the recipient of couriered messages and public statements from bin Laden and passed messages to bin Laden from both senior lieutenants and rank-and-file members. Some of his work almost certainly required personal meetings with bin Laden or Zawahiri, a privilege reserved since 2002 for select members of the group.[123]

Abu Faraj al-Libi also commanded al Qaeda's forces in Afghanistan, where they fought under the overall command of Afghan Taliban leader, Mullah Muhammad Umar. According to the information presented by the prosecution against Abu Faraj at an enemy-combatant hearing in Guantanamo, Abu Faraj's duties included "[v]etting and transporting al Qaeda fighters to Afghanistan. Individuals wanting to fight in Afghanistan were required to be sponsored by an al Qaeda member and be interviewed by the detainee [Abu Faraj al-Libi] to verify their bona fides."[124]

However, Abu Faraj al-Libi's primary job was to take care of al Qaeda's families in Pakistan, who could not be supported by their male patrons. In addition to these duties, Abu Faraj al-Libi oversaw the assassination attempt against Pakistani President Pervez Musharraf. This double suicide attack against President Musharraf's motorcade on 25 December 2003 was ordered by Abu Faraj al-Libi but was planned and executed by members from the Pakistani groups Jamiat ul-Furqan, Harakat ul-Jihad ul-Islami, and Jamiat ul-Ansar. The groups were under the leadership of Abu Faraj al-Libi's Pakistani lieutenant, Amjad Faruqi, who was killed in September 2004 inside Pakistan.[125] Besides being close to KSM, Abu Faraj al-Libi also had frequent meetings with KSM's successor, Hamza Rabia. According to information published by the Office of the Director of National Intelligence in the United States, "Abu Faraj searched for operatives on Rabi'a's behalf, including those who could travel to the United States for attacks, and he also asked now-deceased al-Qa'ida in Iraq leader Abu Mu'sab al-Zarqawi to target US interests outside of Iraq."[126] The prosecution in Guantanamo supplied further information on Abu Faraj's relations with Abu Musab al-Zarqawi, stating that "[i]n September 2004, several members of al Qaeda involved in terrorist operations, including the detainee met in Syria to discuss a variety of terrorist operations, including planned operations in the United States, Europe and Australia."[127]

During the 1980s, Abu Faraj al-Libi fought against the Soviet and Afghan communist forces in Afghanistan. During the 1990s, he trained at al Qaeda's Muaskar al-Badr (Badr training camp) complex in Khost (destroyed by US cruise missiles in August 1998), where he taught orientation and map reading.[128] Abu Faraj al-Libi later helped rebuild the al-Faruq camp in Mes Aynak near Kabul. He also provided training in the camp and administered the Bait al-Shuhadah while it was situated near Kabul.[129]

Abdul Hadi Al-Iraqi

After the arrest of Abu Faraj al-Libi in May 2005, the Egyptians Hamza Rabia and Abu Abd-al Rahman al-Muhajir assumed roles as numbers three and four in the organization. However, after the death of Hamza Rabia in December 2005, his post as head of external operations was assumed by Nashwan Abdulrazaq Abdulbaqi, aka Abd al-Hadi al-Iraqi.[130] Abd al-Hadi is a former officer in Saddam Hussein's army who left his Baathist leanings and joined the Mujahideen who were fighting the Soviet army in Afghanistan during the late 1980s. During the 1990s, he rose inside al Qaeda's hierarchy and later became head of al Qaeda's military forces in Kabul and a member of al Qaeda's ruling Majlis al-Shurra.[131] Abd al-Hadi and Ammar al-Ruqa'i, aka Abu Layth al-Libi, worked mainly from bases in the Shakai Valley in the South Waziristan Agency and from Sedgi and the Shawal Valley in the North Waziristan Agency of Pakistan's FATA.[132] al Qaeda's operations in Afghanistan were conducted under the overall leadership of Taliban leader Mullah Muhammad Umar. Abd al-Hadi conducted attacks in southeastern Afghanistan, and Abu Layth al-Libi commanded al Qaeda's operations in southwestern Afghanistan.

Information on the presence of al Qaeda's leaders in the FATA, and specifically Abd al-Hadi al-Iraqi's presence in Waziristan during 2002–2004, derives from the findings of the British Security Service investigation called "Operation Crevice." Operation Crevice investigated a group of mainly British citizens of Pakistani origin. Eight individuals from the Operation Crevice group were arrested in March 2004, suspected of planning attacks in the United Kingdom.[133] Several of those involved in the group traveled to Pakistan during June 2003, where the Pakistani American, Muhammad Junaid Babar, from New York, arranged a three-week training course in the Upper Dir district of Pakistan's Malakand Division, located in the North West Frontier Province.[134] The group's members trained on small arms and on making IEDs from aluminum powder and ammonium nitrate and aluminuim.[135] After finishing the training, some of the group's members traveled with Muhammad Junaid Babar to meet Abd al-Hadi al-Iraqi and one of Abd al-Hadi's lieutenants, Abu Munthir al-Maghrebi, in South Waziristan. During the trip, they visited both the Shakai Valley and the town of Angor Adda, which is situated sixty kilometers west of Wana, South Waziristan's main town.[136]

In August 2004, Abd al-Hadi al-Iraqi was removed from his position as leader of al Qaeda's operations in Afghanistan. Abd al-Hadi is a brilliant military commander, but we believe his personality is very rough. He was often at odds with other senior commanders in al Qaeda. However, his very direct and candid nature also made him a natural choice when al Qaeda was negotiating with the leaders of other militant groups who had similar personalities. After the US invasion of Iraq in March 2003, Abd al-Hadi acted as a conduit between Osama bin Laden and Ahmed Fadil Nazzal al-Khalayleh, aka Abu Musab al-Zarqawi, the leader of the Jamiat Tawhid wal Jihad (which would later become Tanzim Qaedat fi Bilad al-Rafidayn, or The al Qaeda Organization in the Land of the Two Rivers/al Qaeda in Iraq).[137] Abd-al Hadi was essentially a broker in bringing Osama bin Laden and al-Zarqawi into the agreement, which served as the basis for bringing Abu Musab's organization into al Qaeda.[138] We believe that during 2005, Abd-al Hadi al-Iraqi was intent on returning to his native country and serving with Abu

Musab. However, because of his knowledge about the disapproval of his actions among al Qaeda's leadership in Pakistan, Abu Musab thought that Hadi al-Iraqi was replacing him, and he subsequently refused to assist with his entry into Iraq. In Abd al-Hadi's absence, Osama bin Laden appointed the Egyptian, Khalid Habib, as al-Iraqi's replacement. Khalid Habib was a very able commander and a close friend of both Hamza Rabia and al-Zawahiri, but we believe he is more introverted than Abd al-Hadi and a much less inspiring military commander. When Abd al-Hadi returned to northern Waziristan, we assessed that al Qaeda's leadership decided that his military skills were too important to leave unused and therefore decided to reappoint him as the commander of al Qaeda's operations in southwestern Afghanistan, while Khalid Habib remained in overall command of operations in Afghanistan and regionally focused in southeastern Afghanistan.[139]

In August 2006, Abd al-Hadi was described as al Qaeda's number three by the *New York Times*, and we believe that he and Abu Ubayda al-Masri planned the previously described "Liquid/Airline Plot," which was foiled in the United Kingdom in August 2006.[140] In April 2007, a leading British investigator stated that Abd al-Hadi al-Iraqi was the one who had retasked the 7 July 2005 bombers, Muhammad Sadiqque Khan and Sheezad Tanvir, to execute suicide attacks in the United Kingdom.[141] This retasking was likely to have taken place during Saddique Khan and Sheezad Tanwir's visit to Pakistan from November 2004 until February 2005. This could indeed be a likely scenario, as Saddique Khan could have known Abd al-Hadi al-Iraq from his visit to Pakistan, with Umar Khayam and Muhammad Junaid Babar in 2003, but it is still odd that Abd al-Hadi would assume this role at a time when he was not head of external operations.

In April 2007, US authorities announced that they detained Abd al-Hadi and that he was moving to the US detention facility at Guantanamo Bay in Cuba. Abd al-Hadi al-Iraqi was captured in late 2006 while traveling to Iraq, where he was serving in al Qaeda's local branch.[142] Abd-al-Hadi was likely replaced by one of the Egyptians, Abu Ubayda al-Masri, Khalid Habib, or the Gulf Arab Hamza al-Jawfi, as head of al Qaeda's external operations.

Abu Yahya Al-Libi

Abu Yahaya Al-Libi took over as the number two leader in al Qaeda after the former number two, Atiya Abdul Rehman, was killed in a US drone strike in the Northern Waziristan Agency of the FATA on 10 December 2012.[143] He was the deputy of Ayman al-Zawahiri. On 4 June 2012, Abu Yahya al-Libi, al Qaeda's second in command and top religious ideologue, was killed in a US drone strike in Hassu Khel village, situated in the Mirali area of the North Waziristan Agency of Pakistan. Al-Libi was critically injured and died at a local private hospital.

He played a critical role in the group's planning against the West by providing oversight for the efforts of external operations. He was a key link between al Qaeda and its regional affiliates, including the dreaded al Qaeda in the Arabian Peninsula. Al-Libi's religious credentials gave him the authority to issue fatwas (religious edicts), operational approvals, and guidance to the core group in Pakistan and al Qaeda's regional affiliates.

He also served as al Qaeda's "general manager," overseeing operations in Pakistan's tribal belt, and he was responsible for liaising with the other militant groups in the area. He effectively utilized his prolific video messages and writings. Among the contemporary global jihadists, al-Libi was the most vocal and visible among all the jihadi groups worldwide.

Al-Libi, whose real name is Mohamed Hassan Qaid, was reportedly born in 1963. He made numerous appearances in al Qaeda propaganda videos and became a key target for Western intelligence services after the death of Osama bin Laden. He rose in al Qaeda's ranks after his successful escape in 2005 from Bagram Airfield in Afghanistan after three years of imprisonment.[144]

In the late 1980s or early 1990s, al-Libi fought against Soviet forces, which occupied Afghanistan for a decade, and became part of the Libyan Islamic Fighting Group. Al-Libi was a key motivator in the global jihadi movement. He was an Islamic scholar who used his religious training to influence people and legitimize the actions of al Qaeda. The US State Department placed a bounty on his head of $1 million.

Atiya Abd al-Rahman

Atiya Abd al-Rahman was killed in a US drone strike in the North Waziristan Agency of the FATA on 22 August 2011, delivering another big blow to a terrorist group that the United States believes to be on the verge of defeat. He became al Qaeda's number two leader under Ayman al-Zawahiri, who succeeded bin Laden. He also used the name Abu Zaid al-Kuwaiti.[145]

Atiyah, whose real name is Jamal Ibrahim Ashtiwi al Misrati, also uses the name Atiyah Allah. He was a senior leader for the Libyan Islamic Fighting Group before rising to the top ranks of al Qaeda's leadership. Atiyah was described as al Qaeda's "operations chief" and second in command in most press reports, where his role in plotting terrorist attacks has been repeatedly noted. Nonetheless, according to one senior US intelligence official contacted by the *Long War Journal*, Atiyah was al Qaeda's "general manager," and also served as Osama bin Laden's "chief of staff."[146]

He joined al Qaeda in the early 1990s and fought in Afghanistan. In 1993, he moved to Algeria to serve as a liaison between al Qaeda and Algerian radicals fighting a civil war against the military government located there. Instead of welcoming him, an Algerian rebel network, known as the Armed

Islamic Group (GIA), placed Rahman under detention and threatened to execute him for reasons that remain unclear. He and a handful of other Libyan prisoners escaped after five months and subsequently fled the country.[147]

A Libyan national, al-Rahman never had the worldwide name recognition of bin Laden or bin Laden's successor, Ayman al-Zawahiri. Al-Rahman was an instrumental figure in the terrorist organization and was trusted by bin Laden to oversee al Qaeda's daily operations. When the US Navy SEALs raided bin Laden's compound, they found evidence of al-Rahman's deep involvement in running al Qaeda.[148]

He eventually returned to Afghanistan and fell under al Qaeda's influence. He assumed a leadership role after the 9/11 hijackings. In addition to serving as the primary liaison to al Qaeda's organization in Iraq and network in Iran, he returned to Algeria and tried to bolster al Qaeda's presence there. He was successful, brokering a partnership between al Qaeda and the Salafist Group for Preaching and Combat—a successor organization to the faction that threatened to kill al-Rahman a decade earlier. In September 2006, al Qaeda announced a formal alliance with the Algerian Salafist group. In January, the Algerian network changed its name to al Qaeda in the Islamic Maghreb.[149]

Born in Libya, al-Rahman joined bin Laden as a teenager in Afghanistan to fight the Soviet Union. He once served as bin Laden's personal emissary to Iran. Al-Rahman moved freely in and out of Iran as part of that arrangement and operated out of Waziristan for some time according to official accounts.

He was the head of al Qaeda's religious affairs wing. He was also in frequent contact with bin Laden in the months prior to his death in Abbottabad, Pakistan. Thousands of electronic files recovered at bin Laden's compound revealed that bin Laden had communicated frequently with al-Rahman. They also indicated that bin Laden had relied on al-Rahman to get messages to other al Qaeda leaders and to ensure that bin Laden's recorded communications were broadcast widely.[150]

The files captured in Abbottabad revealed that bin Laden and al-Rahman had discussed brokering a deal with Pakistan: al Qaeda offered to refrain from mounting attacks in the country in exchange for protection for al Qaeda leaders hiding in Pakistan.[151] Al-Rahman also served as bin Laden's liaison to al Qaeda's affiliates. In 2010, according to US officials, al-Rahman notified bin Laden of a request by the leader of al Qaeda's affiliate in Yemen to install Anwar al-Awlaki, the radical American-born cleric, as the leader of the group in Yemen.[152]

Mustafa Abu Yazid

Mustafa Abu Yazid became al Qaeda's number three leader after the death of Osama bin Laden, in addition to the head of al Qaeda in Afghanistan. He died after a US drone strike on 1 June 2010, in North Waziristan Agency.[153] Aged 51, Yazid was part of the Egyptian contingent that dominated al Qaeda's leadership since the network's founding. He served time in prison in the early 1980s with the current al Qaeda chief, Ayman al-Zawahiri, for their role as conspirators in the 1981 assassination of Egyptian President Anwar Sadat. The September 11th Commission identified Yazid as al Qaeda's "chief financial manager" and said he had opposed the 9/11 hijackings "because he feared the US response to an attack."

Mustafa Abu Yazid, also known as Sheikh Saeed, was an original member of al Qaeda's Shura leadership council and a trusted adviser to bin Laden for more than a decade. When bin Laden and al Qaeda's leadership were exiled from Pakistan to Sudan in the 1990s, Yazid served as the financial manager for some of bin Laden's business enterprises there.[154]

Yazid was also close to Taliban leader Mullah Omar, and he feared, correctly, that US retaliation would result in the Taliban's downfall according to Yasser al-Sirri, an Egyptian political exile who runs the Islamic Observatory Center for Human Rights in London. Yazid maintained his loyalty after the attacks and made a rare public appearance in May, when al Qaeda released an Internet video that named him as the network's commander in charge of operations in Afghanistan. Security analysts said he continued to lead al Qaeda's global fund-raising efforts. Sirri described Yazid as an amiable personality who was popular among al Qaeda's core command. This stands in stark contrast to Zawahiri, who is a more polarizing figure. His public appointment by al Qaeda is likely a sign that he has taken on a greater role as the liaison to other militant networks, such as the Taliban and the Islamic Movement of Uzbekistan, both of which are active along the Afghanistan–Pakistan border.[155]

Ilyas Kashmiri

Ilyas Kashmiri died as the result of a US drone strike near the South Waziristan Agency on 5 June 2011. He was commander in chief of al Qaeda's global operations, whereas others say he was chief of al Qaeda's military wing.[156] Kashmiri used to provide logistical support to al Qaeda and coordinated attacks against Pakistani installations, including a strike against the Pakistani ISI in 2009. He spearheaded efforts for the string of high-profile attacks against Western targets, as well as attacks inside Pakistan and India. He carried a bounty of 50 million rupees for his capture and was an active member of Harkat-ul-Jihad-e-Islami before forming his 313 Brigade.[157]

Kashmiri's death was a huge loss for the militants fighting against foreign forces in Afghanistan.[158]

Ilyas completed the first year of a mass communications degree at Allama Iqbal Open University, Islamabad. He did not continue because of his heavy involvement in jihad activities. Afghan jihad was his first exposure to armed jihad. He was an expert on the mines supplied to the Afghan Mujahedeen by the United States. He lost one eye during the jihad against Russian invaders.[159] Kashmiri was based in the Miramshah area of North Waziristan, where he was working as an instructor at a training camp. In 1994, Kashmiri launched the al-Hadid operation in the Indian capital, New Delhi, to get some of his jihadi comrades released. His group of twenty-five people included Sheikh Omar Saeed, the abductor of US reporter Daniel Pearl in Karachi in 2002, who served as his deputy. The group abducted several foreigners including American, Israeli, and British tourists and took them to Ghaziabad near Delhi. Then they demanded that the Indian authorities release their colleagues, but instead they attacked the hideout. Sheikh Omar was injured and arrested. (He was later released in a swap for the passengers of a hijacked Indian aircraft.) Kashmiri escaped unhurt. On 25 February 2000, the Indian army killed fourteen civilians in Lonjot village, located in Pakistan-administered Kashmir, after commandos crossed the Line of Control that separates the two Kashmirs. They returned to the Indian side with abducted Pakistani girls and threw the severed heads of three of them at the Pakistani soldiers. The next day, Kashmiri conducted a guerilla operation against the Indian army in the Nakyal sector, after crossing the Line of Control with twenty-five fighters from the 313 Brigade. They kidnapped an Indian army officer who was later beheaded, and his head was paraded in the bazaars of Kotli, back in Pakistani territory. Maulana Zahoor Ahmad Alvi, of Jamia Muhammadia, Islamabad, issued a fatwa in support of slitting the throats of Indian army officers. However, the most significant operation involving Kashmiri was in the Aknor cantonment, located in Indian-administered Kashmir. This was an attack against the Indian armed forces following the massacre of Muslims in the Indian city of Gujarat in 2002. Two generals were injured. Of note, the Pakistani army could not injure a single Indian general in three years of war. In addition, several brigadiers and colonels died. This was a significant setback for India in the long-running history of the Kashmiri insurgency.[160]

His outfit was banned by President Musharraf after 9/11. He was arrested after an assassination attempt against President Pervez Musharraf in December 2003. He was tortured during the interrogation.[161] The United Jihad Council, led by Syed Salahuddin, strongly protested the arrest of Kashmiri, and because of the pressure of Kashmiri militants, he was released in February 2004. He was a shattered man after his release. He disassociated himself from the Kashmiri militants and remained silent for at least three years. It was the Lal Masjid operation in July 2007 that totally transformed Kashmiri.

He moved to North Waziristan, where he spent many years as a jihad instructor. This area was full of his friends and sympathizers.[162] He reorganized his 313 Brigade and joined hands with the Taliban, but he was never close to al Qaeda's leadership. He attracted many former Pakistan army officers to join ranks with him. The strength of the 313 Brigade in North Waziristan was more than three thousand. Most of his fighters were hired from the Punjab, Sindh, and Azad Kashmir.

According to some unconfirmed media reports, Kashmiri was a former Special Services Group (SSG) commando from the Pakistan army.[163] However, such claims have been refuted by former SSG commandos and the journalists who interviewed Kashmiri.[164] Kashmiri is ranked fourth on the Pakistan Ministry of Interior's most-wanted list. His foremost attachment remained with the Indian-held Kashmir (IHK), probably because he is a Kashmiri and he has spent most of his time fighting against the Indian forces in the IHK.

Kashmiri believed in waging jihad against non-Muslims who occupied Islamic countries or Muslim lands. He wanted enforcement of shariah law in the Muslim world because he believed that all the ills of society could be overcome by enforcing Islamic law. He stood against the Pakistani government, which he believed was selling out the cause of the Kashmiri struggle by negotiating with the Indian government, thereby restraining jihad in Kashmir and working to strike a deal with India over Kashmir.

Kashmiri was a veteran of the Kashmir jihad and had spent several years in an Indian jail. He was arrested by the Pakistani authorities after the December 2003 twin suicide attacks on General Musharraf's presidential cavalcade in Rawalpindi but was released later, in February 2004, because of a lack of evidence. However, according to Pakistani militant circles, Kashmiri was released upon the intervention of the United Jihad Council (UJC). It is alleged that he organized many terrorist attacks in various areas of Pakistan, including the assassination of Major General (Retired) Faisal Alvi in Rawalpindi. Alvi was also from the Pakistan army's SSG, and he led the first-ever army operation in North Waziristan in 2004. Kashmiri planned attacks on Alvi, after demands by the Taliban in North Waziristan.[165]

In May 2009, Kashmiri was accused of plotting the assassination of Army Chief General Ashfaq Parvez Kayani, in collusion with al Qaeda, largely because of his lead role in the ongoing war against terrorism.[166] General Kayani's daily visits to a gymnasium were reportedly tracked by an al Qaeda cell in Pakistan, and it was decided that he would be targeted by a suicide bomber as soon as he would step out of his car. However, the plan did not materialize after it was leaked to the intelligence agencies.[167]

Ustad Ahmed Farooq

Farooq was an important member of a homegrown terrorist cell in the United States that traveled to Pakistan to receive training to fight against coalition forces in Afghanistan. Farooq, an accounting student at George Mason University, was born in Sargodha. His parents, Khalid and Sabria, owned a computer store in northern Virginia and had recently returned to Pakistan. His mother told reporters in Pakistan that she and her husband had come to the United States twenty years ago but that they had returned to Pakistan in September 2009 to start a computer business. Farooq's mother also rebuffed the allegations of her son's involvement with a terrorist cell. She told the media her son was in Pakistan to get married, not to plot terror attacks as Pakistani police alleged. She said her husband traveled with Farooq to arrange the marriage. Farooq's mother may be telling the truth from her perspective because she might not be aware that her son joined the homegrown radicals while working as a volunteer youth coordinator at the family's Alexandria, Virginia, mosque. Farooq might have misled his mother by telling her that he was traveling to Pakistan to marry a Pakistani girl. In fact, Farooq booked the room in Karachi's Saddam Hotel, where the radicals stayed on the night of 1 December 2009. Farooq used the cover story of getting married in Pakistan to hide his real intentions. This was the first of many steps taken to execute the attack.

The young men first tried to contact jihadist groups through Facebook and YouTube, and then traveled to Pakistan to attempt personal meetings. The group applied for travel visas in the week leading up to Thanksgiving. On their visa applications, the stated reasons for their travel were to attend a friend's marriage and to go sightseeing. They arrived in Pakistan on 30 November 2009 and traveled to Pakistan to join Islamist militants in the country's tribal area, prior to crossing into Afghanistan.

In Karachi, the group stayed in room number 207 of the Saddam Hotel, located on Iraq Road. The next day, the group members abandoned their luggage in the hotel room and made their way to the nearby city of Hyderabad, where they met with a member of the banned group Jaish-e-Muhammad and asked for training. They were turned away because they lacked references from trusted militants. After their rejection in Hyderabad, the next destination for the group was Lahore, where they met with representatives of a related group, Jamat-ud-Dawa, and asked to be recruited, trained, and sent on jihad. They were also rebuffed in Lahore.

Out of options, the men went to Sargodha, where they seemed to surprise Farooq's parents, who had traveled to their hometown to arrange a marriage between their son and his cousin, the daughter of Khalid Farooq's brother-in-law, Faheem. It was at Faheem's house, a government-owned bungalow that came with his job as a midranking employee in the local highway department, that the men were arrested. The home is next to a major air force base that was a target for extremists in the past. "They [Farooq's parents] came for the engagement, but the boys started talking about jihad. . . . He [Farooq] had something else on his mind, not a wedding," said a local resident, who knows the family well and spoke only on the condition of anonymity because of the sensitivity of the issue.

Although Farooq had intentions to carry out attacks against US forces in Afghanistan, he was apprehended before turning his plans into reality. During the initial investigation, the men claimed they had come to Pakistan because "they were about to look for a girl, to get married." However, they changed their position and proudly declared that they had come to Pakistan for jihad.

Farooq and four of his friends were arrested on 9 December 2009 in the city of Sarghoda, about 190 kilometers (120 miles) southeast of the capital, Islamabad. Pakistani authorities believe that Farooq, along with four of his American friends, tried to meet up with terror groups but were turned away. The men wanted to conduct jihad, or holy war, in northwestern Pakistan and against American troops in Afghanistan. According to Usman Anwar, the chief of police in the town of Sargodha, these five men were planning a big attack and were seeking a link to an ultra-radical jihad group, possibly al Qaeda. "It's above Jaish. It's something more serious than that," Anwar said in a telephone interview, referring to Jaish-e-Mohammad, the group that's been implicated in the 2002 murder of American journalist Daniel Pearl.

Badar Mansoor

On 9 February 2012, a US drone strike killed Badar Mansoor, a notorious militant commander, along with four other associates, in the Miramshah area of the North Waziristan Agency. The strike took place when Mansoor and others gathered at the hujra (Pushto for *guesthouse*) of Qari Imran at Zafar Colony market in Miramshah.[168] Besides Mansoor, others killed in the strike were identified as Qari Fayaz, Maulvi Faisal Khorsani, Qari Mushtaq, and Yasir Khorasani, who were some of the top commanders of the Badar Mansoor Group.[169] The wife and daughter of Mansoor were living in a nearby house and were also injured in the attack.

Badar Mansoor, whose real name was Fakher Zaman, was forty years old at the time of his death. He came into the limelight in 2008 after he joined the Taliban's struggle in Afghanistan and the FATA of Pakistan. He belonged to the Dera Ghazi Khan district of the Punjab province.[170] Mansoor was a former member of Harkat-ul-Mujahideen (HuM)—a Pakistani militant group that formed during the so-called Afghan jihad against the former Soviet Union in the 1980s. Later, the HuM also fought against Indian security forces in Indian-administered Jammu and Kashmir (J&K), and Mansoor took part in militant attacks. After the rise of the Taliban in Afghanistan in 1995, HuM also fought alongside the Taliban in Afghanistan against anti-Taliban forces comprising the Northern Alliance. While HuM remained involved in attacks against US and NATO forces and after the post-September 2001 overthrow of the Taliban regime, its involvement was limited and mainly confined to eastern Afghanistan.

In 2007, Mansoor split from the HuM in the aftermath of counterterrorism operations by Pakistani security forces against Lal Majsid in Islamabad in July 2007. He developed differences with HuM's head, Maulana Fazlur Rehman Khalil, when the latter distanced himself from the Lal Masjid clerics, Maulana Abdul Aziz and Abdul Rashid Ghazi, by refusing to support their cause against the government.[171] Subsequently, Mansoor established the Al-Badar[172] group, under the tutelage of the Haqqani Network and al Qaeda. He reportedly had two hundred militants under his command.[173] Most of his rank and file were non-Pushtun and came from the Punjab and Sindh provinces of Pakistan; hence he and his group came to be known as the Punjabi Taliban. Similarly, because ethnic identity plays an important role within the spectrum of militant landscapes in the FATA, his non-Pushtun associates used to refer to themselves as Khorasani(s)—a widely held Islamic belief centered on an Islamic army rising from Khorasan[174] and paving the way for the khilafat of Al-Mahdi (A.S.) by fighting the infidels, Zionists, and crusaders.

Mansoor's Al-Badar group established training camps and maintained presences in places in and around Miramshah, Boya, Datakhel, Mir Ali, Tapi, and other areas of the North Waziristan Agency.[175] Initially, the group mainly concentrated its fight in Afghanistan, and Mansoor sent fighters to Afghanistan after training them in the North Waziristan Agency.[176] Al-Badar also cooperated closely with the Haqqani Network and the North Waziristan Taliban, led by Hafiz Gul Bahadur. Subsequently, Badar Mansoor and militants belonging to Al-Badar's group were targeted by US drones. On 12 September 2008, a US drone attack killed twelve Al-Badar militants in Tol Khel village in the North Waziristan Agency.[177] On 3 October 2008, sixteen militants from Al-Badar's groups were killed in the North Waziristan Agency after a drone strike.[178] On 24 February 2010, Badar Mansoor was targeted in a drone strike in the Dargah Mandi area near Miramshah. Initial reports claimed that Mansoor, along with Qari Zafar and Rana Afzal, aka Noor Khan, of the sectarianist militant outfit Lashkar-e-Jhangvi (LeJ), were killed in the attack.[179] However, it seems that Mansoor survived the attack. Similarly, in another drone strike on 2 October 2010, nine militants of Al-Badar's group were killed in the Datta Khel area of the North Waziristan Agency.[180]

Sometime in 2010–2011, Badar Mansoor became a member of al Qaeda. This could mean that he brought his entire Al-Badar group within the fold of al Qaeda. Although US and Pakistani officials claim that he succeeded Ilyas

Kashmiri, this could not be confirmed. The Pakistan Taliban also denied that Mansoor took over Kashmiri's responsibilities after the latter's death.[181] According to a senior Pakistani official, "His [Badar Mansoor's] death is a major blow to al Qaeda's abilities to strike in Pakistan."

At the time of his death, Mansoor was acting as head of al Qaeda's internal operations in Pakistan. His major efforts were concentrated against Pakistan, and his involvement in Afghanistan had tapered off considerably. Before joining al Qaeda, Mansoor worked closely with Sheikh Isa al-Masri, an Egyptian militant who did not belong to al Qaeda but enjoyed cordial relations with many militant outfits, including al Qaeda, and he is presently detained in Egypt.[182]

Mansoor's main responsibilities under al Qaeda were to raise finances and fresh recruits for its global operations. He developed strong links with militant networks in the Punjab and Sindh provinces, as well as with the leadership of other militant groups, such as Brigade 313, Lashkar-e-Jhangvi, Jaish-e-Muhammad, and Harkatul Mujahideen. These links helped him channel resources to al Qaeda in North Waziristan. Mansoor also developed strong links with Tehrik-e-Taliban Pakistan (TTP), which is an anti-Pakistan militant outfit involved in attacks against Pakistan's government. Mansoor's role was crucial for al Qaeda during this period because Pakistan is viewed by the group as its lifeline to keep itself afloat through fund-raising efforts and inducting new recruits.[183]

After Mansoor's focus on Afghanistan had shifted to Pakistan, his group conducted terrorist activities in Pakistan. While his involvement in terror attacks against security forces is not clearly known, his name did appear in attacks against Muslim minorities in the country. He was indicted in a May 2010 terrorist attack against two places of worship of the Qadiani/ Ahmedia sect[184] in Lahore, the provincial capital of the Punjab province. The twin attacks killed ninety-eight worshippers. One of the attackers, Abdullah, aka Muhammad, confessed during a police interrogation that he was trained by Badar Mansoor's group for the attack. It was also confided that Abdullah's younger brother, Muneeb, worked for Badar Mansoor and imparted training to Abdullah in the North Waziristan Agency.[185]

In Karachi, terrorists associated with Badar Mansoor were arrested in various incidents that included terrorism and criminal activities to raise finances, as well as recruiting efforts for the group. For example, in May 2011, the Karachi police arrested four terror suspects belonging to the group. The group was led by Maaz Ali, alias Irfan, who planned and orchestrated the December 2010 attack against Shia Muslim students belonging to the Imamia Student Organization, on the campus of Karachi University.[186] Maaz told police investigators that he and his other associates had received training in North Waziristan at a training camp run by Badar Mansoor and that he even saw Mansoor from a distance of ten feet but never got the opportunity to engage him in a conversation.[187]

Maaz also spread hate and propaganda literature, such as booklets and pamphlets, in Karachi and on the Karachi University campus on behalf of the Badar Mansoor group. Through the Internet, Maaz downloaded videos containing hate material, which he would burn to CDs and send to people throughout the country. In addition to this activity, the group's leaders provided him with a USB flash drive containing videos of militant training camps in Iraq and Afghanistan, as well as speeches made by prominent extremist leaders. Maaz was also instrumental in delivering electronic goods to Badar Mansoor. The militant outfit's leaders delivered cash to Maaz, and it was his responsibility to procure items, such as remote controls, capacitors, resistors, and integrated circuits used to make bombs and other weapons of destruction. He gained expertise in manufacturing bombs and prepared a number of explosive devices.[188] Maaz further told investigators that the instructions from Badar Mansoor were clear. Mansoor wanted him to increase the organization's manpower by distributing hate material and exhorting youngsters toward terrorism. Up until his arrest, Maaz had been ordered to prepare bombs and suicide jackets to prepare for operations targeting police and military installations. Among their targets was the Police Training Centre in Saeedabad.

In August 2011, Karachi police arrested three suspected terrorists associated with Badar Mansoor and recovered a huge cache of arms and explosives from their possession. The arrested suspects admitted that they were trained in Waziristan and were sent to Karachi to target political and religious leaders.[189] One of Badar Mansoor's cell, Al-Mukhtar, was active in Karachi and was assigned the tasks of collecting extortion money, kidnapping people for ransom, and conducting bank robberies. Al-Mukhtar was involved in a bomb blast in an illegal gambling den in the Ghas Mandi area on 21 April 2011, which killed twenty-two people and injured dozens of others. The attack took place after the owner of the gambling den refused to pay extortion money to the militants.[190]

In June 2011, Badar Mansoor reportedly attended a meeting attended by Ilyas Kashmiri, Asmatullah Maavia, and Amjad Farooqui in North Waziristan. The meeting discussed forming a new terrorist outfit, Lashkar-e-Osama, to avenge the death of Osama bin Laden in May 2011 by conducting attacks in Pakistan.

The death of Badar Mansoor will deal a severe blow to al Qaeda's internal operations in Pakistan. There is a chain of Pakistani leaders available within the Badar Mansoor group to fill his position; however, it would be hard to replace his experience and contacts.

Younis al-Mauritani

Younis al-Mauritani, a senior al Qaeda leader and foreign minister of the organization, was captured by Pakistani security forces from the southwestern Balochistan province. He played a central role in the group's plots against the West. He was the highest profile al Qaeda figure who was arrested in Pakistan in 2011, following the death of Osama bin Laden in a US raid on 2 May 2011.[191]

Younis al-Mauritani planned and executed international operations for the global terror network, the military said in a statement. Al-Mauritani was tasked personally by bin Laden to focus on hitting targets of economic importance in the United States, Europe, and Australia. Al-Mauritani was also involved in planning multiple attacks against European countries similar to those of 2008 in Mumbai, India, according to European intelligence officials in interviews with CNN last year. The man at the center of the alleged al Qaeda plot, Afghan German Ahmed Sidiqui, was detained in July 2010, and he told interrogators that al-Mauritani had helped with planning and coordination.[192]

Previously, al-Mauritani had been an unknown figure. He was catapulted into the spotlight after he was identified as directing a plot by al Qaeda to attack multiple targets in Europe in a Mumbai-like terror assault. Several news reports incorrectly claimed that he was al Qaeda's "number three," or third in command. The number three designation is often assigned by Western officials and media to al Qaeda's suspected operations chief.[193]

POLITICAL OBJECTIVES

Al Qaeda was established 18 August 1988 in Peshawar, Pakistan.[194] It was established as an organized Islamic faction with the aim of training Mujahideen, who could later be recruited into the group and serve Muslims all over the world.[195] However, after the entrance of Western and particularly military forces from the United States into the Arabian Peninsula, Osama bin Laden started to advocate attacking US interests. This was most explicitly seen in his declaration on 23 August 1996 and from his declaration of total war against Jews and Crusaders on 22 February 1998. Osama bin Laden saw the United States as the head of the snake, with the corrupt and apostate regimes in the Muslim world forming the main body. By unifying the resources of the various militant jihadi groups, bin Laden believed that he could defeat the United States as he had previously defeated another superpower, namely the Soviet Union. Once the United States was defeated and driven from the Muslim world, Muslims would be released from their coercion and be free to topple their weak apostate governments.[196]

GENERAL

Al Qaeda has numerous links with local as well as regional militant groups around the world.

Algeria

Groupe Salafiste pour la Prédication et le Combat (GSPC)—Two militant groups merged with al Qaeda in 2006, and more are likely to merge in the coming years. The second merger was announced in Zawahiri's 11 September 2006 interview with al Qaeda's media arm, al-Sahab (The Cloud), when Zawahiri stated the following:

> Our Amir, mujahid Shaykh and lion of Islam usama Bin Laden, may God protect him, has instructed me to give the good news to Muslims in general, and my brothers the mujahidin everywhere that the Salafi Group for Call and Combat has joined al Qaeda of Jihad Organization. So, praise is due to God, praise is due to God, and praise is due to God for this blessed alliance, which we ask God that it will be a bone in the throats of the Americans and French Crusaders and their allies that would bring on them distress, trepidation, and dejection in the hearts of the traitorous apostate sons of France. We beseech Him Almighty to guide our brothers at the Salafi Group for Call and Combat to success in order to crush the pillars of the Crusader alliance, especially their old immoral leader, America.[197]

Since the accession of the GSPC into al Qaeda, its leadership has changed the emblem for the group. The initial emblem, an oval-shaped symbol centered on an open Quran appearing to be standing on a gray brick wall with a sword and an AK-assault rifle, was changed to a black flag attached to a Kalashnikov machine gun. The Kalashnikov, which presumably reinforces perceptions that victory comes through fighting, tops the icon, confirming the global agenda. The GSPC supports this agenda ever since Hassan Hattab was ousted as the leader of the group in 2003.[198] In January 2007, the GSPC rescinded its previous name to become part of the Tanzim Qaeda bi-Bilad al-Maghreb al-Islami (The al Qaeda Organization in the Islamic Maghreb), which conducted two major attacks against international oil workers in Algeria and the first suicide attacks in Algeria's history.[199] However, despite the new name and the recent attacks against international targets,[200] we believe that GSPC's merger with al Qaeda was merely the last step in a long series of steps taken by the GSPC since 2003. The group has progressed from being a mostly Algeria-focused group to being oriented toward the global agenda of al Qaeda. Since 2003, the GSPC focuses on conducting attacks outside Algeria, culminating in the attack on the Mauritanian army base in Lemgheitty in June 2005.[201]

Libya

Libyan Islamic Fighting Group (LIFG)—With the fall of the Taliban, many members of the LIFG declared an oath of allegiance to the Taliban's leader, Mullah Muhammad Umar. Members of the LIFG fought as part of al Qaeda's internal structure in Afghanistan under the overall command of Mullah Umar, while maintaining their independence on external operations.[202] A letter released by the United States Central Command on 26 September 2006 consisted of correspondence from a Libyan known as Atiyah Abd al-Rahman, written in December 2005. He wrote to the previous leader of al Qaeda in Iraq, Abu Musab al-Zarqawi, making it clear that a major part of the Majlis al-Shurra of the LIFG was and likely still remains in one of the Waziristan agencies, and most likely the North Waziristan Agency. In the letter, Atiyah Abd al-Rahman states that he is with the leadership and urges Abu Musab to send an emissary to the leadership in Waziristan. At the end of the letter, he extends the regards of what we believe are a whole range of senior al Qaeda and LIFG members, including Abu Layth al-Libi and Abu Sahl al-Libi, who are both believed to be part of LIFG's Majlis al-Shurra (Advisory Council) in North Waziristan.[203] In a video interview produced by al Qaeda's media arm al-Sahab (The Cloud) and posted to the Internet on 28 April 2007, Abu Layth al-Libi was featured as one of the leaders of al Qaeda al-Jihad in Khorasan (Afghanistan).[204] During the interview, Abu Layth al-Libi avoids any specific mention of Libya and instead praises Osama bin Laden's strategy, which prioritizes attacks and the defeat of the head of the snake (the United States), to overcome the main body of apostasy (the corrupt rulers in the Islamic world), who are perceived as being completely dependent on their patron, the United States.[205] In this video interview, Abu Layth al-Libi seems to be foretelling the LIFG as the next full member of al Qaeda. We believe such a merger may likely form during the coming year, entailing support for al Qaeda's international operations and its local branch in North Africa.

Morocco

Moroccan Islamic Combatant Group (GICM)—The GICM established relations with Jama'at al Qaeda al-Jihad in the period immediately prior to the attacks in the United States on 9/11.[206] However, despite receiving political, financial, and training assistance from al Qaeda, the GICM consistently refused to join al Qaeda's fight against the United States in the period leading up to the 9/11 attacks. After the 9/11 attacks, some members of the GICM joined al Qaeda's branch on the Arabian Peninsula, known as Tanzim Qaedat fi al-Jazeeratul-Arab (The al Qaeda Organization on the Arabian Peninsula).

However, most of these former GICM members were killed during operations conducted by Saudi security forces in 2005–2006.

Tunisia

Tunisia Combatant Group (TCG)—This group had very strong links to al Qaeda's leadership in Afghanistan. The leadership of the TCG recruited and launched two suicide bombers to kill the military commander of the Northern Alliance, Ahmed Shah Masud, in September 2001. The attack was conducted in close coordination with al Qaeda's leadership and under the direct orders of Osama bin Laden. The group was also responsible for recruiting the bomber who executed a suicide attack using a liquefied gas petrol truck on 11 April 2002 against the oldest Jewish synagogue in Tunisia. The financing and coordination for this attack was by al Qaeda's external operations leader, Khalid Sheikh Muhammad (KSM). However, since these attacks, the TCG has been dismantled, and the leaders and founders of the group were arrested in Belgium and Turkey. (Tarek Maaroufi was arrested in Belgium, and Abu Ayyad al-Tunisi was arrested in Turkey and subsequently extradited to Tunisia.)

Egypt

Egyptian Islamic Jihad (EIJ)—The relationship between the EIJ and al Qaeda formalized in June 2001, when al Qaeda and a faction of al-Jihad merged into a single group, known as Jama'at al Qaeda al-Jihad. Ayman al-Zawahiri had already joined al Qaeda in 1998, and before the merger, al-Jihad's leader was Tharwat Shehata.

Al-Gama'at al-Islamiyya—One faction of Gama'at al-Islamiyah has long-standing relations with al Qaeda. This faction of Gama'at al-Islamiyah was traditionally led by Mustafa Hamza, aka Abu Hazim al-Masri, but he was arrested in Iran and later extradited to Egypt. In early August 2006, this faction merged with al Qaeda when al-Zawahiri announced the following: "the unification of a great faction of the knights of the Gamaa Islamiya . . . with the al Qaeda group."[207] According to al-Zawahiri, the faction of Gama'at al-Islamiyah that joined al Qaeda was led by Muhammad Shawqi Islambouli, aka Abu Jafar al-Masri, the brother of Khalid Islambouli, who took part in the assassination of Egyptian President Anwar Sadat in 1981.[208] However, we do not believe that Muhammad Shawqi Islambouli is anything other than a figurehead for this faction. He has not delivered any video, audio, or written statement. We believe this is because he is currently detained in Iran, which makes it more difficult for him to communicate.[209] So far, the forty-five-year-old Gama'at al-Islamiyah member Muhammad Khalil Hakaymah, aka Abu Jihad al-Masri, has been the main spokesperson for this faction of Gama'at, which broke away from the main group after it declared a unilateral cease-fire with the Egyptian government in 1997. The Gama'at faction that joined al Qaeda was named Tanzim Qaedat al-Jihad fi-Ard al-Kinanah (The al Qaeda Organization for Jihad in the land of Kinanah [Egypt]). The strategy for this organization outlined by Abu Jihad al-Masri is on the group's website, Thabitun ala al-Ahd, under the following title: "Toward a New Strategy in Resisting the Occupier."[210] In this publication, Hakaymah continues and mirrors the strategic vision presented in al-Zawahiri's letter from 9 July 2005 and his subsequent speeches.[211] He legitimizes attacks against civilians and in countries that occupy Muslim lands. Considering the international security situation and the problems related to the establishment of hierarchical organizations, he suggests that such attacks can be conducted by individuals or small groups.[212]

It is unknown where Abu Jihad al-Masri and the rest of the Gama'at al-Islamiyah faction are currently located. Members of this Gama'at faction stayed near Peshawar in Pakistan's North-West Frontier Province. However, most of them were captured, and the rest have moved to the Bajaur Agency. We believe that Abu Jihad's faction is likely based in Iran, as suggested by al-Sharq al-Awsat's sources. This was supported by an April 2007 article in the *New York Times* in which US intelligence officials confirmed the following: "Several other important Qaeda figures may be operating in Iran, including an Egyptian known as Abu Jihad al-Masri and a Libyan explosives expert named Atiyah Abd al-Rahman, who is thought to travel between Iran and Pakistan's tribal areas."[213] However, we have no information suggesting that Abu Jihad's faction is receiving support from Iranian authorities, although we do believe relations existed between Gama'at al-Islamiyah and Iran's Ministry of Intelligence and National Security of the Islamic Republic of Iran.

Ethiopia

Islamic Union of the Mujahideen of Ogaden—In the early to mid-1990s, al Qaeda fostered cooperation between various groups in the region. One example was the Islamic Union of the Mujahideen of Ogaden. It brought together Islamist groups of Somalia, Western Somalia, and Ethiopia, to whom al Qaeda provided training and financial support. The relations between Mujahideen in the Ogaden province of Ethiopia and al Qaeda's structure in the Horn of Africa is currently unclear.

Somalia

Al-Itihaad al-Islamiya (AIAI)—The AIAI was considered a support group for al Qaeda in Somalia. Former AIAI commander Hassan Dahir Aweys had strong relations with members of al Qaeda. Before the bombing of the USS *Cole* in Yemen, AIAI agents in northern Somalia were identified with al Qaeda operatives. AIAI members also assisted al Qaeda in the Mombasa hotel bombing, which killed fifteen, and in an unsuccessful attempt to bring down a passenger jet using missiles on 28 November 2002. However, the AIAI no longer exists as an organized group, and its leader, Sheikh Hassan Dahir Aweys, instead plays a central role in the Union of Islamic Courts (UIC), which ruled Somalia during 2006. However, in late 2006, Ethiopian forces and Somali forces loyal to the Transitional Federal Government ejected the UIC's leadership. The UIC's leadership fled Somalia and moved its headquarters to Yemen and later to Eritrea. However, the faction of the UIC most closely aligned with al Qaeda, Harakat Shabab al-Mujahidin, is still operating in Mogadishu and in the Lower Jubba Region of Somalia.

Harakat Shabab al-Mujahidin—Adnan Hashi Ayro is the leader of Shabab's youth militia.[214] The Shabab emerged around 2003 and is known for training young, die-hard Islamists for specialized assignments.[215] Unlike the rest of the UIC, the Shabab is a cross-clan entity, which provides elite elements and commissars who maintain discipline.[216] The group was seen to be instrumental in defeating the US-backed Alliance for Restoration of Peace and Counter Terrorism (ARPCT) and ousting them from Mogadishu in June 2006. Ayro was made commander of the Ifka Halane court militia in July 2005 and rose to prominence when he and his fighters desecrated three hundred Italian graves in Mogadishu in January 2005. This was done to embarrass his clan for failing to defend him against the forces of the US-backed ARPCT, who raided his house in search of a senior al Qaeda suspect.[217] Despite denouncing Aweys and his group for the incident, in July 2005, the Islamic Courts accepted the appointment of Ayro as commander of the Ifka Halane militia without any protest.[218] This could be because of Ayro's connection with Hassan Dahir Aweys, who is an influential leader in the Ifka Halane Court. According to the International Crisis Group (ICG), Adnan Hashi Ayro and the Shabab militia "hosted a steady trickle of foreign volunteers eager for jihad"[219] into the area around Kismayu in November–December 2006.[220] Shabab fighters suffered heavily during the battles with Ethiopian forces, and many are believed to have deserted. However, according to the ICG, some units "[a]ppear to have withdrawn in good order on several fronts and the core leadership remains intact."[221] The remaining leadership of the Shabab is, according to the ICG, centered around individuals such as Abdullahi Mo'alin Ali Abu Utayba, Muktar Robow, Ibrahim Haji Jamah al-Afghani, Fuad Muhammad Qalaf, and Adnan Hashi Ayro.[222]

Adnan Hashi Ayro has twice been targeted by US air strikes. According to a report by the ICG, Adnan Hashi Ayro was wounded in an 8 January 2007 air strike, which killed eight of his guards, while a second air strike on 23 January 2007 missed him completely.[223] The exact locations of these air strikes are unknown, but we believe they were executed in either Ras Kamboni, which is a group of six rocky islands where AIAI and UIC had training camps, or near the quiet town of Afmadow in the Lower Juba region, close to the Kenyan border. One of those wounded in these air strikes was the chairman of the Islamic Courts Council in the southern town of Kismayu, Sheikh Ahmed Mohamed Madobe. He was later captured by Ethiopian forces and subsequently paraded in front of the press and the citizens of Kismayu. During this event, Sheikh Madobe described how he was wounded in the face during one of the two US air strikes.[224] Harakat Shabab al-Mujahidin were likely behind the first suicide attacks in Somalia's history, when they executed a double suicide attack in September 2006 in an attempt to assassinate the Somali president Abdullahi Yusuf Ahmed.[225] They have since executed intermittent suicide attacks against the Transitional Federal Government and Ethiopian targets in Somalia, but in June 2007 the group also stated that they had infiltrated operatives deep into Ethiopia.[226]

Eritrea

Eritrean Islamic Jihad Movement—This group was created and sponsored by al Qaeda and other regional and international Islamic groups to perpetrate subversive acts in Eritrea. In 1994, Eritrean security forces intercepted an assorted group of terrorists, who included in their ranks al Qaeda-trained nationals of several countries.

Lebanon

Osbat al-Ansar—A Palestinian militant Salafi group that recruited, trained, and sent fighters to Iraq, where they fought with Tanzim Qaedat fi Bilad al-Rafidayn (the al Qaeda organization in the land between the two rivers, or al Qaeda in Iraq). It is the only group that is allowed to honor its own shuhadah (martyrs) who have died fighting for al Qaeda in Iraq. Its headquarters are in the Ein el-Hilweh Palestinian Refugee camp near Sidon.

Diniya—A Lebanese militant Salafi group that recruited, trained, and sent fighters to Iraq, where they fought with Tanzim Qaedat fi Bilad al-Rafidayn (the al Qaeda organization in the land between the two rivers, or al Qaeda in Iraq). Most members of the Diniya group are from northern or eastern Lebanon, but the organization's headquarters are in the Ein el-Hilweh Palestinian Refugee camp near Sidon.

Jund al-Sham—A Palestinian militant Salafi group that recruited, trained, and sent fighters to Iraq, where they have fought with Tanzim Qaedat fi Bilad al-Rafidayn. Its headquarters are in the Ein el-Hilweh Palestinian Refugee camp near Sidon.

Fateh al-Islam—A militant Salafi group that broke out of the secular Palestinian group Fatah Intifadah. It trained many Jihadis from Syria and Saudi Arabia who subsequently traveled to Iraq and joined Tanzim Qaedat fi Bilad al-Rafidayn.

Yemen

Aden-Abyan Islamic Army (AAIA)—Formed by Yemeni and other Arab fighters who helped the Afghans oust the Soviets in 1989. This group is no longer operational.

Tanzim al Qaeda al-Jihad fi-Ard al-Yemen—This group sprang into notoriety when it executed two sets of nearly simultaneous suicide attacks at two different oil installations in Yemen on 15 September 2006. The suicide attacks were poorly executed, using low-grade IEDs, and did not manage to inflict significant damage. The organization's contacts and command relations with al Qaeda remain undetermined, but the attacks came only four days after Ayman al-Zawahiri warned of these impending attacks.

Iraq

Jama'at Ansar al-Sunnah—The leadership of Jama'at Ansar al-Sunnah has long-standing ties to al Qaeda in Afghanistan and Pakistan. These relations date as far back as during the 1990s, when Jama'at Ansar al-Sunnah's predecessors, The Second Soran Unit and the Tawhid Islamic Front, established contact with al Qaeda. Later, these contacts were strengthened with direct communications between Ansar al-Sunnah's leader Abbas bin Farnas bin Qafqas, aka Ali Wali, and al Qaeda's leaders in Pakistan during 2005. However, Ali Wali died during a counterterrorism raid in Baghdad in May 2006.[227]

Tanzim Qaedat fi Bilad al-Rafidayn (TQBR)—Became a branch of al Qaeda when its predecessor, Jama'at Tawhid wal Jihad, merged with Jama'at al Qaeda al-Jihad in October 2004. It is led by the Egyptian Abd-al Munim Izzidine Ali Ismail, aka Abu Hamza al-Muhajir. It is responsible for most suicide attacks and generally most spectacular attacks in Iraq. During the tenure of Ahmed Fadil Nazzal al-Khalayleh, aka Abu Musab al-Zarqawi, al Qaeda's leadership in Pakistan had great difficulty controlling this branch. Aside from attacking coalition and Iraqi security forces, Abu Musab al-Zarqawi also led an extremely confrontational policy against civilian Shiites and Iraqi nationalist resistance groups. Al Qaeda's leadership discouraged his actions, but he refused to change course. Although this relationship changed somewhat after Abu Hamza al-Muhajir assumed control, the organization is still executing the same massacres as it did during Abu Musab's tenure, and it remains generally disliked among other militant groups in Iraq.

These other militant groups have on many occasions appealed to Osama bin Laden for him to censor TQBR, but al Qaeda's leadership supported TQBR's unpopular establishment of Dawlat al-Iraq al-Islamiyah (The Islamic State of Iraq), which TQBR tried to entice and coerce other militant groups to join.

Afghanistan

Taliban—Hosted al Qaeda in Afghanistan and provided refuge for the group after 9/11. Currently, they have a joint alliance with al Qaeda against the United States and its allies. Al Qaeda's branch in Afghanistan, Tanzim al Qaeda al-Jihad fi al-Khorasan, fights subservient to the commands of Mullah Muhammad Umar. Many al Qaeda members, including Osama bin Laden, have sworn an oath of allegiance to Taliban leader, Mullah Umar. He is the Amir al-Muminin (The leader of the Faithful) within the Emirate of Afghanistan. When fighting inside Afghanistan, al Qaeda fight under his leadership, while operating independently outside.

Tanzim al Qaeda al-Jihad fi al-Khorasan—The establishment of this branch of al Qaeda was announced indirectly and directly in a series of videos from leaders within this branch. In April 2007, Ammar al-Ruqa'I, aka Abu Layth al-Libi, was announced as one of the leaders of this organization by al Qaeda's media arm al-Sahab (The Cloud).[228] This was later followed by an announcement from the leader of this branch Mustafa Abu-al-Yazid, aka Abu Said al-Masri, in May 2007.[229] Abu Said al-Masri was previously the head of al Qaeda's Financial Committee.

Hezb-e-Islami-Gulbuddin Faction—After Gulbuddin Hekmatyar's return to Afghanistan, al Qaeda initially brokered an agreement between him and his enemies from the Taliban. However, this alliance has since broken down, and Hezb-e-Islami is currently fighting independently of the Taliban. Hekmatyar claims that members of his party assisted al Qaeda's fugitives in their escape after the fall of the Taliban in Afghanistan.

Hezb-e-Islami-Yunus Khalis Faction—There was a long-standing and close relationship between the head of this faction, Yunus Khalis, and Osama bin Laden. When Osama returned to Afghanistan from the Sudan, Yunus Khalis allowed him access to the Tora Bora complex, in the heart of Yunus Khalis's territory. After Yunus Khalis's death, his eldest son, Anwarul Haq Mujahid, changed his father's passive policy and formed the Tora Bora Military Front in February 2007.[230] Since its formation, the group has executed several attacks in the Nangarhar province of Afghanistan, including suicide attacks.

China

East Turkistan Islamic Movement (ETIM)—Islamic separatists operating from Xinjiang, China, get training and financial and material aid from al Qaeda. The ETIM train in the North Waziristan Agency of Pakistan, where they also have a close relationship with al Qaeda and the Libyan Islamic Fighting Group leader, Abu Layth al-Libi.

Uzbekistan

Islamic Movement of Uzbekistan (IMU)—Both of the IMU's founders, Namangani and Yuldashev, worked with Osama bin Laden in 1999. IMU fighters supported the Taliban against the Northern Alliance and coalition forces. After the IMU was expelled from Afghanistan in 2001, the group moved its headquarters to the Wana plains in the South Waziristan Agency of Pakistan. Despite moving to Pakistan, the IMU remained focused on the local jihad in Central Asia. In March–April 2007, Uzbek, Tajik, Uighur, and Chechen fighters were dislocated from their main base on the Wana plains, near the town of Azam Warsaq, by tribesmen from the Darikhel subclan of the Zalikhel clan and local Taliban loyal to Mullah Nazir from the small Kakakhel subclan of the Zalikhel clan. These local Taliban and tribal militants fought and defeated other local Taliban forces from the much larger Yargulkhel subclan of the Zalikhel clan and Uzbeks, Tajiks, Uighurs, and Chechens loyal to the IMU and its leader, Tahir Yuldashev.[231] The forces loyal to the IMU became increasingly unpopular among the Darikhel and Kakakhel subclans, because they participated in the killing of tribal leaders and battles for power among the local Taliban and within the Zalikhel clan, where they built their own power base and structures in the form of land holdings and prisons.[232] It is not clear where the IMU moved, but we believe they sought shelter either in the Mehsud territory or among members of the Uzbek Islamic Jihad Union, in North Waziristan.

Islamic Jihad Union (IJU)—The IJU is a faction from the IMU, which broke away and formed a separate group under the name Islamic Jihad Group (IJG). In 2005, it changed its name to Islamic Jihad Union (IJU). It is led by Uzbek national Nadzhmiddin Kamilidinovich Janov, aka Commander Janov, and Mansur Suhail.[233] Their base is in North Waziristan and specifically in the Mir Ali area, where they direct the groups' operations in Pakistan and in Central Asia.[234] IJU was the first global jihadi group to use female suicide bombers, and the group targeted both local and international targets in Uzbekistan, most significantly in three suicide attacks against the US–Israeli embassies and the Uzbek General Prosecutors office in Tashkent on 30 July 2004.[235] IJU augmented its local ambitions with the global vision of al Qaeda, whereas the main goal of the other Uzbek group, the IMU, remains the local Jihad in Central Asia.

Chechnya

Islamic International Brigade—Khattab, the late founder of the group, had close ideological, tactical, and financial relations with Osama bin Laden. In fact, bin Laden and Khattab fought together side by side in Afghanistan. Khattab was killed and was succeeded by Abd al-Aziz Al-Ghamdi, aka Abu Walid.

However, Abu Walid died in late 2003 and was succeeded by Faris Yusuf Amirat, aka Abu Hafs al-Ordoni, who was killed a few years later. The jihad in Iraq and Afghanistan drew most of the money and mujahideen to these arenas, leaving the international presence in Chechnya greatly diminished and currently relatively insignificant.

India and Pakistan

Jaish-e-Mohammed (JEM), Harakat ul-Jihad ul-Islami (HuJI), and Jamiat ul-Ansar (JuA)—These groups were trained by al Qaeda. Maulana Masood Azhar, the leader of JEM, received training in Yemen with al Qaeda members. In 2002, after Jaish Muhammad was banned, the group changed its name to Khuddam ul-Islam, and Maulana Masud Azhar refocused the group on the Kashmir/India conflict. This was unacceptable to the group's second in command, Maulana Abdul Jabbar, who focused on countering what he perceived as the Western occupation of Afghanistan and Musharraf's support for the United States. Abdul Jabbar broke with Azhar, forming Jamiat ul-Furqan. During 2002, and later in 2003, the leadership of Harakat ul-Jihad ul-Islami and Jamiat ul-Furqan increasingly found difficulty operating because of Pakistan's security agencies. The operational work of these groups was led by twenty-eight-year-old Amjad Faruqi, who was a member of HuJI. He headed a heterogeneous group of members from Jamiat ul-Furqan, HuJI, Jamiat ul-Ansar (previously known Harakat ul-Mujahidin), and the sectarian group Laskhar e-Jhangvi. He was assisted by Osama Nazir from Jamiat ul-Furqan and Qari Zafar, who had extensive contacts into Laskhar e-Jhangvi's structure in Sindh and southern Punjab. They became the interface between the Pakistani groups and the leadership of Jama'at al Qaeda al-Jihad, and specifically the successive heads of al Qaeda's Military Committee, Khalid Sheikh Muhammad and Abu Faraj al-Libi (captured respectively on 1 March 2003 and in May 2005 in Pakistan). It was only through Amjad Faruqi's structure that al Qaeda could continue to operate in Pakistan after al Qaeda's members were forced to flee into the FATA after the arrests of Khalid Sheikh Muhammad and Tawfiq bin Attash in the spring of 2003. Amjad Faruqi also had extensive contacts among the Pakistani community in Europe. These contacts, and particularly his contacts among Pakistani Hawala owners in Spain, were used to pass money from Khalid Sheikh Muhammad to the Tunisian, Nawaz Naur, who carried out the April 2002 bombing of a synagogue in Djerba, Tunisia. Amjad Faruqi and his men were heavily involved in the string of attacks against Christian targets in Pakistan during 2002, the killing of Daniel Pearl in Karachi on 1 February 2002, and the second assassination attempt against Pervez Musharraf in December 2003. Faruqi was killed in a gun battle in the southern part of Sindh province on 26 September 2004. Prior to this, Qari Saifullah Aktar was detained in Dubai in August 2004 and was later extradited to Pakistan. There are indications that this attrition and the subsequent arrest of the head of al Qaeda's Military Committee, Abu Faraj al-Libi, temporarily severed or hampered collaboration between al Qaeda and the militant Pakistani groups. Initially, Osama Nazir, from Jamiat ul-Furqan, assumed Faruqi's role, but he was arrested in Faisalabad in November 2004. Subsequently, Muhammad Zafar, aka Qari Zafar, assumed the leadership. Qari Zafar subsequently masterminded the attack on the US consulate in Karachi on 2 March 2006 and attempted suicide bombings in Karachi in January 2007.

Lashkar-e-Taiba (LeT)—This group used training facilities in Afghanistan and received funding from al Qaeda. Abu Zubaydah, then number three in al Qaeda, was arrested in the house of an LeT leader at Faisalabad in Pakistan's Punjab. However, from 2002–2005 Pakistan's ISI arrested most of the members of the LeT faction that were giving support to al Qaeda's members in Pakistan.

Lashkar-e-Jhangvi (LeJ)—A sectarian group trained by al Qaeda personnel. Many LeJ members were recruited into Qari Zafar's structure, and just like Qari Zafar, the group found a new base in the South Waziristan Agency, where they are assisted by Pakistan Taliban Commanders Qari Hussein Mahsud and Abdullah Mahsud from the Mahsud tribe, and Javed Karmazkhel and Commander Maulavi Abbas from the Ahmadzai-Wazir tribe.

Bangladesh

Harkat-ul-Jihad-al-Islam-B (HuJI)—Osama bin Laden sent his private secretary to attend a meeting of HuJI in Bangladesh to draft a strategy in the region. HuJI likely receives funding from al Qaeda. A twenty-five-member team of al Qaeda/Taliban fighters were sent to Bangladesh in June 2001 to provide small-arms training to the HuJI. HuJI-B members were placed under arrest in Bangladesh, and the group is not assessed to be assisting al Qaeda. However, the group is likely assisting Pakistani militant groups by conducting attacks in India. These groups specifically include Khuddam ul-Islam of Maulana Masud Azhar and Lashkar-e-Taiba.

Indonesia

Jemaah Islamiah (JI)—This group is headed by Abu Bakar Ba'asyir, who is currently free after detainment for his alleged involvement in the Bali and Marriott bombings. Hambali, the head of the JI faction, was closest to al Qaeda, and coordinated al Qaeda's activities in Southeast Asia. In August 2003, Thai authorities captured him, and then he was transferred to the CIA. In 2006, he went to the US detention facility in Guantanamo Bay in Cuba.

Philippines

Abu Sayyef Group (ASG)—Deceased founder and leader Abduragak Abubakar Janjalani was a veteran of the Afghan war and a friend of Osama bin Laden. The group allegedly received funding from Mohammad Jamal Khalifa, Osama bin Laden's brother-in-law, who is now deceased.

Moro Islamic Liberation Front (MILF)—MILF members trained in al Qaeda's camps in Afghanistan and the Egyptian Sayf al-Adl, who headed al Qaeda's Security Committee, provided training for the MILF in the Philippines in 1998. The MILF also has strong links with al Qaeda affiliated factions of JI.

Malaysia

Kumpulan Mujahideen Malaysia (KMM)—Al Qaeda was previously believed to be a source of financial and military support. Members trained in al Qaeda camps in Afghanistan and gained combat experience as mujahideen. The group's current relations with al Qaeda are unclear, but we believe they are very tenuous, if ties remain.

Saudi Arabia

Tanzim Qaedat fi al-Jazeeratul Arab (The al Qaeda Organization on the Arabian Peninsula)—This is a branch of al Qaeda with its main structure in Saudi Arabia. During the period from the late 1990s until 2004, the group's leadership maintained close ties to al Qaeda's leaders in Afghanistan, Pakistan, and Iran. From Iran, Sayf al-Adl, in 2003, helped relay orders from Ayman al-Zawahiri to Tanzim Qaedat fi al-Jazeeratul Arab (The al Qaeda Organization on the Arabian Peninsula), telling al Qaeda's branch on the Arabian Peninsula to initiate attacks in Saudi Arabia.[236] From Iran, Sayf al-Adl was also involved in mediating a dispute between the head of al Qaeda on the Arabian Peninsula, Yusuf Salih Fahd al-Ayiri, aka Abu Qutaybah al-Makki, and his military chief, Ali Abd al-Rahman al-Faqasi, aka Abu Bakr al-Azdi, concerning the strength needed to engage Saudi Arabian security forces.[237] The organization conducted its first attacks inside Saudi Arabia in

May 2003, when it struck a compound inhabited by Westerners with car bombs. Effective counterterrorism measures and intelligence operations have considerably weakened Tanzim Qaedat fi al-Jazeeratul Arab.

ORGANIZATIONAL STRUCTURE

Vertically, al Qaeda was organized with Osama bin Laden as the emir (prince), at the top, followed by nine other al Qaeda leaders in the Majlis al-Shurra (Consultative Council). The structure served as the means for coordinating functions and providing material support to operations. Once a specific operation was decided upon, it would be assigned to a carefully selected clandestine cell, headed by a senior al Qaeda operative who reported personally to bin Laden. The diagram below[238] illustrates the structure of al Qaeda:

- Shura/Advisory Council—Osama bin Laden's inner circle; they direct the overall strategy of the organization.
- Sharia/Political Committee—Responsible for issuing fatwas.
- Military Committee—Responsible for conceiving and planning operations, as well as managing training camps.
- Finance Committee—Responsible for fund-raising and the concealment of assets.
- Foreign Purchases Committee—Responsible for the acquisition of foreign arms and supplies.
- Security Committee—Physical protection, intelligence, and counterintelligence.
- Information Committee—In charge of propaganda.[239]

While the organization weakened considerably since the 9/11 terrorist attacks against the United States, al Qaeda remains a structured organization. The Consultative Council no longer assembles, as the organization has adapted to the war on terrorism. Instead, coordination on the strategic direction of al Qaeda is communicated via couriers. At least four of the six committees remain intact.

COMMAND AND CONTROL STRUCTURE

Bin Laden held the top position in the command structure (now headed by Zawahiri), followed by the Shura Council. The Shura Council serves as the board of directors for al Qaeda, with bin Laden serving in the position of the chief executive officer. While it existed in rudimentary form prior to the entry of Ayman al-Zawahiri into al Qaeda, the structure underwent a dramatic change during the summer of 2001, when Ayman al-Zawahiri's faction of al-Jihad formally merged with al Qaeda's command structure, and their joint leadership was integrated into the former organization. Bin Laden's sequestration in the aftermath of the 9/11 attacks forced operational commanders and cell leaders to assume greater authority. They are now making command decisions previously made by him. The following list of key leaders and current assessed locations are as follows:

Key Leader Locations

Name: Osama bin Laden
Function: Martyred figurehead
Status: Killed in a US Navy SEALs raid on 2 May 2011 in Pakistan
Location: Pakistan as of June 2007

Name: Ayman al-Zawahiri
Function: Amir
Status: At large
Location: Pakistan, probably the Bajaur Agency as of June 2007

Name: Thirwat Salah Shirhata
Function: Egyptian Islamic Jihad deputy emir
Status: Imprisoned in Iran as of June 2003

Name: Rifa Ahmed Taha
Function: Gamaa al-Islamiyyah secretary-general
Status: Arrested in Syria in November 2001 and extradited to Egypt

Name: Mustafa Hamza
Function: Gamaa al-Islamiyyah deputy emir
Status: Arrested in Iran and extradited to Egypt

Name: Mohammed Atef
Function: Supreme Military Commander
Status: Dead (November 2001)

Name: Saif al-Adel
Function: Formerly the second in command of al Qaeda's military leadership, assumed the position of Supreme Military Commander upon Mohammed Atef's death
Status: Detained in Iran

Name: Abd al-Aziz al-Jamal
Function: Member of al-Jihad and commanded a Taliban unit
Status: Arrested in Yemen and handed over to Egypt

Name: Abu Zubaydah
Function: Global operations chief
Status: Apprehended in Pakistan (March 2002)

Name: Abu Musab Zarqawi
Function: Head of Tanzim Qaedat fi Bilad al-Rafidayn
Status: Dead in Iraq, June 2006 by coalition forces

Name: Abu Zubair al-Haili
Function: Part of Tanzim Qaedat fi al-Jazeeratul Arab
Status: Apprehended in Morocco (June 2002)

Name: Tawfiq Attash Khallad
Function: Part of external operations structure
Status: Apprehended in Pakistan (April 2003)

Name: Abd al-Rahim al-Nashiri
Function: Head of Tanzim Qaeda fi al-Jazeeratul-Arab
Status: Apprehended in the United Arab Emirates (November 2002)

Name: Abu Mohammed al-Masri (Abdullah Ahmed Abdullah)
Function: Head of Training Subsection
Status: Detained in Iran

Name: Tariq Anwar al-Sayyid Ahmad
Function: Balkans operations chief
Status: Dead (February 2002)

Name: Mohammed Salah
Function: Foremost explosives expert and Central African operations chief
Status: Dead (December 2001)

Name: Mahfouz Ould al-Walid (Abu Hafs the Mauritanian, Mr. Mauritania)
Function: Leader of al Qaeda's Religious and Political Committee
Status: Detained in Iran

Name: Muhammad Abdallah Rajab (Abu Kayr al-Masri)
Function: Member of the Religious and Political Committee
Status: Detained in Iran

Name: Abd al-Aziz al-Masri
Function: Head of the Nuclear Subsection
Status: Detained in Iran

Immediate Inner Circle of Leader Locations

These are bin Laden's aides, security chiefs, and immediate family members—some of whom performed some of the most sensitive and trusted functions for al Qaeda.

Name: Amin al-Haq
Function: Close associate of Osama bin Laden
Status: At large

Name: Abdallah Tabarak
Function: Tora Bora commander in chief
Status: Apprehended in December 2001, sent to Guantanamo Bay detention facility, extradited to Morocco in August 2004, where he was charged in December 2004 and released on bail

Name: Abu Bashir al-Yemeni
Function: Political adviser to Osama bin Laden
Status: Most likely detained in Iran and extradited to Yemen

Name: Saad bin Laden (son)
Function: Operations chief and heir apparent
Status: Captured in Iran

Name: Mohammed bin Laden (son)
Function: Security chief
Status: Captured in Iran

Name: Hamza bin Laden (son)
Function: Unknown
Status: Captured in Iran

Name: Saif bin Laden (son)
Function: Unknown
Status: At large

Name: Abdallah bin Laden (son)
Function: Unknown
Status: Not wanted, living in Saudi Arabia

Note: Osama bin Laden likely had up to four wives and as many as twenty-three sons, though only five are listed by counterterrorism sources. According to *Time* magazine, documents recovered from Khalid Sheikh Mohammed's residence indicate that during December 2001, most of bin Laden's family escaped to Iran with several hundred al Qaeda fighters, a charge made by Secretary of Defense Donald Rumsfeld at the time. Iranian authorities detained three of bin Laden's sons and a number of his wives.

Financial Committee Leaders

Al Qaeda typically had a great deal of money at their disposal. These financial resources emanated from a wide variety of sources, including everything from legitimate businesses to an elaborate network of Islamic charities and NGOs created solely to supply funds to the organization. This committee is responsible for the administration and distribution of the group's funds, as well as for transferring assets to avoid law enforcement seizure. However, since the fall of the Taliban in Afghanistan and the subsequent retreat of al Qaeda into the tribal areas, al Qaeda's leaders often struggled to maintain their financial freedom.

>Name: Sheikh Said al-Masri (Mustafa Abu al-Yazid)
>Function: Chief of the Financial Committee and head of Tanzim al Qaeda al-Jihad fi al-Khorasan
>Status: At large
>Location: Most likely in the FATA in Pakistan

>Name: Abu Said (Mustafa Ahmed al-Hawsawi)
>Function: Member of the Financial Committee
>Status: Detained in Pakistan in March 2003

Media Committee Leaders

This committee acts as al Qaeda's unofficial press representative and is responsible for the spread of its ideology throughout the Islamic world. Other unofficial members of the committee not listed here are members of the Khalifah, Hizb-ut-Tahrir, and Salafist movements.

>Name: Abu Abd al-Rahman al-Maghrebi (Muhammad Abaytah)
>Function: Emir of the Media Committee
>Status: At large
>Location: Most likely in the FATA of Pakistan

Nuclear Subsection Leaders

Al Qaeda employed a number of Muslim scientists of various nationalities, principally Egyptians, to assist them in the creation and procurement of chemical, biological, radiological, and nuclear weapons.

>Name: Abd al-Aziz al-Masri
>Function: Emir of the Nuclear Subsectio
>Status: Detained in Iran

Military Committee Leaders

Al Qaeda's Military Committee maintains its structure, which oversees its terror and military operations. After the death of Muhammad Atef, the structure was divided into internal and external operations. However, in May 2007, the internal operations structure likely transformed into another branch of al Qaeda, named the al Qaeda and Jihad organization in Afghanistan or Tanzim al Qaeda al-Jihad fi Ard al-Khorasan. Al Qaeda's external operations seem to be headed by the following leaders:

Name: Khalid Habib
Function: Head of external operations
Status: At large
Location: Most likely in the FATA of Pakistan

Name: Abu Ubayda al-Masri
Function: External operations and possibly head of al Qaeda operations in Kunar Province.
Status: At large
Location: Most likely in the FATA of Pakistan

Name: Hamza al-Jawfi
Function: External operations structure
Status: At large
Location: Most likely in the FATA of Pakistan

Al Qaeda also has other structures in various parts of the world including:

The Horn of Africa

Name: Harun (Fazul Abdallah Muhammed)
Function: Chief on the Horn of Africa
Status: At large
Location: Somalia

Name: Abu Talha al-Sudani
Function: Chief on the Horn of Africa
Status: At large
Location: Somalia

Name: Ali Saleh Ali Nabhan
Function: Deputy to Fazul Abdallah Muhammad
Status: At large
Location: Somalia

Egypt

Name: Muhammad Shawqi Islambouli
Function: Leader of Tanzim al Qaeda al-Jihad fi Ard al-Kinnah
Status: Imprisoned
Location: Iran

Name: Muhammad Hakaymah
Function: Spokesman for Tanzim al Qaeda al-Jihad fi Ard al-Kinnah
Status: At large
Location: Iran

Name: Sayfallah Abd al-Rahman
Function: Top member of Tanzim al Qaeda al-Jihad fi Ard al-Kinnah and son of Umar Abd al-Rahman
Status: At large
Location: Iran

Afghanistan/Pakistan

Name: Abu Said al-Masri (Mustafa Abu al-Yazid)
Function: Head of Tanzim al Qaeda al-Jihad fi al-Khorasan
Status: At large
Location: Pakistan's FATA

Name: Abu Layth al-Libi (Ammar al-Ruqa'I)
Function: Member of Tanzim al Qaeda al-Jihad fi al-Khorasan
Status: At large
Location: Pakistan's FATA

Name: Atiyah Abd al-Rahman
Function: Close associate to Ayman al-Zawahiri
Status: At large
Location: Iran

Iraq

Name: Abu Hamza al-Muhajir (Abd-al Munim Izzidine Ali Ismail)
Function: Leader of Tanzim Qaedat fi Bilad al-Rafidayn and Minister of War for Dawlat Islamiyah al-Iraq
Status: At large
Location: Iraq

Maghreb

Name: Abu Musab Abd-al Wadud (Abd al-Malik Droukdel)
Function: Leader of Tanzim Qaedat bi-Bilad al-Maghrebi Islami
Status: At large
Location: Algeria

Name: Haythem Abu Yahya (Abd al-Hamid Saadaoui)
Function: Leader within Tanzim Qaedat bi-Bilad al-Maghrebi Islami
Status: At large
Location: Algeria

Name: Moktar Belmoktar
Function: Leader within Tanzim Qaedat bi-Bilad al-Maghrebi Islami
Status: At large
Location: Mali

Name: Abid Hammadou
Function: Leader within Tanzim Qaedat bi-Bilad al-Maghrebi Islami
Status: At large
Location: Mali

Yemen

Name: Abu-Basir Nasir al-Wuhayshi
Function: Leader of Tanzim al Qaeda al-Jihad fi Ard al-Yemen
Status: At large
Location: Yemen

Name: Abu-Hurayrah al-San'ani
Function: Leader of Tanzim al Qaeda al-Jihad fi Ard al-Yemen and one of the ten remaining fugitives from the February 2006 prison break in

Yemen. Convicted for involvement in the USS *Cole* or the Limburg attacks.
Status: At large
Location: Yemen

HISTORY AND DEVELOPMENT

From 1982–1984, Azzam founded Maktab al Khidmat lil-mujahidin al-Arab (MAK), known commonly as the Afghan Service bureau. As MAK's principal financier, Osama bin Laden was considered the deputy to Azzam. Other leaders included Abdul Muizz, Abu Ayman, Abu Sayyaf, Samir Abdul Motaleb, and Mohammad Yusuff Abass. At the height of the foreign Arab and Muslim influxes into Pakistan and Afghanistan from 1984–1986, bin Laden spent time traveling widely and raising funds in the Arab world. He recruited several thousand Arab and Muslim youths to fight the Soviet Union, and MAK channeled several billion dollars' worth of Western financial and material resources for the Afghan jihad. MAK worked closely with Pakistan, especially the Inter-Services Intelligence Directorate (ISID), the Saudi and Egyptian governments, and the vast Muslim Brotherhood network. Moreover, MAK established recruitment offices around the world, including the United States, the United Kingdom, Germany, and Pakistan.

Bin Laden's relationship with Azzam suffered toward the end of the anti-Soviet Afghan campaign. The dispute was over Azzam's support for Ahmad Shah Massoud, leader of the Tajik forces in the Panshir Valley in northern Afghanistan. Bin Laden and especially his Egyptian supporters preferred Gulbuddin Hekmatyar, who would later become prime minister. Gulbuddin Hekmatyar leads the Islamic Party (Hizb-e-Islami) and was both anti-communist and anti-Western. Another major cleavage developed because bin Laden wanted to develop a separate Arab group instead of merely facilitating the entry of Arabs into Afghanistan, as MAK had previously done. Azzam was vehemently against this because he believed this would lead the Arabs to become a party to the infighting among Afghan mujahideen commanders.

As tensions between mentor and protégé grew, bin Laden distanced himself from Azzam and moved to Peshawar and established independent training camps and infrastructure for al Qaeda. Bin Laden decided to form a group that could unite the mujahideen into a single group, and in 1988 formed al Qaeda to continue the work of the struggle. While Azzam continued to focus on support to Muslims in Afghanistan, bin Laden turned his attention to carrying the war to other countries. In September 1989, Abdallah Azzam died in a car bomb attack, generally blamed on the Egyptian who was close to bin Laden.

Although Soviet troops withdrew in 1989, they installed the procommunist leader Najibullah in Kabul. MAK strengthened to fight the Najibullah regime and to channel resources to other international campaigns, whereas Muslims were perceived to be victims. In addition to benefiting from MAK's pan-Islamic vision, as opposed to pan-Arab ideology, al Qaeda drew from the vast financial resources and technical expertise mobilized during the decade-long anti-Soviet campaign.

As the infighting among the Afghan mujahideen commanders increased in the period after the Soviet withdrawal, bin Laden decided to return to the Middle East. Here he helped create the first mujahideen group in South Yemen, which fought against forces from North Yemen in the Yemeni civil war. Prior to this, Iraq invaded Kuwait in August 1990. Harboring great opposition toward Saddam Hussein and the Baathist ideology, bin Laden approached the Saudi royal family to seek their support for his ambition of forming a coalition of mujahideen to oust Saddam Hussein from Kuwait. His proposal was rejected, and instead US troops were invited into the Holy Kingdom, which bin Laden found humiliating and in opposition to the teachings of Islam.

The refusal by the royal Saudi family to allow bin Laden to fight Saddam's forces and the subsequent entry of thousands of US troops into Saudi Arabia infuriated bin Laden, and he subsequently led a campaign against the House of Saud. He accused the Saudi rulers of being apostates (Munafiqin), whose replacement was a necessity. Moreover, he considered the US presence on the Arabian Peninsula as offensive. In 1991, he sneaked out of Saudi Arabia to Pakistan and subsequently relocated to Sudan. Together with his family and a large band of followers, bin Laden moved to Khartoum. In 1992, he led al Qaeda into a new role, with the stated purpose of driving US forces from the Arabian Peninsula. Because of bin Laden's criticism, the Saudi rulers revoked his citizenship in 1994.

In Sudan, bin Laden set up factories and farms, some of which were established solely to supply jobs to out-of-work mujahideen. Osama bin Laden's construction company el-Hijrah for Construction and Development Ltd., together with the National Islamic Front and the Sudanese military, also built the new airport at Port Sudan, as well as a 1,200-kilometer-long highway linking Khartoum to Port Sudan. Osama bin Laden also set up the Wadi al-Aqiq Company, an export-import firm. He ran the Taba Investment Company Ltd., as well as the el-Shamal Islamic Bank in Khartoum, in which he is said to have invested $50 million. In Sudan, bin Laden also bought the Damazine Farm, which served both as a farm and as a training camp and meeting point for al Qaeda's leadership. However, as Sudan began to open to the West, the government feared his presence would complicate their new policies, and the Sudanese leadership therefore requested his departure. As a result, in May 1996, bin Laden moved to Afghanistan, leaving behind in

Sudan a network of Afghan veterans and several successful factories and corporations.

While in Afghanistan, al Qaeda established links with the Taliban, providing the Taliban with finances, military support, and other resources. Initially, bin Laden assisted his close friends Yunus Khalis and Jalaluddin Haqqani. Jalaluddin Haqqani hosted al Qaeda's training infrastructure in the Khost province during the period bin Laden spent in Sudan. These facilities, which included the Jihad Wal, Abu Bakr al-Sadiq, and the al-Faruq camps were expanded after bin Laden returned to Afghanistan in 1996. Yunus Khalis allowed bin Laden the use of his fortress in the Tora Bora mountains of the Nangarhar province.

However, in late 1996, the Taliban arrived in Nangarhar, and despite a great initial aversion toward the Taliban's practice of Islam, bin Laden and al Qaeda eventually established a relationship with the Taliban. In this relationship, al Qaeda could continue to run training camps, but during 1997 Mullah Muhammad Umar ordered bin Laden to stop giving media interviews. Following Mullah Umar's direction, bin Laden continued to provide videotaped responses to questions sent by the international media. Despite this breach of orders, the relationship between bin Laden and Mullah Umar seems to have grown after bin Laden moved to Kandahar in 1997. In return for the strong relationship, al Qaeda set up the 055 Brigade to assist the Taliban in their fight against the Northern Alliance. The Taliban regime reciprocated this support by providing al Qaeda sanctuary, weapons, equipment, and training resources. Osama bin Laden based himself in an area called Tarnak Farms, near the airport of Kandahar. In 1999, bin Laden moved al Qaeda's al-Faruq camp and Beit al-Shuhadah (House of Martyrs) from Mes Aynak to an area near Kandahar airport.

While in Afghanistan, bin Laden not only established an alliance with the Taliban but also formed the front known as "The Islamic World Front for the struggle against the Jews and the Crusaders" (Al-Jabhah Al-Islamiyyah al-'Alamiyyah li-Qital al-Yahud wal-Salibiyyin), on 23 February 1998. The fatwah, which was the basis of this front, stated that the group called upon "Muslim ulema, leaders, youths, and people" to "kill the Americans and their allies civilian and military. This is in accordance with the words of Almighty God." With the creation of this front, it was apparent that al Qaeda had a wider reach than previously imagined. The announcement of the group was made by Osama bin Laden, Dr. Ayman Zawahiri, Rifa'I Ahmad Taha (a leader in the Egyptian Al-Gama'ah al-Islamiyah), Munir Hamzah (the secretary of the Association of Pakistani Clerics), Fazul Rahman Khalil (the leader of Jamiat ul-Ansar group in Pakistan), and Sheikh Abd al-Salam Muhammad Khan (the leader of the Jihad Movement of Bangladesh). The US campaign in Afghanistan, which started in late 2001, dispersed al Qaeda temporarily and destroyed the group's training facilities. However, al Qaeda since restructured and built new training opportunities in the North Waziristan Agency of the FATA of Pakistan, where the group is empowering fighters from the West with bomb-making skills, which are increasingly more sophisticated than those of the mujahideen who have not been to training camps in the FATA.

FINANCIAL

Sources of Supply

Al Qaeda relies on several sources of funding for its operations. They include direct funding from Arab supporters of al Qaeda and contributions through Islamic charitable organizations. Arab supporters of al Qaeda supply financial resources to the organization. Much of this allegedly comes from citizens of countries situated on the Arabian Peninsula and from Europe and North America.

Islamic charities were previously used to finance al Qaeda. Generally, funds were used legitimately for the humanitarian causes these charities support, but some money was channeled to pay for terrorist activities. For example, one Chicago-based charity, the Benevolence International Foundation, was accused of creating a list of orphans to justify expenses paid to an injured terrorist fighter. Illicit charities have proven difficult for authorities to identify and close, because it has proven difficult to tie illegal money transfers directly to a charity and because charities can easily reregister under a new name.

East Africa, the Indian subcontinent, Southeast Asia, and parts of the Middle East all have a tradition and empathy with alternative remittance systems and basic Hawala banking practices. This often is used by al Qaeda to transfer money in these areas. In this context, the cross-movement of terrorist funds is made by the most available and efficient methods, often under alternative remittance systems such as Hawalas. These systems were already in use by Islamic terrorist groups before the 9/11 attacks, albeit on a smaller scale than today.[240] However, couriers are the main vehicle for the transfer of funds to al Qaeda's leaders in Pakistan. It is relatively uncomplicated to travel with cash or with credit cards, where money can be withdrawn in Pakistan or Syria.

External Support

Al Qaeda solicits donations from like-minded supporters and illicitly siphons funds from donations to Muslim charitable organizations across the globe. It is estimated that al Qaeda received millions of dollars in external support that is distributed to affiliates and operational elements throughout the world.

STRATEGY

In the post-9/11 environment, al Qaeda's leaders refined the terrorist organization's strategy to use small-scale attacks to destabilize—and ultimately overthrow—the secular governments in Islamic countries, while continuing to plan both small and larger sophisticated attacks against Western targets. This leads to a general feature of a strategy that still seems largely unrecognized. Al Qaeda seems to be specifically interested in inciting greater US and Western military action anywhere in the Islamic world. It is not expecting to defeat the United States in the short term. Quite to the contrary, it seeks an increased confrontation as a means of greatly increasing support for both its long- and medium-range goals. Al Qaeda is well aware that the US and Western responses to terrorist attacks will further alienate Muslims in the world and eventually push moderates to their side.

The group initially emphasized the symbolic targets in the West when making their selections (US embassies, the World Trade Center, military barracks, USS *Cole*). However, the measures and countermeasures taken by governments made al Qaeda change its strategy and pursue a dual strategy of planning both smaller attacks against soft targets and more sophisticated, bigger attacks against hardened targets.

Al Qaeda also finds it less costly to operate in parts of Asia, Africa, and the Middle East, where there is a lack of security controls and a vacuum of state authority. Therefore, most attacks will be against Western targets located where al Qaeda has infrastructure, but government supervision is not rigid. While the focus on Western targets will remain a priority, al Qaeda will also conduct operations against Muslim rulers and regimes supporting the US-led war on terror. The physical security of Iraqi, Pakistani, and Afghan leaders Nuri al-Maliki and President Hamid Karzai remains particularly vulnerable, and their regimes will come under sustained political challenges. A number of Pakistani groups, who were previously fighting in the Kashmir or against Shiites, have come under greater control of al Qaeda. Through these Pakistani groups, al Qaeda recruited fighters among the convert and diaspora communities in the West. South Asian and particularly the Pakistani communities in the West are penetrated by militant Pakistani groups like HuJI, Laskhar e-Jhangvi, or Jamiat ul-Furqan, who act as the interface between al Qaeda and these communities.

MILITARY CAPABILITIES

Many of al Qaeda's operatives attended training camps in Afghanistan. There was a mutually reinforcing relationship between the camps and terrorist operations. The camps provided operatives for terrorist attacks, and successful attacks in turn boosted camp recruitment and attendance. The training at these camps was multifaceted in nature. Training primarily focused on conventional warfare. Advanced terrorist training was provided to the best and most ardent recruits. Trainees and personnel were allowed to think creatively of ways to commit mass murder. In addition, equal emphasis was given to ideological and religious indoctrination. It is estimated that perhaps as many as twenty thousand men trained in Afghan camps during the 1990s. Of these trainees, only a small percentage went on to receive advanced terrorist training, and an even smaller percentage became members of al Qaeda.[241]

Al Qaeda's members are familiar with modern communications and are reported to use encrypted e-mail, cellular phones, satellite communications, and training manuals on CD-ROMs. However, their use of satellite phones was discouraged after several of al Qaeda's leaders were tracked, detained, and killed because of their use of satellite phones.

Al Qaeda has operatives that are extremely skilled in the development of IEDs. They use the pressure cooker bombs as roadside IEDs, and in 2004–2006, al Qaeda's members are believed to have instructed several like-minded individuals from the United Kingdom in the development of hydrogen peroxide IEDs. Hydrogen peroxide (oxidant) and black pepper, chapatti flour, and sugar (fuels) were used as the main charge in the 7 and 21 July bombings in 2005 in the United Kingdom and in the liquid IED's in the 2006 airline attacks over the Atlantic.[242] These kinds of high concentration hydrogen peroxide IEDs were not previously seen in the United Kingdom.[243] We believe that its use in at least two terrorism cases, where the bomb makers were trained in Pakistan, makes it a signature source for bomb makers trained in Pakistan during the period from 2004–2005.

Al Qaeda also operates across the technological spectrum, and it is likely to use low-tech, high-impact attacks, especially using civilian infrastructure to attack civilian society and critical infrastructure. With greater border controls after 9/11, members and associate members of al Qaeda will use items easily purchased off the shelf, especially from pharmacies, chemist shops, and hardware stores. Al Qaeda's members will live off the environment and turn commercially available material into weapons. A Tunisian member of al Qaeda conducted a suicide attack against the oldest Jewish synagogue in Djerba, Tunisia, using a commercial LPG truck, and it was detonated by high explosives. Similarly, JI used a consignment of chlorate purchased from the port city of Surabaya in Indonesia against targets in Bali in October 2002. Using multiple identities, al Qaeda's members will travel to Pakistan or Iraq, receive training, and then return to their native countries. Here they will manufacture IEDs or chemical, biological, radiological, or nuclear weapons (CBRN) that they learned to manufacture in Pakistan and Iraq and then subsequently plan and prepare attacks.

Tactics

The structure and nature of al Qaeda enable it to use a wealth of operational knowledge. As such, the tactics used by al Qaeda are broad and diverse. Al Qaeda selects whichever tactics suit its requirements according to the objective or target. Moreover, al Qaeda is a learning organization; it carefully studies the target's environment and the security levels of its target. For example, in the case of the surface-to-air missile attacks against the Israeli airline in Mombassa on 29 November 2002, the attackers realized that rather than orchestrating an attack inside the airport, it would be more effective to orchestrate an attack from the outside, where there was less security. Al Qaeda operates like a modern organization and values the importance of cost efficiency. For example, the October 2000 attack on the USS *Cole*, a ship valued at $1 billion to build, cost the organization only $5,000 to significantly damage.

As such, al Qaeda's operations utilize tactics that it can execute effectively and efficiently. One example of such a tactic is simultaneous suicide attacks. Al Qaeda will also conduct coordinated simultaneous suicide attacks with the intention of inflicting maximum damage to human and physical infrastructure. For instance, al Qaeda executed two simultaneous suicide attacks in East Africa in August 1998. Similarly, Turkish jihadis, who received direction from al Qaeda and training in Afghanistan, executed two double suicide attacks in November 2003 in Istanbul.

In conclusion, al Qaeda uses a diverse array of tactics. The tactics used in al Qaeda's incidents are merely a sample of the tactics the group effectively employs. Al Qaeda will continue to innovate and venture into new techniques. Al Qaeda weakened in the period after 9/11. However, the group is resilient, and a new leadership and structure have emerged. Al Qaeda may still be capable of orchestrating new terrorist operations on a scale similar to that of the 9/11 attacks.[244]

Targets

Al Qaeda engages in symbolic bombings that not only create significant physical destruction but also inflict massive psychological and financial cost. Among its targets are major banks and financial institutions, embassies, and military installations—particularly from the West and the secular governments of Muslim countries that are perceived as supporters of the US war on terror.

Training

Prior to America's military incursion into Afghanistan, al Qaeda operated a total of six–seven training camps in Afghanistan. However, most of them were destroyed during the August 1998 US cruise missile attack against Jihad Wal, Abu Bakr al-Saddiq, Khalid ibn Walid, and the al-Faruq camps in the Khost province of Afghanistan. Al Qaeda subsequently moved its al-Faruq camp to an old copper mine at Mes Aynak, near Kabul. The camp was small and often on the front line between the Taliban and the Northern Alliance. In 1999, al Qaeda moved the al-Faruq camp near Kandahar and placed it outside the city, near the airport and Tarnak Farms, where Osama bin Laden lived. After the admission of Ibn Sheikh al-Libi and Abu Zubaydah into al Qaeda in 2000, completion of the Khalden complex solidified his leadership role in the organization. The Khalden complex located in Khost was closed and moved to Rishkor, near Kabul. The Khalden camp never regenerated itself after the move and never again became the significant provider for training and brotherhood that it had previously had been.

In the camps mentioned above, al Qaeda's training included the use of deception and denial in its operational techniques, similar to those employed by intelligence services. Al Qaeda's training manuals carry detailed instructions on the use of deception by terrorists, particularly in Western target countries. The training manuals are primarily concerned with one main goal: "to avoid detection at all costs when infiltrating an enemy state."[245] The manuals contain an abundance of tactical lessons on how to use disguises, elude deception as a virtue, and execute a wide range of missions.

The following are examples of the content of a typical training manual. The introductory section of the training manual recites stories from the Qu-ran and ancient proverbs that extol deception as a virtue. Lesson two discusses the importance of keeping secrets and concealing information. Lesson three touches on the issue of counterfeit currency and forged documents. Lesson four discusses the correct use of apartments and hiding places. The manual advises the member to avoid being conspicuous and to blend into the society concerned. Lesson five focuses on the importance of communications and transportation, and talks about the advantages and disadvantages of the different forms of communications. Other lessons in the manual touch on the execution of assassination, assault, kidnapping, bombing, intelligence, and espionage.[246]

Al Qaeda was able to conduct its training in Afghanistan because of a historically unique factor: being a benign Islamic movement in Afghanistan that enjoyed support across the porous borders and into Pakistan. Compounding this was the Sahwah–Islamic awakening—which emerged during the Soviet jihad and reenergized a violent ideology, with powerful backers in the Middle East. These factors were exacerbated by a profound lack of interest in the region, especially on the part of Western powers.

In subsequent years, al Qaeda was able to induce various separatist Islamic groups across the world—especially in Central and Southeast Asia. Al Qaeda assisted these groups by providing financial support, establishing training facilities, and providing training to them. Among the groups were the Libyan Islamic Fighting Group; the Moroccan Islamic Fighting Group, the Abu Sayyaf, the Moro Islamic Liberation Front of the Philippines, and Jemaah Islamiyah and what it calls "jihad militants" from Burma, Bosnia, Chechnya, Indonesia, Iraq, Jordan, Lebanon, Pakistan, Somalia, Tajikistan, Turkey, Turkmenistan, and Uzbekistan.

In the 1990s, Osama bin Laden asked the Moro Islamic Liberation Front (MILF) chairman Hashim Salamat to set up training camps in the Philippines for al Qaeda, because it was becoming harder for his operatives to travel secretly to Afghanistan for training. Al Qaeda established a terrorist training camp at the MILF's Camp Abu Bakar, in the Philippines. This camp was a sprawling complex, run by the largest Muslim separatist group. According to CNN news, the MILF reopened two training camps in the southern Philippines, in addition to one training camp in Indonesia. This information was verified by various militants now in custody. Singaporean intelligence similarly reported that al Qaeda's close ally, Jemaah Islamiyah, and specifically the Hambali faction, was training militants in Indonesia—in the areas of Poso and Ambon, both of which are flashpoints for Muslim–Christian violence. A videotape discovered by CNN in Afghanistan revealed an al Qaeda training camp in Indonesia. Rohan Gunaratna, an al Qaeda expert, postulated that the video is of a training camp in Indonesia. It is very likely that the camp is the Poso, Sulawesi, training camp run by al Qaeda until July 2000.

In fact, al Qaeda's activities in Southeast Asia in particular were part of a larger plan to move al Qaeda's base of operations from Afghanistan to Southeast Asia. Ayman al-Zawahiri, Osama bin Laden's right-hand man, and Mohammed Atef, al Qaeda's former military chief, visited Indonesia in 2000. The visit was a fact-finding mission to assess the possibility of moving al Qaeda's base of operations to Southeast Asia. Southeast Asia's topographical peculiarities (porous borders, slack immigration controls, etc.) were an advantage. Indonesia, for example, is a sprawling archipelago of more than thirteen thousand islands and has relatively porous borders and plenty of potential hiding places beyond the routine control of any of the security agencies that made it ideal for establishing training bases. Though the term "camp" implies a complex filled with tents and temporary structures, the camps that Southeast Asian militants use/d were often large and sophisticated installations containing not only classrooms, prayer halls, bunkers, testing fields, and firing ranges but sometimes underground tunnels and concrete storage facilities for weapons and chemicals—items mostly off limits to the hosts themselves.

Such camps became the lifeblood of local militants, providing indoctrination and training for many of the estimated five thousand plus foot soldiers, go-betweens, planners, document forgers, communications specialists, scouts, technicians, bombers, and even hijackers who passed through enroute to conduct terrorist attacks. An estimated five thousand militants from more than fifty countries have passed through the camps, spending from two weeks to more than six months learning the general and specific skills that modern terrorism requires.

POLITICAL

Ideology

The goal of the global Islamist jihadist movement is to create an international Islamic caliphate system.

Political Affiliations

Al Qaeda is known to receive state sponsorship from two countries, namely South Yemen and Sudan. The group also maintains close ties to political parties such as Jamiat Ulema al-Islami (Fazl) and Jamiat Ulema al-Islami (Samiul Haq).

Support Base

Before the 9/11 attacks against the United States, al Qaeda's membership was estimated to be between three thousand and five thousand men. Most of these men fought alongside the Taliban against the Northern Alliance. Since the 9/11 attacks, 70 percent of al Qaeda's original senior leadership and 3,400 of its lower-level operatives and associates were killed or detained.[247] Today al Qaeda has around three to four thousand members in Iraq, fighting as part of the Dawlat al-Iraq al-Islamiyah (the Islamic State of Iraq). In Pakistan, the group has around two to three hundred members, while Tanzim Qaedat bi-Bilad al-Maghrebi Islami is around two thousand members strong. Al Qaeda's cadre in the Arabian Peninsula is believed to number a few hundred, including the members of the new branch, Tanzim al Qaeda fi-Bilad al-Yemen, which first rose to prominence in September 2006 when the group conducted four suicide bombings that targeted multiple oil installations in one day. The membership of Tanzim al Qaeda al-Jihad Ard al-Kinanah is believed to number below one hundred members, who are currently either in Pakistan or Iran.

RESPONSES TO AL QAEDA

The response against al Qaeda has been very robust. Since the attacks of 9/11, many countries, particularly the United States, have set up policies of countering the efforts of terrorist organizations, particularly al Qaeda, regardless of where they are based and operate. While the United States led the military response, such as the Operation Enduring Freedom, to remove terrorist training camps and infrastructure within Afghanistan, the capture of al Qaeda's leaders and the cessation of terrorist activities in other countries remains a challenge. Efforts to address the terrorist threat through a series of legislative and other practical measures, including financial measures, airline security, security and intelligence cooperation, and the protection of critical infrastructure must remain to mitigate the long-term threats from these groups.

In addition, the UN stepped up its counterterrorism measures through the UN Security Council Resolution 1373, which calls on states to take specific actions against terrorists, focusing principally on disrupting their funding and support networks to curb the threat of terrorism.

Other multilateral organizations, such as the G8 and the European Union (EU), have also come up with policies to confront terrorism. The G8 has been one of the leading players to announce that officials should draw up a list of specific measures to enhance counterterrorism cooperation. On 6 October 2001, G8 finance ministers and central bank governors issued statements and an action plan to combat the financing of terrorism. Progress toward the agreement led the G8 to develop a twenty-five-point action plan on counterterrorism in January 2002, covering issues such as the support for the UN's role, financing of terrorism, aviation security, migration, drugs, cybercrime, and judicial cooperation.

Although all EU countries are engaged in some military response to the fight against terrorism, Europeans shrewdly understand that terrorism cannot be fought through military means alone. As such, Europe's multilateral response toward terrorism is gaining positive results.

Following the 9/11 attacks, much greater efforts undertaken in Southeast Asia by individual countries and between nations to counter terrorism and al Qaeda have been successful. Indonesia, particularly after months of insistence that al Qaeda did not operate in the country, endorsed a public statement in December 2001, in which the intelligence agency admitted the presence of al Qaeda training camps in the country. In February 2002, Indonesia signed a pact with Australia to fight international terrorism. There have also been mass arrests of individuals with links to JI, an al Qaeda-affiliated group. Other countries like the Philippines passed antimoney laundering legislation to block the flow of terrorist money. In addition, the Philippines government offered US intelligence and logistical support, along with the use of Philippine airspace for efforts to counter terrorism. Additionally, they opened two former US military bases: Clark Air Force Base and Subic Bay. On a regional level, all ASEAN members adopted the ASEAN Declaration on Joint Action to Counter Terrorism at the Brunei summit in November 2001. However, the Philippine legislature still has not passed specific terrorism legislation, which greatly hampers counterterrorism operations in the country.

The counterterrorism efforts undertaken by various countries led to the arrests of senior leadership and prominent figures. However, new leadership emerged to replace the old generation of al Qaeda leaders.

Current Assessment

Al Qaeda and its affiliated groups are under increasing international pressure. Most of the gains from the war on terror include isolating al Qaeda politically and continuing pressure to strain al Qaeda's ability to organize and connect to the rest of the Muslim world. The killings of several high-profile al Qaeda leaders, especially the 2 May 2011 assassination of al Qaeda chief Osama bin Laden in a US Navy SEAL special operations mission, and arrests of several hundred members have dealt severe blows to the group. In spite of this, at the ideological level, the ghost of transnational jihad refuses to go away.

Almost a decade after 9/11, analysts are still divided in their assessments of al Qaeda's current situation. Nonetheless, a majority believe organizationally al Qaeda is weaker than ever, but ideologically it is at its strongest. This comment outlines a brief front-by-front rundown of al Qaeda's strengths and weaknesses to argue after weakening al Qaeda organizationally and operationally, through military means, effective countermeasures are needed in the political domain to discredit and defeat the transnational terrorist group.

Since the bombings against London's transportation system on 7 July 2005, al Qaeda has not conducted a successful attack in the West. Also, the group has not succeeded in attacking the United States for more than a decade. Most of al Qaeda's attack attempts in the West are lone wolf–style attacks, involving one gunman or inept bombers. Several of these attempted terrorist attacks either failed or were foiled by security and law enforcement agencies. Al Qaeda's outreach to its supporters and sympathizers to their jihadi ideologues and mentors is now largely limited to the virtual world of the Internet.

In 2007, the national intelligence estimate declared the Pakistani tribal belt as al Qaeda's global headquarters. The success of the US-led eight-year-old drone campaign against al Qaeda in the FATA heralds a gradual shift of focus against the al Qaeda. During the past two years, the central gravity of al Qaeda's operations against the West shifted from the Pakistani tribal areas to Yemen and Somalia, where most of the terror plots were conducted. Today, the most lethal of al Qaeda's franchises are the Yemen-based al Qaeda in the Arabian Peninsula (AQAP). Therefore, with the removal of al Qaeda's top leaders, except al-Zawahiri, is the downfall of al Qaeda in sight?

Some of the terrorist organizations are built around a cult of personality, similar to Peru's Shining Path or the Turkish Kurdistan Workers' Party

(PKK), which were virtually crippled after the loss of their top leadership. The arrest of the Shining Path's head in 1992, Abimael Guzman, and the PKK leader, Abdullah Oclan, in 1999, led to the demise of the two groups.

Insurgent groups like Hamas and Hizballah have hierarchical organizational structures and a devout affiliation with their cause. They survived the loss of their top leaders. In 2004, Israel eliminated Sheikh Ahmed Yaseen, Hamas's founder, and then his successor, Abdul Aziz Rantisi, through helicopter-fired missiles. Similarly, in 1992, Israel killed the secretary-general of Hizballah, Abbas Mussawi, in a helicopter strike and its director of military operations, Imad Mughniyeh, in a car bomb in 2008. However, both organizations are intact and fully active. Like Hamas and Hizballah, al Qaeda survived the loss of its top leaders.

Al Qaeda has collective leadership and remains united and ideologically motivated to forward its cause of global jihad, despite suffering enormous losses and losing its key leaders. Therefore, the elimination of top leaders will not do much damage to the organizational structure of al Qaeda. In fact, today al Qaeda is ideologically stronger than ever, and its influence is also expanding beyond the Afghanistan–Pakistan region. It is spreading its wings in Yemen, Iraq, and the Horn of Africa. Killing the top leadership harms al Qaeda, but it will not defeat them unless steps are taken to weaken their ideological propaganda and its ability to exploit ungoverned spaces, like the tribal areas of Pakistan, Somalia, Iraq, Afghanistan, and Yemen.

The physical damages done to al Qaeda's organizational structure will set the organization back several years. Most of al Qaeda's training centers and sanctuaries in the Afghanistan–Pakistan region are dismantled. A handful of members from al Qaeda's core leadership remain on the run to evade US drone strikes and arrests. As a result, al Qaeda is nearly devoid of any formal command and control structure.

One key factor accounting for the failure of al Qaeda's terrorist operations in the West is the improved international coordination of intelligence agencies. The speed and accuracy of identifying and locating persons of interest and members of al Qaeda has improved exponentially since 9/11. Globally focused intelligence operations created an environment hostile to al Qaeda's operations. The attack attempts launched by al Qaeda throughout the world met with swift and harsh responses by the governments and societies under attack, thus further weakening al Qaeda's organization.

Al Qaeda is also searching for relevance in the face of intense international pressure. Al Qaeda does not present itself convincingly as a resilient, long-term organization with a clear vision for the future. Its agenda for global jihad is too vague and obscure. Moreover, it not only challenges its ability to attain such overambitious goals but also strains the means to attain them in a very charged international atmosphere. Moreover, the United States led the charge to stop the funding streams worldwide and with far-reaching consequences for individuals connected to terror organizations.

The central challenge for the group is the increasing disruption of the degree of connectedness with the rest of the world. Al Qaeda's core leadership remains distant and out of touch with the tactical and operational aspects of the fight. Therefore, its ability to provide strategic vision and direct resources is limited. This is increasingly important because strategic attacks may need coordinated resources across wide geographic areas and the operational security risks are too great for the core leadership to play a more prominent role. Even though al Qaeda's leadership remains in place, it is not likely to recover its position of power enjoyed in 2001. No matter how inspirational and charismatic the leadership is, without maintaining active contacts with their followers, leaders and organizations lose their support base. Al Qaeda lost its secure base and a reliable means of contact with its supporters. Issuing video messages on the Internet or releasing statements issued to print media does not suffice. Their outreach to their supporters and sympathizers is largely in decline, and the organization's best avenues to connect with the masses are through digital means.

Prior to his assassination, Osama bin Laden had become almost a mythical figurehead of symbolic and iconic value inside al Qaeda. In the wake of his death, lingering questions of legitimacy loom over al Qaeda's remaining leadership. The group's image is waning and frayed. They stand to lose credibility if they are unable to follow through with their threats and warnings. With a view of long-term futuristic thinking, al Qaeda's leadership failed to create and train a confident and trusted cadre of younger and fresher second- and third-tier leaders. Apart from bin Laden, Ayman al-Zawahiri, and perhaps Abu Yahya al-Libi, even its most ardent supporters might find it hard to name or recognize another living hero of al Qaeda's terrorism.

Increasing steps for the Afghan Taliban to distance itself from al Qaeda is highly indicative of the problems the group is facing. The strong bonds that used to hold these groups together is now weaker than ever. During the past thirteen years, the links between the Afghan Taliban and al Qaeda have weakened. After bin Laden's death, the Afghan Taliban have parted their ways with al Qaeda to avail chances of becoming political stakeholders for a negotiated settlement in Afghanistan's endgame. The death of al Qaeda's chief opened some avenues for political solutions to end the decade-long war. A content analysis of statements issued by the Shura of the Afghan Taliban after bin Laden's death provides insights into the divergent goals of the two jihadist movements. It was a well-crafted message eulogizing the services of bin Laden for jihad but did not vow any reprisal attacks to avenge his death. Instead, they reaffirmed their commitment to continue their struggle against the US-led international coalition forces inside Afghanistan.

While al Qaeda focuses on worldwide jihad against the West and establishment of a religious superstate in the Muslim world, the Afghan Taliban focus on their own country and show little to no interest in attacking targets outside Afghanistan. They portray themselves as a local nationalist resistance movement of Afghanistan. However, despite losing a number of its prominent leaders and suffering countless setbacks, al Qaeda remains a potent threat and a trendsetter for transnational jihad in the world. Al Qaeda is still evolving. Moreover, it still maintains the capability to attract aspiring jihadists to its cadres in different forms and manifestations. Moreover, notwithstanding the dormant nature of its operations, it had achieved technological sophistication and the ability to adapt to changing environments, use innovative methods for carrying out terrorist operations, and improve its ideological articulation and novel ways of propaganda dissemination.

Al Qaeda's Robin Hood image won it sympathizers and supporters from around the Muslim world. In his book *Good Muslim, Bad Muslim*, Mehmood Mamdani maintains that "[i]nitially, al Qaeda started as a political movement declaring three main objectives: to liberate occupied Muslim territories through jihad, withdrawal of US forces from the Arabian Peninsula and demanding an end to double dealings of the United States with the Muslim World." At that time, al Qaeda openly challenged the questionable policies of the inept and corrupt Muslim rulers and provided the Muslim masses with much-needed alternative voices. People looked up to it as an agent of change—a needed panacea for decades of tyranny and oppression. However, al Qaeda failed to provide a plan of action to actualize its stated objectives into reality.

As time passed, al Qaeda reduced its size and support base in the 1990s, which further shrank after 9/11. Because of its overambitious goals of creating a universal Islamic caliphate, it lost its appeal to the wider Muslim world. It degenerated from a widespread political movement to a jihadist movement, with a few pockets of active supporters and a fair level of sympathizers from around the Muslim world, especially in the Muslim diaspora communities of the West. Today, its point of strength is not its global infrastructure and membership but rather its overarching and appealing ideology. It is constantly seeking to reinvigorate the global jihad movement by exploiting the widespread suffering, resentment, and anger in the Muslim world and turning it against the United States and its allies. Now al Qaeda is an umbrella organization providing all like-minded militant outfits an ideological platform to join hands with it in its cause of global jihad.

For various Islamist militant organizations around the globe, the stature of al Qaeda is that of an ideological motivator providing religious justification for their violent acts. Considering the sympathy and new recruits gathered from Islamist groups in Asia, Africa, the Middle East, and elsewhere, the ideological campaign unleashed by al Qaeda has been partially successful. Al

Qaeda's radical ideology—sustained internationally by anti-Western and anti-Semitic rhetoric—has adherents among many individuals and groups. They merely follow al Qaeda's precepts, models, and methods and act in the style of al Qaeda.

Moreover, after 9/11, al Qaeda is no longer a hierarchical organization. It is decentralized and compartmentalized and is a group that no longer falls or fits into the category or classical definition of a terrorist outfit per se. Much has changed in al Qaeda's organizational structure and functional matters for the organization and its leadership hierarchy. It does not have a unified body with a coherent structure. Over the years, it has splintered, giving rise to many other groups.

Currently, al Qaeda has five to six autonomous organizations operating in different parts of the world, namely al Qaeda in the Arabian Peninsula (AQAP), al Qaeda in Islamic Maghreb (AQIM), al Qaeda in Somalia or Al-Shabab (AQSA), the Libyan Islamic Fighting Group (LIFG), and al Qaeda in Yemen. Moreover, there are various other militant factions in different regions of the world aligned with al Qaeda. For instance, Tehrik-e-Taliban Pakistan (TTP)—a conglomerate of antistate militant movements based in Pakistan's tribal areas adjacent to the Afghanistan–Pakistan border, and JI of Malaysia. These organizations are loosely affiliated and more or less work autonomously within their own local context and set of environments.

Another incipient indicator of concern regarding recruiting is al Qaeda's appeal to the Muslim diaspora communities of America and Europe. Close scrutiny and analysis of attacks on the World Trade Center in 2001, Madrid bombings in 2004, bombings of London commuter trains in London in 2005, and the botched bomb attack in New York's Time Square in 2010 depict that the perpetrators of these attacks were holders of dual nationalities who had hardly met bin Laden or visited al Qaeda's training camps. Expecting that bin Laden's death will result in subsiding violence is a fallacy.

An overwhelming majority of analysts and experts on al Qaeda believe the 2 May death of bin Laden is the single-most devastating blow to the jihadist group. This school of thought argues that bin Laden's death deprived al Qaeda of charismatic and inspiring leadership. It upholds that Dr. Ayman al-Zawahiri, the current patron in chief of the organization, does not have the aura, inspiration, and leadership qualities that bin Laden had. In our estimation, al-Zawahiri will not be able to command the respect that bin Laden enjoyed. As a result, al Qaeda will further weaken and disintegrate.

However, a compelling counternarrative suggests that militancy has not died with bin Laden, even if his death delivered a demoralizing blow to its affiliated militant organizations. They regard his death as a significant symbolic victory for America and its allies, which will have minimal effects on al Qaeda's worldwide operations. Experts of this tradition consider the al Qaeda-led terrorist threat as "franchised terrorism," whereby previously identified al Qaeda leaders serve as examples and provide ideological rather than material support to terrorist operatives around the world. Bin Laden's stature as commander in chief of al Qaeda was of an iconic figurehead and that of a spiritual leader. His death elevates him further from an iconic spiritual figurehead to a martyred figurehead.

In counterinsurgency operations, counting casualties or removal of key leaders is hardly the best measure to map the road to success or measure victory. Recent history of various insurgencies is a glaring example of this assertion. Assassinations of Nawab Akbar Bugti on 27 August 2006 in the Baloch insurgency, the execution of former Iraqi president Saddam Hussein on 30 December 2006, and the death of TTP chief Baitullah Meshed in a US drone strike on 25 August 2009 added fuel to these insurgencies instead of diminishing them.

Al Qaeda's key strength is its global outreach. Hardly any terrorist group today is truly multinational with branches all over the world. Most violent extremist groups are die-hard nationalist extremists who would never accept foreigners in their ranks. Al Qaeda is an exception. From its start, al Qaeda was a multinational and multiethnic enterprise, even if Arabs, especially Saudis and Egyptians, have always dominated the upper echelons of the organization. The fact that membership in al Qaeda is open to virtually everyone, irrespective of ethnicity and nationality, is a key selling point for al Qaeda, because it strengthens the credibility of its pan-Islamic rhetoric. It greatly expands the recruitment base for the organization. As long as one is willing to accept its extremist ideology, anyone can become an al Qaeda member. Hence, al Qaeda succeeded in recruiting followers from a large number of countries.

In recent years, al Qaeda worked consistently to establish cooperative networks with other groups of Muslim extremists in many parts of the world, from Southeast Asia to Northern Africa. It succeeded in finding local partners by offering training facilities, military expertise, and financial support. The organization also offered media services and increasingly lent its brand name to local groups willing to work with al Qaeda. Al Qaeda's abilities to sustain cooperative relationships with local partners and to insert itself as a relevant actor in local and regional contexts were the key to its survival.

In Sudan, bin Laden established an Islamic Army Shura, which was to serve as the coordinating body for the consortium of terrorist groups with which he was forging alliances. It was composed of his own al Qaeda Shura, together with leaders or representatives of terrorist organizations that were still independent. In building this Islamic army, he enlisted groups from Saudi Arabia, Egypt, Jordan, Lebanon, Iraq, Oman, Algeria, Libya, Tunisia, Morocco, Somalia, and Eritrea. Al Qaeda also established cooperative but less formal relationships with other extremist groups.

Though al Qaeda lacks the sophisticated military hardware of the United States, it still has at its disposal significant capabilities to remain a force to reckon with. Some of these capabilities involve using the Internet and related information technologies to facilitate achievement of their objectives. In addition, al Qaeda central keeps in contact with franchises and affiliates through an interlocking network of media production and distribution entities. Al Qaeda central, its regional franchises, and affiliated movements all place a high premium on media and release a constant stream of media products, from political statements to films. Three key entities connect al Qaeda and affiliated movements to the outside world through the Internet. Three media entities—Fajr, the Global Islamic Media Front, and Sahab—receive materials from more than one armed group and post those materials to the Internet.

Undoubtedly, al Qaeda's appeal owes a great deal to its shrewd media strategies and exploitation of the Internet. The importance of "the jihadi web" for al Qaeda's widespread appeal cannot be overstated. The organization demonstrates an ability to exploit the potential of the Internet for a wide variety of purposes. Al Qaeda and its online sympathizers produce enormous amounts of material on the Internet. Al Qaeda's Internet resources include thousands of audiovisual products, tens of thousands of audio files, and probably millions of written documents. They span a wide range of genres, all designed to cater to the needs of jihadi sympathizers, recruits, operatives, and not the least, the recruiters.

Though video is an important component of jihadist media, text products comprise the bulk of the daily media flow. Within text products, periodicals focused on specific "fronts" of the jihad are an important genre that deserves more attention from researchers. Al Qaeda also uses Internet chat rooms and e-mails to plan and coordinate operations. Many chat rooms are available for anonymous login and can be accessed from cyber cafes, libraries, or other Internet connections not traceable to a suspected terrorist group or member. Free e-mail hosting is also popular and available from a variety of sources.

A threat assessment of al Qaeda's status of its capabilities, intentions, and opportunities reveals that it clearly lacks capabilities and has fewer opportunities at its disposal; however, it still has the intentions to carry forward its agenda of transnational jihad. Effective and efficient responses to al Qaeda's threat at political and ideological levels have isolated the terror network. As mentioned in previous pieces, al Qaeda's staunchest ally, the Afghan Taliban, distanced themselves from its ideology of global jihad and portray themselves as nationalist resistant movements. Currently, al Qaeda's closest ally in Pakistan, the Tehrik-e-Taliban Pakistan (TTP), is also suffering desertions and dissentions. Internal divisions are quite visible within TTP's ranks, and the group finds it difficult to keep its act together. In such a scenario, it will be difficult for the TTP to protect and shelter al Qaeda in the Afghanistan–Pakistan border regions.

Starting with capabilities, al Qaeda does not possess both manpower and firepower to carry out large-scale terror attacks against targets. It is weak at the center but strong at the fringes. However, because of the continuous threat of CIA-led predator drone strikes and fear of being spotted, key leaders remain underground. Most of the time their focus is on how to survive and keep themselves alive and, every now and then, to appear in video messages to address their followers and operatives. This in turn weakens their ability to manage operational matters for al Qaeda and actively coordinate with its worldwide cells. Even before his death, former al Qaeda chief Osama bin Laden was leading the life of a recluse, and he was hardly in touch with the leadership of his group.

After 9/11, al Qaeda failed to conduct any major attacks beyond the Gulf. The great counterterrorism cooperation among security agencies across the world ensured that nearly all of the planned attacks were thwarted. Moreover, countless other operations never reached an operational stage because of the detention or disruption of preparation activities regarding attacks. According to research carried out by the Heritage Foundation, since the terrorist attacks of 9/11, at least thirty-nine terror plots against the United States were stopped. Moreover, lone wolf–style terror acts by al Qaeda operatives were also unsuccessful. The failed attempts of Richard Reid and Faisal Shahzad are two cases in point. Richard Reid failed to light a fuse protruding from his shoe on a Paris-bound American Airlines Flight Number 63. The flight crew and passengers overpowered Reid, hence diverting the flight to Boston. Faisal Shahzad's attack attempt against Times Square in New York City failed, and he was subsequently arrested by security authorities. Even though these attacks ultimately failed, they highlight the evolution of attack tactics and technology advancements to carry out attacks against their intended targets. Moreover, it underscores an unflinching desire to continue the fight against the West.

Looking at al Qaeda's intentions, the group still desires to implement its espoused vision of global jihad and to target its enemies around the globe. However, it has not been able to recover from various setbacks it suffered during the past decade. Various attempts, failed or otherwise, establish this fact beyond any doubt. Despite all odds and difficulties, al Qaeda has not given up on its stated goals and objectives. A worrying factor in this regard is the breakdown of state institutions in Muslim countries located in Africa and the Middle East. Moreover, the spread of radicalization in Muslim diaspora communities of the West and United States is of great concern. Al Qaeda thrives in failed or failing Muslim states, where the state security apparatus does not possess the expertise to pursue terrorists. The increase of incompetent and corrupt Muslim leaders and poor governance created huge vacuums, which al Qaeda masterly exploited to further its own interests. Currently, the abysmal state of affairs in several Muslim countries provides an ideal opportunity for al Qaeda and its like-minded groups to recultivate their influence. However, at the other end of the spectrum, the masses have the ability to heighten awareness against corrupt regimes or rogue terror entities that can precipitate demands for more democratic governance institutions—which is against everything that al Qaeda stands for. The Arab Spring is a case in point, where not even al Qaeda could shape the perception or momentum of the masses in Libya.

The most heartening thing to notice in the Arab Spring was minimal to no al Qaeda influence in these movements. Though these protests varied from country to country in their agendas and motivations, one thing in common from these mass movements was that they sprouted from their own set of problems in local contexts. The major demands in these movements were better job opportunities, the right to elect their representatives, and an end to decades of dictatorial rules and monarchies. None of these movements attributed the ills to external forces (read America), and all demanded solutions that do not provide al Qaeda any groundswell. However, a concern about this situation is the transition phase. If the public mandate is not respected and the peaceful transfer of power to elected public representatives is not facilitated by interim arrangements, then prolonged transition phases can provide al Qaeda with an opportunity to inject its influence to manipulate the process of power transition from old to new regimes.

Another lesson learned from the Arab Spring is the rise of Islamist forces in elections. Any attempt to sideline these Islamist forces would pave the way for al Qaeda to manipulate the circumstances to its benefit. A case in point is the suppression of the Islamic Salvation Front (FIS) in Algeria by the Algerian military, which over the years brought Algeria's Islamists closer to al Qaeda. Al Qaeda in the Islamic Maghreb (AQIM) grew out of a conflict in Algeria between the government and Islamist militants.

Furthermore, the decision of Egypt's Muslim Brotherhood to tone down its ideological rhetoric and show a moderate face in the form of the Justice and Development Party indicates its willingness for political compromises and accommodations. Previously, Hizballah in Lebanon and Hamas and Al-Fateh in Palestine transformed from armed resistance movements to political organizations. Currently, the Afghan Taliban movement in Afghanistan is undergoing the same transformation as well. Efforts should engage and work with these Islamist forces, if voted to power in the Muslim world, rather than efforts from outside to sideline them. In turn, it will deprive al Qaeda of any ground to cultivate its influence.

Most significantly, amicable solutions to the long-standing issue of Palestine, Indian Occupied Kashmir, and other occupied Muslim territories must also be explored. In the absence of judicious solutions to these problems, the issue of transnational militancy and terrorism cannot be resolved.

PROJECTED ACTIVITIES

Since the 9/11 attacks in the United States, al Qaeda's strength has weakened significantly as a result of the counterterrorism efforts undertaken by many countries. The US-led military efforts in Afghanistan shortly after 9/11 destroyed al Qaeda's base in Afghanistan. Al Qaeda has not been able to replace the base since the commencement of hostilities. The base in Afghanistan was not only a place for training but was used by al Qaeda to develop more powerful tools such as biological and chemical weapons. Evidence of this was found when the Taliban was overthrown in late 2001.[248]

However, not long after the fall of the Taliban and the expulsion of al Qaeda from Afghanistan, the group resettled in the FATA of Pakistan. Today, al Qaeda has once again successfully carved out a semisafe haven in the FATA. The Afghanistan–Pakistan border has emerged as the new headquarters of the global jihad movement. The subject of al Qaeda dominates the international media, but until five years after 9/11, its presence in the FATA has not been the subject of intense international debate. In the meantime, al Qaeda's determination to attack the West has recruited global fighters and struck its enemies through its inspiration for distant cells.

From the FATA, particularly North Waziristan, the group is resting, reorganizing, and regenerating. Compared to the Afghan Taliban and the Pakistan Taliban in the FATA, al Qaeda's presence and influence in Pakistan and across the border into Afghanistan is relatively weak.[249] The local Taliban has grown significantly in strength, and in the coming years it will be a significant factor influencing both Afghanistan and Pakistan.

The terror effect of al-Zawahiri's continuing threats is slowly wearing off. As such, al Qaeda's leadership must show that the group retains capabilities to strike against Western targets outside of its normal areas of operation in Iraq and Afghanistan. Jama'at al Qaeda al-Jihad seems intent on showing its relevance by creating new structures and linking up with existing platforms globally. Al Qaeda's leadership wants to create the perception that al Qaeda is the headquarters of the global jihadi movement.

In terms of directing attacks, al Qaeda is using the FATA to impart training and direction to a new generation of both a traditional and homegrown cadre. From this sanctuary, al Qaeda is building capacity and empowering a new, albeit small, generation of Western recruits. In addition to imparting propaganda and working to increase support for al Qaeda and its movement globally, al Qaeda is providing operational tactics and IED knowledge, which make young jihadis from the West able to plan and conduct attacks that are much more sophisticated than what are normally capabilities of homegrown groups.

Al Qaeda currently seems to be following a dual strategy of planning both smaller attacks against soft targets and larger, more sophisticated plots against hardened targets. During the past three to four years, the central leadership in Pakistan has focused on training and finding recruits from the United Kingdom to conduct attacks in their home country. However, although the United States and the United Kingdom remain major targets for al Qaeda, the focus on attacking the United Kingdom is likely due to the availability of recruits. As al Qaeda seeks recruits from Western nations to conduct attacks, the strategic focus of the group will still target Western countries in the hope of finding the recruits that will provide the capability to conduct spectacular attacks against the West.

PROFILE 3

HAQQANI NETWORK GROUP PROFILE

BY ABDUL BASIT

Fact Sheet

Name(s):	Haqqani Network, also refers to itself as "Islamic Emirate of Afghanistan"
Date of creation:	2001
Leader:	Jalaluddin Haqqani and Sirajuddin Haqqani
Estimated strength:	Between 2,000 and 4,000 fighters
Area of operation:	The Haqqani Network conducts operations in almost all regions of Afghanistan. However, its principal region of strength is in the Greater Paktia area.
Symbols	Flag
Overview of ideology	The Haqqani Network is ideologically affiliated with the Taliban group, but it is independent operationally. The Haqqani Network's leaders describe the US-led invasion in 2001 as an attack on their homeland and religion, and justify jihad to liberate the homeland and defend the religion. In the words of Maulavi Jalaluddin Haqqani: "We will retreat to the mountains and begin a long guerilla war to reclaim our pure land from the infidels and free our country as we did against the Soviets. . . . We are eagerly awaiting the American troops to land on our soil, where we will deal with them in our own way. . . . The Americans are creatures of comfort. They will not be able to sustain the harsh conditions that await them."[1]

1. Scott McDonald, "Minister's Visit Hints at Taliban Split," Reuters, Islamabad, 20 October 2001. Also, "Taliban Official in Talks Over Leadership," *OC Register*, 20 October 2001.

History

War with the Soviet Union (1979–1989)

Seven Pakistan-based Afghan mujahideen groups, assisted by Pakistan, Saudi Arabia, and the United States, fought against Soviet forces from 1979 to 1989.[250] One of these groups was Hezb-i-Islami, led by Maulawi Younus Khalis. The group conducted a remarkably successful guerrilla war in the southeastern region of Afghanistan through its regional commander Jalaluddin Haqqani.[251] In the summer of 1985, Jalaluddin Haqqani gathered several thousand fighters and attacked the city of Khost, overrunning the Soviet's and the Afghan's outposts. Subsequent heavy fighting continued until early 1986. On each occasion, Haqqani and other key leaders in his group would withdraw to the FATA of Pakistan, when the temporary Soviet firepower would overwhelm them and again stage a comeback to continue fighting. Fighting this way, Haqqani and his group did not allow the Soviets to maintain military dominance in the greater Paktia region over the long term.[252] This raised him to prominence as a strong military leader in Afghanistan.[253] After the Soviet withdrawal in 1989 and the collapse of President Najibullah's government in 1992, the unity of the mujahideen disintegrated and intramujahideen fighting erupted between 1992 and 1994. However, Jalaluddin Haqqani's group remained largely impartial and was not involved in the factional fighting until the Afghan Taliban emerged in 1994.

Joining the Taliban in 1994

When the Afghan Taliban emerged, Jalaluddin Haqqani unconditionally surrendered and supported the Afghan Taliban in their fighting during the subsequent years. Jalaluddin Haqqani later became commander in chief of the Afghan Taliban's armed forces and then remained the minister for borders and tribal affairs until 2001, when the Afghan Taliban regime collapsed.[254] In 1997, the Haqqani network used its influence and links to the Pakistani religious elements to recruit soldiers for the Afghan Taliban after their massive defeat in Mazar-e Sharif city of the northern Balkh province.[255]

In 2001, the Haqqani group fled to its traditional sanctuaries in North Waziristan Agency of the FATA in Pakistan and launched insurgency against the Afghan government and the ISAF post-2001—thus becoming known to world as the Haqqani Network. In September 2012, the United States designated the Haqqani Network as a terrorist entity. A senior Haqqani commander called the designation a sign of US "lame tactics." He said, "Americans are claiming that by declaring us terrorist, we would lose support of some Muslim countries. Let me assure everyone that we only seek Allah's and the Afghan nation's support."[256]

The Haqqani Network Leadership

The Haqqani Network is founded by and named after Jalaluddin Haqqani.[257] However, his son, Sirajuddin Haqqani, has taken over most of the leadership responsibilities and is the de facto leader of the Haqqani Network now. There were reports of Jalaluddin Haqqani's fragile health, but so far there are no confirmed reports of his death. In March 2008 he appeared in a video speech, countering rumors that he had died of hepatitis.

The Haqqani Network is built around close familial, clan and tribal connections, and it is believed to plan operations through face-to-face meetings among the top leadership. Sirajuddin Haqqani is said to be responsible for military operations overall, giving operational guidance to subcommanders and coordinating logistics for their operations. The US Department of State and/or US Department of the Treasury designated six Haqqani Network leaders as terrorists/supporters of terrorism. They include Jalaluddin Haqqani, Sangeen Zadran (one of the top commanders), Abdul Aziz Ahbasin (commander), Haji Mali Khan (commander), Sirajuddin Haqqani (de facto head of the Network), Khalil al-Rahman Haqqani (fund-raiser in the Persian Gulf/Arabian Peninsula), and Nasiruddin Haqqani (son of Jalaluddin Haqqani and logistical head).[258]

Target Killings and Their Effect on Haqqani Network Leadership Structures

The Haqqani Network leaders have shown themselves to be highly adaptive in a fluid and dangerous environment. However, they remained vulnerable to CIA drone strikes in the FATA. The drone strikes in the FATA led to the killing of a number of high-ranking leaders of the Haqqani Network. A drone strike in September 2013 killed Sangeen Zadran in North Waziristan Agency. Zadran was a senior commander of the Haqqani Network and shadow governor of the Paktia province. He was said to have held the American soldier, Bowe Robert Bergdahl, in June 2009 as hostage. Zadran was among five killed in the drone strike.[259] Badruddin Haqqani, son of Jalaluddin Haqqani, was also killed by a drone strike in North Waziristan Agency of the FATA in summer 2012.[260] Badruddin Haqqani was the day-to-day operations commander for the Haqqani Network. He and his elder brother Sirajuddin Haqqani were said to have expanded the network in terms of its operation since 2005.[261]

Personnel

There are reports that the manpower of the Haqqani Network stands around ten thousand fighters.[262] The accurate number of fighters is estimated to be between two thousand and four thousand.[263] The Network recruits fighters from madrassas in Pakistan but also from local people who sympathize with their cause in the Afghanistan–Pakistan region. The Haqqani Network itself is running a madrassa, where hundreds of students are educated with the jihadi ideology. The Network established several training camps in North Waziristan Agency, where these camps provide training to newly joined volunteers and include children. The volunteers are trained on both traditional and modern insurgency tactics including how to make homemade explosive devices.

Equipment

The Haqqani Network's fighters possess light weaponry, including AK-47s, rocket propelled grenades (RPGs), and IEDs. The most effective weapon of the Haqqani Network remains explosives and suicide bombers.

FUNDING AND ASSOCIATIONS

Financing

While the Haqqani Network obtains the bulk of its logistical supplies in Pakistan and the tribal areas, it also operates extensive fund-raising activities in the broader Afghanistan–Pakistan region and beyond. On 22 July 2010, the US Department of Treasury labeled three important individuals for "supporting acts of terrorism and for acting for or on behalf of the Taliban or the Haqqani Network."[264] One of these leaders was Nasiruddin Haqqani, who was placed on the financial sanctions list.[265] The Network's financial activities can be broken down into six broad categories: 1) extortion business that operates in Afghanistan's southeast and in Pakistan's tribal areas; 2) kidnapping for ransom; 3) taxing illicit drug smugglers; 4) ownership stakes in dozens of real estate holdings, both commercial and residential; 5) fundraising from ideological supporters in Pakistan and across the Gulf region; and 6) money laundering in its area of operations.[266] The Network has also been connected to the narcotics trade in Afghanistan, which is supplying more than 90 percent of the world's opium. Most of the opium produced in Afghanistan is trafficked to Pakistan (southern/southeastern route), Iran (western route), and Central Asia (northern route). The southeastern route enters the FATA from Afghanistan's southeastern provinces, which is the key opium smuggling route to several destinations worldwide, including Iran, China, India, the Middle East, and Europe.[267] The Haqqani Network has a strong presence on both sides of the border between the FATA and the southeastern provinces of Afghanistan. It charges the traffickers protection fees during shipments and for running the processing laboratories in its areas of control.[268]

ASSOCIATIONS

The Taliban

The Haqqani Network is ideologically affiliated to the Afghan Taliban group, but it is independent operationally. It makes its own operational strategies and implements them largely in the southeastern (also known as Greater Paktia) region as the main area of operations. There has been some debate recently over whether or not a disaggregation of the Afghan Taliban should include the Haqqani Network as an independent militant group operating in Afghanistan or as a subset of the wider Afghan Taliban movement. The Afghan government separately reached out to the Haqqani Network for negotiations. However, the Haqqani Network responded by stating that it would be willing to negotiate only if the Quetta Council agrees, somewhat eliminating the hope that the Network could be negotiated with independently of the Afghan Taliban's leadership.[269] This message strongly suggests that the Haqqani Network is just a subset of the larger Afghan Taliban movement.

AL QAEDA

Al Qaeda reportedly has close relations with the Haqqani Network, and its fighters have been involved in coordinating militant activities with the Network in southeastern Afghanistan. Haqqani established a close relationship with Osama bin Laden in the 1980s, and the first camp that bin Laden created in Afghanistan, Lion's Den, was in the Haqqani's territory.[270] Osama bin Laden settled in the Jalalabad area in 1992 at the invitation of Hezb-e-Islami, led by Maulawi Younus Khalis, the mujahideen party to which Jalaluddin Haqqani was affiliated during the Soviet war.

Mustafa Abu al-Yazid, general leader for al Qaeda in Afghanistan in 2007, was reportedly involved in establishing relations with local militant groups on both sides of the Afghanistan–Pakistan border, including the Haqqani Network. In a few cases, Mustafa claimed responsibility for attacks carried out jointly by al Qaeda and the Haqqani Network. The suicide attack on a CIA base in Khost province in December 2009 is one example. The attack killed seven CIA operatives and was engineered by al Qaeda, the Haaqani Network, and the TTP. Mr. Yazid issued a statement praising the work of the bomber, Humam Khalil Abu Mulal al-Balawi, and said that the bombing was revenge for the killing of TTP leader Baitullah Mehsud.

In addition to al Qaeda, other foreign groups are part of both the Haqqani Network's operations and training. These foreign entities include the TTP, the Islamic Movement of Uzbekistan (IMU), the Islamic Jihad Union (IJU), Tehrik Nefaz-e-Shariat Muhammedi (TNSM), and the Eastern Turkistan Islamic Movement (ETIM).[271]

INTERACTIONS WITH INTELLIGENCE SERVICES

Pakistan and Inter-Services Intelligence

Pakistan's Inter-Services Intelligence (ISI) is widely known for its involvement with the Haqqani Network. The Haqqani Network's relationship with the ISI traces back to the Soviet's war in Afghanistan. At that time, the Haqqani Network was supported by the ISI, the Saudis, and the CIA. It received considerable funds from CIA and Saudi intelligence through ISI.[272] The ISI's relationship with the Haqqani group faded with the emergence of the Afghan Taliban, but it revived after 2001 with the US-led invasion of Afghanistan. Telephonic intercepts by US and Indian intelligence agencies reportedly confirm a strong link between ISI's elements and the Haqqani Network. There have been claims that the Haqqani Network and ISI jointly planned and executed the deadly suicide attack on India's embassy in Kabul on 7 July 2008. During the US Senate Armed Services Committee hearing, Admiral Michael Mullen, former chairman of the Joint Chiefs of Staff, highlighted the ISI's role in sponsoring the Haqqani Network, including its attacks in Afghanistan. He said the Haqqani Network is serving as proxies of Pakistan and attacks both Afghan and ISAF forces.[273] Admiral Mullen said that ISI played a direct role in supporting the Haqqani Network militants who carried out the attack on the American Embassy in Kabul in September 2011.[274]

TARGETS, TACTICS, AND PROCEDURES

Targets

In addition to combatant targets, including Afghan and ISAF forces and their bases, the Haqqani Network increasingly targeted Afghan government civilian officials and progovernment personalities and tribal elders. The Network also targeted hotels, guesthouses, and banks. The Haqqani Network claimed responsibility for most of the deadliest attacks in Afghanistan, including the attacks on the Serena Hotel, the Inter-Continental Hotel, the Indian Embassy, and the US Embassy.[275]

Tactics and Procedures

The Haqqani Network utilizes suicide bombing in urban areas and roadside bomb ambushes in the rural areas of Afghanistan. It is also involved in extortion, kidnapping, and smuggling to financially support its operations. The group is thought to have pioneered the use of suicide bombing in Afghanistan and routinely uses foreigners (Pakistani nationals mostly) in their suicide attacks. Additionally, Haqqani Network technologies, specifically in regard to bomb making and remote detonation, are highly advanced. It frequently uses remote detonation through cellular phone signals and radio frequency.[276]

Peace Process and the US/Afghanistan Strategic Partnership

The Haqqani Network remains silent regarding recent developments related to the peace talks between the United States and the Afghan Taliban and the Afghan government. The Afghan Taliban opened a political office, and all the members of the delegation appeared to have been dispatched by the Afghan Taliban's Quetta Council. There was no mention made that the Haqqani Network also had a representative among them or that it did not have a representative. The Afghan government separately reached out to the Haqqani Network for negotiations. The Haqqani Network responded, stating it would be willing to negotiate only if the Quetta Council agrees.[277] The rising role of the Haqqani Network can have an influential impact on the overall leadership of the Afghan Taliban movement. Some of these effects are already emerging. In regions that are between the spheres of influence of the different leaders of the Afghan Taliban's movement, insurgents are referred to as "Haqqani's men" or "Mullah Omar's men." This could signify a decentralization or fractionalization of the Afghan Taliban movement, which could have important consequences for any counterinsurgency measures that may be implemented, especially the proposed government peace process.

Threat Assessment/Outlook

The Haqqani Network remains a complex and capable threat in Afghanistan. The Network is focused on attacking local enemies, with no ambition to attack the United States. Its ties with al Qaeda are a concern to the Afghan government and to the United States. The Network believes in al Qaeda's global jihad ideology. It is predominantly comprises Afghans, but it also trains and incorporates foreign militants, including Arabs, Chechens, Uzbeks, and Pakistanis influenced by al Qaeda's ideology. In addition, the Haqqani Network's fighters seem to be sophisticated and better trained. It demonstrated proficiency in the past several years by making lethal explosive devices and homemade bombs, and used them against the Afghan government and ISAF forces in Afghanistan.

UPDATED KILL/CAPTURE LIST OF SENIOR HAQQANI NETWORK MILITANTS[278]

Updated Kill/Capture List of Senior Haqqani Network Militants

No.	Name/Position	Date Killed/Capture	Circumstances/Means
1.	Mullah Sangeen Zadran — Senior Haqqani Network leader who was on the US list of specially designated global terrorists for supporting al Qaeda	5 September 2013	Killed by a drone strike in North Waziristan
2.	Badruddin Haqqani — One of the top military commanders of the Haqqani Network and son of Jalaluddin Haqqani	24 August 2012	Killed by a drone strike in North Waziristan
3.	Miraj Wazir — Senior Commander	27 October 2011	Killed by an air strike in the FATA, Pakistan
4.	Ashfaq Wazir — Senior Commander	27 October 2011	Killed in air strike
5.	Jan Baz Zadran — Sirajuddin Haqqani's deputy, who served as the number three for the terror network	13 October 2011	Killed by a drone strike in Waziristan
6.	Saifullah Haqqani — A Haqqani Network military commander in Afghanistan and a cousin of Sirajuddin Haqqani	14 September 2010	Killed by an air strike in Pakistan
7.	Mohammed Haqqani — A midlevel Haqqani Network military commander and son of Jalaluddin Haqqani	18 February 2010	Killed by an air strike in Pakistan

PROFILE 4

HEZB-E-ISLAMI GULBUDDIN GROUP PROFILE

BY ABDUL BASIT

Fact Sheet

Name(s):	Hezb-e-Islami Gulbuddin (HIG)
Date of creation:	1975
Leader:	Engineer Gulbuddin Hekmatyar
Estimated strength:	Between 1,500 and 2,000 fighters
Area of operation:	Hezb-e-Islami Gulbuddin conducts operations largely in the eastern and northern provinces of Afghanistan.
Symbols	Flag Hezb-e-Islami "coat of arms"
Overview of ideology	Hezb-e-Islami declared jihad against the US-led forces in Afghanistan in 2001. It considers Afghanistan to be occupied by the United States and its allies, and believes that the military incursion into Afghanistan was not an attempt to drive out the Taliban or al Qaeda but rather was an effort to lead the region. Hezb-e-Islami likens the US invasion to that of the Soviet Union and believes jihad should be waged against the United States, just like against the Soviet Union.[1] In the words of Gulbuddin Hekmatyar in 2009,[2] "If foreign forces insist on continuing the war, we don't have any other way than fighting."

1. "US Came to Lead the Region, Not Beat the Taliban: Hizb-e-Islami," *Tolo News*, 28 May 2013. http://tolonews.com/en/afghanistan/6387-us-came-to-lead-the-region-not-beat-the-taliban-hizb-e-islami
2. "Profile: Gulbuddin Hekmatyar," *BBC News*, 23 March 2010. http://news.bbc.co.uk/2/hi/south_asia/2701547.stm

HISTORY

War with the Soviet Union (1979–1989)

Hezb-i-Islami was founded in Pakistan in 1975 and is the oldest group participating in the current insurgency in Afghanistan. Hezb-e-Islami was the most radical of the seven mujahideen parties fighting the Soviets in 1980s.[279] Like the Muslim Brotherhood, Hezb-e-Islami focused on the establishment of an Islamic state in Afghanistan. Built around a small cadre of educated elites, Hezb-e-Islami fractured in 1979, and the different factions came to be known by the name of their leaders: Hezb-i-Islami Gulbuddin Hekmatyar (referred to as HIG currently) and Hezb-i-Islami Maulawi Khalis, which joined the Taliban movement in 1994.

After the Soviet's withdrawal and the collapse of the Afghan communist government, Hezb-e-Islami Gulbuddin, with the alleged support of the Pakistani government, fought in Kabul to topple the mujahideen government, led by Jamiat-e-Islami from 1992 to 1996.[280] Pakistan's government, however, abandoned Hekmatyar in 1994 and shifted support to the Taliban when they emerged victorious in southern Kandahar province. After the Taliban seized Kabul in 1996 and overthrew the mujahideen government, many of the Hezb-i-Islami Gulbuddin commanders either joined the Taliban or fled to Pakistan. Hekmatyar himself escaped to Iran in 1997 and lived there in exile until 2001.[281]

HEZB-E-ISLAMI GULBUDDIN AFTER 9/11

After the US-led invasion of Afghanistan in 2001, Iran expelled Hekmatyar, and he returned to the Afghanistan–Pakistan region in February 2002.[282] Hekmatyar declared jihad against US-led forces in December 2002 and reactivated its previous recruiting and training camps in Peshawar, of which the Shamshatoo camp is the most well known.[283] On 19 February 2003, the United States designated Hekmatyar a specially designated global terrorist,[284] and as a group of concern, but not a foreign terrorist organization.[285] Hezb-e-Islami Gulbuddin's main areas of operation against the Afghan government and the ISAF forces have been the eastern and northern provinces. Its fighters are active in provinces such as Nangarhar, Kunar, Laghman, Kapisa, and Paktia (eastern province) and Kunduz, Baghlan, and Parwan (northern provinces).

HEZB-E-ISLAMI GULBUDDIN LEADERSHIP

Hezb-e-Islami Gulbuddin (HIG) has been weakened both militarily and politically, and many of its loyalists broke away from it during the past twelve years. When HIG declared Jihad against US-led forces in Afghanistan post-2001, a number of its commanders formed and registered a new political party under the name Hezb-i-Islami Afghanistan (HIA) and declared support for President Karzai in the 2004 presidential elections.[286] Mohammad Amin Waqad, who was a former deputy leader of Hezb-e-Islami, was a vice presidential candidate for the 2004 presidential elections in Afghanistan.[287] HIA claims to have no ties with HIG.[288] HIA evolved politically and opened offices in Kabul and other major cities of Afghanistan,[289] and its members now occupy many high-ranking positions in the Afghan government, including ministerships, governorships, and many other important posts.[290] Members of HIA likened their wing to Sinn Fein and the Irish Republican Army (IRA), where the militant wing is led by its founder, Gulbuddin Hekmatyar. Others, however, counter the claim by HIA, arguing that HIG and HIA are one group serving each other's interests in two different capacities.[291] In 2009, Hekmatyar also disassociated himself from HIA and stated that it does not represent him or his party, which he claims is the true Hezb-e-Islami.[292]

PERSONNEL

HIG seems stronger politically than militarily. It claims to have a force of eighteen thousand fighters as of 2002, but ISAF sources estimated their numbers at just three hundred to four hundred fighters in 2006. A 2003 estimate puts HIG as holding between 15 percent and 25 percent of the total number of militants fighting in Afghanistan. In 2008, the group's forces were estimated at around fifteen hundred fighters. Many HIG militants are part-time fighters and maintain civilian jobs by day.[293]

EQUIPMENT

Hezb-e-Islami Gulbuddin fighters possess light weaponry, including AK-47s, RPGs, and IEDs, including suicide bombers.

FUNDING AND ASSOCIATIONS

Financing

Opium production is facilitated in Afghanistan due to factors like poverty, state fragility, high demand, and easy access to buyers' markets. This makes the nexus between the militant groups and drug syndicates very difficult to trace and to delineate clear hierarchies.[294] Private donations are a source of the Hezb-e-Islami Gulbuddin in the Af–Pak region, although not a major source of income. The trafficking of narcotics is believed to be providing substantial financing to the group, which receives income for traffickers' protection fees during shipments and for running the processing laboratories in their areas of control.[295] HIG has several drug processing laboratories in Nangarhar and controls the drug trafficking routes into Pakistan.[296] In 2011, Afghanistan accounted for 82 percent of the global opium production.[297] Only 4.3 percent (priced at $2.9 billion) of the total $60 billion average annual volume of the global market for Afghan opium remained in Afghanistan. Most of this income was earned by drug traffickers and militant groups.[298]

ASSOCIATIONS

The Afghan Taliban

Both Hezb-i-Islami Gulbuddin and the Afghan Taliban are formed around Islamist agendas. There is some cooperation between them at the operational level, but Hezb-i-Islami Gulbuddin in 2010 denied any strategic cooperation, claiming that Hezb-i-Islami is a party, while the Afghan Taliban is merely a movement. Members of Hezb-i-Islami tend to have a higher level of education than the Afghan Taliban because Hekmatyar built its leadership from university educated and politically active urban Afghans.[299]

Al Qaeda

HIG established a close relationship with Osama bin Laden in the 1980s. Hezb-e-Islami and al Qaeda distanced from each other because the latter got close to the Afghan Taliban when they emerged in 1994. The Afghan Taliban fought against Hezb-e-Islami Gulbuddin and forced Hekmatyar to go into exile in Iran. However, after 2001, Hezb-e-Islami continued to reiterate its ties with al Qaeda. In a 2006 interview, Hekmatyar claimed his fighters helped Osama bin Laden escape from Tora Bora in Nangarhar, which was one of the strongholds of Hezb-e-Islami Gulbuddin during the Soviet war.[300]

INTERACTIONS WITH INTELLIGENCE SERVICES

Pakistan and Inter-Services Intelligence

Hezb-e-Islami Gulbuddin was a favorite group of Pakistan's ISI during the Soviet war and thus received the largest portion of US and Saudi assistance for the mujahideen.[301] It is alleged that the group still has support from the Pakistan government, which provided it freedom of movement, fund-raising, and training on Pakistan's soil. HIG reportedly has bases in Pakistan's Swat Valley, as well as in the tribal agencies of Bajaur, Mohmand, and North and South Waziristan.[302]

TARGETS, TACTICS, AND PROCEDURES

Targets

HIG designate their attacks according to their targets and the theaters of operation. In addition to combatant targets, which include Afghan and NATO forces and their bases, unlike the Afghan Taliban and the Haqqani Network, HIG largely limited attacks to targeting the ISAF, as well as Afghan forces. In his Eid message on 6 August 2013, Gulbuddin Hekmatyar asked HIG fighters to target ISAF troops and cautioned them on bombings that take civilians' lives: civil service workers, teachers, judges, scholars, doctors, engineers, and journalists.[303] The group does not have a record of targeting hotels, guesthouses, banks, and Afghan government installations. This may not be because these targets are not HIG's priorities but likely because it does not have the capabilities to engineer these attacks.

Tactics and Procedures

HIG fighting tactics include ambushes, suicide bombings, and roadside bombs. HIG claimed responsibility for a suicide attack in Kabul on 18 September 2012, which was executed by a female. At least twelve people, mostly foreign workers, were killed in the attack. Engineer Haroon Zarghoon, a spokesman for the HIG, said the attack was carried out by a twenty-two-year-old woman named Fatima and that it was conducted to avenge a controversial film released on YouTube that depicted the life of the Prophet Mohammed in a negative light.[304]

Peace Process and the US/Afghanistan Strategic Partnership

Unlike the Afghan Taliban, who have always refused to talk to the Afghan government and call it a "puppet"regime, HIG publicly reached out to the Afghan government for talks, beginning in March 2010. Since then, HIG has sent seventeen delegations to Kabul, some of which also met with President Hamed Karzai. With the government's priority to bring the Afghan Taliban to the negotiation table, however, negotiations with Hezb-e Islami reached a deadlock despite the latter's openness to talks and flexibility on terms of a possible political accommodation. Thus, HIG was not able to reach any agreement with the government during its many meetings in Kabul between March 2010 and May 2012, nor did the government respond to HIG's fifteen-point peace plan.[305] The peace plan included full withdrawal of ISAF forces from Afghanistan by the end of 2010.[306]

In May 2012, Ghairat Bahir, Hekmatyar's son-in-law and currently his second in command, said that the party suspended talks with the government in objection to its signing of the US–Afghan Strategic Partnership Agreement (SPA). He blamed the failure of talks in May 2012 on the "dishonesty and breach of promises'" by the Kabul government and, more specifically, on Kabul's rejection of HIG's terms for peace. The Afghan government's reason for refusing HIG's peace overtures was its priority to reconcile with the Afghan Taliban, who represents the bulk of the insurgency. The government's disinterest in striking a deal with HIG is also grounded in the fact that it has already been able to lure a faction of former Hezb-e Islami and many of its individual members into the current political system. The breakaway group, HIA, led by the Minister of Economy Abdul Hadi Arghandiwal, aligned itself with President Karzai in the past two elections. HIA holds three ministries—the other two being the Ministry of Education (Faruq Wardak as minister) and the Ministry of Agriculture and Livestock (Asef Rahimi as minister). It has forty-seven members in both houses of parliament as well as almost one quarter of the 420 members of all provincial councils.[307]

Threat Assessment/Outlook

Based on the information presented in this profile, unlike the Taliban and the Haqqani Network, HIG does not remain a complex and capable threat in Afghanistan. HIG has small areas of influence and manpower. Its estimated strength is between one thousand and two thousnd fighters. There does not seem to be cooperation between HIG and the Afghan Taliban/Haqqani Networks. There might be instances of cooperation at the tactical level, which could be out of necessity. However, HIG clearly states that it pursues a different ideological purpose, sharing no affinity with that of the Afghan Taliban. HIG supports a republic governing system and believes in elections, while the Afghan Taliban and the Haqqani Network firmly stand on establishing an Islamic emirate of Afghanistan and have shown no willingness toward a democratic government.

ANNEXES

HIG's Fifteen-Point Peace Plan proposed to the Afghan government:[308]

1. Foreign troops must start withdrawal in July of this year and complete the process in six months.
2. They should quit main cities and populated area and move to military bases.
3. Security issues must be completely handed over to the Afghan army and the police. Foreign troops will have no rights to carry out military operations and house search and arrests on their own anywhere in Afghanistan.
4. The parliament and the incumbent government will continue to function unless new elections are held and new a government is formed. But those people should not be part of the government who are controversial and accused of corruption and war crimes and who have secular ideas. And those people should not be in top military leadership who support a group against other.
5. A seven-member National Security Council will be formed with the consensus of all Afghan factions, which will have the power to make

final decisions on key issues. The Council's center will be in a province where security will be completely under Afghan forces, and there will be no foreign troops there.

6. After the withdrawal of foreign troops, elections for the office of the president, national assembly, and provincial assemblies will be held simultaneously on a proportional representation basis in March 2011.
7. Only cabinet members and governors who resign three months before the polls can be allowed to take part in the elections.
8. Every party will be represented in the first elected government in accordance with their seats in the parliament, and they will secure a trust vote from the parliament. And the largest group will not be bound to form a coalition government.
9. That group or alliance will have the right to take part in coming elections, which will secure up to 10 percent of the votes in the first election.
10. During this period there will be a complete cease-fire among the warring factions, all political prisoners will be freed, and all sides will make a commitment that they will not fight against rival factions and that they will not use illegal channels to grab power.
11. The first elected parliament will have the right to review the constitution and to make the final decision about the constitution.
12. No foreign country will have the right to establish its jails in Afghanistan. Foreign countries will not arrest or put on trial any Afghan national and will not take any Afghan outside of the country for trial.
13. Those accused of war crimes, drug smuggling, corruption, and plundering national wealth will be tried in Islamic courts. No side will defend them covertly or overtly.
14. Foreign fighters will not stay in Afghanistan after the withdrawal of foreign troops.
15. Any internal and external elements who are opposed to this agreement and insist on fighting will be jointly dealt with as war mongers to save our homeland from their curse.

HAFIZ GUL BAHADUR GROUP PROFILE

BY ABDUL BASIT

Fact Sheet	
Name(s):	Hafiz Gul Bahadur or the Muqami Taliban
Date of creation:	June 2008
Leader:	Hafiz Gul Bahadur
Estimated strength:	2,000 to 3,000 (approximately)
Area of operation:	North Waziristan Agency, FATA
Overview of ideology	Anti-US, Pro-Afghan Taliban

The Gul Bahadur Group is the most powerful group in North Waziristan. The Gul Bahadur Group is an Afghanistan-focused group and does not attack Pakistani security forces. The group's organization consists of fifteen to twenty smaller groups. Most of its supporters are from the Uthmanzai and Daur Wazir tribes of North Waziristan, based in the mountains between Miram Shah and the border with Afghanistan.[309] The total strength of its fighters is around three thousand. Of these fighters, Gul Bahadur commands approximately fifteen hundred fighters; commander Sadiq Noor, eight hundred; Abdul Khaliq Haqqani, five hundred; Wahidullah Wazir, two hundred; Halim Khan Daur, one hundred fifty; and Saifullah Wazir, four hundred.[310]

HISTORY

The foryt-eight-year-old Hafiz Gul Bahadur is a cleric and hails from the Uthmanzai Wazir tribe of North Waziristan. He is a resident of Lwara, a region bordering Afghanistan. He studied at a Deobandi madrassa in the Punjabi city of Multan. Bahadur fought in Afghanistan during the civil war that followed the Soviet withdrawal. After returning to North Waziristan, he became a political activist in the Islamist party Jamiat, known as the Ulema-e-Islam (Fazel ur-Rahman), or JUI-F. He rose to prominence in 2004, following Pakistan's military operations in North Waziristan, and he coordinates closely with the Haqqanis on both strategy and operations in Afghanistan.[311]

During Pakistan's 2004–2005 military offensive, Hafiz Gul Bahadur led a militia against Pakistani security forces. In 2006, Gul Bahadur, along with other Taliban groups of North Waziristan, agreed to a cease-fire arrangement with the Pakistani government, commonly called the 2006 North Waziristan Peace Agreement. The Afghan Taliban and the Haqqani Network brokered this agreement. The agreement asked for the removal of foreign fighters from

North Waziristan. However, Gul Bahadur continued to host and support Afghan Taliban and al Qaeda fighters, some of whom are ethnic Saudis.

In 2009, the Afghan Taliban attempted to bring the TTP, Hafiz Gul Bahadur, and Mullah Nazir under a new alliance, known as the Shura Ittihad-ul-Mujahadeen (Council for United Holy Warriors). However, the Shura collapsed after the death of Baitullah Mehsud by a drone attack in August of that year.

During Operation Rahe-Nijat in 2009, against the TTP, Hafiz Gul Bahadur remained neutral. The situation led to Mehsud's TTP fighters gaining a foothold within North Waziristan and attempting to recruit local fighters.

LEADERSHIP

Hafiz Gul Bahadur Group Leadership

Name	Designation/Position
Hafiz Gul Bahadur	Chief
Maulana Sadiq Noor	A close aide of Hafiz Gul Bahadur
Saeed Khan Daur	Midranking commander
Maulana Abdul Khaliq Haqqani	Commander, Miran Shah
Halim Khan Daur	Commander, Mir Ali
Wahidullah Wazir	Commander, Mir Ali
Saifullah Wazir	Commander, Shawal

IDEOLOGICAL AND POLITICAL LEANINGS

Hafiz Gul Bahadur is closer to Maulana Fazlur Rehman's–led Jamiat Ulema-e-Islam (JUI) leadership. The group shares similar broad goals as the Mullah Nazir Group. They support the insurgency in Afghanistan and work for the implementation of sharia law in Pakistan. As with Mullah Nazir, Gul Bahadur set up parallel administrations in those areas under his control, in which sharia law and a conservative code of ethics are enforced. Additionally, Gul Bahadur's group banned polio vaccinations in North Waziristan until all US drone attacks in the region cease. The group is linked to the Haqqani Network and fights against the US forces in Afghanistan under the command of the Haqqanis.

As with the Mullah Nazir group, Gul Bahadur's made the decision to disassociate from attacks on Pakistani forces. He focuses instead on the Afghanistan insurgency, leading a label of the so-called "good Taliban." Ittehad-e-Mujahedeen-e-Khurasan (IMK), an alliance of local and foreign fighters in the FATA, have, in consequence, targeted members of the Uthmanzai Wazir and Daur tribes for spying on behalf of the US and Pakistani governments. Gul Bahadur reportedly responded by abandoning his links with the IMK.

STRATEGY, TRAINING, AND TACTICS

After the TTP, the Hafiz Gul Bahadur Group is the single-largest militant outfit in the FATA. The group is host to al Qaeda and abides by the Afghan Taliban's directives, thus making it favorable to receive tremendous support in terms of IED technology and finances. These advantages make it militarily stronger than the TTP.

Similarly, the Gul Bahadur Group also controls the entire border region adjoining Afghanistan, and the TTP's militants have to cross the Wazir Tribal territory to conduct cross-border attacks. This element provides the former with the strength to control the actions of the latter. The support base for the Gul Bahadur Group exists in the North Agency. Similarly, there are a considerable number of Wazir tribesmen living in the adjoining settled districts of the KP. Some of these settlers are sympathizers of the Taliban's movement and provide political, moral, financial, material, and human resources to the Muqami Tehrik-e-Taliban. Most attacks conducted by the Hafiz Gul Bahadur Group include hit-and-run operations, which entail the employment of small arms and IEDs. Most of the attacks of the militant organization focus on the adjoining provinces of Khost, Paktia, and Paktika.

Militants of the Gul Bahadur Group infiltrate in these area under the cover of night or using unfrequented passages along the rugged Afghanistan–Pakistan border to conduct attacks and retreat immediately. The targets of the Gul Bahadur Group include US and ISAF-NATO troops and installations, Afghan security forces, and alleged "spies" working for US forces in Afghanistan or Pakistan. Pakistan views Hafiz Gul Bahadur favorably because both dissuade their groups not to carry out attacks in Pakistan nor Talibanize Pakistan's Khyber Pakhtunkhwa province.

FUNDING AND ASSOCIATIONS

Gul Bahadur has troubled relations with the TTP since the time of the latter's inception. He negotiated a peace deal with the Pakistani government, resulting in cessation of hostilities and military operations in exchange for the expulsion of foreign fighters from the area (which never fully occurred). However, his serious differences with Baitullah Mehsud over attacks against Pakistan's security forces were in blatant violation of the agreement brokered by him. He returned to Pakistan in late 2007 and attempted to distance himself from the TTP after the group began to attack the government that he previously agreed to observe in 2006.[312]

THREAT ASSESSMENT/OUTLOOK

Currently, Hafiz Gul Bahadur maintains a neutral stand in the ongoing military battles between Pakistan's army and the TTP. The Pakistani military responds to ensure its continued freedom of movement through his area, but neither side seeks open conflict with the other. As a result, neither a true peace agreement nor a complete defeat of Bahadur seems likely any time soon.[313]

His neutrality toward the TTP and Pakistan's government allows the TTP to reconstitute its sanctuaries and command and control structure in the Mir Ali area of North Waziristan. The TTP carried out attacks against Pakistan's security forces from this location. Gul Bahadur continues to look the other way during the TTP's attacks against Pakistan.

So far, the army has not moved into North Waziristan to dismantle the TTP's hideouts. In case of a military intervention, which looks imminent given the scale of attacks the TTP has carried out in past two years, the truce between Gul Bahadur and Pakistan's army is strained. However, it is likely that Pakistan's army will ask the Gul Bahadur group to force the TTP to vacate its North Waziristan sanctuaries.

After the drawdown of US forces in Afghanistan, Gul Bahadur will be one of the militant groups Pakistan can rely on to secure the western borders adjacent to North Waziristan, in case of a civil war in Afghanistan. At the same time, the group will be pivotal for Pakistan's bid against the TTP, which uses the slogan of jihad to fight Pakistan's security forces. Pakistan can engage Gul Bahadur to discredit the jihadi narrative of the TTP once the fighting in Afghanistan ends. Gul Bahadur's close ties with Mullah Umar and the Haqqani Network will also put him in an advantageous position to survive in his stronghold of North Waziristan after 2014.

MULLAH NAZIR GROUP PROFILE

BY ABDUL BASIT

Fact Sheet

Name(s):	Mullah Nazir Group or the Waziri Taliban
Date of creation:	December 2007
Leader:	Bhawal Khan
Estimated strength:	3,000 to 4,000 (approximately)
Area of operation:	Ahmed Zai Wazir tribal territory of South Waziristan Agency
Overview of ideology	Afghanistan-focused group

HISTORY

In June 2008, the Afghanistan-focused Mullah Nazir Group was formed, and is also known as the Muqami Tehrik-e-Taliban. Initially, Mullah Nazir joined the TTP, but serious differences emerged between him and the TTP's founder Baitullah Mehsud. These differences centered on the presence of Uzbek militants of the Islamic Movement of Uzbekistan (IMU) in the Waziri tribal areas of South Waziristan.

The Mullah Nazir Group has a strong presence in Wana, the capital of South Waziristan, and in other southern parts of the agency. It is also active in hit-and-run operations in the Khost, Paktia, and Paktika provinces of Afghanistan that adjoin North and South Waziristan.

On 3 January 2013, a drone strike killed Nazir in South Waziristan.[314] A senior militant commander of the group, Bahawal Khan, also known as Salahuddin Ayubi, is his successor. Bahwal is in his mid-thirties and belongs to the Kaka Khel subdivision of the main Wazir tribe. He was very close to Nazir for more than sixteen years.[315] In February 2013, the US State Department added the Mullah Nazir Group to the list of foreign terrorist entities.[316]

LEADERSHIP

Mullah Nazir Group Leadership

Name	Designation/Position
Bhawal Khan	Bhawal Khan, aka Salahuddin Ayubi, is the head of the Mullah Nazir Group. The shura of the Mullah Nazir Group appointed Ayubi as the new chief of the terror group after the assassination of Nazir in a drone attack.
Commander Malang Wazir	Deputy chief

IDEOLOGY

The Mullah Nazir Group is ideologically akin to the Afghan Taliban. It believes in enforcement of the Taliban's style of sharia in Pakistan. It imposed Taliban sharia laws in the areas under its control.

STRATEGY, TRAINING, AND TACTICS

According to the US State Department, the Mullah Nazir Group runs training camps in the Ahmedzai Wazir tribal territory in South Waziristan. The group fights under the command of the Haqqani Network in Afghanistan and provides the Haqqanis with mercenary fighters. The group dispatched suicide bombers to Afghanistan to target ISAF forces. In addition to its attacks against international forces in Afghanistan, the group is also responsible for assassinations and intimidation operations against civilians in Afghanistan and Pakistan.[317]

FUNDING AND ASSOCIATIONS

As mentioned earlier, the Mullah Nazir Group has ethnic and ideological rivalries with the Mehsud-dominated TTP. The local Waziri tribesmen stand against the presence of Uzbeks in their area. The growing influence of Uzbeks in their areas irritated them. Baitullah Mehsud wanted to keep the Uzbeks there. Mullah Nazir formed a militia of the Waziri tribesmen, duly supported by the Pakistan army, and drew Uzbeks out of the Waziri-dominated areas of South Waziristan. This resulted in open hostility between him and the TTP. Later on, the TTP carried out several abortive assassination attempts against Mullah Nazir.

Nazir's group maintains close affiliations with the Afghan Taliban, the Tanzim al Qaeda al-Jihad, the Libyan Islamic Fighting Group (LIFG), and the Islamic Jihad Union. The Nazir Group maintains a close alliance with the Hafiz Gul Bahadur Group. This alliance is the Waziri alliance because both Nazir and Bahadur belong to the dominant Wazir tribe.

While both Nazir and Bahadur were committed to conduct attacks on ISAF-NATO and US presence in Afghanistan, both dislike the TTP's terrorist attacks in Pakistan. The policy of Nazir and Bahadur conforms to the broader policy of the Afghan Taliban, who advised the Pakistan Taliban to shun fighting Pakistani security forces and to focus their energy and resources on Afghanistan. However, some Taliban militants, especially Baitullah Mahsud, recently moved closer to al Qaeda, which advocates conducting terrorist attacks against the Pakistani government and conducting a global jihad.

The Mullah Nazir faction is one of the four major Taliban groups that joined the Shura-e-Murakeba, an alliance brokered by al Qaeda in late 2011. The Shura-e-Murakeba also includes Hafiz Gul Bahadar's group, the Haqqani Network, and the TTP. The members of the Shura-e-Murakeba agreed to cease attacks against Pakistani security forces, refocus efforts against the United States in Afghanistan, and end kidnappings and other criminal activities in the tribal areas.[318]

THREAT ASSESSMENT/OUTLOOK

Currently, Maulvi Nazir maintains a neutral stand between the army and the TTP. The Ahmedzai Wazir tribe succeeded in convincing Taliban leader Maulvi Nazir to stay neutral and not to side with the TTP before the start of the operation Rah-e-Nijat. Pakistan's military launched its offensive against Hakimullah from the western, eastern, and northern parts of the agency. However, Maulvi Nazir's "support" to the military comes at a price. Before brokering the cease-fire, the KP government agreed to a number of demands forwarded by the Ahmedzai Wazirs, including reopening blockaded roads and launching several development schemes worth millions in their areas.

UPDATED KILL/CAPTURE LIST OF SENIOR COMMANDER NAZIR NETWORK MILITANTS[319]

Updated Kill/Capture List of Senior Commander Nazir Network Militants

No.	Name/Position	Date Killed/Capture	Circumstances/Means
1.	Mullah Nazir, founder of the group	3 January 2013	Killed in a drone strike in South Waziristan
2.	Rahmanullah Wazir, a midranking commander	2 June 2012	Killed in a drone strike in North Waziristan
3.	Ghulam Jan Wazir, a midranking commander	25 June 2009	Killed in military operation Rah-e-Nijat (Path to Salvation)

TEHRIK-E-TALIBAN PAKISTAN GROUP PROFILE

BY ABDUL BASIT

Fact Sheet

Name(s):	Tehrik-e-Taliban Pakistan (TTP) or the Pakistan Taliban
Date of creation:	December 2007
Leader:	Hakimullah Mehsud
Estimated strength:	10,000 to 15,000 (approximately)
Area of operation:	Federally Administered Tribal Areas of Pakistan (FATA) and some areas of Khyber Pakhtunkhwa (KP) province
Symbols	Flag
Overview of ideology	Pro-Al Qaeda

HISTORY

The Tehrik-e-Taliban Pakistan (TTP) is a conglomerate of around forty to fifty local and foreign anti-Pakistan militant groups. The TTP is based in Pakistan's FATA and parts of the northwestern Khyber Pakhtunkhwa (KP) province. The tribal militant commander Baitullah Meshud founded it on 14 December 2007 in the South Waziristan Agency.

The TTP has stated objectives that include the liberation of Afghanistan from the US occupation, fighting defensive jihad against Pakistan's security forces, and pursuing Talibanization in Pakistan, particularly in the FATA and the KP. The breakaway factions of the Kashmiri jihadi groups such as Lashkar-e-Taiba (LeT, Army of the Pure), Jaish-e-Muhammad (JeM, Army of Muhammad), and Harkatul Mujahideen (HuM) boosted the strength for the TTP in the initial years of its formation.[320]

Having close links with al Qaeda, the TTP is extensively brutal toward local tribesmen, political leaders, and Pakistani security forces in the FATA. It even targets those militant groups that did not join its cause in fighting against Pakistani security forces.

The TTP is very strong in almost all the agencies of the FATA, except Khyber, where they gained a recent foothold but are relatively weak compared to the local militant factions of the Khyber Agency. A frontier region is a buffer zone between seven tribal agencies of the FATA's and the KP's settled district. The TTP also established its strongholds in Peshawar, Nowshera, Charsadda, Hangu, Bannu, Laki Marwat, Dera Ismail Khan, Kohat, Tank, Swat, and Dir districts of the KP.

INTERNAL SPLITS

At the time of the TTP's formation, security experts in Pakistan believed that the organization would fall apart within a few years of its formation. Just seven months after its inception, in July 2008, internal clashes erupted between pro-Baitullah Taliban and pro-LeT Taliban, resulting in internal splits. The pro-LeT Taliban opposed the idea of fighting Pakistani security forces, and they wanted to help the Afghan Taliban in their fight in Afghanistan. On the contrary, the supporters of Baitullah were keen to wage jihad against the Pakistani state and its security forces for supporting the United States against the Afghan Taliban.

In October 2008, the TTP witnessed another major leadership split. The TTP's second deputy leader, Hafiz Gul Bahadur, parted ways with the TTP because of Baitullah Mehsud's violent policies against the Pakistani security forces. Gul Bahadur believed Baitullah's policies weakened the Afghan resistance against ISAF forces in Afghanistan.

On 1 November 2008, the TTP offered a unilateral cease-fire to the Pakistani government. In a media interview, the then TTP spokesperson Maulvi Omar informed journalists that in a meeting with the TTP's Shura Council, they decided to lay down arms and hold talks with the government. He said, "TTP is not against Pakistan, it, rather, is waging its struggle against the US imperialism."

Because of intensifying attacks of the TTP against Pakistan's security forces and sabotage activities spreading to almost all parts of the country, the Pakistani government imposed a ban on the TTP under the Anti-Terrorism Act. The state bank froze all assets and accounts of the organization on 25 August 2008. Announcing the ban on the TTP, the Federal Interior Minister Rehman Malik (2008–2013) said, "The Tehrik-e-Taliban Pakistan (TTP) will have its bank accounts and assets frozen. The organization and persons belonging to it are forbidden to collect money or raising funds for their activities. TTP is involved in a series of suicide attacks. They themselves have claimed responsibility for several suicide attacks and the government cannot engage in a dialogue with such people. TTP has created mayhem against the public life."[321]

After the death of Baitullah Mehsud from a US drone strike on 5 August 2009 in South Waziristan, the TTP's Shura Council chose his cousin Hakimullah Mehsud as the group's new chief. Hakimullah proved to be more brutal than his predecessor was. He made waves with a series of high-profile terrorist attacks across Pakistan. The TTP's suicide campaigns not only attacked high-value targets but also resulted in noncombatant deaths in its assaults.[322]

On 29 June 2013, a US drone attack killed the TTP's number two commander and leading ideologue Waliur Rehman.[323] The TTP's Shura chose Khan Said to succeed Waliur Rehman. Khan Said belongs to the Shabikhel clan of the Pashtun Mehsud tribe and resides in Dwa Toi village in South Waziristan. Khan Said was previously the TTP's commander in Miran Shah, the headquarters of the North Waziristan Agency.[324]

In additional to several small-scale counterterrorism operations, a few major military operations such as Rah-e-Rast (Path of Righteousness) in Malakand Division, Rah-e-Nijat (Path of Deliverance) in South Waziristan, Operation Sher Dil (Lion's Heart) in Bajaur, Operation Barekhna (Lightning) in Orakzai Agency, and Operation Koh-i-Safiad (White Mountain) in Kurram Agency have inflicted heavy losses on the TTP.

These military operations considerably reduced the TTP's ability to carry out major military operations in Pakistan's cities between 2009 and 2011. The destruction of the physical infrastructure and command and control systems for the TTP degraded from these operations. It forced several TTP leaders to flee Afghanistan from the tribal areas. For instance, the TTP's head for Bajaur Agency Faqir Muhammad, the TTP's swat chapter chief Maulana Fazlullah, and the TTP's Mohmand agency chief Qari Omar Khaid Khurasani fled to the Kunar, Nuristan, and Khost provinces of Afghanistan, respectively.

In 2012, the indecision and reluctance of the Pakistan People's Party (PPP) led the coalition government (2008–2013) to continue counterterrorism operations ahead of the May 2013 parliamentary elections in Pakistan.

During the election campaign, TTP's terrorist attacks against liberal-secular parties such as the PPP, Mutahidq Qaumi Movement (MQM), and the Awami National Party (ANP) further created divisions between promilitary operations and protalks among political parties. Namely, the Pakistani Muslim Leagues Nawaz (PML-N), Imran Khan's Pakistan Tehrik-e-Insaf (PTI, Party of Justice), and other religious political parties favored peace talks with the TTP.

Since 2012, the Awami National Party, on 14 February 2013, Jamiat-e-Ulama-e-Islam Fazal Faction (JUI-F), on 28 February 2013, and the Pakistani Mulism League Nawaz, on 9 September 2013 convened three All Parties Conferences (APCs) to lay out a framework on how to tackle militancy and terrorism. The APCs decided to resolve the issue through talks. Ironically, the TTP has shown little interest in government peace talk offers, and it continues its terror campaign with impunity. Currently, the debate on the topic is confused in the event of mounting terrorist attacks across Pakistan.

The government's peace talk offer to the TTP created divisions within the group. The head of the TTP's Punjab chapter Asmatullah Muavia welcomed the peace talks. The TTP's Shura council expelled Muavia for individually welcoming the peace talks offer and distanced itself from his decision. Similarly, serious differences exist between the Waliur Rehman faction and the Hakimullah Mehsud faction of the TTP.[325] The former is in favor of negotiations, while the latter opposes peace talks tooth and nail. The Mohmand and swat chapter of the TTP are also against talks.[326]

TEHRIK-E-TALIBAN PAKISTAN (TTP) LEADERSHIP

Tehrik-e-Taliban Pakistan (TTP) Leadership

Name	Designation/Position
Hakimullah Mehsud	Chief
Omar Khalid Khurasani	Head in Mohmand Agency
Sahidullah Shahid	Central spokesperson
Sajjad Mohmand alias Ihsanullah Ihsan	Member of TTP Central Shura
Asmatullah Muawiya	Head of the Punjabi Taliban
Mullah Fazlullah	Head of TTP Malakand chapter

Name	Designation/Position
Khan Said alias Sajna Mehsud	TTP chief in South Waziristan
Haji Mangal Bagh Afridi	Head of his own faction Lashkar-e-Islam and TTP in Khyber Agency
Mullah Noor Jamal alias Mullah Toofan	Head of TTP Orakzai and Kurram Agency
Maulana Abu Bakar	TTP chief in Bajaur Agency

IDEOLOGICAL AND POLITICAL LEANINGS

Ideologically, the TTP is an ultraconservative militant organization that subscribes to a puritanical interpretation of Islam. They believe in Takfirya. The TTP's main targets have not only been the US and NATO forces in Afghanistan but also include ambushes of Pakistan's security forces, convoys, and checkpoints in the tribal areas and the NWFP. The organization executed terrorist attacks in different parts of Pakistan as well. Their political aim is to establish a Taliban-style caliphate in the tribal areas of Pakistan. While justifying its stance against Pakistan's security forces, the TTP's spokesperson insisted that "[o]ur main aim is to target the US allies in Afghanistan but the government of Pakistan's ill-strategy has made us to launch a defensive Jihad in Pakistan."[327]

STRATEGY, TRAINING, AND TACTICS

The TTP use a variety of tactics to spread their tentacles over the FATA. Their aim is to spread terror to repress the civilians but also to implement their authority. The TTP use their training facilities in the FATA to train their foot soldiers in guerrilla warfare and suicide attacks. They also maintain training facilities for bomb-making homegrown jihadis. Basic military training performed in these camps prepares potential suicide bombers for further training in South Waziristan for an additional four months of training.

The TTP claim responsibility for attacks by videos of killing and kidnapping hundreds of soldiers. The TTP also were involved in high-profile terrorist attacks such as the assassination of Benazir Bhutto, suicide attacks on Pakistan's former Interior Minister Aftab Sherpao, Asfand Yar Wali, head of the Awami National Party, Bashir Bilor, leader of Awami National Party and many others. The TTP has also attacked the ISI, Pakistan's premier external intelligence agency.

FUNDING AND ASSOCIATIONS

In the initial years of its formation, major financing for the TTP came from al Qaeda and charity donations from the Arab countries in the Gulf and Middle East. With the passage of time, the TTP diversified its sources of financing. Now it is involved in kidnapping for ransom, bank robberies, money extortion, forced taxes, and funding from the sources hostile to Pakistan.[328] The TTP believes in al Qaeda's ideology of transnational jihad and carries out terrorist activities on its behalf.

The Afghan Taliban and the TTP have one major difference in their ideology. Despite possessing the same ideology, their goals differ. Unlike the TTP, the Afghan Taliban possess no ambitions beyond Afghanistan.[329]

THREAT ASSESSMENT/OUTLOOK

Currently, the TTP is the most potent and organized entity that continues to pose stiff resistance to Pakistan's security forces in the FATA, despite suffering numerous setbacks and internal disputes. Traditionally, the TTP is very strong in almost all the agencies of the FATA except Khyber. The TTP recently gained a foothold in Khyber, but they are too weak to challenge local militant factions of the Khyber Agency. The TTP also established its strongholds in Peshawar, Nowshera, Charsadda, Hangu, Bannu, Laki Marwat, Dera Ismail Khan, Kohat, Tank, Swat, and Dir districts of the KP. In 2012, the TTP also registered a strong presence in Pakistan's most populous city and country's financial capital, Karachi.[330]

As the war on terror progresses, the TTP developed and cultivated itself as a Neo-Islamist militant group in Pakistan. It is no longer a reactionary group attacking Pakistani forces supporting the US war in Afghanistan. Ending the alliance with the United States will not end the TTP's struggle against the Pakistani state and its political and military leadership. The TTP's core demand is Islamization of Pakistan through talks or through jihad. The TTP will not stop short of anything except the implementation of a shariah system in Pakistan.

In its various statements issued during the past few years, along with criticizing the country's secular political forces, the TTP has also been very critical of Pakistan's religious-political parties. The TTP accused the religious-political leadership of paying lip service to the cause of Islamization in Pakistan. It asserted itself as an alternative stakeholder for creation of an Islamic state in Pakistan through jihad.

In a video message released by TTP's Al-Umar Studio in May 2012, the TTP's chief Hakeemullah Mehsud, openly criticized religious political parties for ambiguity toward the Pakistan alliance with the United States. He criticized Qazi Hussain Ahmed (late), the former chief of the Jamaat-e-Islami (JI), for his overtures to revive the Milli Yakjehti Council (MYC), an alliance of different religious schools of thought to ensure sectarian harmony in the country, and offering his prayers alongside the Shia Muslims. He also criticized Qazi for his fatwa (religious ruling) declaring jihad was allowed in Afghanistan, a Muslim land under non-Muslim occupation, and not in Pakistan.

Contrary to unfounded popular narrative in Pakistan, the US withdrawal from Afghanistan in 2014 will not put the TTP out of business. In fact, this will likely further aggravate the threat of homegrown militancy and terrorism. If implementation of the appropriate policies and measures against the TTP fail, it will be difficult to counter the TTP through only military means and methods. A political counternarrative and ideological rebuttal of the TTP's policies will also be required to limit and checkmate their growth after 2014.

ANNEX

Updated Kill/Capture List of Tehrik-e-Taliban Pakistan (TTP) [331]

Tehrik-e-Taliban Pakistan (TTP) Leadership

Name	Designation/Position
Hakimullah Mehsud	Chief
Omar Khalid Khurasani	Head in Mohmand Agency
Sahidullah Shahid	Central spokesperson
Sajjad Mohmand alias Ihsanullah Ihsan	Member of TTP Central Shura
Asmatullah Muawiya	Head of the Punjabi Taliban
Mullah Fazlullah	Head of TTP Malakand chapter
Khan Said alias Sajna Mehsud	TTP chief in South Waziristan
Haji Mangal Bagh Afridi	Head of his own faction Lashkar-e-Islam and TTP in Khyber Agency
Mullah Noor Jamal alias Mullah Toofan	Head of TTP Orakzai and Kurram Agency
Maulana Abu Bakar	TTP chief in Bajaur Agency

Notes

1. WHAT DOES THE FUTURE HOLD FOR AFGHANISTAN?

1. "Afghans Take Nationwide Security Lead from Nato," *BBC News*, 18 June 2013. http://www.bbc.co.uk/news/world-asia-22942013

2. According to an AP-GfK poll released on 9 May 2013, support for war in Afghanistan was at its lowest in the United States and is on par with the support for the Vietnam War in the early 1970s. Only 27 percent of Americans say they back the war effort, and 66 percent oppose the war.

3. "Corruption in Afghanistan: Recent Patterns and Trends," United Nations Office on Drug and Crime, Islamic Republic of Afghanistan High Office of Oversight and Anti-Corruption, December 2012. http://www.unodc.org/documents/frontpage/Corruption_in_Afghanistan_FINAL.pdf

4. William Dalrymple "A Deadly Triangle: Afghanistan, Pakistan and India," The Brookings Institution, 25 June 2013. http://www.brookings.edu/research/essays/2013/deadly-triangle-afghanistan-pakistan-india-c

5. Ahmad Ramin, "Taliban Does Not Want to Seize Power in Afghanistan: Mullah Omar," *Tolo News*, 6 August 2013. http://tolonews.com/en/afghanistan/11472-taliban-does-not-aim-to-disintegrate-afghanistan-mullah-omar

6. "Taliban Vows to Unleash Jihad in Kashmir, Implement Sharia," *Rediff News*, 8 January 2013. http://www.rediff.com/news/report/taliban-vows-to-unleash-jihad-in-kashmir-implement-sharia/20130108.htm

7. "US Warned Against Reconciliation with Taliban," *Pajhwok Afghan News*, 24 July 2013. http://www.pajhwok.com/en/2013/07/24/us-warned-against-reconciliation-taliban

8. Dean Nelson, "Afghanistan is a Proxy War between India and Pakistan," *The Telegraph*, 2 November 2011. http://www.telegraph.co.uk/news/worldnews/asia/afghanistan/8863073/Afghanistan-is-a-proxy-war-between-India-and-Pakistan.html

9. Amie Ferris-Rotman, "Insight: Iran's 'Great Game' in Afghanistan," *Reuters*, 24 May 2012. http://www.reuters.com/article/2012/05/24/us-afghanistan-iran-media-idUSBRE84N0CB20120524

10. "The Official Visit of Taliban to Iran in the Eyes of the Analysts," Islamic Emirate of Afghanistan, 10 June 2013. http://shahamat-english.com/index.php/articles/32565-the-official-visit-of-taliban-to-iran-in-the-eyes-of-the-analysts

11. "Former Afghan Warlord Remobilizes Militia," Radio Free Europe Radio Liberty Afghanistan, 14 November 2012. http://www.rferl.org/content/afghanistan-former-mujahedin-warlord-recalls-militia/24771179.html

12. Ahmad Quraishi, "Karzai Most Influential Afghan Leader: Poll," 4 May 2013. http://www.pajhwok.com/en/2013/05/04/karzai-most-influential-afghan-leader-poll

13. Mark Sedra, Geoff Burt, and Mike Lawrence, "The Afghan Exit Strategy is Fraught with Peril," *The Globe and Mail*, 7 December 2011. http://www.theglobeandmail.com/commentary/the-afghan-exit-strategy-is-fraught-with-peril/article4238618/

14. This is the fourth time in the past 160 years that Afghanistan is reestablishing its military force following its total disintegration caused by foreign invasions or civil wars. In the 1870s, Amir Sher Ali Khan reestablished the Afghan military, which disintegrated during the second Anglo-Afghan War (1878–1880). The military was remodeled under King Amanullah following the third Anglo-Afghan War (1919), but it suffered a fatal blow during the civil war of 1929. King Nader Shah created a new military establishment after his accession in 1929. The Soviets started to sponsor modernization of the Afghans in the 1960s and continued through the Moscow-backed communist rule. It was totally disintegrated during the civil war of 1992–2001. Ali A. Jalali, "Rebuilding Afghanistan's National Army," Strategic Studies Institute, 2002.

15. Ali A. Jalali, "Rebuilding Afghanistan's National Army," Strategic Studies Institute, 2002. http://strategicstudiesinstitute.army.mil/pubs/parameters/articles/02autumn/jalali.pdf

16. Miriam Arghandiwal, "As Foreign Aid Dries Up, Afghan NGOs Fight to Survive," *Reuters*, 5 July 2013. http://www.reuters.com/article/2012/07/05/us-afghanistan-aid-tokyo-idUSBRE8640G720120705

17. "Karzai: NATO Should Scale Back, Hasten Handover," *CBS/AP*, 15 March 2012. http://www.cbsnews.com/8301-202_162-57397892/karzai-nato-should-scale-back-hasten-handover/

18. After the Soviet withdrawal from Afghanistan in 1989, the Afghan communist government headed by President Najibullah Ahmadzai sustained his power for a little over two years. With the dissolution of the Soviet Union in 1991, the Soviet aid to President Najib's government stopped and the government collapsed in 1992. The United States decided it had no further interests in Afghanistan and abandoned the region. The Mujahideen parties disagreed profoundly on the power sharing, leading to internal fighting against each other, and the neighboring countries—Pakistan, Iran, India, and Saudi Arabia—continued to deliver financial and material support to their preferred proxies. The intra-Mujahideen fighting continued until 1994, when the new religious militia movement, the Taliban, emerged from the south of Afghanistan and started fighting against the Mujahideen parties and their local warlord until it captured Kabul in 1996. Steve Coll, *Ghost Wars: The Secret History of the CIA, Afghanistan, and bin Laden, from the Soviet Invasion to September 10, 2001*.

19. Michael Semple, "Soldierless Jihad," *Foreign Affairs*, 26 July 2013. http://www.foreignaffairs.com/articles/139606/michael-semple/soldierless-jihad

20. "Afghanistan in 2012: A Survey of the Afghan People," The Asia Foundation, October 2012. http://www.asiafoundation.org/resources/pdfs/Surveybook2012web1.pdf

21. "Taliban Moderate Mullah Agha Jan Motasim Calls for End to War," Policy Research Group, 17 August 2012. http://policyresearchgroup.com/newscomment/taliban_moderate_mullah_agha_jan_motasim_calls_for_end_to_war.html

22. Caroline Wyatt, "Afghanistan Eyes Taliban Peace Ahead of Nato Withdrawal," *BBC News Asia*, 4 April 2013. http://www.bbc.com/news/world-asia-22030845

23. Sami Yousafzai, "Afghanistan: A Moderate Defies the Taliban," *The Daily Beast*, 25 April 2012. http://www.thedailybeast.com/articles/2012/04/25/afghanistan-a-moderate-defies-the-taliban.html

24. Myra MacDonald, "Pakistan's Arrest of Mullah Baradar: Tactics or Strategy?" *Reuters* 17 February 2010. http://blogs.reuters.com/pakistan/2010/02/17/pakistans-arrest-of-mullah-baradar-tactics-or-strategy/

25. Ghanizada, "US Commander Insists for Significant Post-2014 Presence in Afghanistan," *Khaama Press*, 14 August 2013. http://www.khaama.com/us-commander-insists-for-significant-post-2014-presence-in-afghanistan-1755

26. Ben Farmer, "Karzai to Allow US Bases in Afghanistan after Nato Withdrawal," *The Telegraph*, 9 May 2013. http://www.telegraph.co.uk/news/worldnews/asia/afghanistan/1004

7898/Karzai-to-allow-US-bases-in-Afghanistan-after-Nato-withdrawal.html

27. Ghanizada, "Top US General Says Afghan-US Security Agreement Vital," *Khaama Press*, 10 August 2013. http://www.khaama.com/top-us-general-says-afghan-us-security-agreement-vital-2336

28. "Gen. Dempsey Asks Afghanistan to Sign BSA by October," *Afghan Tolo News*, 23 July 2013. http://tolonews.com/en/afghanistan/11315-gen-dempsey-asks-afghanistan-to-sign-bsa-by-october

29. Jim Lobe, "US-Taliban Talks Set to Begin," Inter Press Service News Agency, 19 June 2013. http://www.ipsnews.net/2013/06/u-s-taliban-talks-set-to-begin/

30. "Statement of Leadership Council of Islamic Emirate Regarding 'Khalid bin Waleed' Spring Operation," Islamic Emirate of Afghanistan, 27 April 2013. http://www.shahamat-english.com/index.php/paighamoona/30919-statement-of-leadership-council-of-islamic-emirate-regarding-%E2%80%98khalid-bin-waleed%E2%80%99-spring-operation

31. Ghanizada, "Top Afghan Officials Resume Talks on New Phase of Security Agreement with US," *Khaama Press*, 20 August 2013. http://www.khaama.com/top-afghan-officials-resume-talks-on-new-phase-of-security-agreement-with-us-1771

32. Zalmay Khalilzad, "Afghanistan Deal Faces Many Hurdles," *The Washington Post*, 26 July 2013. http://www.washingtonpost.com/opinions/afghanistan-deal-faces-many-hurdles/2013/07/25/0f7b565c-f476-11e2-a2f1-a7acf9bd5d3a_story.html

33. Zalmay Khalilzad, "Afghanistan Deal Faces Many Hurdles," *The Washington Post*, 26 July 2013. http://www.washingtonpost.com/opinions/afghanistan-deal-faces-many-hurdles/2013/07/25/0f7b565c-f476-11e2-a2f1-a7acf9bd5d3a_story.html

34. Kamran Yousaf, "Pak, Russia Army Chiefs Discuss US Exit in Afghanistan," *The Express Tribune*, 6 August 2013. http://tribune.com.pk/story/587112/pak-russia-army-chiefs-discuss-us-exit-in-afghanistan/

35. Zalmay Khalilzad, "Afghanistan Deal Faces Many Hurdles," *The Washington Post*, 26 July 2013. http://www.washingtonpost.com/opinions/afghanistan-deal-faces-many-hurdles/2013/07/25/0f7b565c-f476-11e2-a2f1-a7acf9bd5d3a_story.html

36. Patrick Goodenough, "Contrary to Obama's 'Narrative,' Al Qaeda Threat Getting Worse, Say GOP Critics," *CNSNews*, 12 August 2013. http://www.cnsnews.com/news/article/contrary-obama-s-narrative-al Qaeda-threat-getting-worse-say-gop-critics

37. Mark Thompson and Bobby Ghosh, "The CIA's Silent War in Pakistan," *Time*, 1 June 2009. http://content.time.com/time/magazine/article/0,9171,1900248,00.html

38. Piotr Smolar, "Key US Base in Central Asia Faces Closure after Kyrgyz MPs' Vote," *The Guardian*, 16 July 2013. http://www.theguardian.com/world/2013/jul/16/us-base-closure-kyrgyzstan-manas

39. "US Loses Key Base in Central Asia," *BBC News*, 31 July 2013. http://news.bbc.co.uk/2/hi/asia-pacific/4732197.stm

40. Piotr Smolar, "Key US Base in Central Asia Faces Closure after Kyrgyz MPs' Vote," *The Guardian*, 16 July 2013. http://www.theguardian.com/world/2013/jul/16/us-base-closure-kyrgyzstan-manas

2. PAKISTAN'S INEXTRICABLE ROLE IN AFGHANISTAN'S FUTURE

1. Amy Willis, "Taliban: We Cannot Win War in Afghanistan," *The Telegraph*, 11 July 2012. http://www.telegraph.co.uk/news/worldnews/al Qaeda/9391093/Taliban-We-cannot-win-war-in-Afghanistan.html; Stephen Biddle, "Ending the War in Afghanistan: How to Avoid Failure on the Installment Plan," *Foreign Affairs*, September–October 2013. http://www.foreignaffairs.com/articles/139644/stephen-biddle/ending-the-war-in-afghanistan

2. Moeed Yusuf, Huma Yusuf, and Salman Zaidi, "Pakistan, the United States and the Endgame in Afghanistan: Perception of Pakistan's Foreign Policy Elite," Peace Brief, United States Institute of Peace, 25 July 2011. http://www.usip.org/sites/default/files/PB100.pdf

3. Matan Chorve and Jake Sherman, "The Prospects for Security and Political Reconciliation in Afghanistan: Local, National, and Regional Perspectives," a workshop report by the Belfer Center for Science and Technology, Harvard Kennedy School, May 2010, p. 10. Accessed 15 July 2013. http://belfercenter.ksg.harvard.edu/publication/20111/prospects_for_security_and_political_reconciliation_in_afghanistan.html

4. Shantie Mariet D'Souza, "Transition in Afghanistan: A War of Perceptions," *Small Wars Journal*, 10 January 2013, p. 1. http://smallwarsjournal.com/jrnl/art/transition-in-afghanistan-a-war-of-perceptions

5. Ioannis Koskinas and Kamal Alam, "Reconciliation Foolosophy: Fishing without Bait," *Af-Pak Channel*, 14 June 2013. http://afpak.foreignpolicy.com/posts/2013/06/14/reconciliationfoolosophy_fishing_without_bait

6. Shantie Mariet D'Souza, "Transition in Afghanistan."

7. Arian Sharifi, "US Needs to Clear its Vision on Afghanistan," *Khama Press*, Afghanistan, 28 July 2013. http://www.khaama.com/us-needs-to-clear-its-vision-on-afghanistan-9090

8. Jair van der Linj, "Afghanistan Post-2014: Groping in the Dark?" Netherlands Institute of International Relations, p. 20. http://www.clingendael.nl/sites/default/files/Afghanistan%20post%202014%20Groping%20in%20the%20dark.pdf

9. Ioannis Koskinas and Kamal Alam, "Reconciliation Foolosophy: Fishing without Bait," *Af-Pak Channel*, 14 June 2013. http://afpak.foreignpolicy.com/posts/2013/06/14/reconciliationfoolosophy_fishing_without_bait

10. "Talking About Talks: Toward a Political Settlement in Afghanistan," Asia Report No. 221, International Crisis Group, 26 March 2012, p. 38. http://www.crisisgroup.org/~/media/Files/asia/south-asia/afghanistan/221-talking-about-talks-toward-a-political-settlement-in-afghanistan.pdf

11. Ten Years Since 9/11: Our Collective Experience (Pakistan's Perspective), a white paper that Pakistan Army chief General Kayani presented to President Obama during his US visit in December 2010, p. 5. https://archive.org/stream/329645-pakistan-document/329645-pakistan-document_djvu.txt

12. Radha Kumar and Kalish K. Parsad, "Afghanistan 2012: Looking to the Future," a report by Delhi Policy Group Publication, 2012, p. 22. http://www.delhipolicygroup.com/pdf/regional_conference_report.pdf

13. Khadim Hussain, "Post-2014 AfPak," *Dawn*, Pakistan, 12 August 2013. http://dawn.com/news/1035358

14. Randall Joyce, "Afghanistan-Taliban Peace Talks: Too Many Cooks in the Kitchen," *CBS News*, 5 February 2013. http://www.cbsnews.com/8301-202_162-57567661/afghanistan-taliban-peace-talks-too-many-cooks-in-the-kitchen/

15. Carlotta Gall and Ruhullah Khapalwak, "US Has Held Meetings with Aide to Taliban Leader, Officials Say," *New York Times*, 26 May 2011. http://www.nytimes.com/2011/05/27/world/asia/27taliban.html

16. Eric Schmitt and David E. Sanger, "US Seeks Aid from Pakistan in Peace Effort," *New York Times*, 30 October 2011. http://www.nytimes.com/2011/10/31/world/asia/united-states-seeks-pakistan-spy-agencys-help-for-afghan-talks.html?pagewanted=1&_r=1&ref=world

17. "Afghan Taliban Open Office in Qatar," *The News*, Pakistan, 18 June 2013. http://www.thenews.com.pk/article-105842-Afghan-Taliban-open-office-in-Qatar

18. Yusuf, Yusuf, and Zaidi, "Pakistan, the United States and the End Game in Afghanistan, p. 10. http://www.usip.org/sites/default/files/resources/PB100.pdf

19. Anatol Lieven, "Afghanistan: The War after the War," *The New York Review of Books*, 9 July 2013. http://www.nybooks.com/blogs/nyrblog/2013/jul/14/afghanistan-war-after-war/

20. Michael Crowley, "America and Pakistan after Bin Laden: Still Frenemies," *Time*, 2 May 2011. http://swampland.time.com/2011/05/02/america-and-pakistan-after-bin-laden-still-frenemies/

21. Britta Peterson, "A Study of Pakistan's Interests in Afghanistan: Fear Prejudice," *Henrich Boll Stiftung*, Germany, 26 October 2011. http://pk.boell.org/2011/10/26/study-pakistans-interests-afghanistan-fear-and-prejudice

22. For the complete transcript of Hillary Clinton's remarks with Afghan President Hamid Karzai see, http://www.state.gov/secretary/20092013clinton/rm/2011/10/175893.htm, 11 October 2011 (retrieved on 28 July 2013).

23. "Afghan Army Chief: 'Pakistan Controls Taliban,'" *BBC News*, 3 July 2013. http://www.bbc.co.uk/news/world-asia-23152159

24. "Joint Chiefs Chairman Adm. Michael Mullen Says Pakistan 'Exporting Violence,'" ABC News, 22 September 2011. http://abcnews.go.com/Politics/joint-chiefs-chairman-adm-michael-mullen-pakistan-exporting/story?id=14583906&page=2

25. "John Kerry Urges Bigger Afghan Role for India; Hyphenates India & Pakistan," *The Economic Times*, 24 June 2013. http://articles.economictimes.indiatimes.com/2013-06-24/news/40166755_1_climate-change-john-kerry-us-rebalance

26. Asif Haroon Raja, "Hamid Karzai Has Preferred India over Pakistan," *Pak Tribune* (Online Newspaper), 27 October 2011. http://paktribune.com/articles/Hamid-Karzai-has-preferred-India-over-Pakistan-242802.html

27. Suba Chandran, "Af-Pak Diary: Are Regional Differences over Afghanistan Irreconcilable?" Institute of Peace and Conflict Studies, India, 19 December 2012. http://www.ipcs.org/article/afghanistan/af-pak-diary-are-regional-differences-over-afghanistan-irreconcilable-3780.html

28. After these moves, Pakistan arrested the number two leader of the Afghan Taliban, Mullah Abdul Ghani Baradar from Karachi in 2010. While Kabul considered his arrest as a sabotage move, Pakistan clearly indicated that it was not in favor of talks that bypassed Islamabad. Unlike the widespread misperception that the Afghan Taliban are the proxies of the Pakistani state, relations between the two are very strained and tense. Since 9/11, the Afghan Taliban do not trust the Pakistani government, especially the Pakistan army and the ISI. After the 9/11 al Qaeda attacks on the United States, Pakistan, under the military regime of General (Retired) Pervez Musharraf, took a U-turn on its Afghan policy and sided with the United States against the Taliban regime in Afghanistan. Pakistan provided the United States with intelligence and logistical support. Even before 9/11, despite their heavy dependence on Pakistan, the Afghan Taliban have always pursued an independent path. They accepted only those decisions of the Pakistani state that suited their interests. From the bombing of the Bamiyan Buddhas in Central Afghanistan in 2001 to the refusal to hand over al Qaeda chief Osama bin Laden to the United States, the Afghan Taliban have followed an independent path. Like previous Afghan governments, during their rule (1996–2001) the Taliban did not recognize the Durand Line as a de jure international border between Afghanistan and Pakistan.

29. Bruce Ridel, "Pakistan Seeks Control of Its Afghanistan Endgame," *Yale Global Online*, 30 September 2011. http://yaleglobal.yale.edu/content/pakistan-seeks-control-its-afghanistan-endgame

30. Ishtiaq Ahmed, "As Western Withdrawal Gains Momentum, Peace in Afghanistan Hinges on One Factor: Pakistan," *Politics in Spires*, University of Oxford, UK, 18 February 2013. http://politicsinspires.org/as-western-withdrawal-gains-momentum-peace-in-afghanistan-hinges-on-one-factor-pakistan/

31. William Dalrymple, "A Deadly Triangle: Afghanistan, Pakistan and India," Brookings Institute, 25 June 2013. http://www.brookings.edu/research/essays/2013/deadly-triangle-afghanistan-pakistan-india-c

32. Aryaman Bhatnagar, "Afghanistan: India-Pakistan Rivalry Reignited," Observer Research Foundation, India, 19 August 2013. http://orfonline.org/cms/sites/orfonline/modules/weeklyassessment/WeeklyAssessmentDetail.html?cmaid=56076&mmacmaid=56077&volumeno=VI&issueno=33

33. Ibid.

34. Larry Hanauer and Peter Chalk, "India's and Pakistan's Strategies in Afghanistan: Implications for the United States and the Region," Center for Asia Pacific Policy, RAND Corporation, 2013, p. 11. http://www.rand.org/content/dam/rand/pubs/occasional_papers/2012/RAND_OP387.pdf

35. "India's Growing Stake in Afghanistan," *BBC*, 22 June 2012. http://www.bbc.co.uk/news/world-asia-18622573

36. Dalrymple, "A Deadly Triangle."

37. Sajjad Ashraf, "India and Pakistan Compete for Influence in Afghanistan," *East Asia Forum*, 25 April 2013. http://www.eastasiaforum.org/2013/04/25/india-and-pakistan-compete-for-influence-in-afghanistan/

38. In his 2013 Eid al-Fitr, the Muslim religious festival marking the end of the holy month of Ramadan, the leader of the Afghan Taliban, Mullah Umar, maintained, "We have already said that the Islamic Emirate does not think of monopolizing power. We believe in reaching understanding with the Afghans regarding an Afghan-inclusive government based on Islamic principles." See full text: http://shahamat-english.com/index.php/paighamoona/35234-message-of-felicitation-of-amir-ul-momineen-may-allah-protect-him-on-the-occasion-of-eid-ul-fitr

39. Matt Waldman, "Taliban Qatar Office: A Small Step Forward," Chatham House, London, 20 June 2013. http://www.chathamhouse.org/media/comment/view/192553

40. Anthony H. Cordesman, "Transition in the Afghanistan-Pakistan War: How Does This War End?" Center for Strategic and International Studies, 11 July 2012, p. 33. http://csis.org/files/publication/120111_Afghanistan_Aspen_Paper.pdf

41. Talal Hussain, "Afghanistan Complex Situation and Its Implications on Pakistan," Unpublished master's thesis, p. 26.

42. Stability should be seen in the Afghan context.

43. Ayaz Wazir, "Afghanistan: Handle with Care," *The News*, Pakistan, 1 August 2013. http://www.thenews.com.pk/Todays-News-9-193664-Afghanistan-handle-with-care

44. An excerpt from former Pakistani Foreign Minister Hina Rabbani Khar's speech at Chatham House, London on 22 February 2013. For more details see http://www.chathamhouse.org/sites/default/files/public/Meetings/Meeting%20Transcripts/220212khar.pdf (retrieved on 28 June 2013).

45. Conditioned upon the Taliban's renunciation of violence, scuttling ties with al Qaeda and accepting the Afghan constitution.

46. Anatol Liven, "Afghanistan: What Pakistan Wants," *The New York Book of Reviews*, 2 May 2013. http://www.nybooks.com/blogs/nyrblog/2013/jul/15/Afghanistan-what-pakistan-wants/

47. For the complete text of the paper visit http://s3.documentcloud.org/documents/329645/pakistan-document.pdf (retrieved on 29 July 2013).

48. Steve Coll, "What Does Pakistan Want?" *The New Yorker*, 29 March 2012. http://www.newyorker.com/online/blogs/comment/2012/03/classified-document-our-collective-experience.html

49. "Afghanistan and Pakistan After the 2014 NATO Drawdown," *Stratfor Global Intelligence*, 15 April 2013. http://www.stratfor.com/analysis/afghanistan-and-pakistan-after-2014-nato-drawdown

50. Safdar Sial, "Pakistan's Role and Strategic Priorities in Afghanistan Since 1980," Norwegian Peacebuilding and Resource Centre, June 2013, p. 7. http://www.peacebuilding.no/var/ezflow_site/storage/original/application/daf97b6b68b9445f85c58923a3afdeb3.pdf

51. Najmuddin A. Shaikh, "What Does Pakistan Want in Afghanistan?" *The Express Tribune*, Pakistan, 15 December 2011. http://tribune.com.pk/story/307077/what-does-pakistan-want-in-afghanistan-2/

52. Brajesh Upadhyay, "Pakistani Fears over India Afghan Role 'Not Groundless,'" *BBC*, 7 August 2013. http://www.bbc.co.uk/news/world-asia-india-23598521

53. "India Finances Trouble in Pakistan: Hagel," *Dawn*, Pakistan, 27 January 2013. http://beta.dawn.com/news/788984/india-finances-trouble-in-pakistan-hagel

54. Saba Imtiaz, "MPs Told Russia, India and UAE Involved in Baloch Insurgency," *The Express Tribune*, Pakistan, 3 December 2010. http://tribune.com.pk/story/84902/wikileaks-india-russia-supporting-baloch-insurgency/

55. Declan Walsh, "WikiLeaks Cables Reveal Afghan-Pakistani Row over Fugitive Rebel," *The Guardian*, 30 November 2010. http://www.theguardian.com/world/2010/nov/30/wikileaks-cables-afghan-pakistani-fugitive

56. Moeed Yusuf, "No Regional Framework," *Dawn*, Pakistan, 20 November 2011. http://beta.dawn.com/news/674667/no-regional-framework

57. Ibid.

58. Daud Khattak, "For Pakistan, a Change of Heart in Afghanistan?" *Af-Pak Channel*, 17 December 2012. http://afpak.foreignpolicy.com/posts/2012/12/17/pakistans_change_of_heart_in_afghanistan

59. Sial, "Pakistan's Role and Strategic Priorities," p. 1.

60. Kamran Yousuf, "New Envoy: Drones Impede Pakistan's Role in Afghan Peace, Says Nawaz," *The Express Tribune*, Pakistan, 31 May 2013. http://tribune.com.pk/story/556905/new-envoy-drones-impede-pakistans-role-in-afghan-peace-says-nawaz/

61. Mona Kanwal Sheikh, "Where Are We Now: Reintegration, Reconciliation and Negotiation with the Taliban," in *Taliban Talks: Past, Present and Prospects for the US, Afghanistan and Pakistan*, Mona K. Shiekh and Maja T. J. Greenwod (eds.), a report by the Danish Institute for International Studies, May 2013, p. 22. http://reliefweb.int/sites/reliefweb.int/files/resources/RP2013-06-Taliban-Talks_web.pdf

62. Najmuddin A. Shaikh, "What Does Pakistan Want?" *Dawn*, Pakistan, 27 June 2013. http://beta.dawn.com/news/729835/what-does-pakistan-want

63. The Durand Line is a 2,500-kilometer-long unmarked border agreed to by Sir Mortimer Durand of British India and Afghan Amir Abdur Rahman Khan in 1893, and is not recognized by Afghanistan.

64. Aziz Hakimi, "Af-Pak: What Strategic Depth?" *Open Democracy*, 4 February 2010. http://www.opendemocracy.net/opensecurity/aziz-hakimi/af-pak-what-strategic-depth

65. No objection to Indian development role should not be confused with India's anti-Pakistan activities in Afghanistan.

66. Ishtiaq Ahmed, "Pakistan's Afghan Outreach Program," *Weekly Pulse*, Pakistan, 2–8 November 2012. http://www.ishtiaqahmad.com/item_display.aspx?listing_id=855&listing_type=1

67. Jennifer Rowland, "Pakistan Outreach Could Aid Afghan Settlement," *Af-Pak Channel*, 29 October 2012. http://southasia.foreignpolicy.com/posts/2012/10/29/pakistan_outreach_could_aid_afghan_settlement

68. Arshad Ali, "Endgame in Afghanistan: Pakistan's New Approach," *RSIS Commentaries*, Singapore, 19 December 2013. http://dr.ntu.edu.sg/bitstream/handle/10220/11815/RSIS 2302012.pdf?sequence=

69. "Pakistan Releases Four More Afghan Taliban Prisoners," *The Nation*, Pakistan, 31 December 2012. http://www.nation.com.pk/pakistan-news-newspaper-daily-english-online/national/31-Dec-2012/pakistan-releases-four-more-afghan-taliban-prisoners

70. Baqir Sajjad Syed, "7 Taliban Freed to 'Facilitate' Peace Talks," *Dawn*, Pakistan, 8 September 2013. http://dawn.com/news/1041342/7-taliban-freed-to-facilitate-peace-talks

71. Larry Hanauer and Peter Chalk, "India's and Pakistan's Strategies in Afghanistan: Implications for the United States and the Region," Occasional Paper, Center for Asia Pacific Policy, RAND Corporation, 2012, p. 27. http://www.rand.org/content/dam/rand/pubs/occasional_papers/2012/RAND_OP387.pdf

72. Yusuf, Yusuf, and Zaidi, "Pakistan, the United States and the Endgame in Afghanistan," p. 12.

73. Shabbir Mir, "Gunmen Kill 9 Foreign Tourists, Guide in Gilgit-Baltistan," *The Express Tribune*, Pakistan, 23 June 2013. http://tribune.com.pk/story/567190/ten-tourists-shot-dead-at-fairy-meadows/; Ali Hazrat Bacha, "Carnage at church after Sunday mass," *Dawn*, Pakistan, 23 September 2013. http://dawn.com/news/1044808/carnage-at-church-after-sunday-mass

74. "Junood ul Hifsa New Wing Set Up to Attack Foreigners, Claims TTP," *The Express Tribune*, Pakistan, 23 June 2013. http://tribune.com.pk/story/567366/junood-ul-hifsa-new-wing-set-up-to-attack-foreigners-claims-ttp/

75. Faisal Aziz, "'Punjabi Taliban' a Growing Threat for Pakistan," *Reuters*, 30 May 2010. http://www.reuters.com/article/2010/05/30/us-pakistan-militants-punjab-idUSTRE64T0QT20100530

76. For the full text of Mullah Omar's Eid message visit http://www.shahamat-english.com/index.php/paighamoona/35234-message-of-felicitation-of-amir-ul-momineen-may-allah-protect-him-on-the-occasion-of-eid-ul-fitr (retrieved on 9 August 2013).

77. Mark N. Katza, "Lessons of Soviet Withdrawal from Afghanistan," Middle East Policy Council, 19 March 2011. http://www.mepc.org/articles-commentary/commentary/lessons-soviet-withdrawal-afghanistan

78. Dr. Farrukh Saleem, "Capital Suggestion . . . Post-2014," *The News*, Pakistan, 18 August 2013. http://www.thenews.com.pk/Todays-News-9-196486-Post-2014

79. Rahul Roy-Chaudhury, "Pakistan," in *Afghanistan to 2015 and Beyond*, Nicholas Redman and Toby Dodge (eds.) (London: The International Institute for Strategic Studies, 2012), p. 171.

80. Taken from the text of Hina Rabbani Khar's speech available at http://www.chathamhouse.org/sites/default/files/public/Meetings/Meeting%20Transcripts/220212khar.pdf (retrieved on 13 August 2013).

81. "Displaced Persons: Afghan Repatriation Deadline Extended Till Dec 2015," *The Express Tribune*, Pakistan, 14 August 2013. http://tribune.com.pk/story/589806/displaced-persons-afghan-repatriation-deadline-extended-till-dec-2015/

82. Rizwan Zeb, "Is India-Pakistan 'Competition' over Afghanistan Inevitable?" *Daily Times*, Pakistan, 21 July 2013. http://archives.dailytimes.com.pk/editorial/21-Jul-2013/comment-is-india-pakistan-competition-over-afghanistan-inevitable-rizwan-zeb

83. Sadika Hameed, "Prospects of Indian-Pakistani Cooperation in Afghanistan," Center for Strategic and International Studies, August 2012, p. 9. http://csis.org/files/publication/120821_Hameed_ProspectsIndianPakistan_Web.pdf

84. Ishtiaq Ahmed, "Good Neighbour Policy," *Weekly Pulse*, Pakistan, 29 July 2013. http://www.weeklypulse.org/details.aspx?contentID=3898&storylist=2

85. Sheikh, "Where Are We Now," p. 27.

86. Tim Foxley, "Messaging the Taliban," in *Taliban Talks: Past, Present and Prospects for the US, Afghanistan and Pakistan*, Mona K. Shiekh and Maja T. J. Greenwod (eds.), a report by the Danish Institute for International Studies, May 2013, p. 34. http://reliefweb.int/sites/reliefweb.int/files/resources/RP2013-06-Taliban-Talks_web.pdf

87. Ibid., p. 36.

3. AN AMERICAN PERSPECTIVE FOR AFGHANISTAN'S FUTURE

1. The views expressed in this chapter are those of the author and do not necessarily reflect the views of the Department of Defense or any of its agencies.

2. James A. Michener, *Caravans* (New York: The Random House Publishing Group, 1963), p. 58.

3. "Pakistan Ready to Release Mullah Baradar at 'Appropriate' Time," *Daily Times Monitor*, 21 July 2013. http://www.dailytimes.com.pk (accessed 21 July 2013).

4. Tom Vanden Brook, "Afghan 'Insurgents' Now Called 'Enemies of Afghanistan,'" *USA Today*, 12 August 2013. http://www.stripes.com/news/middle-east/afghan-insurgents-now-called-enemies-of-afghanistan-1.235023 (accessed 12 August 2013).

5. Robert Burns, "Commander Encouraged by Anti-Taliban Uprising," Yahoo News, 13 March 2013. http://news.yahoo.com/commander-encouraged-anti-taliban-uprising-165413103--politics.html (accessed 12 July 2013).

6. Bill Gertz, "Anti-Taliban Movement Gaining Strength in Afghanistan, US Says," *The Washington Free Beacon*, 12 July 2013. http://freebeacon.com/anti-taliban-movement-gaining-strength-in-afghanistan-u-s-says/ (accessed 21 July 2013).

7. Stephanie McCrummen, "International Donors Pledge $16 Billion in Aid to Afghanistan over Four Years," *The Washington Post*, 8 July 2012. http://articles.washingtonpost.com/2012-07-08/world/35487477_1_mutual-accountability-framework-donor-afghanistan (accessed 11 November 2013).

8. Associated Press, "International Community Affirms Afghan Funding but Concerned over Corruption," Fox News. 3 July 2013. http://www.foxnews.com/world/2013/07/03/international-community-affirms-afghan-funding-but-concerned-over-corruption/ (accessed 20 July 2013).

9. BBC News Update, "China Workers Die in Afghan Raid," BBC News, 10 June 2004. http://news.bbc.co.uk/2/hi/south_asia/3792901.stm (accessed 20 July 2013).

10. Jessica Donati, "Three Chinese Murdered in Afghan Capital, One Missing—Embassy," Yahoo News, 10 August 2013. http://uk.news.yahoo.com/three-chinese-murdered-afghan-capital-two-missing-embassy-052959380.html#AxzfOpT (accessed 12 August 2013).

11. Jere Van Dyk, "As America Fights, China Gets Contracts," CBS News, 19 July 2013. http://www.cbsnews.com/8301-505123_162-57591567/as-america-fights-china-gets-contracts/ (accessed 21 July 2013).

12. Kevin Seiff, "Karzai Backers Seek Delay in Afghan Vote," *The Washington Post*, 31 July 2013. http://articles.washingtonpost.com/2013-07-31/world/40912914_1_president-hamid-karzai-top-afghan-officials-april-election (accessed 7 August 2013).

13. Aazem Arash, "Afghan-Iran Strategic Agreement Will Damage Relations with the West: Political Parties," *Tolo News*, 7 August 2013. http://tolonews.com/en/afghanistan/11485-afghan-iran-strategic-agreement-to-hamper-relation-with-western-allies-political-parties. (accessed 12 August 2013).

14. Mushtaq Yusufzai and Fakhar Rehman, "Taliban Spin? Mullah Omar Supports Education, Respects Other Religions," *NBC News*, 7 August 2013. http://worldnews.nbcnews.com/_news/2013/08/07/19908176-taliban-spin-mullah-omar-supports-education-respects-other-religions?lite (accessed 8 August 2013).

15. Zheng Limin, "Chinese President Raises Proposal on SCO Cooperation," *Xinhua*, 13 September 2013. http://english.cntv.cn/20130913/104853.shtml (accessed 14 September 2013).

16. Zheng Limin, "Chinese President Raises Proposal on SCO Cooperation," Xinhua, September 13, 2013. Information Office of the State Council, China 2013. http://english.cntv.cn/20130913/104853.shtml (accessed 14 September 2013).

17. Limin 2013.

18. Mark Mazzetti and Matthew Rosenburg, "US Considers Faster Pullout in Afghanistan," *The New York Times*, 8 July 2013. http://www.nytimes.com/2013/07/09/world/asia/frustrated-obama-considers-full-troop-withdrawal-from-afghanistan.html?pagewanted=all&_r=0 (accessed 12 August 2013).

19. Magsie Hamilton-Little, "Taking Tea with Afghanistan's Most Fearsome Warlord, General Abdul Rashid Dostum," *The Telegraph*, 29 July 2012. http://www.telegraph.co.uk/news/worldnews/asia/afghanistan/9435387/Taking-tea-with-Afghanistans-most-fearsome-warlord-General-Abdul-Rashid-Dostum.html (accessed 15 July 2013).

20. Ibid.

21. Ronald E. Neumann and Vanda Felbab-Brown, "Fair Afghan Elections Are a Must," *The Post and Courier*, 29 July 2013. http://www.postandcourier.com/article/20130729/PC1002/130729412/1021/fair-afghan-elections-are-a-must&source=RSS (accessed 10 August 2013).

22. Lynne O'Donnell, "Afghanistan's Plan to Jumpstart Economy with Chinese Mining Investment under Threat," *South China Morning Post*, 20 September 2013. http://www.scmp.com/news/asia/article/1313161/afghanistans-plan-jumpstart-economy-chinese-mining-investment-under-threat (accessed 25 September 2013).

23. Rupakjyoti Borah, "India's Challenges in Afghanistan Post-2014," *East Asia Forum*, 6 August 2013. http://www.eastasiaforum.org/2013/08/06/indias-challenges-in-afghanistan-post-2014/ (accessed 11 November 2013).

24. Aazem Arash, "Afghan-Iran Strategic Agreement Will Damage Relations with the West: Political Parties," *Tolo News*, 8 August 2013. http://www.tolonews.com/en/afghanistan/11485-afghan-iran-strategic-agreement-to-hamper-relation-with-western-allies-political-parties (accessed 11 November 2013).

25. Andrew Bowen, "Why Russia is Worried About 'Zero Option' in Afghanistan," *The Interpreter*, 9 August 2013. http://www.interpretermag.com/why-russia-is-worried-about-zero-option-in-afghanistan/ (accessed 12 August 2013).

26. Ben Blanchard and John Ruwitch, "China Hikes Defense Budget, to Spend More on Internal Security," *Reuters*, 5 March 2013. http://www.reuters.com/article/2013/03/05/us-china-parliament-defence-idUSBRE92403620130305 (accessed 15 July 2013).

27. Ibid.

4. INDIA'S KEY ROLE AND SOUTH ASIA'S SECURITY CONCERNS

1. Interview with Indian analyst, 26 September 2013.

2. Pakistani support for Afghan Taliban is well known. When the Afghan Taliban came to power in Afghanistan, Pakistan was the first country to recognize them. In Pakistan the insurgency in Afghanistan is called "jihad" (holy war), and the Afghan Taliban are called "Shahid" (martyr). Though the Pakistan government denies that it supports the Afghan Taliban, the Afghan authorities strongly believe that the Afghan Taliban have support and sanctuary in Pakistan. The Afghan Taliban enjoy the support of Pakistani militant groups and Islamist political parties as well as a group of Ulema or Islamic clerics. For example the Tahir Ashrafi, chairman of Pakistan's Ulema Council, suicide attacks were lawful in Afghanistan but not in Pakistan. For details see, http://www.tolonews.com/en/afghanistan/9627-pakistan-ulema-permits-suicide-attacks

3. Rohan Gunaratna, "Terrorists to Bounce Back in 2013," *Counter Terrorist Trends and Analysis*, Vol 5, Issue 1, January 2013, http://www.pvtr.org/pdf/CTTA/2013/CTTA-January13.pdf

4. Interview with Afghan analyst, 19 August 2013.

5. It is difficult to determine the exact strength of the Taliban. However, many Afghan analysts believe that the Taliban's current strength is 25,000–30,000.

6. See briefing by Major General Michael Flynn, director of intelligence for the ISAF, "State of the Insurgency: Trends, Intentions and Objectives," 22 December 2009, for an overview of the insurgent threat.

7. "Lashkar behind Jalalabad Attack, Afghans Tell India," *The Hindustan Times*, 9 August 2013, http://www.hindustantimes.com/india-news/newdelhi/lashkar-behind-jalalabad-attack-afghans-tell-india/article1-1105487.aspx

8. This paper considers Talibanization as a process that encompasses Islamist political endeavors, including the resort to violence and terrorism that is legitimized through selective reading and interpretation of Islam. For details, see Bilveer Singh, *Talibanization in Southeast Asia: Losing the War on Terror to Islamist Extremists* (Westport, CT: Paeger Security International), 2007, p. 14.

9. For an excellent narrative on foreign fighters in Afghanistan and Pakistan see Brian Glyn Williams, "On the Trail of the Lions of Islam: Foreign Fighters in Afghanistan and Pakistan 1980–2010," *Orbis*, Vol. 55, No. 2, Spring 2011.

10. US Department of State, "Designations of Harakat-ul Jihad Islami (HUJI) and its Leader Mohammad Ilyas Kashmiri," 6 August 2010, http://www.state.gov/r/pa/prs/ps/2010/08/145779.html

11. Toby Dodge and Nicholas Redman (Eds.), *Afghanistan: To 2015 and Beyond* (Oxford: Routledge, 2012) p. 232.

12. Ali Riaz, "Long Shadow of a Distant World," in *Islamist Militancy in Bangladesh: A Complex Web* (Oxford: Routledge, 2008).

13. "South and Central Asia: Background Briefing: Senior State Department Officials and Senior Administration Official on Bilateral Security Agreement," US Department of State, http://www.state.gov/r/pa/prs/ps/2013/10/215361.htm

14. The exact number of people killed by these devices is difficult to calculate, but the Afghan interior ministry says they were responsible for killing most of 1,800 Afghan national police personnel who died in 2012. About 900 Afghan National Army soldiers were killed by roadside bombs during the same time period estimates suggest.

15. The US Department of Defense has identified 2,273 American service members who have died as a part of the Afghan war and related operations. "US Military Deaths in Afghani-

stan," New York Times, http://www.nytimes.com/2013/10/22/us/us-military-deaths-in-afghanistan.html?_r=0

16. US Department of Defense, *Report on Progress Toward Security and Stability in Afghanistan*, July 2013. http://www.defense.gov/pubs/Section_1230_Report_July_2013.pdf

17. The ANSF has a desertion rate of 30 percent, a third of the force is to be found new and trained annually. The recruits owe loyalty to the tribe or the warlord instead of to a central authority.

18. Interview with Indian analyst, 26 September 2013.

19. Author's interview with Indian analyst, 26 September 2013.

20. Interview with Indian analyst, 26 September 2013.

5. THE ENDGAME IN AFGHANISTAN WILL AFFECT CENTRAL ASIA

1. Caroe, Sir Olaf Kirkpatrick Kruuse, *The Pathans: 550 B.C.-A.D. 1957*, London: Macmillan, 1964, p. 397.

2. Statement by the Press Secretary on the attack in Kabul, The White House, Office of the Press Secretary, 18 January 2014, http://www.whitehouse.gov/the-press-office/2014/01/18/statement-press-secretary-attack-kabul

3. "US, Taliban to Hold Talks in Doha," *The Huffington Post*, 18 June 2013, http://www.huffingtonpost.com/2013/06/18/us-taliban-talks_n_3459383.html

4. Stefan Olsson, Erika Holmquist, *Afghanistan after 2014: Five Scenarios*. Sweden, 2010, https://www.academia.edu/3488447/Afghanistan_After_2014_Five_Scenarios

5. "A Test for the Meaning of Victory in Afghanistan," *The New York Times*, 13 February 2010, http://www.nytimes.com/2010/02/14/weekinreview/14sanger.html

6. "Al Qaeda is 'Morphing,' Not on the Run, Intel Chiefs Say," *CBS News*, 11 February 2014, http://www.cbsnews.com/news/al Qaeda-is-morphing-not-on-the-run-intel-chiefs-say/

7. Houssain Kettani, *2010 World Muslim Population*, Proceedings of the Eighth Hawaii International Conference on Arts and Humanities, Honolulu, Hawaii, January 2010, p. 9, at http://www.pupr.edu/hkettani/papers/hicah2010.pdf

8. Ahmed Rashid, "Annals of Terrorism. They're Only Sleeping," 14 January 2002, http://www.newyorker.com/archive/2002/01/14/020114fa_FACT

9. S. Frederick Star, *Introducing the Ferghana Valley*, p. xii, http://www.mesharpe.com/extra/004Starr-Intro.pdf

10. Guido Steinberg, "A Turkish al Qaeda: The Islamic Jihad Union and the Internationalization of Uzbek Jihadism," July 2008, p. 3. http://www.hsdl.org/?view&did=487277

11. "Amriddin May Be Link between Tajik, Waziri Extremists," *Central Asia Online*, 28 January 2013, http://centralasiaonline.com/en_GB/articles/caii/newsbriefs/2011/01/28/newsbrief-01

12. "Kyrgyzstan Ends Inquiry into Suspected Terrorist Group," *Central Asia Online*, 2 May 2011, http://centralasiaonline.com/en_GB/articles/caii/features/main/2011/05/02/feature-01

13. Yelena Altman, "Kyrgyzstan Mujahideen Swear Allegiance to Amir of the Islamic Emirate of Afghanistan, Mullah Omar, Islam," *Islamism and Politics in Eurasia Report*, No. 37, Monterey Terrorism Research and Education Program (MonTREP), Monterey Institute for International Studies, 30 March 2011, https://csis.org/files/publication/110330_Hahn_IIPER_37.pdf

14. "Jund al Khilafah Emir Killed in 'Treacherous Raid,'" *The Long War Journal*, 17 October 2012, http://www.longwarjournal.org/archives/2012/10/jund_al_khilafah_emi.php

15. "General Security Situation in Afghanistan and Events in Kabul," *European Country of Origin Information Network*, 17 March 2014, http://www.ecoi.net/news/188769::afghanistan/101.general-security-situation-in-afghanistan-and-events-in-kabul.htm

16. Inomzhon Bobokulov, "The Afghan Transformation: Priorities and Key Problems," *Central Asia and the Caucasus*, Vol. 14, Issue 2, 2013, p. 35.

17. Author's interview with Afghanistan analyst, 19 April 2014.
18. Tahir Mehdi, "Why the Taliban Won't Succeed in Afghanistan Now," *Dawn*, Pakistan, 2 April 2014, http://www.dawn.com/news/1048279/why-the-taliban-wont-succeed-in-afghanistan-now
19. Syed Hussain Shaheed Soherwordi, "Withdrawal of American Forces from Afghanistan (Endgame): Issues and Challenges for Pakistan." *Journal of Political Studies*, Vol. 19, Issue 1, 2012, 129:141, p. 1. http://pu.edu.pk/images/journal/pols/pdf-files/Endgame%20in%20Afghanistan%20for%20by%20Dr.%20Suharwardi_Vol_19_Issue_1_2012.pdf
20. "Konstantin Syroezhkin: Civil War in Afghanistan Is Inevitable," *Ferghana*, Russia, http://www.fergananews.com/article.php?id=7017
21. Martha Brill Olcott, "Is Threat of Jihad in Central Asia Potential?" *Polit.ru*, Russia, 23 September 2009, http://polit.ru/article/2009/09/23/dzhihad/
22. "Tajikistan on the Brink of Civil War," *Tvrainru*, Russia, 22 August 2012, http://tvrain.ru/articles/tadzhikistan_na_grani_grazhdanskoj_vojny-329554/
23. "Pakistan's Darra Adam Khel Is World's Largest Illegal Arms Market," *Indiatvnews*, 14 December 2013, http://www.indiatvnews.com/news/world/pakistan-s-darra-adam-khel-is-world-s-largest-illegal-arms-marke-14283.html?page=4
24. Sayfiddin Shapoatov, *The Tajik Civil War: 1992–1997* (Master's thesis). Middle East Technical University: METU, Turkey, June 2004, http://etd.lib.metu.edu.tr/upload/12605036/index.pdf
25. The World Factbook, 2014, https://www.cia.gov/library/publications/the-world-factbook/geos/af.html
26. "Lack of Justice Can Lead to Further Clashes in Kyrgyzstan, Amnesty International Warns," *Human Rights House Foundation*, 13 June 2011, humanrightshouse.org/Articles/16570.html
27. "Taliban Militants Kill 3 Border Guards of Turkmenistan," *Khaama Press*, Afghanistan, 2 March 2014, http://www.khaama.com/afghan-taliban-rejects-killing-turkmenistan-border-guards-2848
28. "Central Asia and the Transition in Afghanistan," A Majority Staff Report prepared for the use of the Committee on Foreign Relations, United States Senate, 2011, US Government Printing Office, Washington, p. 4.http://www.fdsys.gpo.gov
29. Alexander Cooley, *Great Games, Local Rules: The New Great Power Contest in Central Asia*, Oxford University Press, 23 July 2012, p. 158.
30. World Drug Report 2013, UNODC (United Nations Office on Drugs and Crime), p. 30, http://www.unodc.org/unodc/secured/wdr/wdr2013/World_Drug_Report_2013.pdf
31. "Opium Production in Afghanistan Hits Record High," *Time*, 13 November 2013, http://world.time.com/2013/11/13/opium-production-in-afghanistan-hits-record-high/
32. Bobi Perseyedi, "Small Arms Problem in Central Asia Features and Implications," United Nations Institute for Disarmament Research, 4 August 2000, http://unidir.org/files/publications/pdfs/the-small-arms-problem-in-central-asia-features-and-implications-117.pdf
33. Inomjon Bobokulov, "Central Asia as a Security Complex: Theory and Practice," *Central Asia and the Caucasus*, Vol. 13, Issue 3, 2012, p. 11.
34. Inomzhon Bobokulov, "The Afghan Transformation: Priorities and Key Problems," *Central Asia and the Caucasus*, Vol. 14, Issue 2, 2013, p. 37.

6. IRAN'S STRATEGIC DESIGNS FOR AFGHANISTAN

1. "The Long Goodbye in Afghanistan," *The New York Times*, 23 November 2013. http://www.nytimes.com/2013/11/24/opinion/sunday/the-long-goodbye-in-afghanistan.html?_r=0
2. "Afghan President Karzai Reiterates Preconditions for Inking BSA with U.S.," *Xinhua*, 25 January 2014. http://news.xinhuanet.com/english/world/2014-01/25/c_133073336.htm
3. Mohd. Ahsan, "U.S.-Iran Rivalry and Afghan Government's Silence," *Daily Outlook Afghanistan*, 14 September 2011. http://outlookafghanistan.net/topics.php?post_id=1852
4. Ibid.

5. "Afghanistan's Other Neighbors: Iran, Central Asia, and China," a conference report of The Hollings Center for International Dialogues and the American Institute of Afghan Studies, February 2009. http://www.hollingscenter.org/wp-content/uploads/2010/03/07-2008_Afghanistans_Other_Neighbors.pdf

6. Alireza Nader and Joya Laha, *Iran's Balancing Act in Afghanistan*, RAND National Defense Research Institute, 2011. http://www.rand.org/content/dam/rand/pubs/occasional_papers/2011/RAND_OP322.pdf

7. Ibid.

8. "Iran Seeks Its Share of Hirmand Water," *Press TV*, 15 April 2011. http://www.presstv.com/detail/174852.html

9. Sumitha Narayanan Kutty and C. Christine Fair, "Iran's Interests in Afghanistan Post 2014," 7 November 2013. http://papers.ssrn.com/sol3/papers.cfm?abstract_id=2351445&download=yes

10. Saman Sepehri, "The Iranian Revolution," *International Socialist Review*, Issue 9 August-September 2000. http://www.isreview.org/issues/09/iranian_revolution.shtml

11. Ali Omidi, "Iran's Narrative of Security in Afghanistan and the Feasibility of Iranian–U.S. Engagement," *SIPRI Afghanistan Regional Dialogue*, September 2013. http://www.sipri.org/research/security/afghanistan/afghanistan-regional-dialogue-1/publications-1/adr02.pdf

12. Ibid.

13. Ibid.

14. Mohsen M. Milani, "Iran's Policy towards Afghanistan," *Middle East Journal*, Vol. 60, Issue 2 (2006), p. 237. http://scholarcommons.usf.edu/cgi/viewcontent.cgi?article=1106&context=gia_facpub

15. Amie Ferris-Rotman, "Insight: Iran's 'Great Game' in Afghanistan," *Reuters*, 24 May 2012. http://www.reuters.com/article/2012/05/24/us-afghanistan-iran-media-idUSBRE84N0CB20120524

16. Kutty and Fair, "Iran's Interests in Afghanistan Post 2014."

17. Nader and Laha, *Iran's Balancing Act in Afghanistan*.

18. Zachary Laub, "The Taliban in Afghanistan," Council on Foreign Relations, 25 February 2014. http://www.cfr.org/afghanistan/taliban-afghanistan/p10551

19. Andrew Hill, "Taleban Leader Warns Iran of 'Serious Steps,'" *Reuters/Afghanistan News Center*, 5 October 1998. http://www.afghanistannewscenter.com/news/1998/october/oct5n1998.htm

20. Ibid.

21. James Dobbins, "Engaging Iran," *Iran Primer*, The United States Institute of Peace. http://iranprimer.usip.org/resources

22. "Afghanistan's Other Neighbors."

23. Ferris-Rotman, "Insight."

24. "Iran's Unavoidable Influence over Afghanistan's Future," *Carnegie Endowment for International Peace*, 15 August 2013. http://carnegieendowment.org/2013/08/15/iran-s-unavoidable-influence-over-afghanistan-s-future/gii0

25. "Afghanistan's Other Neighbors."

26. F. Milad, "Official: Tehran-Kabul Trade to Hit $3 Billion," *The Daily Trend*, 8 September 2012. http://en.trend.az/regions/iran/2063182.html

27. Ellen Laipson, "Iran & South Asia #3: After U.S. Withdrawal from Afghanistan," *United Institute for Peace*, 16 December 2013. http://iranprimer.usip.org/blog/all/Ellen%20Laipson

28. Daniel Wagnerand and Giorgio Cafiero, "The Paradoxical Afghan/Iran Alliance," *The Huffington Post*, 15 November 2013. http://www.huffingtonpost.com/daniel-wagner/the-paradoxical-afghanira_b_4277936.html

29. Seyed Hossein Mousavian, "Engage with Iran in Afghanistan," *The National Interest*, 30 May 2013. http://nationalinterest.org/commentary/engage-iran-afghanistan-8528

30. Njdeh Asisian, "Russia & Iran: Strategic Alliance or Marriage of Convenience," *Small Wars Journal*, 23 November 2013. http://smallwarsjournal.com/jrnl/art/russia-iran-strategic-alliance-or-marriage-of-convenience

31. Kutty and Fair, "Iran's Interests in Afghanistan Post 2014."

32. "Afghanistan Not to Halt Iran Trade Due to US Sanctions," *Press TV*, 4 September 2012. http://www.presstv.com/detail/2012/09/04/259813/afghanistan-will-not-halt-iran-trade/
33. Nader and Laha, "Iran's Balancing Act in Afghanistan."
34. "Taliban Confirms FNA Report on Recent Visit to Tehran," *FARS News Agency*, 3 June 2013. http://english2.farsnews.com/newstext.php?nn=9202247052
35. "Taliban Confirm Team's Visit to Tehran," *Pajhwok Afghan News*, 3 June 2013. http://www.pajhwok.com/en/2013/06/03/taliban-confirm-team%E2%80%99s-visit-tehran
36. Mina Habib, "Iran Flexes Muscle with Taliban Meeting," *Asia Times*, 13 June 2013. http://www.atimes.com/atimes/South_Asia/SOU-02-130613.html
37. "The Official Visit of Taliban to Iran in the Eyes of the Analysts," *Islamic Emirate of Afghanistan*, 10 June 2013. http://shahamat-english.com/index.php/articles/32565-the-official-visit-of-taliban-to-iran-in-the-eyes-of-the-analysts
38. "Afghanistan's Other Neighbors."
39. Shakeela Abrahimkhil, "Karzai Confirms Receiving Cash from the US," *Tolo News*, 30 April 2013. http://www.tolonews.com/en/afghanistan/10330-karzai-confirms-receiving-cash-from-the-us-
40. Manoj Kumar Mishra, "Iran's Changed Perception Concerning its Role in Afghanistan Following Soviet Disintegration," *Afro Eurasian Studies*, Vol. 1, Issue 2, Fall 2012, pp. 76–96.
41. Sunil Dasgupta, "India Readjusts Ties with Iran," *Asia Times*, 1 December 2013. http://www.atimes.com/atimes/South_Asia/SOU-01-121213.html
42. Dr. Rupakjyoti Borah, "Afghan Great Game: Huge Stakes for Russia, India," *Russia & India Report*, 16 May 2011. http://indrus.in/articles/2011/05/16/afghan_great_game_huge_stakes_for_russia_india_12517.html
43. Ibid.
44. Ibid.
45. Dasgupta, "India Readjusts Ties with Iran."
46. Borah, "Afghan Great Game."
47. Scott Warren Harold and Alireza Nader, *China and Iran: Economic, Political, and Military Relations*, RAND Cooperation, 2012. http://www.rand.org/pubs/occasional_papers/OP351.html
48. Akio Kawato, "The China Factor in Afghanistan-2014," *Eurasia Outlook*, 25 October 2013. http://carnegie.ru/eurasiaoutlook/?fa=53424
49. "China to Help Afghanistan Fight 'Terrorism,'" *Aljazeera News*, 8 March 2014. http://www.aljazeera.com/news/asia-pacific/2014/03/china-help-afghanistan-fight-terrorism-20143883457182295.html
50. Jugal R. Purohit, "Afghanistan Post-NATO: India Remains Hopeful, Russia Unconvinced," *India Today*, 25 February 2014. http://indiatoday.intoday.in/story/afghanistan-nato-troops-pullout-russia-taliban-northern-alliance-us/1/345424.html
51. Rajeev Agarwal, "Could Iran and India be Afghanistan's 'Plan B'?" *The Diplomat*, 14 February 2014. http://thediplomat.com/2014/02/could-iran-and-india-be-afghanistans-plan-b/
52. Harsh V. Pant, "India's Changing Role: The Afghanistan Conflict," *Middle East Quarterly*, Spring 2011, pp. 31–39. http://www.meforum.org/2895/india-afghanistan
53. Purohit, "Afghanistan post-NATO."
54. Jaideep A. Prabhu, "Defending Interests in Afghanistan: India Can Play Key Role in Bringing Together an Anti-Taliban Alliance," *The Economic Times*, 11 August 2013. http://articles.economictimes.indiatimes.com/2013-08-11/news/41268674_1_afghanistan-afghan-troops-kabul
55. Njdeh Asisian, "Russia & Iran: Strategic Alliance or Marriage of Convenience," *Small Wars Journal*, 23 November 2013. http://smallwarsjournal.com/jrnl/art/russia-iran-strategic-alliance-or-marriage-of-convenience
56. Barnett R. Rubin and Sara Batmanglich, "The US and Iran in Afghanistan: Policy Gone Awry," *MIT Center for International Studies* 3 (2008), p. 3.
57. Scott Peterson, "Iran President Ahmadinejad Attacks US during Afghanistan Visit," *Christian Science Monitor*, 10 March 2010. http://www.csmonitor.com/World/Middle-East/2010/0310/Iran-President-Ahmadinejad-attacks-US-during-Afghanistan-visit

58. Ahmad Reza Taheri, "Baloch Insurgency and Challenges to the Islamic Republic of Iran," *Society for the Study of Peace and Conflict*, April 2012. http://www.academia.edu/7638705/Baloch_Insurgency_and_Challenges_to_the_Islamic_Republic_of_Iran_SSPC_ISSUE_BRIEF

59. Nader and Laha, "Iran's Balancing Act in Afghanistan."

60. "Iran, Afghanistan Sign Strategic Agreement," *Press TV*, 5 August 2013. http://www.presstv.com/detail/2013/08/05/317291/iran-afghanistan-sign-strategic-pact/

61. Thomas Ruttig, "Can Kabul Carry Two Melons in One Hand? Afghanistan and Iran Sign Strategic Cooperation Document," *Afghanistan Analysts Network*, 6 August 2013. http://www.afghanistan-analysts.org/can-kabul-carry-two-melons-in-one-hand-afghanistan-and-iran-sign-strategic-cooperation-document

62. Omidi, "Iran's Narrative of Security in Afghanistan and the Feasibility of Iranian–US Engagement."

63. "Iran Calls for Afghan Nation's Vigilance against Enemies' Divisive Plots," *FARS News Agency*, 18 January 2014. http://english.farsnews.com/newstext.aspx?nn=13921028001096

7. WHY AFGHANISTAN MATTERS

1. Interview, Arnaud de Borchgrave, 2008. Borchgrave interviewed the Taliban leader, Mullah Mohammad Omar Akhund, 13 June 2001. http://www.upi.com/Business_News/Security-Industry/2001/12/10/Mullah-Omar-bin-Laden-Null-and-void/UPI-70171008031323/#ixzz30d7qJWnN

2. Linda J. Bilmes, "The Financial Legacy of Iraq and Afghanistan: How Wartime Spending Decisions Will Constrain Future National Security Budgets," HKS Faculty Research Working Paper Series RWP13-006, March 2013.

3. "Afghan Taliban Denies Killing Turkmenistan Border Guards, Comments on Taverna du Liban Restaurant Attack," *SITE Monitoring Service*, 1 March 2014. http://ent.siteintelgroup.com/Jihadist-News/afghan-taliban-denies-killing-turkmenistan-border-guards-comments-on-taverna-du-liban-restaurant-attack.html

4. http://shahamat-english.com/, accessed on 1 March 2014.

5. Humeyra Pamuk and Hamid Shalizi, "Karzai Rejects U.S. Warnings Over Freed Afghan Detainees," Reuters, 13 February 2014.

6. "Abdullah Abdullah: Talks With Taliban Futile." National Public Radio (NPR). 2010-10-22.

7. "The Solid Base" (al Qaeda), *Al-Jihad* (journal), April 1988, n. 41.

8. "Jihadists React to Reported Death of TTP Leader in U.S. Drone Strike," *SITE*, 1 November 2013.

9. Ibid.

10. Ibid.

11. Sheikh Jalaluddin Haqqani, "The Defeat of America in Afghanistan Will Be Swifter than the Defeat of the Collapsed Soviet Union," *Interviews and Reports*, Islamic Emirate of Afghanistan, 4 May 2011.

12. "The Message of Mawlawi Jalaluddin Haqqani—A Member of the Islamic Emirate's Leadership Council and a Scholar and Mujahid of Afghanistan—To the Valiant Afghan Nation on the Occassion of Doctor Naseeruddin Haqqani's Martyrdom," Press Release, *Islamic Emirate of Afghanistan*, 14 November 2013.

13. Ibid.

14. National Consortium for the Study of Terrorism and Responses to Terrorism (START) counted 9,707 terrorist attacks around the world in 2013, resulting in more than 17,800 deaths and more than 32,500 injuries. Most of those occurred in Afghanistan, India, Iraq, Nigeria, Pakistan, the Philippines, Somalia, Syria, Thailand, and Yemen. In 2012, the figures were 6,771 terrorist attacks, with more than 11,000 deaths and more than 21,600 injuries. Most of those were in the same ten countries as in 2013. http://www.dailystar.com.lb/News/

International/2014/May-01/255030-us-warns-of-new-generation-of-global-terrorists. ashx#ixzz30dbZsvDh

15. "Australian Cleric in al-Nusra Front Gives Comprehensive Interview on Issues with ISIL, Infighting in Syria," *SITE*, 12 April 2014.

16. Jihadi forum al-'Areen on 25 April 2014.

17. "Shabaab Promotes Westgate Raid, Threatens More Attacks in Kenya," *SITE*, 17 April 2014.

18. The MILF under Hashim Salamat established a working partnership with al Qaeda, but the MILF under Haji Murad broke ties with al Qaeda and decided to work with the Philippines government to establish peace between the Moros and other communities.

19. Interview, Aviv Oreg, former head of al Qaeda desk, Israeli IDF Military Intelligence, 5 May 2014.

20. Jason Burke, "Al-Qaida Leader Zawahiri Urges Muslim Support for Syrian Uprising," *The Guardian*, 12 February 2012.

21. Ibid.

22. "Zawahiri Advises Kidnapping Westerners for Prisoner Exchanges," *SITE*, 25 April 2014.

23. Ibid.

24. "Jihadist Leader in Indonesia Calls to Kill Special Forces, Claims They are American and Australian Agents," *SITE*, 22 April 2014.

25. "The Americans Can No Longer Conceal Their Defeat in the Kandahar Operations," *Weekly Analysis, Islamic Emirate of Afghanistan*, 19 November 2010.

26. "True Position of the Islamic Emirate Regarding the Negotiations," *Weekly Analysis, Islamic Emirate of Afghanistan*, 23 March 2012.

27. Ibid.

28. Ibid.

29. "Jihadists React to Reported Death of TTP Leader in U.S. Drone Strike," *SITE*, 1 November 2013.

30. Qari Yousuf Ahmadi, "When the Head of an Imperial Power Lies!" *Weekly Analysis, Islamic Emirate of Afghanistan*, 29 January 2014.

31. "America is Concealing Her Defeat in Afghanistan," Press Release, *Islamic Emirate of Afghanistan*, 31 January 2014.

32. Shahidullah Shahid, Central spokesman for Tehrik-e-Taliban Pakistan, 2 February 2013.

33. Syed Adnan, Ali Shah, and Khuram Iqbal, " Marriott Hotel Suicide Bombing in Islamabad ," *ICPVTR Spot Report* , 20 September 2008 . http://www.pvtr.org/pdf/RegionalAnalysis/SouthAsia/Marriott%20Hotel%20Suicide%20Bombing%20in%20Islamabad.pdf

34. "Demographics of Suicide Terrorism," *Dawn*, Pakistan, 5 August 2010. http://www.dawn.com/news/844531/demographics-of-suicide-terrorism

35. "Ansar al-Tawhid in Hind Releases Video of Attack, Incites Lone-Wolves," *SITE*, 28 April 2014.

36. Ibid.

37. Ibid.

38. "The Kunming Attack, 12 Minute, 56 Second, Uyghur-Language Video," *TIP's Islam Awazi Media Center*, 11 March 2014, translated by SITE.

39. Ibid.

40. Michael Martina, "China's Xi Says Xinjiang is Front Line on Terrorism, Hails Police," *Reuters*, 29 April 2014.

41. Abū Dhar 'Azzām, "We Are Coming, Oh Buddhists," *SITE*, 24 February 2014.

42. Ibid.

43. Ibid.

44. "The Kunming Attack."

45. David Cook. (2002). *Studies in Muslim Apocalyptic*. Princeton, NJ: Darwin Press. p. 153.

8. THREAT GROUP PROFILES

1. Steve Coll, *Ghost Wars: The Secret History of the CIA, Afghanistan and bin Laden*, Penguin Publishing, 2005.
2. Ibid.
3. William Maley, "The Foreign Policy of the Taliban," Council for Foreign Relations; see also Position Paper regarding IEA's Recognition at the United Nations presented by Abdul Hakim Mujahid, Permanent Representative/Designate of the Islamic Emirate of Afghanistan to the UN.
4. Ibid.
5. Ahmed Rashid, *Taliban: The Power of Militant Islam in Afghanistan and Beyond*, IB Tauris & Co. Ltd., 2010.
6. Shahamat (Taliban Website) Online, 2006.
7. Antony Cordesmen, "Afghanistan: A Progress Report," CSIS, 2010.
8. Al-Jazeerah interview with Mullah Dadullah on military strategy (ca 02:40), 31 May 2005.
9. "Taliban Fighters Estimated at 36,000," UPI, March 2010.
10. Declan Walsh, "Afghan Militants Attack Kandahar Prison and Free Inmates," *The Guardian*, 13 June 2008.
11. "The Taliban's Information Warfare," Institute for Military Operations Faculty of Strategy and Military Operations, Royal Danish Defence College, December 2007.
12. Ibid.
13. Ibid.
14. Ibid.
15. "Iraq-Style Bomb Found in Afghanistan," AP, February 2007.
16. Alexi Malashenko, "Afghanistan: Ways Out of the Crisis," 10 May 2011.
17. Ahmed Rashid, *Taliban: The Power of Militant Islam in Afghanistan and Beyond*, IB Tauris & Co. Ltd., 2010.
18. US Embassy (Islamabad), cable, Meeting with the Taliban in Kandahar: more questions than answers, 15 February 1995.
19. Ahmed Rashid, *Taliban: The Power of Militant Islam in Afghanistan and Beyond*, IB Tauris & Co. Ltd., 2010.
20. Ibid.
21. Ibid.
22. George Gavrilis, "The Good and Bad News about Afghan Opium," Council on Foreign Relations, 10 February 2010.
23. Ibid.
24. Abdullah bin Muhammad Al-Ghunayman, "Fatwa Concerning the Taliban," July 2004.
25. Antony Cordesmen, "Afghanistan: A Progress Report," CSIS, 2010.
26. Bill Roggio, "US adds Haqqani Network, Taliban Leaders to List of Designated Terrorists," *Long War Journal*, 22 July 2010.
27. Lolita C. Baldor, "US Targets Afghan Taliban Leaders with Sanctions," ABC News, 22 July 2010.
28. The transfer of money via this system is very simple. For instance, one person gives a certain amount of money to a money exchanger in country (A). In return he gets a special code, which is then given to another person in country (B). Upon showing the code of country (A) to a specific money exchanger of country (B), an individual can easily receive money without paying a high fee to a formal money transfer company.
29. "Afghanistan: Veteran Mujahideen Defies West," Adnkronos International, 2008.
30. Haqqani Network to Support Afghanistan Peace Process," *Tolo News*, 17 September 2011.
31. Antony Cordesmen, "Afghanistan: A Progress Report," CSIS, 2010.
32. D. Byman, *Deadly Connections—States that Sponsor Terrorism*, Cambridge University Press, 2005, pp. 187–218.

33. Bill Roggio, "How Many al Qaeda are in Afghanistan Again?" *Long War Journal*, 4 September 2011.
34. Ibid.
35. Sonil Haidari, "Taliban Have Captured Waigal District of Nuristan Province in Eastern Afghanistan on Monday Midnight, Provincial Officials Said," *Tolo News*, 29 March 2011.
36. "Taliban Set Afire Dist Offices of Muqur," *Afghanistan Islamic Press*, 26 August 2011.
37. Jane Jamison, "The Taliban's Response to Obama Afghanistan Policy," *American Thinker*, 5 December 2009.
38. Ibid.
39. CAPS Suicide Attack Database 2001 to 2011.
40. Ibid.
41. Ibid.
42. "77 US Troops Wounded in Attack on Afghan Base," NBC, 9 September 2011.
43. Jason Burke, "Seven Bombers Killed as Taliban Switch Tactics with Attack in East," *The Guardian*, 26 July 2008.
44. "Karzai Orders Release of 20 Would-be Youth Suicide Bombers," CNN World News, 25 August 2011.
45. "Karzai Pardons 5 Would-be Suicide Bombers," ToloNews.com, 24 August 2011.
46. Abdul Haleem and Zhang Jianhu, "Using Children as Suicide Bombers to Expose Other Face of Afghan Teens' Plight," *Xinhua*, 27 August 2011.
47. "Martyr Attack Hits Department of Spy Agency; 5 Spies Killed, Several More Hurt," alemara1.com, 29 October 2011.
48. "Twin Suicide Attacks Hit Afghanistan," Al Jazeera, 29 October 2011.
49. Bill Roggio, "Afghan, US Forces Hunt al Qaeda, Taliban in Northeast," *Long War Journal*, 2 August 2011.
50. Bill Roggio, "Taliban: 'Mujahida Sister' Executed Kunar Suicide Attack," *Long War Journal*, 4 June 2011.
51. "Kandahar Mayor Killed in Suicide Attack," *Pajhwok*, 27 July 2011.
52. "The Fallout From the AWK Murder," *The Daily Beast*, 14 July 2011.
53. CAPS Suicide Attack Database, 2011.
54. "Afghan Overture: Behind Karzai's Appeal to Mullah Omar," *Time*, 17 November 2011.
55. "Taliban Reject Peace Council as a Ploy," *Pajhwok*, 29 September 2010.
56. Taliban statements on 28 January 2010 and 6 July 2011 to reject any negotiations and condemned the Afghan government peace process.
57. "Taliban Doubt Safety of Peace Talks with Afghan Govt.," *Tolo News*, 4 June 2011.
58. "Afghanistan Welcomes Taliban Office in Turkey," *Tolo News*, 3 March 2011.
59. "Mullah Omer Willing to Hold Peace Talks: Peace Council," *Tolo News*, 5 August 2011.
60. "World Leaders Condemn Rabbani Assassination," ABC News, 21 September 2011.
61. "Quetta Shura Linked to Rabbani Death: NDS," *Pajhwok*, 22 September 2011.
62. Taliban statements on response of Islamic Emirate of Afghanistan about the secret talks between Kabul stooge administration and America regarding permanent bases, 9 Febrauny 2011.
63. "Attacker Killed Near Venue As Opponents Try to Sidetrack Afghan Jirga," RFERL, 20 November 2011.
64. This information is taken from *Tolo News*, *Pajhwok News*, the *Long War Journal*, the ISAF website, and *Dawn News*.
65. This information is compiled from the *Long War Journal*, *Pahjwok News*, and *Tolo News*.
66. Gunaratna, Rohan, "Al Qaeda in the Tribal Areas of Pakistan and Beyond," *Studies in Conflict and Terrorism*, Volume 31, Issue 9, 2008. Material in this section was pulled for use by the analysts from the center to provide an updated perspective on the threat dynamics in the Tribal Areas and al Qaeda. Analysts at the center also used http://therationale.org/june_ver/after_osma.html, http://www.gctat.org/fr/component/content/article/1-latest-news/179-badar-mansoor-or-the-confusion-of-words-2.html, and http://weeklypulse.org/details.aspx?contentID=1525&storylist=10.

67. Elisabeth Bumiller, "In Bin Laden's Compound, Seals' All-Star Team," *New York Times*, 4 May 2011. http://www.nytimes.com/2011/05/05/world/middleeast/05seals.html?pagewanted=all&_r=0#
68. Bergen, Peter, 2006, p.16, *The Osama bin Laden I Know*, New York, Free Press.
69. Ibid., p. 26.
70. *Sawt al-Jihad*, Issue 30, 8 February 2007.
71. Bergen, Peter, 2006, p.67, *The Osama bin Laden I Know*.
72. Ibid., p. 80.
73. Ibid., p. 81.
74. Ibid., p. 67.
75. Kobs, David Marts, 2005, p. 54, *Terrorist Support of the State: The al Qaeda Network and Failed States* and *Jane's Security and Terrorism Monitor*, February 2007, "al Qaeda's East Africa Cell."
76. Bergen, Peter, 2006, p. 167, *The Osama bin Laden I Know*.
77. Ibid, p. 166.
78. Ibid, p. 165.
79. Ibid, pp. 193–194.
80. Ibid, pp. 195–196.
81. Ibid, p. 196.
82. Ibid, p. 202.
83. "Inside al Qaeda's Hard Drive," *The Atlantic Monthly Online*, September 2004.
84. Bergen, Peter, 2006, p. 285, *The Osama bin Laden I Know*.
85. "Profile on Khalid Sheikh Muhammad," Office of the Director of National Intelligence, September 2006.
86. Bergen, Peter, 2006, pp. 261–262, *The Osama bin Laden I Know*.
87. "Profile on Adb al-Rahim al-Nashiri," Office of the Director of National Intelligence, September 2006.
88. "Inside al Qaeda's Hard Drive," *The Atlantic Monthly Online*, September 2004.
89. Ibid.
90. Gary Berntsen, 2005, pp. 283–284, *Jawbreaker*, New York, Three Rivers Press.
91. Ron Suskind, 2006, p. 74, *The One Percent Doctrine*, New York, Simon & Schuster.
92. Ibid, p. 75.
93. "Hekmatyar Says His Men Helped Bin Laden and Zawahri Escape," *Daily Times*, 12 January 2007.
94. "Spy Chief Pushes for Action in Pakistan," AP, 27 February 2007.
95. "Abbottabad Commission Report," Pakistan, leaked by Al-Jazeera News Network on 13 July 2013, pp. 35–47, available at http://www.aljazeera.com/programmes/aljazeerainvestigates/2013/07/2013713122728648778.html.
96. "Al Jazeera Net Posts Extended Report of Bin Laden's Audiotape," 23 April 2006, Al-Jazeera Net WWW-Text in Arabic.
97. Bergen, Peter, 2006, p. 66, *The Osama bin Laden I Know*.
98. Ibid., p. 67.
99. Ibid., pp. 80–84.
100. "Islamists' Attorney Views Changes Taking Place in Egyptian Al-Jihad Movement," Al-Sharq al-Awsat, 16 August 2006.
101. "Egypt's Most Wanted," *Al-Ahram Weekly Online*, 18–24 October 2001.
102. "Islamic Groups Operate in Albania Under Cover of Charity," *Gazeta Shqiptare*, 20 November 2004.
103. "Muhammad al-Zawahiri and Hussain al-Zawahiri," Human Rights Watch.
104. "Inside al Qaeda's Hard Drive," *The Atlantic Monthly Online*, September 2004.
105. Ibid.
106. Ibid.
107. Ron Suskind, 2006, p. 251, *The One Percent Doctrine* and "US Frustrated in al Qaeda Anthrax Case," *Global Security Newswire*, 31 October 2006.
108. "Sufaat, Yazid," MIPT Terrorism, key leader profile.
109. Ibid.

110. Verbatim Transcript of Combatant Status Review Tribunal Hearing for ISN 10024.
111. "Inside al Qaeda's Hard Drive," *The Atlantic Monthly Online*, September 2004.
112. Verbatim Transcript of Combatant Status Review Tribunal Hearing for ISN 10024.
113. "The Drone, the CIA and a Botched Attempt to Kill Bin Laden's Deputy," *The Guardian Unlimited*, 15 January 2006.
114. "Bajaur Seminary Was Producing Suicide Bombers; National Security Sources Produce Evidence to Media," *Jang*, 2 November 2006.
115. "Pakistan: Villagers Start Rebuilding Seminary Destroyed in Bajaur Airstrike," *The News* (Internet Version-WWW), 18 November 2006.
116. Bergen, Peter, 2006, pp. 75–85, *The Osama bin Laden I Know*.
117. "Profiles on Abu Faraj al-Libi and Khalid Sheikh Muhammad," Office of the Director of National Intelligence, September 2006.
118. Verbatim Transcript of Combatant Status Review Tribunal Hearing for ISN 10024.
119. Ibid.
120. "Profile on Khalid Sheikh Muhammad," Office of the Director of National Intelligence, September 2006.
121. Verbatim Transcript of Combatant Status Review Tribunal Hearing for ISN 10024.
122. "Profile on Abu Faraj al-Libi," Office of the Director of National Intelligence, September 2006.
123. "Profile on Abu Faraj al-Libi," Office of the Director of National Intelligence, September 2006.
124. Verbatim Transcript of Open Session Combatant Status Review Tribunal Hearing ISN 10017.
125. Musharraf, Pervez, 2006, pp. 254–262, *In the Line of Fire*, New York, Simon & Schuster.
126. "Profile on Abu Faraj al-Libi," Office of the Director of National Intelligence, September 2006.
127. Verbatim Transcript of Open Session Combatant Status Review Tribunal Hearing ISN 10017.
128. Ibid.
129. Ibid.
130. "Footage Showing al Qaeda Leader in Afghanistan Abd al-Hadi al-Iraqi Downing an American Fighter Jet," Middle East Media Research Institute, 29 May 2005.
131. Interrogation Report from Interrogations of Nurredin Nafei, Moroccan Justice Department, 2003.
132. "Accounts after 2005 London Bombing Point to al Qaeda Role from Pakistan," *New York Times*, 13 August 2006.
133. "British Terror Trial Traces a Path to Militant Islam," *New York Times*, 25 November 2006.
134. "Accounts after 2005 London Bombing Point to al Qaeda Role from Pakistan," *New York Times*, 13 August 2006.
135. Ibid.
136. Ibid.
137. "Terror Broker," *Newsweek*, 11 April 2006.
138. Ibid.
139. Karzai, Hikmat, "Afghanistan and Globalisation of Terrorist Tactics," Institute for Defence and Strategic Studies, Nanyang Technological University, 4 January 2006.
140. "Accounts after 2005 London Bombing Point to al Qaeda Role from Pakistan," *New York Times*, 13 August 2006.
141. "7/7 'Mastermind' is Seized in Iraq," *The Times*, UK, 28 April 2007.
142. Ibid.
143. "Al Qaeda's Khaled bin Abdul Rahman 'Killed by Drone,'" *BBC News*, 10 December 2012. http://www.bbc.com/news/world-asia-20667672
144. "Dead or Alive: Who is al Qaeda's Abu Yahya al-Libi?," *Al-Arabiya News*, 12 June 2012. http://english.alarabiya.net/articles/2012/06/05/218803.html.

145. "Al Qaeda's Khaled bin Abdul Rahman 'Killed by Drone,'" *BBC News*, 10 December 2012. http://www.bbc.com/news/world-asia-20667672.
146. Bill Roggio, "Al Qaeda Announces Death of Atiyah Abd al Rahman," *Long War Journal*, 1 December 2011. http://www.longwarjournal.org/archives/2011/12/al_qaeda_announces_d.php
147. "Atiyah Abd al-Rahman, Liaison to Iraq and Algeria Nationality: Libyan," *Washington Post*, 2011. http://www.washingtonpost.com/wp-srv/world/specials/terror/rahman.html
148. "Atiyah Abd Al-Rahman Dead: Al Qaeda Second in Command Killed in Pakistan," *The Huffington Post*, 28 August 2011. http://www.huffingtonpost.com/2011/08/27/atiyah-abd-al-rahman-al Qaeda-dead_n_939009.html
149. Ibid.
150. Mark Mazetti, "C.I.A. Drone Is Said to Kill al Qaeda's No. 2," *New York Times,* 27 August 2011. http://www.nytimes.com/2011/08/28/world/asia/28qaeda.html?_r=0
151. Ibid.
152. Ibid.
153. Huma Yusuf, "Drone Strike Reportedly Killed al Qaeda No. 3 Mustafa Abu al-Yazid," *Christian Science Monitor*, 1 June 2010. http://www.csmonitor.com/World/terrorism-security/2010/0601/Drone-strike-reportedly-killed-al Qaeda-No.-3-Mustafa-Abu-al-Yazid
154. Craig Whitlock and Munir Ladaa, "Mustafa Abu al-Yazid, Liaison to Taliban Nationality: Egyptian," *Washington Post*. http://www.washingtonpost.com/wp-srv/world/specials/terror/yazid.html
155. Ibid.
156. Syed Saleem Shahzad, "Al Qaeda's Guerrilla Chief Lays Out Strategy," *Asia Times Online*, www.atimes.com/atimes/South_Asia/KJ15Df03.html, last visited 26 November 2009.
157. "Drone Strike Kills Ilyas Kashmiri," *Dawn*, Pakistan, 5 June 2011. http://www.dawn.com/news/634299/ilyas-kashmiri-killed-in-us-drone-strike
158. Ibid.
159. Hamid Mir, "Who was Ilyas Kashmiri?," *The News*, 20 September 2009.
160. Ibid.
161. Ibid.
162. Ibid.
163. Hamid Mir, "How an Ex-Army Commando Became a Terrorist," *The News*, 20 September 2009.
164. Colonel (R) Imam an Ex-SSG officer rejected the claim made by Hamid Mir and termed it "total disinformation." Similarly, Syed Salim Shehzad, a journalist associated with *Asia Times Online* wrote, "Ilyas was never a part of Pakistan's special forces, nor even of the army." See Syed Saleem Shahzad, "Al Qaeda's Guerrilla Chief Lays Out Strategy," *Asia Times Online*, www.atimes.com/atimes/South_Asia/KJ15Df03.html, last visited 26 November 2009.
165. Mudassir Raja, "Lashkar-e-Taiba Killed Gen Alvi, Court Told," *Dawn*, 13 May 2009.
166. Amir Mir, "Ilyas Kashmiri Had Planned to Attack COAS," *The News*, 18 September 2009.
167. Ibid.
168. "Pakistan: Taliban Commander, Three Others Killed in Drone Attack," *The News*, 10 February 2012. http://www.thenews.com.pk/TodaysPrintDetail.aspx?ID=12350&Cat=13
169. "Badr Mansoor, al Qaeda Commander in Pakistan, Reported Killed," *Central Asia Online*, 9 February 2012. http://www.centralasiaonline.com/en_GB/articles/caii/features/pakistan/main/2012/02/09/feature-02
170. "Death of Badar Mansoor 'al Qaeda' Commander in Pakistan US Missile Strike," *Al-Seyassah*, 10 February 2012. http://www.al-seyassah.com/AtricleView/tabid/59/smid/438/ArticleID/177191/reftab/36/Default.aspx
171. Deadly Drone Strike Signals Renewed US-Pakistan Cooperation," *Boston Herald*, 9 February 2012. http://www.bostonherald.com/news/international/asia_pacific/view/201202 09us_drone_strike_kills_key_al Qaeda_operative/srvc=home&position=recent
172. Badar Mansoor's Al-Badar is in no way associated or part of Al-Badr mujahideen group active in Indian-administered Jammu and Kashmir. The latter is led by Bakht Zameen and is believed to be a splinter group of Hizbul Mujahideen (HuM) led by Syed Salahuddin.

173. "US Kills al Qaeda-Linked Militant in Pakistan," *U-T San Diego*, 9 February 2012. http://www.utsandiego.com/news/2012/feb/09/us-kills-al Qaeda-linked-militant-in-pakistan/?print&page=all

174. The Greater or Ancient Khorasan was a province of Persia during the Sassanid Dynasty (AD 224 to AD 651). It comprised parts of present-day Iran (Nishapur and Tus), Afghanistan (Balkh, Heart, and Ghazni), Turkmenistan (Merv), Uzbekistan (Samarqand and Bukhara), and Tajikistan. However, a strong belief based on findings of some Arabic geographers exists within the Taliban, al Qaeda, and Pakistani militants that all of Afghanistan, as well as the present-day FATA and Khyber-Pakhtunkhwa province, was part of the Ancient Khorasan, and they therefore consider themselves to be the Islamic army of Al-Mahdi.

175. "Badr Mansoor, al Qaeda Commander in Pakistan, Reported Killed," *Central Asia Online*, 9 February 2012.

176. "Pakistan al Qaeda Chief Killed by US Drone," *Times Live*, 9 February 2012. http://www.timeslive.co.za/world/article3919625.ece

177. "Drone Strike Data Analysis," http://dronedata.wordpress.com/

178. "Covert Drone War Data," The Bureau of Investigative Journalism. http://www.thebureauinvestigates.com/2011/08/10/the-bush-years-2004-2009/

179. "3 Top Taliban Militants among Nine Killed in Drone Attack," *Zee News*, 25 February 2012. http://zeenews.india.com/news/south-asia/3-top-taliban-militants-among-nine-killed-in-drone-attack_607089.html

180. "US Drone Attacks Kill 17 Militants in Pakistan," *New York Times*, 2 October 2010. http://www.nytimes.com/2010/10/03/world/asia/03pstan.html

181. "Pakistan: Taliban Commander, Three Others Killed in Drone Attack," *The News*, 10 February 2012. http://www.thenews.com.pk/TodaysPrintDetail.aspx?ID=12350&Cat=13

182. Telephonic interview with an intelligence official, 12 February 2012.

183. Ibid.

184. Qadianis/Ahmedia consider themselves Muslim, but have been disowned by mainstream Islam because the sect differs on several core beliefs, notably the status of Holy Prophet Muhammad (SAW) as the final messenger of God.

185. "Lahore Attacker Reveals Key Information," *The News,* Pakistan, 4 June 2010. http://www.thenews.com.pk/TodaysPrintDetail.aspx?ID=29263&Cat=13&dt=6/4/2010

186. "Four TTP Suspects Remanded," *The News*, 14 May 2011. http://www.thenews.com.pk/TodaysPrintDetail.aspx?ID=46852&Cat=4&dt=5/14/2011

187. "From Promising Student to Feared Militant," *The News*, Pakistan 23 May 2011. http://old.thenews.com.pk/23-05-2011/ethenews/e-48493.htm

188. Ibid.

189. Ibid.

190. "Three LJ Activists Arrested," *The News*, 28 August 2011. http://www.thenews.com.pk/TodaysPrintDetail.aspx?ID=64993&Cat=4

191. Saeed Shah, "Al Qaeda 'Foreign Minister' Captured by Pakistani Forces," *The Guardian*, 5 September 2011. http://www.theguardian.com/world/2011/sep/05/al Qaeda-foreign-minister-captured-pakistan

192. "Top al Qaeda Leader Arrested in Pakistan," *CNN*, 5 September 2011. http://edition.cnn.com/2011/WORLD/asiapcf/09/05/pakistan.al.qaeda.arrest/

193. Bill Roggio, "Pakistani Forces Capture Senior al Qaeda Leader Younis al Mauritani in Quetta," *Long War Journal*, 5 September 2011. http://www.longwarjournal.org/archives/2011/09/pakistani_forces_cap.php#ixzz2ypJZYaRh

194. Bergen, Peter, 2006, p. 80, *The Osama bin Laden I Know.*

195. Ibid., pp. 83–84.

196. Interrogation Report from the Former Head of the Moroccan Islamic Fighting Group, Nuriddin Nafai, Moroccan Justice Department, August 2003, and Nabil al-Haq's posting to the Islamic Renewal Organization forum on 25 May 2005 in which "Detained Al-Qa'ida Leader Sayf al-Adl Chronicles Al-Zarqawi's Rise in Organization."

197. "Al-Zawahiri Calls on Muslims to Wage 'War of Jihad,' Reject UN Resolutions," Jihadist Websites—OSC Report, 12 September 2006.

198. ICPVTR Group Profile on GSPC/al Qaeda Organization of the Islamic Maghreb.

199. "Algeria Hit by Bombings, Six Dead," Reuters, 13 February 2007.
200. ICPVTR Analysis of 11 April 2007 attacks by Tanzim al Qaeda al-Jihad bi Bilad al-Maghreb al-Islami in Algiers, available in ICPVTR database.
201. Ibid.
202. ICPVTR profile on "Libyan Islamic Fighting Group."
203. "Letter Exposes New Leader in Al-Qa`ida High Command," and S. Rajaratnam School of International Studies, ICPVTR profile on "Libyan Islamic Fighting Group," Combating Terrorism Center, United States Military Academy, 25 September 2006.
204. "Al-Qa'ida's Al-Libi Discusses 'Jihad' in Iraq, Afghanistan, Other Issues," Jihadist Websites—OSC Summary, 29 April 2007.
205. Ibid.
206. Interrogation Report, Moroccan Justice Department, August 2003.
207. "Al Qaeda's No. 2 Welcomes Egyptian Group," AP, 6 August 2006.
208. Ibid.
209. "Son-in-Law of Zawahiri was Mastermind," *Dawn*, 19 August 2006.
210. "Toward a New Strategy in Resisting the Occupier." http://www.althabeton.co.nr/
211. "Al-Jazirah Airs New Al-Zawahiri Tape," 4 August 2005.
212. "Toward a New Strategy in Resisting the Occupier." http://www.althabeton.co.nr/
213. "Al Qaeda is Seen as Restoring Leadership," *New York Times*, 2 April 2007.
214. Steward Bell, "Canadian among Islamists: Toronto Man 'Key Player' with Group in Somalia," *National Post*, 19 October 2006.
215. Sunguta West, "Hardline Islamist Militia Group Shabbab Emerges in Somalia," Jamestown Foundation "Terrorism Focus," 8 August 2006, Vol. 3 (31).
216. "Somalia: The Tough Part is Ahead," AP, 9 January 2007, and "Helicopters Strafe al Qaeda in Somalia," International Crisis Group, 26 January 2007.
217. Abdirisak Suleman, "US Can't Afford to Ignore Young Militant, Somali leaders Say," *Somaliland Net*, 16 June 2006. http://www.somalilandnet.com/news/wnews/headline/13371863.shtml
218. "Somalia's Islamist," International Crisis Group, December 2005.
219. "Somalia: The Tough Part is Ahead," AP, 9 January 2007, and "Helicopters Strafe al Qaeda in Somalia," International Crisis Group, 26 January 2007.
220. Ibid.
221. Ibid.
222. Ibid.
223. Ibid.
224. "Ethiopians Parade Captured Islamist Cleric in Somalia," Reuters, 6 February 2007.
225. "Somalia on the Brink as Suicide Attack Hits Government Seat," AFP. 30 November 2006.
226. "Mujahidin Youth Movement Response to Alleged Reconciliation Conference," Jihadist Websites—OSC Summary, 14 June 2007.
227. http://www.defenselink.mil/news/newsarticle.aspx?id=15837
228. "Al-Qa'ida's Al-Libi Discusses 'Jihad' in Iraq, Afghanistan, Other Issues," Jihadist Websites—OSC Summary, 29 April 2007.
229. "Afghan 'General Official' Says Al-Qa'ida's Goal is 'Annihilation' of America," Jihadist Websites—OSC Summary, 30 May 2007.
230. "New Taliban Group Named after Tora Bora," *The News*, 26 February 2007.
231. "Pakistan's Tribal District of South Waziristan, on the Border with Afghanistan, Is in the Throes of Turmoil Once Again," BBC, 5 April 2007.
232. Ibid., "Tribal Militants Pledge to Evict Uzbeks from Wana," *The News* (Internet version), 29 March 2007, and "Letter Explains Drive Against Foreign Militants in Waziristan," *The News* (Internet version), 7 April 2007.
233. "Al Qaeda Affiliate behind Pakistan Rocket Plot: Report," Reuters, 4 November 2006.
234. "Pakistan: Urdu Press Roundup on Fighting in Waziristan," Pakistan—OSC Summary, 26 March 2007.
235. "Suicide Bombers Hit Uzbek Capital, Leaving at Least Five Dead," Eurasianet.org, 30 July 2004.

236. Suskind, Ron, 2006, p. 235, *The One Percent Doctrine*.
237. Ibid.
238. "Staff Statement No. 15," National Commission on Terrorist Attacks upon the United States, 16 June 2004.
239. "Al Qaeda Organizational Structure," GlobalSecurity.org. http://www.globalsecurity.org/military/world/para/al Qaeda-structure.htm
240. "Al Qaeda—Profile," Jane's World Insurgency. www.janes.com, accessed on 28 December 2003.
241. "Staff Statement No. 15," National Commission on Terrorist Attacks upon the United States, 16 June 2004.
242. "Heathrow Terror Suspect Set to Be Extradited," *The Times*, 13 December 2006; "'Panic' as Plotters' Bomb Attempts Failed," *Daily Mail*, 16 January 2007; "The Hydrogen Peroxide Bombs that Link 21/7 Terror Plot to 7/7 Suicide Bombers," *Daily Telegraph*, 25 March 2007.
243. Ibid.
244. Ben Venzke and Aimee Ibrahim, *The al Qaeda Threat: An Analytical Guide to al Qaeda Tactics and Targets*, Tempest Publishing, 2003.
245. Richard H. Shultz, Jr., and Ruth Margolies Beitler, "Tactical Deception and Strategic Surprise in Al-Qai'da's Operations," *Middle East Review of International Affairs*, Vol. 8, No. 2 (June 2004).
246. Ibid.
247. "Black Says al Qaeda Weaker, but Still a Potent Force," United States Consulate Mumbai-India Press Releases and Briefings, April 1, 2004. http://mumbai.usconsulate.gov/wwwhwashnews1556.html
248. James Dunnigan, "al Qaeda Without al Qaeda," StrategyPage.com, 18 October 2004. http://www.strategypage.com/search.asp?target=d:\inetpub\strategypageroot\dls\docs\2004101822.htm&search=al%20qaeda%20without%20al%20qaeda
249. "Pakistani President Hopes for More Trade with the EU," European Parliament Website, 13 September 2006.
250. Steve Coll, *Ghost Wars: The Secret History of the CIA, Afghanistan and bin Laden*, Penguin Publishing, 2005.
251. Ibid.
252. Ibid.
253. "Haqqani Network," Institute for the Study of War. http://www.understandingwar.org/haqqani-network
254. "Through the Eyes of the Taliban," *Asia Times*, 5 May 2004. http://www.atimes.com/atimes/Central_Asia/FE05Ag02.html
255. "Haqqani Network," Institute for the Study of War. http://www.understandingwar.org/haqqani-network
256. Declan Walsh and Eric Schmitt, "US Blacklists Militant Haqqani Network," *New York Times*, 7 September 2012. http://www.nytimes.com/2012/09/08/world/asia/state-department-blacklists-militant-haqqani-network.html?ref=haqqaninetwork&_r=0
257. "Afghanistan: Veteran Mujahideen Defies West," *Adnkronos International*, 2008.
258. "Mapping Militant Organization: Haqqani Network," Stanford University, 23 July 2012. http://www.stanford.edu/group/mappingmilitants/cgi-bin/groups/view/363
259. "US Drone Kills Haqqani Commander Sangeen Zadran," BBC News, 6 September 2013. http://www.bbc.co.uk/news/world-asia-23983388
260. Bill Roggio, "Taliban Confirm Death of Badruddin Haqqani in Drone Strike Last Year," 8 September 2013. http://www.longwarjournal.org/archives/2013/09/taliban_confirm_deat_1.php#ixzz2fWaD02A9
261. Sebastian Abbot, "Badruddin Haqqani Dead: Pakistani Officials Confirm Death of Key Militant," Associated Press, 30 August 2012. http://www.huffingtonpost.com/2012/08/30/badruddin-haqqani-dead-pakistan_n_1842469.html
262. "Official: Haqqani Network Behind Deadly Afghanistan Attacks," *Euro News*, 16 April 2012. http://www.euronews.com/2012/04/16/official-haqqani-network-behind-deadly-afghanistan-attacks/

263. Sebastian Abbot, "A Glance at the Pakistan-based Haqqani Network," Associated Press, 7 September 2012. http://bigstory.ap.org/article/glance-pakistan-based-haqqani-network
264. Roggio, Bill. "US Adds Haqqani Network, Taliban Leaders to List of Designated Terrorists," *Long War Journal*, 22 July 2010.
265. Lolita C. Baldor, "US targets Afghan Taliban Leaders with Sanctions," ABC News, 22 July 2010.
266. Gretchen Peters, "Haqqani Network Financing: The Evolution of an Industry," Combatting Terrorism Center at West Point, July 2012.
267. Andrea Mancini, "Afghanistan after 2014: The Narco-Dimension," ISPI, July 2011.
268. "The Role of Illicit Trafficking in the Af-Pak Context," IEEE.ES, April 2012.
269. "Haqqani Network to Support Afghanistan Peace Process," *Tolo News*, 17 September 2011.
270. "Haqqani Network," Institute for the Study of War. http://www.understandingwar.org/haqqani-network
271. "Country Reports on Terrorism 2010," United States Department of State, Office of the Coordinator for Counterterrorism, August 2011.
272. Sharif Amiri, "US Senators Admonish Obama Over Haqqani-ISI Relationship," *Tolo News*, 14 July 2013. http://www.tolonews.com/en/afghanistan/11217-us-senators-admonish-obama-over-haqqani-isi-relationship
273. Thomas Joscelyn, "Admiral Mullen: Pakistani ISI Sponsoring Haqqani Attacks," 22 September 2011. http://www.longwarjournal.org/archives/2011/09/admiral_mullen_pakis.php#ixzz2fXALDj97
274. Elisabeth Bumiller and Jane Perlez, "Pakistan's Spy Agency Is Tied to Attack on US Embassy," 22 September 2011. http://www.nytimes.com/2011/09/23/world/asia/mullen-asserts-pakistani-role-in-attack-on-us-embassy.html?pagewanted=all
275. Thomas Joscelyn, "Admiral Mullen: Pakistani ISI Sponsoring Haqqani Attacks," 22 September 2011. http://www.longwarjournal.org/archives/2011/09/admiral_mullen_pakis.php#ixzz2fXALDj97
276. "Mapping Militant Organization: Haqqani Network," Stanford University, 23 July 2012. http://www.stanford.edu/group/mappingmilitants/cgi-bin/groups/view/363
277. "Haqqani Network to Support Afghanistan Peace Process," *Tolo News*, 17 September 2011.
278. This information is taken from *Tolo News*, *Pajhwok News*, *Long War Journal*, the ISAF website, and *Dawn News*.
279. "Hizb-i-Islami Gulbuddin (HIG)," Terrorist Research and Analysis Consortium. http://www.trackingterrorism.org/group/hizb-i-islami-gulbuddin-hig
280. Ibid.
281. Ibid.
282. Ibid.
283. "Afghan Authorities Report Presence of Hezb-e Eslami Terror Camps in Pakistan," Afghan Tolo TV, 28 October 2006.
284. "US Designates Hekmatyar as a Terrorist," *Dawn*, 20 February 2003.
285. "US Designates Foreign Terrorist Organizations," America.gov, 30 April 2007.
286. "Commanders Line Up Behind Karzai," Institute for War and Peace Reporting, 14 September 2004.
287. "Update on the Situation in Afghanistan and International Protection Considerations," UNHCR, June 2005, pp. 48–49, 78.
288. Ibid.
289. See list of licensed political parties at Afghanistan's Ministry of Justice website.
290. "Hizb-i-Islami Members Are Busy with Politics," *Wakht News Agency*, Kabul, 12 July 2008.
291. Matthew Rosenberg, "A Group Taking Politics and Military Strategy to the Same Extremes," *New York Times*, 21 May 2013. http://www.nytimes.com/2013/05/22/world/asia/in-afghanistan-hezb-i-islami-takes-its-extremism-into-politics.html?pagewanted=all&_r=0

292. "Hizb-e Islami Defectors Call for Talks with Opposition," *BBC Persian News*, 12 June 2008.
293. Touzari Janesdatter Greenwood, "The Social Lives of Hezb-e-Islami: Cohesion of an Afghan Insurgent Group," University of Copenhagen, 29 June 2012.
294. "The Role of Illicit Trafficking in the Af-Pak Context," IEEE.ES, April 2012.
295. Afghanistan Opium Survey 2011, World Drug Report, 2011.
296. Ibid.
297. Ibid.
298. "The role of illicit trafficking in the Af-Pak context," IEEE.ES, April 2012.
299. Touzari Janesdatter Greenwood, "The Social Lives of Hezb-e-Islami: Cohesion of an Afghan Insurgent Group," University of Copenhagen, 29 June 2012.
300. "Profile: Gulbuddin Hekmatyar," *BBC News*, 23 March 2013. http://news.bbc.co.uk/2/hi/south_asia/2701547.stm
301. Ibid.
302. Bill Roggio, "Female Suicide Bomber from Hizb-i-Islami Gulbuddin Strikes in Kabul," *Long War Journal*, 18 September 2012. http://www.longwarjournal.org/archives/2012/09/female_suicide_bombe_6.php
303. "Hezb-e Islami Calls for Caution on Noncombatants," *Wakht News Agency*, 8 August 2013. http://wakht.af/en/index.php/security-and-crime/4475-hezb-e-islami-calls-for-caution-on-noncombatants.html
304. Bill Roggio, "Female Suicide Bomber from Hizb-i-Islami Gulbuddin Strikes in Kabul," *Long War Journal*, 18 September 2012. http://www.longwarjournal.org/archives/2012/09/female_suicide_bombe_6.php
305. Borhan Osman, "Adding the Ballot to the Bullet? Hezb-e Islami in Transition," *Afghan Analyst Network*, 6 May 2013. http://www.afghanistan-analysts.org/adding-the-ballot-to-the-bullet-hezb-e-islami-in-transition
306. Bill Roggio, "Hekmatyar's 'Peace Plan' Calls for NATO Withdrawal by 2011," *Long War Journal*, 22 March 2010. http://www.longwarjournal.org/archives/2010/03/hekmatyars_peace_pla.php#ixzz2fgxwp878
307. Borhan Osman, "Adding the Ballot to the Bullet? Hezb-e Islami in Transition," *Afghan Analyst Network*, 6 May 2013. http://www.afghanistan-analysts.org/adding-the-ballot-to-the-bullet-hezb-e-islami-in-transition
308. Bill Roggio, "Hekmatyar's 'Peace Plan' Calls for NATO Withdrawal by 2011," *Long War Journal*, 22 March 2010. http://www.longwarjournal.org/archives/2010/03/hekmatyars_peace_pla.php#ixzz2fgxwp878
309. Anand Gopal, Mansur Khan Mahsud, and Brian Fishman, "Inside Pakistan's Tribal Frontier: North Waziristan," *The Af-Pak Channel*, 23 April 2010. http://afpak.foreignpolicy.com/posts/2010/04/23/inside_pakistans_tribal_frontier_north_waziristan
310. Anand Gopal, Mansur Khan Mahsud, and Brian Fishman, "The Battle for Pakistan Militancy and Conflict in North Waziristan," *New America Foundation*, April 2010, p. 15. http://newamerica.net/sites/newamerica.net/files/policydocs/northwaziristan.pdf
311. Sadia Sulaiman, "Hafiz Gul Bahadur: A Profile of North Waziristani Talibna," *Terrorism Monitor*, 9 April 2010, Volume 7, Issue 9. http://www.jamestown.org/programs/gta/single/?tx_ttnews[tt_news]=34839&tx_ttnews[backPid]=26&cHash=05100a468e
312. "The Pakistani Taliban," Issue Paper, Australian Governmnet, January 2013, p. 21. http://www.refworld.org/pdfid/514313f12.pdf
313. Abdul Basit, "Militant Landscape after Miranshah Agreement," in Amir Rana and Safdar Sial et al. *Dynamics of Taliban Insurgency in FATA* (Islamabad: Pak Institute for Peace Studies, 2010), p. 113.
314. Zahir Shah Sherazi, "Mullah Nazir Killed in South Waziristan Drone Strike: Officials," *Dawn*, Pakistan, 3 January 2013. http://beta.dawn.com/news/776005/drone-strike-kills-four-in-s-waziristan-2
315. "Successor Replaces Mullah Nazir," *The News*, Pakistan, 4 January 2013. http://www.thenews.com.pk/article-82390-Successor-replaces-Mullah-Nazir-

316. Bill Roggio, "US Adds Mullah Nazir Group, Sub-Commander to Terrorism List," *Long War Journal*, 26 February 2013. http://www.longwarjournal.org/archives/2013/02/us_adds_mullah_nazir.php

317. "Terrorist Designations of the Commander Nazir Group and Malang Wazir," US State Department, 26 February 2013. http://www.state.gov/r/pa/prs/ps/2013/02/205195.htm

318. Bill Roggio, "Al Qaeda Brokers New Anti-US Taliban Alliance in Pakistan and Afghanistan," *Long War Journal*, 3 January 2012. http://www.longwarjournal.org/archives/2012/01/al_qaeda_brokers_new.php

319. This information is taken from *Tolo News*, *Pajhwok News*, the *Long War Journal*, the ISAF website, and *Dawn News*.

320. Rohan Gunaratna and Khuram Iqbal, *Pakistan: Terrorism Ground Zero* (London: Reaktion Books, 2010).

321. "Pakistan Government Bans Taleban," *BBC News*, 25 August 2008. http://news.bbc.co.uk/2/hi/south_asia/7580475.stm

322. Ibid.

323. Zahir Shah Sherazi, "US Drone Strike Kills TTP Number Two Waliur Rehman, Six Others," *Dawn*, Pakistan, 29 June 2013. http://beta.dawn.com/news/1014506/us-drone-strike-kills-ttp-number-two-waliur-rehman-six-others

324. Daud Khattak, "A Profile of Khan Said: Waliur Rahman's Successor in the Pakistani Taliban," *CTC Sentinel*, US, Volume 6, Issue 6, June 2013. http://www.ctc.usma.edu/posts/a-profile-of-khan-said-waliur-rahmans-successor-in-the-pakistani-taliban

325. Zulfiqar Ali, "Dissent Within: Punjabi Taliban Ready for Talks," *Express Tribune*, Pakistan, 1 October 2013. http://tribune.com.pk/story/611773/dissent-within-punjabi-taliban-ready-for-talks/

326. "Govt Not Serious in Talks, Says TTP leader," *Dawn*, Pakistan, 28 September 2013. http://dawn.com/news/1046026/govt-not-serious-in-talks-says-ttp-leader

327. Misbah Abdul-Baqi, "Pakistani Taliban Disclosed; Emergence, Objectives, and Leadership," *Islam Online*. www.islamonline.net/servlet/Satellite?c=Article_C&cid=1203757776285&pagename=Zone-English-Muslim_Affairs%2FMAELayout, last visited 28 October 2008.

328. Zahir Shah, "Hostage to Jihad," *Monthly Herald*, Pakistan, October 2008.

329. Katja Riikonen, "Punjabi Taliban and the Sectarian Groups in Pakistan," *Pakistan Security Research Unit (PSRU)*, UK, 12 February 2012. http://www.dur.ac.uk/resources/psru/briefings/archive/Brief55.pdf

330. Abdul Basit, "Militant Landscape after Miranshah Agreement," in Amir Rana and Safdar Sial et al. *Dynamics of Taliban Insurgency in FATA* (Islamabad: Pak Institute for Peace Studies, 2010), p. 99.

331. This information is taken from *Dawn News*, *The News*, and other Pakistan dailies.

Index

055 Brigade, 148
9/11: al Qaeda network effects after, 176; drone use after, 92; mastermind, 90; Pakistan's support after, 129; targets, 86

Abdel Aziz al Masri, 90
Abdul Khaliq Haqqani, 221
Abdul Latif Mansour, 138
Abdullah Abdullah, ix
Abdulloh Fotih, 67
Abu Dujana al-Khorasani, 92
Abu Khair al Masri, 90
Abu Sayyaf, 49, 89
Abu Sayyaf Group, 95
Afghan Local Police, 38
Afghan Ministry of Mines and Petroleum, 40
Afghan sanctuaries, 32
Afghan Taliban: female suicide bombers, 133; interaction with Iran, 129; interaction with Pakistan, 129; peace process involvement, 135; peace talks, x; tactics, techniques, and procedures, 131; targets, 131; threat assessment, 137; turban suicide attacks, 134
Afghan Taliban Group Profile, 113
Afghanistan–Pakistan Transit Trade Agreement, 28
Agha Jan Motasim, 6

Ahmad Shah Masood, viii. *See also* Northern Alliance
Ahmedzai Wazir, 226
Al Andalus Media Foundation, 97
al Qaeda: al Qaeda al Jihad, 89; current assessment, 196; responses to al Qaeda, 194; tactics, 191; threat assessment, 212
al Qaeda in the Arabian Peninsula: as part of al Qaeda, 200; operations, 94
al Sahab, 97
al-Kata'ib Media Foundation, 95
ALP. *See* Afghan Local Police
Amir-ul-Momineen, 100
anti-Taliban: early resistance, 79; movements, 37; political groups, 80; opposing Taliban, 4
Anwarul Haq Mujahid, 171
APTTA. *See* Afghanistan–Pakistan Transit Trade Agreement
AQAP. *See* al-Qaeda in the Arabian Peninsula
Arakan Rohingiya Nationalist Organization, 89
Army War College, xiii
Ashfaq Wazir, 213
Asia Foundation Survey, 6

Badr at Tawheed, 97
Badruddin Haqqani, 208
Bahawal Khan, 225

Baitullah Mehsud: death, 201; relations with Pakistan, 223; retaliation for killing, 210; TTP involvement, 92; Uzbek fighter relationship, 226

Bajaur Agency: Operation Lion's Heart, 230; TTP leadership, 230; Zawahiri, 148

Balkans: al Qaeda, 89; return of fighters from, 106

Baloch: assassinations associated with, 201; extremist groups, 20; India's connections, 23; Iranian involvement, 82; separatists, 20; support to insurgents, 22

Bamiyan: bombing of statues, 241n28; Buddha statue destruction, 86

Baradar: arrest, 6; financial sanctions, 125; role in peace process, 37

Bari Ali, 138

bilateral security agreement: assessment of future scenarios, 36; Loya Jirga back, xi; Pakistan and, 17; post-2014 scenarios, 7

BSA. *See* bilateral security agreement

Buddha statues. *See* Bamiyan

Caravans, 35

Carol Bell partnership model, 28

caucasus: Islamic Emirate of the Caucasus, 95; Caucasus Emirate threat to Central Asia, 66

Central Asia: energy considerations, 3; expansion of terror activity, 66; extremist groups, 56; IMU and, 172; ISAF withdrawal and security, 64; narco-trafficking and, 74; security considerations, 63; trade with Pakistan, 23; US relationship with, 9

Central Asian: militant objectives in, 73; violence spillover, 48

China: China Metallurgical Group Corp, 40; economic influence in South Asia, 40; opportunities for cooperation with US, 44; partnership with Iran, 81; relationship with India, 111; strategic rival, 9; Turkistan Islamic Party and, 106; UN support and global presence, 44; Uyghur separatists, 82; Xinjiang considerations, 73

Christianity Densus 88 perceptions, 99

CIA: coup against Mossadeq in 1953, 78; locations of terror sanctuaries in Afghanistan, 90; suicide bombing in Khost, 92

civil war: Afghan, 17; Afghan future prospects, 29; India–Pakistan proxy fight in Afghansitan, 30; Tajikistan, 71; Yemeni, 186

Dagestan, 81

Daur tribe, 221

Densus 88, 99

Deobandi: Deobandism, 88; Hafiz Gul Bahadur, 221; South Asian region, 114

Department of Treasury: designated terrorists, 125; Haqqani Network and, 209

East Turkestan Islamic Movement: China and separatists, 172; name change, 109; threat to Central Asia, 66; training with Haqqani Network, 210; Turkistan Islamic Party (TIP), 89

elections: Afghan elections, xii; first Afghan parliamentary elections, ix; President Karzai and 2004 elections, 215

ETIM. *See* East Turkestan Islamic Movement

FATA. *See* Federally Administered Tribal Areas

Federally Administered Tribal Areas: Afghan Taliban resurgence, 55; al Qaeda operations in, 65; destabilizing Afghanistan, 16; Fergana Valley, 67; Frontier Constabulary, 27

Frontier Crimes Regulations (FCR), 27

Gerakan Mujahidin Islam Patani (GMIP), 89

Ghazni: Afghan Taliban success, 130; allegations of killing, 101; children used as suicide bombers, 132

GIRoA. *See* Government of the Islamic Republic of Afghanistan

Global Jihad Movement: al Qaeda Networks, 90; FATA and, 205;

ideological motivation, 199
Government of the Islamic Republic of Afghanistan, 36; bilateral security agreement with US, 64

Hagel, 21
Hakimullah Mehsud: faction of TTP, 231; targeted by drone, 92; TTP and, 101
Halim Khan Daur, 221
Haqqani: connections to Pakistan militant groups, 54; Ibrahim, 15; Jalaluddin, 15; network structure, 126; relationship with ISI, 16; Sirajuddin, 54; threat to Central Asia, 66; threat to US Forces, 118
Harakatul Jihad I Islami Bangladesh (HuJI-B), 89
Hezb-i-Islami: association with Afghan Taliban, 217; political group, 215; war with Soviet Union, 207
High Peace Council (HPC), 6, 23
Hizbul Mujahideen, 52
Humam al-Balawi, 92

ICPVTR. *See* International Centre for Political Violence and Terrorism Research
IJU. *See* Islamic Jihad Union
India: Harkat ul Jihad ul Islami and, 56; interests in Afghanistan, 15; Istanbul conference and, 28; Pakistan rivalry, 17; proxy fight using Afghansitan, 43; threat to, 105
India–Afghanistan Strategic Partnership Agreement, 16
Indian Mujahidin, 95
International Centre for Political Violence and Terrorism Research, xii
International Security Assistance Force, 91
Iran: agreement with GIRoA, 42; "axis of evil," 79; Chabahar port, 79; relationship with Northern Alliance, 79; role in Afghanistan, 123; US relationship, 77
ISAF. *See* International Security Assistance Force
Islamic Jihad Union: al Qaeda and, 65; faction of the IMU, 172
Islamic State of Iraq and the Levant, 95

Jaish-e-Mohammed, 95
Jamaat-ud-Dawa, 57
Jamiat-i-Ulema Islam, 128
Jemmah Islamiyah, 89
Junood ul-Hifsa, 24

Kandahar province: Afghan Taliban violence, 101; emergence of the Taliban in 1994, 114; Taliban excesses, 37
Karzai: challenges, 46; credibility, 43; influence on drug trade, 124; release of insurgents, 88
Kayani: interaction with US President Obama, 20; plot to assassinate, 157; statements about security, 17; Talibanization statement, 20
Kazakhstan: Jaish al-Mahdi links, 68; terror activity, 66; terror attacks in, 69
Khalid Sheikh Mohammad and 9/11, 90
Khost: Haqqani operations, 54; militant training, 57; suicide bombing, 92
Khyber Pakhtunkhwa province: Jamiat-i-Ulema Islam Base, 128; Talibanization and, 223; Zawahiri and, 146
Kumpulan Militan Malaysia, 89
Kyrgyz government: order to close Manas, 9; targeted by terrorists, 68
Kyrgyzstan: Fergana Valley, 67; security situation, 72; terrorist threat to, 68; US and Russian connections, 9

Lashkar-e-Taiba: enduring terror threat, 41; linkages to Hezb-e-Islami, 55; part of Punjabi Taliban, 25
Liaquat Ali Khan Engineering University, 23
Loya Jirga: elects Karzai, viii; London conference endorsed, 135; supporting US presence, 43

Maldives: Ali Jaleel and Lahore attack, 59; extremist ideology roots, 58; homegrown militant groups, 52; religious extremist groups, 56
Mazar-e Sharif: collapse of Taliban's hold, 116; defeat of Taliban, 207; Taliban killed Iranians, 79
McRaven, 96
Mehsuds, 101

Michener, 35
Moezeddine Garsallaoui, 69
Moro Islamic Liberation Front: al Qaeda linkages, 193; Philippine insurgent operations, 175; training in South Asia, 89
Morocco: links to Bin Laden, 201; Moroccan Islamic Combatant Group (GICM), 165
Mullah Dadullah: actions involving the peace process, 101; Taliban force claims, 120

Nasir Abdel Karim al-Wuhayshi, 94
NATO: efforts in Afghanistan, 13; end of mission, 51; residual force estimates, 77
New Delhi: operations against, 156; Pakistan views about, 20; relationship with China, 111
Northern Alliance: 055 Brigade and operations against, 187; India's support, 17; Iran's relationship with, 79; leader of, 71; Pakistan military involvement, 20
Nanyang Technological University (NTU), xii

Osama bin Laden: background, 142; killing of, 17; operation in Abbotabad to capture/kill, 96

Panjwai district, 38
Pattani United Liberation Front, 89
People's Liberation Army (PLA), 48

Quetta: Afghan Taliban connections, 54; Shura senior leadership, 118; Shura members, 6

Rabbani: assassination of, 134; Peace Council involvement, 23
Reconstruction Opportunity Zones, 27
Rohingiya Solidarity Organization, 89

Saifullah Wazir, 221
Shanghai Cooperation Organization, 73
Shia: attack against students, 161; militias against Taliban, 114; political leadership in Afghanistan, 4; TTP actions against, 233
South Asian Association for Regional Cooperation, 31
South Waziristan: Central Asian fighter training in, 172; Pakistan's ISI and Hezb-e-Islami, 217; terror leader operations in, 150; TTP leader drone strike, 92
Soviet Union: invasion effects on insurgent groups, 114; invasion of Afghanistan, 55; withdrawal from Afghanistan, 58
Students Islamic Movement of India, 95

Takfirya, 232
Talibanization, 19, 27, 30, 55, 84, 223, 229
Tehrik-e-Taliban, 55, 88, 102, 161, 200, 223, 225
Tohir Yuldoshev, 67
turban suicide, 134
Turkmenistan, 66, 72, 74, 124

United Arab Emirates, 15, 86, 116
United Nations, 56, 86, 120
US forces Iraq, xiv
Usmon Ghazi, 67

village stabilization operations, 91

Wahhabism, 52
Waliur Rehman, 230, 231
Wazir tribe, 174, 221, 223–227
Waziristan: extremist groups, 59; Haqqani Network affiliation, 54; Islamic Jihad Union operations, 67; sanctuary for Afghan Taliban, 24
Western drawdown, xiv
WMD Al Qaeda Committee, 90

Xinjiang: attacks in 2013, 106; East Turkistan Islamic Movement, 172; potential for violence, 48; rise of Islamist militancy, 73; use as sanctuary, 82

zero option, 29, 45

About the Editors and the Contributors

ABOUT THE EDITORS

Dr. Rohan Gunaratna is professor of security studies and head of the International Centre for Political Violence and Terrorism Research at Nanyang Technological University in Singapore. He is also a member of the Steering Committee of George Washington University's Homeland Security Policy Institute and serves on the Advisory board of the International Centre for Counter-Terrorism, The Hague, He is the author and editor of fifteen books including *Inside Al Qaeda: Global Network of Terror*. Admiral William McRaven appointed him to the International Senior Advisory Panel of the US Special Operations Command in 2013. For advancing international security cooperation, he received the Major General Ralph H. Van Deman Award in 2014.

Colonel Douglas Woodall commands a brigade at Fort Hood, Texas. Prior to this appointment, he was a United States Army War College fellow at the International Center for Political Violence and Terrorism Research, Nanyang Technological University, Singapore. He also commanded an intelligence battalion in Afghanistan and was the director of Intelligence Operations for a Special Operations Task Force in Iraq.

ABOUT THE CONTRIBUTORS

Iftekharul Bashar is an associate research fellow at the International Center for Political Violence and Terrorism Research at the S. Rajaratnam School of International Studies, Nanyang Technological University, Singapore.

Abdul Basit is a senior analyst at the International Center for Political Violence and Terrorism Research at the S. Rajaratnam School of International Studies, Nanyang Technological University, Singapore.

Halimullah Kousar is an associate research fellow at the International Center for Political Violence and Terrorism Research at the S. Rajaratnam School of International Studies, Nanyang Technological University, Singapore.

Nodirbek Soliyev is a research analyst at the International Center for Political Violence and Terrorism Research at the S. Rajaratnam School of International Studies, Nanyang Technological University, Singapore.